Mark Borkowski is one of the UK's leadir
and media commentators. He operates hi
brand and celebrity publicity company, Bo
lar list of clients past and present, incl
Norton, Noel Edmonds, Van Morrison,
Macaulay Culkin, Sir Cliff Richard, the Bolshoi Ballet, Cirque du Soleil, the Three Tenors, and that trio of Michaels: Jackson, Flatley and Moore. Mark's roster of the rich and famous even extends to Mikhail Gorbachev and Diego Maradona and he has been responsible for a wealth of quality PR moments in the British media. Corporately, Borkowski PR has represented brands from Daimler, Chrysler, Hasbro and Vodafone to Norwich Union via Selfridges, Virgin Mobile and Thorntons. He is the author of one previous book, *Improperganda: Art of the Publicity Stunt.*

Praise for *The Fame Formula*

'I thought modern-day celebrity PRs were venal, corrupt, incorrigible monsters until I read this book. Now I realise they are just amateur impressionists desperately playing catch-up to their legendary Hollywood predecessors. Those guys spun murder, fixed marriages, hid brawls and would have sold their proverbial grannies if their families hadn't already disowned them. Mark Borkowski has shone a brilliantly illuminating light on the disgraceful, hilarious, and undeniably effective Tinsel Town PR war machines that inspired the current celebrity/PR meltdown we see today. I loved every page'

Piers Morgan

'In this fascinating book, one of Britain's top publicists tells all about what fame is, how to get it, and what to do with it'

Lord Saatchi

'Most people think of Andy Warhol as having the last word on celebrity culture, but he played John the Baptist to Mark Borkowski's Jesus. In this book, Borkowski tells you how to parlay fifteen minutes of fame into a lifetime of pampered luxury'

Toby Young

'The boosters and flacks and the hacks and slebs who served them are the curiously neglected subject of *The Fame Formula*: for people obsessed with media exposure ("don't count the shit, just count the inches" is what they like to say), the publicists' own history is obscure. So Borkowski has excavated some very fine specimens richly deserving scrutiny and awe . . . a compelling read'

Stephen Bayley

'An engrossing and enjoyable stroll in the company of a knowledgeable enthusiast through that weird zone where talent, gullibility and ballyhoo meet'

Evening Standard

'Written by one of the UK's leading PRs, this entertaining riff on celebrity is seen through the eyes of publicists who have steered some of the biggest stars (from Douglas Fairbanks to Tom Cruise) of the past 100 years. PR men and women who, in most cases, were/are as ballsy and maverick as their clients. Case in point, notorious American publicist Jay Bernstein, who staged his own wedding underwater to get publicity'

GQ

'A fascinating and readable insight into the cult of celebrity, from Hollywood legends to the latest Big Brother wannabes. Anyone interested in the rich, famous and infamous will enjoy *The Fame Formula*'

News of the World

'Ain't no one understands the torrid public relationship between fame and publicity like Mr Borkowski. It's one thing knowing where the bodies are buried. Mark knows who sold 'em the shovels. He wears the crown. He wrote the book. This is that book'

Trevor Beattie, BMB Advertising

'This book has it all. Lacing his narrative with humour, history and social and economic analysis, Borkowski demystifies the deceptively simple ideas that create the stars'

Angel Magazine

THE FAME FORMULA

HOW HOLLYWOOD'S FIXERS, FAKERS AND STAR MAKERS CREATED THE CELEBRITY INDUSTRY

Mark Borkowski

PAN BOOKS

First published 2008 by Sidgwick & Jackson

This edition published 2013 by Pan Books
an imprint of Pan Macmillan, a division of Macmillan Publishers Limited
Pan Macmillan, 20 New Wharf Road, London N1 9RR
Basingstoke and Oxford
Associated companies throughout the world
www.panmacmillan.com

ISBN 978-1-4472-4926-9

A CIP catalogue record for this book is available from the British Library.

For Kate, Janek and Joe.

And for the restless, irresistible phantoms and the irreverent shibboleths of promotion which shaped the fame industry.

May the art of creative publicity burn brightly. Let it not be corrupted and corroded by the modern marketing half wits and the cynical elegance of public relations.

Long live the charming mavericks. Let dismal facts never get in the way of a brilliant story.

ACKNOWLEDGEMENTS

The author wishes to acknowledge a profound debt of gratitude to Adam Horovitz without whose patience, diligence and extraordinary creative skill the project would never have been finished. Adam's exceptional and enormous contribution forms a gargantuan component of the finished book.

A very special thanks is also extended to Steve Jaffe without whose assistance I would not have been able to gain access to many of the Hollywood movers and shakers. His reputation and the high regard he is held in was the key to unlocking many doors.

Other invaluable assistance and input came from my precious personal assistant Sarah Bolton; without her good humour, creativity and attentiveness I would have lost my sanity in the first month of the project.

My gratitude is extended to Simon Trewin who believed in the concept and supported the initial idea of the book. It was his hard work that enabled the deal to be struck with Macmillan. I am indebted to the kind, patient support of my editor Ingrid Connell who gave me the freedom to develop the final book. I am grateful to William Hartston for his extraordinary research over a year to help produce the Fame Formula equation, and for the mathematical fine tuning by Neil Procter. Neil also helped reading the manuscript and I appreciate his loving support as a friend.

I would like to thank the countless people who helped with informal reviews and suggestions, and express particular thanks to: Lynda Fairweather, Susan Douglas, Bob Thomas, Dave Andrews, Michael Park, Tim Cooper, Ric Cooper, Chrissy Iley, Joey Skaggs, Mike Gilmore, Stephen Gaydos, Phil and Sarah Thredder of Ross Old Books, Lord Bell, Richard Laver, Victor Davis, Victoria Trow, and the librarians at the Margaret Herrick Library Academy of Motion Picture Arts and Sciences.

I owe a deep debt of gratitude to all my co-workers at Borkowski, especially Dee McCourt, Joanne McNally and Larry Franks, who allowed the time, space and liberty to develop and complete this project.

I am especially grateful to all the people who agreed to be interviewed for the book on and off the record. Finally, thanks to all my close friends. If wealth was measured in friendship I'd be a very rich man.

Contents

PREFACE

> 'A generation of men is like a generation of leaves; the wind scatters some leaves upon the ground, while others the burgeoning wood brings forth – and the season of spring comes on. So of men one generation springs forth and another ceases.'
>
> *The Iliad*

I stumbled into the publicity game in 1979 and it became the heartbeat to my life – I was soon utterly intoxicated by it. It provided an adventure every day, something I still try to maintain in my middle age, be it meeting and dealing with someone famous, being entrusted with a multinational brand or pulling off a scam. The only trouble was that I had no sense of the history of publicity, and history was important to me. I fell into publicity because I failed to get into university to read history. I've always loved the icons of history but I didn't think, working in publicity in a fringe theatre or working as an entertainments publicist, that there was any history to be found.

So in the bushy-tailed days of my youth, I played with the lukewarm heat of a cauldron cooking up publicity scams that involved animals, celebrities, brushes with the law, outrageous things that offended the moral guardians. I was happily submerged in my fishbowl. I never thought that anything was happening anywhere else. This was not out of arrogance, but an absence of context. There was very little media attention on the profession of a publicist. It was only when I started to write that people began to say, 'Have you heard of this, that, or so and so?'

I cut my milk teeth in a beautiful, still backwater, delivering up acres of publicity for a small theatre in Swindon. As a result of the blizzard of hype I created for a long-forgotten pantomime dame, an impresario called Paul Elliott took note and suggested I come to

London; his considered opinion was that my energy was needed in the West End. He felt that no one else had the same huckster spirit I was imbued with, and that if I chose to go to the big city, theatre would be woken up.

Once in London, Elliott got me an interview with Theo Cowan. Cowan was the legendary British film publicist who crafted the extraordinary Rank Charm School, and he was fabled for creating all the Rank starlets, most notably Diana Dors. There's a famous photo of Dors at the Venice film festival wearing a mink bikini in a gondola and, supposedly, Theo Cowan is underneath her in the gondola giving her purchase so the photographers can see all of her and not lose any flesh to the bottom of the boat.

Theo was very generous and kind. Not only did he keep an eye on me and open my eyes to what was happening in London, he also introduced me to some of the important US movie publicists.

And that's where my journey began, in a coffee bar in Soho's Poland Street. My career was really kick-started when Paul Elliott employed me to publicize the West End return of *The Pirates of Penzance*. 'Here's an idea,' I said, 'we should get the cast sword-fighting lessons.'

'Who from?' asked Paul.

'How about a movie star. Douglas Fairbanks Jr or someone like that?' I replied.

'Let's get him,' he said.

And amazingly, Douglas Fairbanks Jr agreed to fly over on Concord and give Paul Nicholas sword-fighting lessons! Naturally, it was staged as an open photo-call and the world and his wife turned up because a great Hollywood swashbuckling legend would be available for interview. I went to meet Fairbanks in the splendour of Claridges and had a very agreeable morning with him. We were talking and he looked at me and said, 'This is a great publicity stunt; reminiscent of the old stuntsters!'

'Stuntster? What's that?' I asked.

After he explained the term, he talked about all the great publicists, people I'd never heard of before, but who had shaped his fame. He told me that my little stunt, born on the spur of the moment, reminded him of those early days. These things are meant to happen, I suppose; the history I longed for, the icons of my chosen profession, suddenly came to life in the words of one of the great icons of the movie industry. Douglas Fairbanks Jr put me on the track of Jim Moran, Russell Birdwell, Harry Reichenbach and more, and later that afternoon I was busy searching out books on all of them.

Surprisingly, another guide on my journey was the late Jeremy Beadle. Greatly misunderstood, Beadle was a great collector of facts and was fascinated by publicity stunts, in all areas of showmanship, huckstering, circus and vaudeville. I got to know him in 1990 and spent hours in his library. He had an encyclopaedic knowledge and passion and loaned me countless books. The publicist he was most fascinated by was Jim Moran, the great wit of the publicity industry, and I rapidly came to share his fascination with this odd and intriguing man and even tried to set up a meeting with him.

It was in 1999, when Chris Evans and Geri Halliwell were supposed to be having an affair. They were playing with the tabloids, and it was obvious hokum and a blatant stunt, but no one wanted to dismiss it because it generated column inches. At the same time the story broke, just as I was due to fly to the US to meet him, Jim Moran died. There were no obituaries in the British press, but America gave him a good send-off. From that moment on I thought, I'm not going to miss another opportunity to meet these people and find out about their lives. And what had been more of a hobby, a diversion for a curious mind starved of historical context, became a quest to understand what it was these publicists had shaped.

I soon realized that I was like these people – maybe not as great or grand because the media had changed so much and there were many more publicists by the time I came on the scene, but I was a stuntster through and through. I shared a connection to the circus, was a ballyhoo aficionado and a showman. I had developed a career along the lines of the original publicists without ever knowing there was a legacy or tradition there.

This book has been a quest to put these people on record, to give them a voice and discover where fame came from, what made it tick and the price it demanded, to mark the graves of the unknown.

Fame is a transient thing that turns the famous person into a walking billboard. It's not about genius or reward, but the process of creating fame *is* a brand of genius. You can become famous for going to a resort, for holding hands in public, for whispering something in someone's ear, for having a baby, for getting invited to a party. Anything can spark the kindling.

Every publicist has realized the financial gain to be made from those with basic human nature who want to leave a mark on the world they live in, to craft a legacy and to be known and loved. The media culture and environment has allowed fame to become an end in itself, and the stimulus behind achieving fame is now hopelessly suspect and shadowy.

It's available to everybody, which has created a limbo where we're all waiting for the opportunity to arise. It has depersonalized citizenship and real work; this is the legacy of the people who worked hard to make an easy route to fame. A nurse is not a hero for cleaning bedpans, but if she hooks up with someone famous, then takes her clothes off in a lad's mag, she can become famous overnight and have a much easier existence.

Different generations have framed and shaped fame by applying different skills and the new mechanisms of the day, but they rarely, if ever, acknowledge the past. Fame does not wait for a man to do something significant. People become famous for what they are prepared to do – it's like an exotic dance and it's not about erudition. It's not about talent any more, it's about publicized routines. The press agents, the suppress agents and the brand-meisters are the people who breathe life into fame. The publicist makes people hanker after it, and that's where their genius lies.

Because of the media agenda, we provide pleasure in the now, and we like the people who most resemble us because, if they can become famous, so can we. People bemoan the phenomenon, but the press are hungry for celebrity because it becomes content that people love to read.

Today's fabulous nobodies can become tomorrow's stars. The whole process is proof against snobbery, because the snobs pale into the unreadable in the face of overpowering fame.

The American screenwriter Ben Hecht wrote, 'Most fame is not a matter of honest laurels won by the dead but dishonest boasts of culture made by the living. The importance to which I aspire is all.' He also wrote, 'Who cares about the moods or problems of a stranger, however glamorous he is? But when a brother speaks, all he says is vital. His trouble, confusions and ventures are our own. It's not a blood tie that makes him important or meaningful to us, it is the fact that we know him well. It is importance I hope for.'

That importance – and the need for that importance – is driven by the publicist. The publicist is the person who delivers, and truly understands, the dark Conradian soul of man, who understands that it's the pressure of people tugging at his elbow that makes him important, and that it creates a mania and greed, a false sense of life and the wrong sort of pride. The publicist supplies immortality in celluloid and print form, the closest thing we get to it, other than in our children.

The publicist's skill is to proactively find, tell and sell the stories that make their clients news, and it's a skill that's more relevant now than ever. Many of the stuntsters who passed into the commercial world took these techniques from the entertainment industry into the corporate arena and turned product into entertainment. This method is driven by an absolute understanding that what most determines media content is entertainment. The job is to provide the media with that material, based on what the client is doing and on the image they wish to present. Whether that material is intellectual, sensational or a mixture of both is determined by the title, the programme or the individual journalist who has been targeted. The publicist should expose every single aspect of the challenge – its provenance and processes – to detailed scrutiny in order to uncover and promote stories that are media-friendly and which provide the hook on which a journalist will hang a news piece, feature item or photo opportunity.

The journey undertaken in this book is a quest to understand how celebrity sprang phoenix-like from the fires of vaudeville, the circus and Hollywood. To paraphrase Ben Hecht, the essence of fame is made up of molecules of flux, natural gas and the breath, not of God but of the publicist. What a publicist can bring is immortality. More often than not they have done so by luck and instinct, but always, it turns out, they have stuck to a formula. Not every publicist in the last one hundred or so years could be covered in this history – there are too many and the taste for long Illiad-like lists has long passed. I have tried to include as many publicists as possible who were innovators rather than imitators. Some of the publicists who are still living would not speak to me, preferring to keep their stories close to their chests and the sanctity of their clients intact. Of the dead, only the most relevant and forward-thinking flacks, as publicity agents are commonly known, have been included.

Just as I found myself echoing the great stunts of the past when I started as a publicist, so other publicists have done the same. Each atom of the fame industry spins to a preset pattern that comes back to the questions: what makes me? How do I become aware of what I've done? What is my place in the scheme of things? How do I begin to understand the mechanisms that were born in me as instinctively as the urge of an animal giving birth to bite through the umbilical chord? It was a joy to discover that there were others out there doing what I'd done by instinct, and that the world of publicity was not a small pool. What concerned me, given my interest in history, was that so few people in the industry were prepared to look beyond the bowl they were swimming in and recognize that what had gone before bore some relevance to what was happening now.

A publicist instinctively knows what to do, but the art risks being lost and denigrated if it is not written down. The aim of this book then is to chart the instincts, analyse them and see how the formula for fame applies to the world of publicity. It is also a brief history of the great ideas publicists have had, of the monsters they became and the monsters they created, and underlines the savage instincts that everybody chooses in their search.

People have accused me, as a publicist, of corrupting minds, but I would answer that I have been involved in shaping thought. It's a very dangerous practice, as we've seen politically with the legacy of politicians like Tony Blair, but 'Wherever ego, I go,' as Russell Birdwell once said.

For better or worse, those who seek notoriety, whether it's a brand or personality, get the publicity they deserve, a prefabricated heaven or inescapable hell. That's what I've come to understand from my unfinished journey.

• Introduction •

THE LAST WILL AND TESTAMENT OF MAYNARD NOTTAGE

Over the years, a number of players have yearned to cast a powerful shadow over Hollywood. Currently, it's the mogul Rupert Murdoch who best understands the art of leveraging money and distribution muscle. But no one's quest for Hollywood influence has been more imaginative or bizarre than the quixotic approach of Maynard Nottage, whose legacy has languished, undiscovered, in an attic until now.

It was remarkable and fortuitous that the full depth of his achievements came to my attention. In one of those moments that can only happen in a place as interconnected and intertwined as Hollywood, a woman approached me in the lobby of the hotel I was staying in, just as I was preparing to depart Los Angeles. She thrust a large package into my hands, telling me she'd heard that I was researching Hollywood publicists for a book and that she had something that might be of interest. She didn't say who she was and disappeared as swiftly as she had arrived, but it demonstrated that my research had caused small ripples to spread out throughout Hollywood. A pebble dropped in a lake never suspects that it could cause a tidal wave, but when I looked through the files on the plane home, I realized that was exactly what I had in my hands. Here was the missing link, the key to unlocking the early days of Hollywood and the beginnings of its publicity industry, hidden in a dusty folder for fifty years and ready to change the perspective on the beginnings of the public relations industry once and for all. Put simply, the file offers a new perspective on the marvels of antiquity; the papers provide a panoramic view into the distorted interior of a forgotten age. The shards of Maynard Nottage's exploded and, finally, rather desperate life lay in my lap. I'd heard whispers of him around Hollywood, from the agent Freddie Fields and a couple of others, but I'd never imagined I would actually find a wealth of material relating to the man. I was, quite simply, stunned.

The papers had remained locked away until Nottage's granddaughter, Lynda Fairweather, my mysterious benefactress, was given custody of the treasure trove in 1964. She sat on the beaten-up selection of moth-eaten papers, cuttings, pictures and letters, unsure of what to do with it, until I turned up looking into the art of the publicist and stuntster. It took me a while to discover who Lynda was, as all I had to go on was a hastily scrawled telephone number in the file she pressed on me, which nobody proceeded to answer for a good week, but the story, when it eventually unfolded, was one of shattered dreams and despair, showing in precise detail how the early, free-wheeling days of the publicist codified and congealed into the studio system and the modern age.

Looking at these files, it's clear that they form a valuable link to the past, though why Nottage didn't leave them to a scholarly institution is a puzzle. Perhaps, in his final despairing days, he considered himself unworthy of attention? Perhaps he didn't want to be dissected by a dry academic who knew nothing of his craft? Looking at it from a practitioner's point of view, I can see that his file might well have a profound influence on the art of the stuntster and may even make a significant contribution to our understanding of the manufacturing of popular culture.

Unlike his successors, Strickling, Brand and Birdwell, Nottage never really conquered Hollywood. His principal legacy rests in the cult of celebrity, something he helped sow the seeds for.

In Lynda Fairweather's twenty-nine years while her grandfather was alive, he seldom spoke about his work. Like a shell-shock victim, one could see the pain in his eyes, the wounded heart beating raggedly behind them, but at Thanksgiving in 1964, all that was about to change. Nottage gave Lynda a huge file of papers, a Pandora's Box of notebooks and photographs. After glancing at the gift, she looked at the old man sitting in the easy chair in his apartment room in Hollywood, guzzling gin from a water glass. Why now? He glanced at her periodically, as if he were on the point of making some long-considered speech.

Nottage's granddaughter was in his apartment in Hollywood by force. Lynda had been so frustrated by his antisocial behaviour at Thanksgiving that she'd descended on the eccentric old man in order to compel him to meet his family and enjoy the holiday season. She was worried about 'MN', as she called him, being holed up in his apartment, drinking for days on end and refusing to answer the telephone. Even his mailbox was crammed with three weeks' worth of letters. Occasionally he would have food and liquor left at his door and, after making sure there was no one around, he'd whisk it inside.

Years earlier, he had been a man of connections and influence. If someone had talked to Nottage in the lobby of the Hollywood Roosevelt Hotel, where he kept lodgings near his friend D. W. Griffith, they would have encountered an entirely different man. He would be breezing around the lobby sporting a jaunty hat and with a cigar hanging loosely from his lips as he discoursed on many subjects in courtly accents.

Now Maynard's rather lordly, arrogant, aquiline features, surmounted by a shining bald head, contrasted with a threadbare suit, which was brought out of the wardrobe on the few family occasions he bothered to attend. At the age of seventy-eight, living alone, drunk and almost forgotten in a tawdry apartment in the suburbs, he rarely sought the company of his family or old friends. Standing around the room were several trunks, and on one of them sat Nottage's beaten-up felt hat while against it leant his cane. In the kitchen were two large crates of film memorabilia containing a rare print of the twelve reels of Joseph Shelderfer's *The Mighty*, made in 1922 with Louise Dresser and Will Rogers.

This was the 1960s; the TV age of publicity where the Rogers & Cowan partnership reigned supreme. Nottage's last campaign was in 1938, for *The Heat*, a groping, violently realistic film about the evils of narcotic addiction in the suburbs. I saw the movie recently at a private screening and it stands up very well and would do credit to the reputations of some highly touted directors today. At the time, however, *The Heat* received poor critical notices and Nottage was made the scapegoat as he failed to generate the necessary column inches the movie's backers craved. Nottage never worked on a significant movie project again.

Hollywood is a place where reputations fade fast. A publicist can have one box-office flop and be out of business, even if he has individuality and integrity. A publicist can make all kinds of unexciting, deceptive, loss-making films look good, and continue to muddle along in Hollywood as long as he genuflects to the proper idols. At that stage in his life, the maverick stuntster had lost the appetite to suck the new-flavour corporate dick. His campaigns, which had excited Hollywood enormously in the early days, were long gone, as were his clients. His old supporters evaporated in the heat of the industry – Gregory La Cava, the febrile director of *My Man Godfrey* and *Stage Door*, who just before he died in 1952 used to sit on Malibu Beach shooting at seagulls with a BB Gun. Ewald André Dupont, director of the classic silent film *Varieté*, who had to take a job as an agent, peddling the talents of men less talented than himself because he couldn't get a job directing at any of the studios. Nottage's old friends had talents too rich and individual for the studio assembly lines, and as a result, they no longer had the power to employ Nottage's talents.

In his later years, Nottage was a familiar but unrecognized figure as he wandered about Hollywood, lost and passé, dropping into bars and ogling the girls while men with not one iota of his ability sat in plush offices in the big studios doing mundane junket work. Nottage was too much of a risk for the vast, gigantically moneyed new movie business. Correspondent Sidney Skoisky tried for several years to sell a movie biography of Nottage, but finally gave up after it was rejected out of hand by the studios. There's nothing Hollywood likes less than to be told their stars are perishable, and it's even more hateful to be told the star makers, too, will be forgotten.

At the start of his self-styled early retirement, Nottage still visited

Hollywood occasionally. He no longer had the influence to run around town and be seen in all the fashionable places; now he had to have a reason to be there, which was either to discuss a screenplay about his career or to have talks with a new director who was trying to get him out of retirement. Nottage could always find an old journalist friend to feed a line worth sinking into some archaic fan publication. On one such occasion he was quoted in a rather satirical vein: 'Gee, where are the kids with real ambition to be stars and not jesters to a studio?' Nottage went on to launch a relentless diatribe, claiming that he was living temporarily in Nevada and doing a great deal of travelling. He said he was still an avid moviegoer and randomly mentioned *The Power and the Glory* as one of a few recent pictures he had liked.

But sat in his smelly room with his granddaughter in 1964, the ravages of time had reduced him to a bitter and twisted old man. Lynda, leafing through the file he had given her, asked him what he thought of the generation of Hollywood publicists that had followed in his wake. 'They were all right,' he said, noncommittally. He still held the view that good pictures were made brilliant by good directors who were allowed to work without interference and was apparently amused by the deferential treatment that had become the norm in Hollywood. 'They didn't know who was boss, the actress, actor, studio or director, so they tried to appeal to them all,' he says in his notes. 'What a waste of energy. Everyone was selling their soul and would take whatever scraps were on offer just to get a ticket to the big time. Yeah, the producers just laughed behind their backs. They were all paper men spilling out press releases and sucking up to Hedda Hopper. They didn't know fiddly squat! I saw Henry Rogers at some dreary launch a while back. He knew his history a little, knew who I was, but he had the gall to come up to me and say he admired my work and had been influenced by me. That was a hell of an insult – he'd never have said that if we'd been rivals. You can only afford to be nice to someone with no power in the publicity game – there was no call to rub in the fact that I had no power. There's no need for these young Turks to belittle me with phoney kindness. Reichenbach would have blacked my eye if I'd said that to him. Hell,

I'd have broken his leg if he'd said it to me. The only satisfaction I have is that Rogers'll end up like me.'

Nottage told Lynda that he had been working on his autobiography as well as some plays, stories and poetry. He needed time away from distractions and he didn't want to know any of his extended family. His writing, looking at it now, reflected a well-guarded sentimentality, though little remains of anything he wrote. 'The simple things, the human things, are important in publicity,' he told her. 'There are supposed to be only seven or eight plots for a successful scam and each one has to work like a potter shapes clay at a wheel. On the surface, they are relatively unimportant. The crucial element is in persuading an audience to love the potential star; the audience must adore the very fibre of the star's being.' Nottage spoke with enthusiasm about Molly Picon, the Yiddish actress, as one of the great contemporary performers. He claimed he had tried, unsuccessfully, to sell her to Hollywood years ago.

On that occasion in 1964, Lynda told me on the phone, Nottage reverted to the graceful, well-mannered gentleman he was said to have been in his youth, both in speech and action. This was something one hadn't seen for years. She remembered long silences as he composed his thoughts, as if he were looking for the answers to his own decline.

Nottage's exile was seedy. He had loved the company of women in his day, the younger the better, but as time passed by and he moved further from the source of his power, his ability to find them failed, though that didn't stop him trying. One diary entry appears now to be a guarded apology to his estranged wife: 'How could I ever have a meaningful relationship with women over the age of twenty-five? So many beautiful women wanted me and they made me feel alive!'

A shaft of sunlight lit up the crooked form of Maynard Nottage in his rooms, highlighting a broken man, his granddaughter thought, but like a spotlight turned on stage, it kicked Nottage into life, and suddenly he started talking about the movies, the old days and the silent films. There were incoherent moments, she remembers, but also a fair measure of eloquence, despite the gin. Lynda Fairweather realized that she was witnessing an unexpected event. She recalls a lot of what was said vividly, despite the intervening years, which is fortunate, as she had only a small address book on which to scribble down his words as fast as possible. The notes cascade all over the small book.

'I can say anything I want about Hollywood,' Nottage told her. 'I don't give a hoot what anyone says about me. I am seventy-eight years old and I can say anything I like about this movie business. It's all nostalgia, but I would love to be again at Forty-fourth and Broadway and love to see D.W. and Gregory walking down the street again. Most of all I would love to see John and Lionel Barrymore crossing the street as they used to be, when they were young and full of youth and vitality, going to a Broadway theatre. They'd stop traffic, arm in arm, in the hallowed days when they were young.'

He paused. 'There is a dreadful sameness in the sunshine out here. I love the rain and the sun. I love the change of seasons. I would love to be in New York again. The most brainless people in the entire world live in Los Angeles. No one has a brain here, unless they come from the East. I am an exile. I was spoiled in my youth. When I first went to New York, I had my first client and I worked hard to succeed. I thought I was a great genius. That was a lot of baloney. Today nobody is interested in Maynard Nottage. I don't kid myself that anybody remembers me. They don't know who I am. Nothing is as sad as poverty. My story would be the story of a fellow who ran away from a safe middle-class home. Now that's a story – how a young fellow shacks up with the rodeo, makes his way in theatre and films and makes a small fortune which he then loses. That's what they might be interested in.'

Nottage earned good money in his years as a publicist and built a lifestyle that was a blow to lose when the studio system took over. Along with Harry Reichenbach, who was more interested in the money than the lifestyle, Nottage helped establish the super-spectacle stunt, to sell what was in the theatres and, later, on the world's movie screens. He left his mark then, but it's been long forgotten. There is much to be learned from Nottage; his best campaigns embodied a boldness of technique and an immoral fervour that would chime well with a modern audience. What powered those campaigns was the fact that Nottage was able, and free, to feed the press with innumerable falsehoods and façades, performing the sort of stunts and hoaxes that would never have met with the approval of a latter-day Hollywood.

Those deliciously carefree days have been erased from Hollywood film history by the censor – now all that remains of them is anecdotal evidence, Harry Reichenbach's autobiography and the incomplete notes and fragmented diaries that Lynda Fairweather pressed on me in Beverly Hills. So much has been forgotten, cut away or hidden.

'There has been no improvement in movies since the old days,' said Nottage from his easy chair. 'We did some crazy things, but underneath it all it was fun and the people loved it. Today it seems you need a soap powder maker to sponsor your career for it to take off,' he chuckled. 'All those soft suds. They haven't improved on the stories. I don't know that they've improved in anything. It's my belief that we have lost the beauty of the craft. Yeah, I made mistakes, but when you've had what I've had, what you want is the chance to come up with big ideas and make new stars with unlimited budgets to play with and complete confidence behind you.'

Nottage sat back, looking weary, and Lynda Fairweather took the opportunity to leave. Nottage grumbled, but she said goodbye and left for Thanksgiving with the rest of her family. Later that night she returned home; Lynda was exhausted, but the session with her grandfather kept running through her mind and she took out the diary and looked at the file, pledging to find someone to pass the treasure on to, somebody who might keep her grandfather's memory alive.

Her quest proved difficult and the file gathered dust.

Lynda didn't see her grandfather again and he died a couple of months later of a cerebral haemorrhage. The funeral was a quiet affair. Nobody from Nottage's lost Hollywood past came to pay him homage. She considered it deplorable, but thought it likely they were all long-gone ghosts themselves.

However, Maynard Nottage was a lost ghost who didn't even have an autobiography to his name. His uncared-for collection of papers showed that he'd started one, but excised and destroyed large chunks of it. His name appears rarely in the annals of showbiz history. He is the worst of things, an unknown early success in the entertainment world, and he suffered the agonies which only achievements of great magnitude can engender once they have passed into obscurity.

His story, as we shall see, is all too familiar in the world of publicity. The media's modes of expression may have changed in the last century, but the passionate embrace that Nottage extended to the art of publicity in his early days – always more of a vocation for the obsessives it attracts than a mere job – crops up again and again throughout the century that followed his arrival on the scene, as does the bitter disillusionment in which he ended his life. It's almost as if a poisoned chalice has been passed on from generation to generation – the scales have tipped erratically back and forth from publicity-as-business to publicity-as-bacchanalian-event, only occasionally finding the necessary balance.

Publicists rarely look to the past, but a glance back in time can be instructive. Publicist's personal stories have rarely been considered important and have, as a consequence, remained hidden, none more successfully than those of Maynard Nottage. Yet it is useful to trace the way that each generation of publicist has embraced the changing century and new ways of telling stories to an ever-changing media. If one exercises the ghosts of PR, rather than exorcising them, one can understand the impact PR has had on the modern world and the formula for fame which they created.

Part One:

IN SEARCH OF THE SONS OF BARNUM

• • •

• One •

BARNUM'S ELEPHANT IN THE ROOM

Where did the PR industry begin? Was it with the *Bible*? Or was it born from the pomp and circumstance of the Roman circus? Did the itinerant bards in the early Middle Ages begin it all, telling stories tailored to the egotistical needs of whichever king they were the guest of? It has its roots in all of these, but the PR industry as we know it today really begins with one man: the great self-publicist, showman and aphorist Phineas Taylor Barnum. It has rarely been in the interests of publicists to admit that the industry started without them, but it is useful, now, to understand the roots of it, and acknowledge that Barnum was the first man to make spectacular use of a new media age where information could travel quickly thanks to the inexorable rise of the newspaper.

Barnum's history is a thing of legend. He was America's second millionaire and he died the richest man in the country with $5 million in the bank. He was friends with Mark Twain, went buffalo hunting with George Custer and hung out with Abraham Lincoln. However, Barnum knew the importance of one thing: connection and how to get people talking about what he did. One of the great untruths about Barnum is that he once said, 'There is a sucker born every minute.' He *did* however say, 'Every crowd has a silver lining.' He believed that in every assembly there was money to plunder, and the bigger the crowd, the mightier the profit. He also considered it foolish for a showman to be disrespectful to the audience that put food on his table.

Barnum loved an audience and he *needed* them to spread his stories around the world. It was no wonder that he had such an impact on later publicists. Those who left the circuses and travelling shows that sprang up towards the end of the nineteenth century, thanks to his influence, had seen how much he earned from wit, chutzpah and a brazen brand of storytelling.

Harry Reichenbach and Maynard Nottage, who were among his immediate successors, were prone to genuflection at the mere mention of his name, for it was he who created the vacuum that sucked in all the talented but unlikely men who created the publicity empire that spawned Hollywood.

In 1825, when he was a mere haberdasher's son, Barnum heard of a story that intrigued him. A plantation owner was putting a slave up for sale and this slave, Joice Heth, claimed to have been the nursemaid of George Washington. She had been offered for sale at $3,000, an awful lot of money in those days. Barnum went upstate to examine the lady, and when he met her, he looked her up and down and did a mental calculation. If this woman was the nursemaid of George Washington, it made her 163 years old. Immediately he began to make arrangements to purchase her. He bartered with the plantation owner, paying the still princely sum of $1,000, then he put her on show. For 25 cents a time, people came from all over the state to poke and prod her, listen to her stories and hear the hymns she'd sung when she was nursemaid to the future president.

When the initial flurry of punters started to die down, letters began appearing in the press, saying that the woman was a fake, an automaton made out of India rubber and whalebone. In answer to these slurs and malicious lies about his prize attraction, Barnum wrote passionate letters to the press, which quickly fuelled a furious discourse. Further stories followed, claiming that she was in fact dying, and Barnum defended the accusations in public. We now know that she wasn't dying, but the debate sparked new interest in Barnum's sideshow attraction and the public began to visit the old woman again.

So who was responsible for writing the letters? Barnum, of course! They provoked the crowds, who flocked in their thousands to re-inspect his oddity. Nearly one and half million people went to see Joice Heth, earning Barnum a fortune in the process. With the money generated, Barnum bought the Scudder Museum in New York and set up the Barnum Museum of American Oddities, which was an extraordinary cornucopia of freaks from all over the globe. The Museum contained two types of freak: tribal people, or previously undiscovered new and unknown races like the Zalumma Agra; and the Circassian Beauties, women who had supposedly been slaves to the Turks during the Circassian War. Part of the intrigue surrounding the exotic Circassian Beauties was their 'not-quite-but-almost slave status'. The primary requirement for the women who played Circassians was that they be attractive, and they obtained their trademark frizzy afro by soaking their hair in beer.

More famously, Barnum exploited people born with physical abnormalities, such as conjoined twins, his most famous being Chang and Eng, the original 'Siamese twins'. The twins were born in 1811 in Siam and arrived in the United States in 1829. They were extremely disagreeable with each other and when they met Barnum they thought him quite stingy. Chang and Eng eventually retired to a plantation in North Carolina, and, aged forty-two, married sisters Addie and Sally Yates, going on to father twenty-one children.

Other natural abnormalities Barnum paraded included Madame Clofullia, the bearded lady, and Jo-Jo the dog-faced boy who was 'The most prodigious paragon of all prodigies secured by P. T. Barnum in fifty years. The human Skye terrier, the crowning mystery of nature's contradictions.' The dog-faced boy, whose real name was Fedor Jeftichew, suffered from a genetic disorder which gave him abnormal amounts of body hair.

Barnum also encouraged performers to do freakish things. Constentenus, the tattooed man, had 288 original designs covering his body. Barnum fabricated his biography, claiming that Constentenus was captured by the Khan of Kashagar and forcibly tattooed as an alternative to death. Constentenus was presented in an exotic fashion with his hair braided, wearing a loincloth to convey a sense of 'untamed' humanity, performing a novelty act involving sword swallowing.

His *tour de force* was the Feejee Mermaid, which was one of Barnum's first 'humbugs'. Before exhibiting the mermaid in 1842, Barnum created a media frenzy by distributing flyers and writing letters to newspapers that claimed a certain 'Dr Griffin, agent of the Lyceum of Natural History in London' would be travelling through New York with a 'veritable mermaid taken from among the Feejee Islands.' In reality, 'Dr Griffin' was Barnum's friend Levi Lyman. The creature, which was nothing more than the upper torso of a monkey sewn to the lower half of a fish, became one of Barnum's biggest attractions, developing his taste for hype and spin.

Barnum's greatest friend was Charles Stratton, aka General Tom Thumb. Barnum began exhibiting General Tom Thumb when he was only a boy of five years old and under two feet tall. At the time he advertised the 'General' as eleven years old for fear that the public wouldn't find a diminutive five-year-old particularly scintillating. Beginning in 1844, Barnum and Tom toured Europe for three years, even meeting Queen Victoria in the 1840s. Tom Thumb married Lavinia Warren, also a midget, in 1863, and Barnum frequently advertised the couple with a child, although Lavinia never bore any children.

The tour with Tom Thumb opened doors throughout Europe for Barnum, which would stand him in good stead when he returned decades later as the proud owner of a circus. Barnum had made and lost fortunes in the intervening years – he'd founded a newspaper, the *Illustrated News*; written a massively popular autobiography; toured the singer Jenny Lind, also known as the Swedish Nightingale, around America; built, lost and regained a museum and written a number of books. He had been reviled and praised in equal measure but always fought back to a position of strength.

The Barnum circus, founded in 1871, was the apotheosis of his career, the perfect refinement of all his interests. It underwent several name and personnel changes before becoming Barnum & Bailey's 'The Greatest Show on Earth' in 1888. It was also the first circus to travel by train, allowing them to reach areas of middle America that were previously inaccessible by anything but the smallest carnivals. What the circus needed, however, was a totem, an icon, a perfect representation of what it stood for.

Back in Britain, touring and visiting royalty, Barnum heard about a problem at the London Zoological Gardens. London Zoo had a problem with their enormous African elephant, Jumbo, who was reputed to be growing too difficult to manage. Jumbo was, by then, over eleven feet high and about six tonnes, making him the largest elephant ever measured in captivity. The bull elephant had been a resident of both Paris and London zoos since he was captured as a baby, and had been nursed from a sickly calf. He was an enormous attraction, but the zoo was anxious that he might escape and kill people, so they wanted to get rid of him.

Barnum saw his opportunity and secretly bought Jumbo for the sum of $10,000 – an enormous amount of money at the time, but a tenth of what he initially offered, thanks to a careful series of negotiations based on the supposition that Jumbo was an awkward and unmanageable beast. As soon as the sale was made public, the British people created a marketing coup for Barnum by demanding the sale be cancelled. Thousands of school children – and even Queen Victoria herself – urged that the beloved elephant be kept on British soil. The outrage was further fuelled when the London *Times* found out: 'How dare this American entrepreneur take our great Jumbo?' it frothed. The rest of the media agreed and the average man on the street became indignant about Barnum's plans to remove Jumbo abroad. Their pleas fell on deaf ears, though, as Barnum now knew what a prize steer he'd lassoed and boasted that he would turn down even an offer of £200,000 to void the sale. So who planted the original letters to the *Times*? Why Barnum of course, giving him exactly the publicity bonanza he craved, and an elephant so well known that it spawned the English phrase, 'Mumbo Jumbo'.

Jumbo departed the British Isles for New York from Southampton docks on the *Assyrian Monarch*. Using the then new telegraph communications, Barnum sped stories out across America announcing his triumphant return with Jumbo. By the time he arrived in New York, the popular press was softened up in readiness for Jumbo's arrival in the city. There were extraordinary scenes when they arrived, as Jumbo had generated such a sentimental hullabaloo on both sides of the Atlantic that he became the single biggest attraction in Barnum's career. The world went Jumbo crazy, and for his part the now gentle Jumbo seemed to love all the attention. For three and a half years he was the much-loved feature in Barnum's travelling circus and menagerie. In the course of his career, he sold millions of souvenirs and photos and gave 'at least a million children' rides on his back, as well as Queen Victoria, Winston Churchill and Teddy Roosevelt.

When Jumbo was killed in Ontario, aged twenty-four, by a passing freight train on 15 September 1885, the gigantic elephant was mourned by millions the world over. Jumbo's stuffed hide eventually went on display at Tufts University, of which Barnum was a trustee, and it remained there until it was destroyed by fire in 1975.

One of Barnum's most durable stunts was to take Jumbo into the town the circus was due to visit next and look for an impoverished farmer so Jumbo could help the farmer plough his fields. One can imagine the scene: everything came to a stop and chaos reigned as the entire population flocked to see such an astonishing and crazy sight. Absolutely no one went to work. In certain states of America it's still illegal to plough with an elephant to this day. Marrying your cousin? Fine. Rigging an election? OK. But elephant ploughing is out. It isn't surprising that Barnum's influence had such a far reach, and it shines through in the work of both Harry Reichenbach and Maynard Nottage.

Towards the end of his life, Barnum's reputation as a purveyor of 'humbug' – his own word for the more hyperbolical side of his operation – was in abeyance and his good works – such as park building, politics, the improvement of public services during his time as mayor of Bridgeport, Connecticut, and a strong anti-slavery stance – were more prominent in the public consciousness.

'I don't believe in duping the public, but I believe in first attracting and then pleasing them,' he once said. By 1891, he had attracted and pleased them in abundance and he still had one more stunt up his sleeve. Knowing that he was dying, he gave permission to the *Evening Sun* to print his obituary in advance, so that he might have the pleasure of reading it. He asked for a rundown of box office receipts on the morning of 7 April, and a few hours later he was dead. The circus was sold sixteen years later for an astonishing $400,000 – over $8 million today.

• Two •

THE RISE OF THE NEW BALLYHOO

Showbusiness was gathering crowds rapidly towards the end of Barnum's life and was heading upmarket, thanks in part to his innovations, away from the sleazy saloon bars romanticized in so many Westerns. It was a natural progression for the people who had drifted out of the circus to take to the lights of vaudeville and, later, to the erupting movie industry.

In the 1880s, vaudeville came into being, thanks in part to Tony Pastor, who had started out singing in minstrel shows and at Barnum's Scudder's American Museum, before leasing, in 1881, the Germania Theatre on 14th Street in New York. There, he alternated between showing operettas and family shows and invited ragtime players to perform. His variety shows took off, but so did innumerable imitators, who created chains and touring shows that soon outstripped his small-time, local outlook and led to the extraordinary vaudeville sensation that, by the time Maynard Nottage and Harry Reichenbach arrived in New York, was crying out for press agents to beat the competition. Tony Pastor, in keeping with his surname, made vaudeville 'respectable for "ladies and gentlemen" '* by the time he died in 1908.

By the turn of the century the king of popular variety was Benjamin Franklin Keith, sitting at the head of the Keith-Albee theatrical empire. Although it seemed omnipresent, Keith's empire had some

---

* Green and Laurie, *Show Biz, From Vaude to Video*, page 4

vibrant competition. Showbusiness had become a cut-throat industry, where the old hands were serenaded by the sound of cash registers but were cautious about the competition. If any upstart moved in on their territory, they were quick to react, and it wasn't uncommon for a ruthless henchman to be employed to take out thunder stealers.

A publicity agent had to be alive to all the trade gossip and quick to formulate an offering under these circumstances. Every impresario's desperation to be top dog was epitomized by the frenzied bidding on the talent auction block. A roster of players, all determined to be kingpin and take Keith's place, wanted to have the best show on the strip. The big guns made up a formidable list: William Morris, Klaw and Erlanger, the Shuberts, Martin Beck and Marcus Loew. All these ruthless impresarios began offering astronomical salaries to corner the star market. The battle between the theatre giants provided an embarrassment of riches for the bewildered yet delighted public. Wooed by affluent theatres, lavish productions and star-studded bills, the public were willingly seduced.

Theatregoing changed from a Saturday-night event to a fixed American habit two and three times a week. Some joked that it was more popular and easier than taking a bath. As the infant *Variety* noted at the time in its colourful 'slanguage', Keith and his competitors had 'deloused Vaud for women and children; with its face scrubbed clean, with satin bows in its hair, Vaud could no longer be scorned as the saloon strumpet of yesteryear!'

Tastes changed so fast that the stars of the legitimate stage, the ones who had formerly looked down at 'vohdville', sought engagements with the 'two a day'. In time, the divinities like Sarah Bernhardt and Lily Langtry shared bills with wirewalkers, contortionists, dog acts and midgets.

The movie industry, meanwhile, began life at Thomas Edison's laboratory in the brain of William K. L. Dickson in 1881, with Barnum's aphorism ringing in their ears. By 1894, Dickson's idea, which Edison said would do 'for the eye what the phonograph does for the ear',* was ready to go, in the shape of the 'kinetoscope'. On

* A. Scott Berg, *Goldwyn*, page 29

23 April Edison shipped twenty-five machines to Atlantic City and Chicago, along with a selection of minute-long films, including one of a man sneezing and a tooth extraction. Nobody had ever seen moving pictures. It was a unique, miraculous event and it's no surprise that people were attracted to it and wanted to put something, anything, on film.

The atmosphere was ripe for men who wanted to make money. Naturally improvements, such as Vitascope, came thick and fast, allowing the time of films shown to expand dramatically. By 1898, there were 5,000 Vitascope parlours across the US, attracting huge numbers of viewers. Initially films, once bought, belonged to the purchaser, but by the early part of the twentieth century, film producers had sniffed money and changed tack, renting out the prints instead of selling them. Demand rapidly became insatiable. In 1904, Carl Laemmle began buying Nickelodeons, and during 1907 and 1908, half the American population went to see a Nickelodeon feature once a week or more. Within two years, as films expanded and their popularity boomed, full-blown theatres took the place of Nickelodeons.

This was the gold-rush period for all forms of showbusiness, although vaudeville dominated until 1913, while the movie industry was merely a foetus. America was loosening up and, new to the experience of mass theatregoing and the miraculous-seeming movie, the nation found it liked the experience. No wonder pioneers eagerly staked their claims to whatever seemed most likely to pay off, be it vaudeville, aviation stunts, the movies or burlesque. Actors, many of whom went on to become household names, had thousands of stages across the country on which to hone their art.

The rise of the newspaper as a means of communication during the previous century, thanks to the Industrial Revolution's speedier printing processes, lead to a flurry of formats in which attention-seeking people could find a public voice. The importance of the press to the entertainment industry began in the so-called Yellow Journalism period, when William Randolph Hearst's *New York Journal* and Joseph Pulitzer's *New York World* fought for the highest circulation in the late 1890s and early 1900s. The pejorative term refers to journalism of an unethical, scandal-mongering nature, designed purely to draw in readers, and is a direct, if somewhat less salubrious, descendant, of Barnum's humbug. It proved a fertile breeding ground for people who had trained under Barnum as spielers and barkers at the circus and who had read his books, such as *The Art of Money-Getting*.

Any paper ready to take any story, however scurrilous, was a prime source of exposure for a press agent and his clients. The newspapers were a primitive medium, despite the technological advances, and apart from a few noble exceptions they were driven by greed. Right up until World War Two, when a more informed, cautious style of journalism took hold, they were a prime target for press agents, and many of the poorly paid journalists soon became press agents instead.

This was a febrile and fertile time in which to be involved in showbusiness and there was so much going on that it was obvious that people would be needed to draw the press and public's attention to the merits of whatever was hot that week, hoping to make it last long enough to make some serious money.

It was a perfect atmosphere for breeding stunts and into this arena stepped great early publicists such as Harry Reichenbach and Maynard Nottage. They were two pioneers, men acclimatized and equipped for the ascent, tempered by a life already lived, both hungry and with a vision of a new epoch. Both men had been conditioned by the sideshow, touched by Phineas Taylor Barnum and his ilk and drawn to New York. Harry Reichenbach was a poor boy from a poor family intent on making his fortune, while Maynard Nottage was escaping a Methodist upbringing and looking for adventure. Without these new pyrotechnicians of publicity, the new world of entertainment would never have sustained itself. Out of their hard graft and wild imaginations came the entertainment industry we know today, a vast juggernaut that started out as a rickshaw bike in the early years of the twentieth century.

One rainy afternoon in December 1902, Harry Reichenbach sauntered down Broadway, nothing in his pockets except his hands. He coolly tramped the asphalt, raising an eyebrow and scowling at the offerings on show. He arrogantly believed he had something to offer to the men behind these trifles and fervently believed they needed his gift. 'New York is the zenith and ideal of every press agent's career, but its doors were double-bolted,' he said.

The young Harry Reichenbach started knocking on doors in order to get an audience with the theatre barons, but the door was unceremoniously slammed in his face. Although he thought he was 'the man', the gatekeepers saw him as a conman, a rough circus spieler. Harry left with his tail between his legs but vowed to return. He went back on the road and further honed his skills on the carnival circuit, teaching ducks to dance and riding the railroads like a hobo. His bravado masked some personal doubts that he would succeed. Did he have the class to break through? Would this kid who had spent an age attracted to the sideshow really find employment?

Whether he had breeding was irrelevant, though, because he had the stuff. Like some religious calling, he had had an epiphany that had drawn him to the big city. When he was nine he had a mystical encounter in his home town of Frostburg, Maryland, which set him on a path that led him years later to this spot.

'A tall, lean fellow in overalls walked along the main street of Frostburg, Maryland, carrying a large roll of paper under his arm and a brick in each hand. Suddenly he stopped, placed one brick on the pavement and walked ten paces ahead to set down the other. Then he returned and looked reassuringly at the two bricks while a small crowd gathered to watch him. He picked up the first brick and placed it ten paces beyond the second, coming back for a new perspective. "They're taking measurements for the new plaza," observed one onlooker. "No, they're marking off fresh coal beds reaching from George's Creek," said another. The lean, gawky fellow ignored these comments and continued methodically to set one brick ten paces beyond the other while more and more people pressed around him. I was a boy of nine then, brush haired, spindly, big eyed, and I wriggled like an eel through the jostling mob, always managing to keep ahead of the others. After four blocks, nearly the whole of Frostburg marched behind the strange surveyor until he paused in front of the local playhouse. There he leisurely put his bricks aside, unrolled the paper under his arm and pasted up a three sheet announcing that the "Cleveland Minstrels" would be in town next week. The man with the bricks taught me the first lesson in attracting attention and the technique of drawing a crowd. Instead of blowing a trumpet, he used two quiet bricks.'

At nine Harry learned that you could make people follow, at twelve he realized an even more important lesson: he discovered that people were gullible.

'In one of Frostburg's store windows, a travelling hypnotist, who took away all ills through mesmerism, offered to place any citizen of our town in a six-day trance. Nobody in town was eager to try it, but a strange young man who said he had come to visit his aunt, was willing to forgo the visit and spend his week sleeping in the window instead of in her parlour. He was hypnotized and stretched out on a table in full view of everybody, and each day crowds stood for hours gazing at his rigid, lifeless form. Even the most hard-boiled cynics of Frostburg succumbed after the second day of proof and visited "The Great Griffith". But the man with the bricks had kindled a spirit for research within me. The third day, I slipped into the store and, through a parting in the curtain, I murmured to the unconscious form on the table, "Say, the Professor would like to know how you're getting along." "Tell the Bozo I'm OK," he replied. I felt I had skipped two grades in the school of ballyhoo. While people were so eager to believe, there was still room in the world for miracles.'

Reichenbach, born in 1882, grew up in small-town America, the son of a storekeeper in a tiny impoverished mining town. Charlie Reichenbach was a generous man and a cherished figure in the community. He empathized with the workers' toil and allowed the miners to run up credit. Unfortunately his sympathies and big heart were over-exposed. While the ruthless pit owners exploited the workers, standing them down at short notice, then reemploying them on lower rates, Charlie tried to help them by opening up his credit book, and when the miners went on to strike to get a fair deal, the owners simply shipped workers in from outside the area to do the extraction instead.

'Out-of-work miners had more time to eat and their appetites increased in proportion to their idleness. Liquor, which used to be a payday luxury, now became an everyday necessity.'

Harry's father kept the work force fed and clothed by digging into his own meagre savings until the whole exercise came crashing down when Charlie fell into bankruptcy. He realized too late that his generosity was insanity and that it had shredded his family life.

Harry grew up captivated by nickel thrillers, transfixed by the adventures of Frank Reade, the teenage hero and inventor, and similar tales of wonder. When he wasn't dreaming of Reade's fantastic mechanical men, who could walk five miles at a step, he was vibrating to the heroism of Frank Merriwell who was always at the point of a gun or with one leg over a precipice.

'That was the life for me! Aladdin combined with Buffalo Bill! Hardship and magic, adventure and miracle! In my hometown, the only excitement I knew was to sit in Hammersmith's coffee house with the boys, talk rough language and eat cream pies. And I often stood at the railroad station watching the long, stark lines of rail streak the distance like mighty spears, and far away – almost three miles – they disappeared in a sudden bend. Around that bend was the world – Baltimore – the great cities of the East, and the centre of the universe, New York.'

Recognizing the family was destitute, the twelve-year old Harry decided to run away from home and not be a burden on his parents. The catalyst for this huge step became his life's passion: 'A carnival came to town. Wanda the palmist, the Girl in Red, Windy Hughes and the spieler, Millie Christine, the Siamese twin, and Mlle. Sutro, the snake charmer. Instinctively, by some magnetic force, I became one of this motley family; when they left town I left with them. I learned that a gypsy is only a poor imitation of a carnival man. Carnival people are the wildest of nomads – they're at home in a tree. They can't eat except in a tent and they're game enough to cheat cowboys under the nozzle of their guns. A new staff of teachers took up my education. Queer, comic figures of the circus lot. Doc Crosby, a former professor of English in a Western University, who was never sober and used a tin cup as a mirror, the frazzled end of a rope as a lather brush and a sharp edge of glass as a razor blade. "Jew" Murphy who taught me that "a guy who shows a gun never uses it, because no one ever uses an ornament in a fight". Doc Hawks who believed "a row of farmers is a circus man's rosary". And Hiki Blitz who thought it was charity to cheat the small town folk a little because it sharpened their wits for bigger deals. They were all children of the ram's horn – trumpeters with magnetic sound waves that turned the ears and heads of country rubes. They devoutly believed the earth's axis was greased with banana oil and the land was covered with applesauce.

'Old Doc Crosby would take me for morning walks to survey each town that we played, and initiate me into the philosophy of the canvas world. "Remember Harry," he'd say in his husky, rum-corroded voice, "if the man who makes 'to let' signs is prospering in a town, nobody else is. Everybody expects graft from circus men. Every place they enter, there's the count of nine against them even before they get a chance to fight, so you have to be quick on the mental trigger to survive." He'd take a chew of black tobacco and stroke his mustache with a curling iron grip. "Never give a sucker an even break. It's dog eat dog all along the line. For every kid born with fifty dollars, there's twins born on the other side of the street scheming to take the fifty from him! So the only way to make a ten strike is to strike up the band!" And I always did. For old Doc Crosby posed as a dentist at street fairs, guaranteeing absolutely painless extractions, and when he pulled a tooth I had to strike up the band, playing a fire alarm march to drown out the patient's yells.'

Harry experienced the raw struggle with sheriffs, cowboys, cattle ranchers, greasers and half-breeds, as he travelled through wide open towns filled with gambling joints and wild women. Here he received the rudiments of a worldly education since he never had a formal education or saw the inside of a school. The odd chemistry of circumstance, the miracles of the nickel thrillers and the wonder books took on a reality and were often duplicated in his own life on the road with the carnival.

Harry soon learned the tricks that drew a crowd; he understood one important thing and that was how to connect with the punters and draw them in, like moths to a flame. If someone would pay money to experience entertainment and enjoyed it, he would tell a friend. This was the power of connection that generated word of mouth. In his days working for the sideshow, Harry learned a crucial fact: that it was all about giving the paying public a story to take away. It was the finding, creating and telling of stories that was important. Stories are irresistible to editors and their readers. Reichenbach understood, well before he turned his hand to the craft, that a skilled publicist can and should be able to deliver a shot directly into the media's artery. It was an alchemy dependent on the subtlety of relationships and reputations, working at the gossamer divide between fact and fiction.

'It was no wonder, therefore,' he wrote, 'that in later life when I adopted the career of a publicity man, I could fool a hundred editors into accepting bits of fancy as front page news, and get a hundred thousand columns in headlines and new stories for things that had never happened.'

In many ways, Harry was driven by the innocence of the age. He was spirited, freewheeling, joyous and random, but he also knew how important his work was. The Doc called it 'a cultural profession' where 'you need an absolute will to achieve the impossible, the surreal and the absurd'. The Doc took the young Reichenbach aside and said, 'Son, it's the great unwashed that have an atavistic longing for heroes, myths and culture. Folklore and anecdote have been central to the human psyche since the Stone Age. They're the great communicators of moral truths, cultural lessons, history and wisdom. They lend order to our random universe.'

Whilst on the road, the Doc schooled Harry in hype and told him about his own hero, Phineas Taylor Barnum. Reichenbach was aware of the great showman, but Crosby dissected his methodology as only a fellow showman could. The Doc understood his power and used it as a template, like so many of his competitors. All the showmen took PT's gospel as their scripture. They were Barnum's disciples, carrying the litany of bunkum across the States of America and sometimes beyond. The mighty PT was the Maharishi of Ballyhoo. As the Doc said, he was 'a man so good at publicity, he's still spinning like a top in his grave'.

• Three •

OUT OF THE OLD WEST

Maynard Nottage's career in showbiz had a slightly more auspicious start than Harry Reichenbach's, although the circumstances bore certain remarkable similarities. Nottage was a tall and wiry boy who left home at sixteen years old, desperate to make an impact on the world. He was, according to the scant notes he left about his early life, fleeing an oppressively religious Methodist upbringing and 'a dreary martinet of a father' in or near Salisbury, Maryland. Every July in his early teens, he had bunked off to be near the Salt Water Cowboys as they rounded up the wild Chincoteague Ponies on Assateague Island, on the borders of Maryland and Virginia. Here, he says, he learned 'which end of a horse would bite'.

Like Reichenbach, he arrived in New York late in 1902, harbouring a fascination with Buffalo Bill Cody's publicist and biographer, John M. Burke, having travelled with Buffalo Bill's Wild West for a season. The Wild West show had hired him because of 'my obvious love of horses and my way with words, which I'd gleaned from my father's sermonizing but spiced with enough profanity to startle even the most equable equine'.

Buffalo Bill's Wild West had an arrangement with the Barnum and Bailey circus – they swapped seasons in Europe and America and shared transportation. Both were huge and relied on a great deal of ballyhoo to draw in a crowd. Little detail remains in Nottage's archives from this time, but it's clear that his imagination was fired by the myth and pathos of the Wild West, which had been built up from nothing more than a few violent and violently self-mythologizing men.

Landing in New York with a head full of ideas and an urgent desire to help create personalities as large as Cody's, he fared better than Reichenbach, initially, because of his skill with horses. That and the fact that, like many boys born in the late nineteenth and early twentieth century, a hard-working, outdoor upbringing had left him looking older than he was. Nottage's aquiline features were marked by a curious hardness and a cynical appearance. It was this same look, born of poverty and hard work from an early age, that allowed fifteen-year-olds to get away with falsifying their age and signing up for the Great War a decade or so later.

In 1903, showbusiness was as desperate as the world's armies were a decade later for bodies to throw into the front line. 'I looked like a mule dressed up as a racehorse,' he wrote in his papers in a rare moment of self-deprecation, 'staggering uncertainly at the tail end of a race, but it was enough to get me work.' Even in these early days he had a strong streak of self-belief that would, in later life, evolve into the arrogant desperation that marked his decline. 'I knew that with a little more luck and a few jobs under my belt I'd be fit to lead the race,' he adds.

The first work he got in New York was as part of the publicity machine behind *The Great Train Robbery*, released in 1903, on the strength of his association with Buffalo Bill's Wild West. Nottage walked out to New Jersey, having heard that they were filming a bandit movie. 'I talked my way into working for that film, showed them a few tricks and pitched a few ideas. I got myself an audience with [director Edwin S.] Porter on a couple of tall tales about Bill Cody and an ability to lasso the prettiest girl on the set and within a few hours I was hired,' he said. The twelve-minute Western, which caused audiences to scream in terror when the train rounded a corner and steamed towards them while a bandit shot directly at them from the screen, was perfect fodder for Nottage's febrile imagination. He had been steeped for the best part of a year in the myths of the West and was ready to pull out all the stops to get some work.

Nottage's main contribution to the film's publicity was concocted in cahoots with Porter and involved a scam with a stuntman. In the company of an old cowboy with a penchant for stunt riding, Nottage – who was passing himself off as a twenty-two-year-old to keep the work – toured a number of cities across the US, getting the cowboy to demonstrate his horsemanship. The name of the cowboy is illegible, but it would seem that he had a major drinking problem and was a serial womanizer. Certainly Nottage had to work extremely hard to spring him from jail on numerous occasions. It taught him the value of sex and alcohol and the sort of stimuli that drove innumerable men and women caught up in the glamour of showbusiness. The industry ran on hookers and booze. Nottage, still escaping his Methodist upbringing, didn't necessarily approve, but he was enough a man of his time to note that 'the most beautiful women seemed to spring like minor goddesses from the poorest places, all desperate for a taste of the godhead of fame'. The sort of outrageous bribes, oiled with bourbon and broken promises, that he produced for small-town officials hell bent on incarcerating the cowboy lothario created a template that was refined to an extraordinary degree a couple of decades later.

As part of the publicity tour, Nottage also staged a safe-cracking exhibition with a reformed outlaw who was a consultant on the production. Unfortunately a bounty hunter spotted the safecracker in the middle of a demonstration in Boston and noisily announced that the self-declared reformer was in fact still a wanted criminal. The bounty hunter stopped the performance and, after a fistfight that Nottage claims increased the takings for the film that night considerably, handcuffed the criminal, turning him in for a handsome reward. To finish the tour, Nottage posed as the safecracker. He claims that he was so good at imitating the act that he was never found out, which leads me to suspect that some of the holes in his papers, which occur mostly in his early years, may well have been made deliberately.

All publicists go through lean patches, and the necessity to survive produces greater tenacity and ingenuity. During Maynard Nottage's hard times, of which there were many, he managed to pay for the groceries by somewhat illicit means. He formulated a method, using drug-store cotton wool and wire, of blocking up the coin returns of subway ticket machines all over New York City. At regular intervals, different ticket machines would be unplugged and handfuls of quarters would fall out. Nottage claims to have regularly raised around $50 a week this way, until his conscience urged him to stop. Conscience notwithstanding, Nottage returned to this thievery later in his career, when times became particularly hard in the late 1920s, in order to invest in certain theatre productions. Every show he invested in with the ill-gotten gains flopped, and attributing the failures to karma, Nottage stopped this caper altogether.

In the early, halcyon days of his career, however, his optimism knew few bounds. 'I knew *The Great Train Robbery* would make money,' he said in his papers, 'and that this sort of visceral entertainment could make me money too. All I needed was a way in.' He had found it. Edwin S. Porter, in gratitude for the extra publicity generated for *The Great Train Robbery*, introduced Nottage to the great vaudeville impresario Willie Hammerstein, and through him Nottage met the actors, dancers, freaks and fools that would haunt his career and later decline.

This was a welcome relief for Nottage after a brief association with the American Mutoscope and Biograph Company (later known simply as the Biograph Company), who were, in late 1902 and early 1903, moving away from documenting real people and starting to make narrative films.

'They took all my best ideas and sucked them dry,' Nottage wrote. 'I was trying to get them to present opportunities for the newspapers to come and take photographs of their stars but they were still of the opinion that film was something people would come to see, regardless of its content, just to be astonished by the mere fact of the moving image. They weren't open to much in the way of publicity, but some of the stunts I pitched at them came back as movies later on. A stunt with a magician following people around, picking their pockets, putting publicity for their films in the wallet and then, just when they're good and panicked about losing their dough, reinserting the wallet, was rejected as "too cumbersome", but when *The Bewitched*

Traveller came out in 1904 I wrote them and demanded royalties. I never saw a cent.'

The trouble was that Nottage's ideas were often too complex; one of the reasons why Reichenbach would flourish later was that his ideas relied on simplicity – even if the set-up was complex, the core idea was simple and effective. Everything Nottage did, or wanted to do, was grand in design and relied on the audience being as bright as he was.

Willie Hammerstein's sense of promotion set high standards. Many looked up to this Goliath of the entertainment world and were inspired to copy him to make serious money, though very few came close to reaching the same level. His theatrical and vaudeville empire, which started with New York's Victoria theatre, was gigantic by modern standards. Willie was Mr Showbiz and his chutzpah knew no bounds, so it wasn't surprising that many tried to emulate him. What wasn't known until I was handed Nottage's papers was how indebted he was to others, Nottage particularly. In the early days, between the opening of the Victoria in 1898 and 1904, Hammerstein operated on his own chutzpah, which was sufficient to make the Victoria a roaring success. Hammerstein wanted more, however, and when Porter introduced Nottage to him, he seems to have encountered someone whose ideas he felt he could exploit to increase his empire.

First, however, he put Nottage to the test, wanting to know whether the way he had managed to promote *The Great Train Robbery* was a one-off. 'I think he knew I wasn't telling the whole truth about my age,' notes Nottage, 'though he was good enough never to mention that failing, at least. So I got me an introduction to one of his copyists and packed my bags for Chicago.'

Waiting for him in Chicago was an attempted Hammerstein clone, Evarts Friedman, a seedy theatrical entrepreneur and owner of three large fleapits in Chicago, whose aspirations for a better life had led him to an association with Hammerstein. This allowed Hammerstein to subtly extend his reach to Chicago and gave Friedman a chance to hit the ground running when he moved from burlesque to vaudeville.

Friedman was, despite appalling personal hygiene, a startlingly charismatic man, and he got audiences, desperate for the thrills of the showbiz world, to come into his theatres despite their rundown appearance. Nottage was taken aback when he was first met Friedman, commenting, 'A singularly unhandsome human, tiny, rotund and overweight, his teeth – those that he had – were brown and his expansive smile was crowned by a scabby, balding pate. He reeked of tobacco and garlic but he had a twinkle in his eye, and with a bundle of worn bills, he contracted me to draw crowds to his houses of fun.

'"I find the acts! You tell their stories," said Friedman in a thick European Jewish accent which became more pronounced the more he tried to hide it. "I got to get ahead and I know what my audience want."'

Friedman was wildly enthusiastic about all the entertainment vogues. He put Nottage through his paces and Nottage responded well, getting more attention for the acts in the papers. His first coup was to resuscitate the flagging confidence of a drunken juggling act, who kept on losing his nerve with the fire and axes, and to bolster his audiences considerably. Nottage presented the juggler, Marshall Gleeman, as a suicidal lunatic intent on taking his own life on stage. Posing as a concerned friend of Gleeman's, he wrote letters to the *Chicago Record Herald*, the *Chicago Tribune*, the mayor of the city and various other dignitaries, claiming that Gleeman was planning to take his own life in spectacular fashion at a performance in a few days' time and that only a full house would stop him carrying it out. Nottage hoped to get his letter published and create a minor stir, but instead the papers ran it as a full story, creating a hoo-ha far surpassing Nottage's timid expectations.

'I had to hide Gleeman away,' he said, 'as he was getting a little too above himself. From a drunk juggler with a case of the creeping yellow he turned into a different sort of monster overnight, thanks mostly to a huge flurry of letters from young women. He wasn't a handsome man but about forty young women offered to do whatever it took to put his mind at rest – I learned a lot about what a touch of fame can do from those young women. They all wanted to be known as the girl who saved Marshall Gleeman. Of course I kept them from him – we needed him clear-headed for the show – but I did keep some of their addresses.'

Come the appointed day for the show, Nottage was pleased to see queues around the block. Friedman was even more pleased. 'You've done me proud,' he told Nottage. 'You can stay!' Gleeman turned in the best performance of his life that night, a dazzling display of twirling fire and metal, but his ego had been so boosted by Nottage's promotion that he immediately demanded a huge fee and a slot higher up the bill. Friedman, however, wasn't keen for a juggler to be more than an opening act, whetting the audience's appetite for the rest of the show, so he let Gleeman go.

The juggler's career came to an end a couple of years later in Florida when he accidentally cut off his hand with an axe. 'I realized later that he had wanted to fail,' wrote Nottage. 'He was bored with what he was good at and wanted to move on, become something greater and more adored. Like so many people, he wanted more than he was capable of and saw, in the giddy lights of Friedman's Chicago theatres, a route to New York and stardom. Trouble was, there was nothing but juggling in him. Last I heard of him after his accident, he was reduced to wrestling alligators in the Everglades for petty cash.'

Nottage stayed with Friedman for a year and a half, pushing acts into the faces of the public and learning how to work the press. He made irregular trips to New York and spotted the Salomé craze early, having seen Gertrude Hoffman dance on a visit to Hammerstein. The Salomé dance was a risqué concoction taking elements of belly dance, the fan dance and a rather chaste striptease. Some of the seven veils were covered in glittery objects, others were as diaphanous as can be, and the overall effect was that of Isadora Duncan on acid. Understandably, it was one of those crazes that gripped America and caused a furore wherever it went, with many producers going on to exploit it well into the latter part of the first decade of the twentieth century.

Nottage took news of Hoffman's reception in New York back to Friedman and Friedman promptly went out and booked himself an exotic dancer. He wanted Nottage to make his Salomé the best known in America and Nottage threw himself into the task, keen to impress Hammerstein as much as Friedman. The raw materials he had to work with were not quite up to the task, however, as the girl engaged to play the part of the seductive hussy, Martha Bradley, may have looked good, but her erotic dancing left a lot to be desired.

'Martha was pretty and innocent looking,' wrote Nottage, 'and when I met her she danced like a tipsy ten year old at a beach party.' So he set to work on her. 'Within a month, I had her casting smouldering looks at any man that passed and dancing on tables like a $3 whore at the drop of a hat – I had even talked her into practising her dances for me in private as well as for work! It never ceases to amaze me what a nice, innocent girl from Des Moines will turn herself into when a whiff of notoriety and money comes her way.'

Having turned Martha from an awkward, virginal eighteen-year-old into a sexually alluring maneater in the space of a month, Nottage set to work getting the Chicago press to take notice. Posing as an outraged parishioner, he approached the church nearest to Friedman's main theatre and, 'wide-eyed and angry', asked the priest to do something about the 'salacious and degrading dancer' who would be performing a 'degenerate Salomé dance for the titillation of the audiences' in the very near future.

Nottage had arranged for Martha to practise her act in the window of a closed shop, priming her to take no notice of the passers-by and protestors he expected to materialize. The shop window was painted out, but there were enough small gaps in the paint for people to catch glimpses of Martha undulating in various states of undress, a seraphic smile – painted by Nottage – fixed on her face. He told the church leaders what he had seen and they went to investigate. With predictable outrage, they went to the papers and then to the shop. The papers, intrigued by anything to do with Friedman's theatre, which was now considered a hotbed of stories and salacious goings-on, flocked to the shop and gleefully reported their glimpses of Martha's flesh and the whirlwind of moral outrage.

Before long, word leaked out and the general populace of Chicago, more tolerant than their spiritual leaders, descended en masse. Fights broke out and eminently sensible young men lost all decorum, publicly declaring their love for Martha and offering outrageous sums of money to buy one of the seven veils she wore. The papers had a field day and tickets for Martha's first show as Salomé were selling for three times their market value within three days. Nottage, watching delighted from an upstairs window at the shop, was forced to whisk Martha away after a couple hours – no one noticed and the papers reported that she remained dancing in the shop all day.

'Martha really wasn't a great dancer,' wrote Nottage, 'but Chicago believed she was. It was an important lesson: if you want people to believe something is glorious, get an authority figure to tell them it isn't, that it's morally degrading and that they mustn't see it. The average man will flock to see it, experiencing the thrill of the illicit far more viscerally than the actual act. Not that street bally ever worked so well as that on the stage – once you get the crowd off the street and into a theatre, the authority figure is able to bring the full weight of the law and licensing to bear. I got Martha her hour on the stage. Many more hours were thrown into closing down her show.'

Whilst in Chicago, Nottage encountered Adolph Zukor. Hungarian-born Zukor had been selling furs in the city until 1903, when he was persuaded to purchase a New York theatre as an investment. Within six months, he owned 500-seat emporiums in Newark, Boston and Philadelphia, and when he met Nottage in early 1905 he was, apparently, in negotiations with Friedman about purchasing his largest theatre. That deal came to nothing, but his encounter with Nottage had a profound impact on both men, according to Nottage's notes.

'I was after some furs,' wrote Nottage, 'for a stunt involving Martha's Salomé act – something big enough to veil her seven veils so she could get into the most public of places dressed in costume and be able to disrobe in a hurry and cause a stir – and something that would go back on in an equal hurry if anyone turned nasty in the street. I wandered into Friedman's dingy office to see if he knew anywhere I could get a good deal. I didn't recognize the guy sat with him, but they were talking with an intensity I'd not seen in Friedman since I arrived. Their accents were thick with old Europe. When they stopped for a moment I took my chance and asked about furs. The new guy turned and looked at me with a crooked smile. "You buy me some lunch when Evarts and I are done," he said, "and then, then we talk about furs."

'I took him to the best dive I could afford, hoping it would be worth my while – somewhere I knew a way to skip out the back and leave him with the check if he was only in it for a free one – but it turned out to be one of the best deals I'd done. His name was Adolph Zukor, he told me, and he ran theatres. He was on the lookout for more of them, and acts to fill them, and he liked my ideas – all this just from a brief mention of getting a semi-naked girl to do a dance in the streets of Chicago to publicize a show. He told me he'd not long ago got out of the fur trade himself and he'd got a small heap of the things choking up a storeroom here in Chicago. One of them could be mine – for a price!

'I looked at him warily and asked what that price might be – you had to be wary of the too good to be true. Still do, I guess. He said he'd give me – straight up – a $100 [worth around $2,000 in today's prices] bear fur that would cover the modesty of three Salomés at least, in exchange for coming to work for him for a fixed time.

'"What do you think of the theatre?" he asked me. "What do you make of vaudeville?" Now, I'd worked in it a while with Friedman – who sure as hell wasn't the best example to bring to mind, having seen Hammerstein's Victoria – and even with Friedman it was wild and full of possibilities. But it wasn't the movies. It didn't have that unadulterated feeling of awe attached to it, in my gut at least. I'd watched *The Great Train Robbery* more times than I care to remember and I saw the audiences screaming – they thought it was all so real for a few seconds. Their disbelief was suspended on rubber and they were immersed from the very first moment the light went down and the flick began. Hell, I'd jumped myself when that bandit pointed his gun out of the screen! Stage work was a whole different ball game, though. At vaudeville, people went to laugh and escape, learn the language – the older Jews flocking in from Russia desperate for a break made a beeline for the theatre and got their kids, always quicker on the uptake as far as the language was concerned, to translate the jokes, which explains how the language of vaude spread so far and so fast. Or they went to have a blast with their pals in a scuzzy dive where they were free to behave as they pleased.

'At the movies, they were absorbed into another world so much more easily than going to see a play, since you couldn't see the film actors sweat or hear them noisily breaking wind in the wings. The only problem was there weren't the stories to go with it – the movies were imitating vaudeville when they should have been imitating the straight theatre. *The Great Train Robbery* was one of the few I'd seen that really hung together as a story.

'I told all this to Zukor in the manner of a locomotive letting off steam, in one big rush. He gave me an odd look, took a slug of his beer and said: "I know what you mean. I've just started bringing in movies from Europe. There's money to be made in movies. Come work for me – I like your ideas and I'd like to have you around to talk more. We'll call the fur a down payment. Get to New York as soon as you can."

'Waiting for the fur to arrive at Friedman's office, I took the chance to quiz him about Zukor. His eyes went wide when I told him what had transpired and that I was still more than a little suspicious of the man. "Don't be a fool, Nottage," he said. "Zukor's going places. There's money to be made with him. Get outta here!" '

Within two months, Nottage had packed his scant belongings, finished up his business with Friedman, left a very happy and considerably less innocent Salomé clutching a fur coat she'd barely earned – for her performance skills at least – and worked his way back to New York to work for Zukor and Hammerstein. In Chicago, he'd got his first taste of the freedom showbiz could give and of the girls he could attract. Aged twenty, but still claiming he was older, he was ready to take on the world.

• Four •

ESCAPES AND ESCAPADES

Reichenbach loved his time with the Doc Crosby, but he was bold enough to want to strike out on his own. In 1904 he met another showman, Colonel Mondy, who was making a huge amount of money with an ambitious Austrian illusionist called the Great Reynard. Harry left the Doc specifically to team up with their act. To shack up with a rival showman was seen as a betrayal by Doc, but Harry had seen someone whom he believed could make his fortune. Harry spent all his spare time building up a rapport with Reynard, who greedily recognized Harry's ambition.

'Colonel Mondy's Animal Show settled in its winter quarters in Olive Street Missouri and was prinking up the old canvas tents and repainting the iron cages for the new season. The show needed an advance agent and my experience with the Doc as spieler, barker and publicity man qualified me.' It was a huge step up and Reichenbach learned a lot from this major-league player. He also found time to visit The World's Fair, a scintillating experience that opened Harry's eyes to a cast of clients he might be able to represent in the future.

'It was at this time that I met Reynard the Great,' wrote Harry in his autobiography, 'the fabulous magician and handcuff king who could step out of sealed boxes, open locked safes, break through bolted prison cells and walk through brick walls with ease, but who couldn't get out of his own hotel room because I had absent-mindedly locked him in. I became his press representative, manager and fixer for twenty-five dollars a week, a salary that only a magician could pay out with grandeur, as if he was shaking diamonds out of my hat.

'Reynard was a stage in my schoolings, a college course in ballyhoo. With him I learned that the fakes of magic and black art made the tricks of the carnival and circus look like the games in a kindergarten. He was always the actor, handsome, bemantled, bejewelled. He made a circus entrance into each town and wore a high silk hat even in bed. He shook more hands than a political candidate and belonged to more secret societies and fraternities than a college freshman. The medals he bought at auctions travelled by freight, and his trunks and hatboxes made a movie actress's wardrobe look like a bundle on a stick. He was so fussy about clothes that for breakfast he wore a brown suit to match the toast. He wouldn't enter a hotel unless he had a diamond in his cravat the size of a drinking glass, another on his finger, a third gem on his fountain pen, a fourth on his cigarette case and a fifth in his tooth. To buy a pack of cigarettes he'd pull out a bankroll the size and colour of a pumpkin and ask for change from a thousand-dollar bill when the heart of the roll was all singles.

'In contrast to his entrance, I'd slip quietly into a town a week early and set the stage for the wizard so that none of his miracles would go wrong. If he planned to perform a jail-break, I'd first befriend the police official and persuade them to let Reynard inspect the locks before undergoing the test. This would give him a chance to see which master key he'd need for the particular lock.

'Normally, he had an average of forty keys dangling about him in concealed places, hanging from his garters, his sleeves, the back of his collar, his shirt-tails and coat lapels. These were pass keys that could open any variation of the thirty-seven standard handcuff and jail-lock contraptions. In cases where he made the jail-break without any clothes on, he'd have only the one key he needed, and while undergoing the final scrutiny by the committee, he'd pin the key to the back of the guard set to watch him. If he had ever been left in a cell without a guard, he might still be there.

'But as it invariably happened, as soon as the committee departed, he'd merely put out his hand, take the key off the guard's back, unlock the door and make his miraculous escape. Another of the great wizard's breath-taking feats was to let himself be bandaged tightly to a bed by strong canvas thongs, moistened so they wouldn't stretch or yield, and it looked as if no human power could release him without cutting those iron ties. But by loosening three slats under him, which held up the springs and mattress, the whole thing began to sag and the real problem was to keep him in bed till the trick was over. Once he nearly fell out through the bottom before we had finished tightening the canvas bonds. After a while the slats got so loose it was dangerous to stay in the bed, so he switched to a safer trick and offered to get out of any regulation straitjacket that any insane asylum would furnish.

'An asylum was insane to furnish it because we never used it, but substituted our own. If by any blunder he had been put into a standard straitjacket, he'd still be in it now. His own jacket looked like the standard kind and seemed to tie him into agonizing knots, but it had a hidden seam worked by a string, and while the mighty Reynard grappled in wild and fierce contortion, pretending to force his giant frame out of the fiendish vice that gripped him, he was really trying to hold the jacket together because once he pulled the string, it was as loose as a nightgown.

'But of all the many and spectacular escapes the Great Reynard performed, the most popular was always the handcuff demonstration. In every town we offered a thousand dollars reward to any man who could wrist-lock Reynard in such a way that he could not release himself within five or ten minutes. We took care to specify that the locks must be the registered, official types of handcuffs, as those were the only ones for which we had keys. But in many small towns they had old-fashioned, medieval types of manacles which gripped tighter on the wrists the more one tried to loosen them. We induced the local police chiefs never to challenge Reynard with these, shaming them into feeling they were behind the times. Instead we used our own up-to-date wristlocks which Reynard, or indeed anyone, could undo with a hairpin.

'To prevent any spite-worker from coming on the stage when we called for volunteers, I'd plant a dozen hand-cuffs with the kindliest and most gullible-looking people in the audience and they would put Reynard to the test. There would be twelve chairs waiting for them on the stage, and they'd all be sitting up front so they could reach the chairs first. As no one could be on the stage who didn't have a chair, this automatically eliminated outsiders.

'When Reynard called for volunteers, the local clerks, grocer-boys and store-keepers marched up with the weirdest array of hardware and iron works the town ever saw. Yet it never occurred to anyone to ask how their neighbours came to have such deadly manacles and wicked gyves. They seemed to take it for granted that the meekest henpeck had a couple of handcuffs lying around the house. In most cases, the trick was not so much getting out of the handcuffs as getting the volunteers not to walk off with them. Only in one instance did a strange and formidable pair of wristlocks suddenly appear on the scene. A blacksmith, anxious to win the thousand dollars forfeit Reynard had posted, worked a whole season to prepare a set of twisted iron pipes which, once enclosed around Reynard's wrists, would come off only with them. When we spied this horrible pair of keyless locks, swift signals passed between us. Suddenly Mrs Reynard, who always did a mind-reading act after the handcuff scene, stepped up to the blacksmith and uttered a cry of wounded dignity. The Great Reynard was startled and the audience took its cue from him. "This man insulted me!" wailed Mrs Reynard, a beautiful and able actress. Reynard rose to his full six feet of manly wrath. "What would any man among you do if a scoundrel insulted his wife?" he demanded of the public. "Kill him!" was the unanimous advice. Before the blacksmith could understand what had happened or have a chance to protest, the mighty Reynard swung his fist like a gate against the victim's eye and closed it. The next instant the blacksmith was hurried out the back way while the public cheered its hero. No handcuff trick ever brought Raymond more applause than this trick of avoiding the only real handcuffs he ever faced.'

Reynard and Harry had a stormy relationship; each had an ego and sometimes it was difficult to fit them both in the same room. But they needed one another and so in some fashion they muddled along, no matter how tough it was on the road. Reynard was in demand from every corner of the globe and Harry saw the world with him in the eight years they were together. The journeys were long and tedious, but Harry used the time to imagine how he would turn his skills to better use back in the States. Harry was desperate to return home. A new chapter would see his career blossom and bloom.

• Five •

TAKING IT FURTHER

Maynard Nottage's relationship with vaudeville from 1905 to 1907 was fraught, as he tried to make his way in the cutthroat world of showbiz. In 1905, according to his notes, Nottage got involved in one of the first forays into celebrity promotion of a brand, helping Murad cigarettes' promotional campaign, which featured Roscoe 'Fatty' Arbuckle, then a vaudeville star and so fine a singer that Enrico Caruso once apparently encouraged him to give up comedy and train to become 'the second greatest singer in the world'. He went on to become one of the great stars of early Hollywood. Also involved in the campaign to extol the virtues of Murad cigarettes in print were the comedian Harry Bulger and actor John Mason.

'I wanted to take it further,' wrote Nottage, 'and get them on the stage smoking – printed paper was all very well but it didn't have the visceral impact of seeing the guy you've come to the theatre to see on stage drawing in a cloud of smoke every night and saying a few sage but enthusiastic words about the product. Murads were keen on it, but it was the performers who nixed the idea, saying they didn't want to spoil their voices, the whiners. They couldn't see how much money there was in it – couldn't see farther than their next pay check. "You can make me praise them in print but don't make me smoke 'em," Arbuckle told me. "I gotta career to think of and it's a live show – what if I cough? They'll stop the money for sure. And those things *make* me cough."'

In late 1905 and early 1906, Nottage began to pull together a group of actors, sideshow freaks and failed performers to use in stunts. These he cherry-picked from the lower echelons of talent he found as a spotter for Zukor and he used them mercilessly to create a hoo-ha wherever he could. His gallery of lesser talents, all of them desperate to make a break in showbiz, were used by Nottage as extras, to be utilized on the streets or planted in the audience of a dying show, as part of his promotional bag of tricks. He wanted to create a factory of famous names, but the people he regularly drew to him were rarely in that league. It seems that, though Nottage understood how to pull people to a nascent phenomenon, he was not so brilliant at finding people who would actually become phenomena in their own right.

At this time, he was also developing what would become a career-long interest in aviation. His notes suggest that he was trying to get work publicizing the 1906 Fields and Wooley vaudeville show which utilized a prop airship. Nottage appears to have approached several manufacturers, hoping to get a cheap deal on his own prop airship to attach it to the theatre where they were performing. No records survive to tell us whether or not he succeeded.

Nottage's time in Chicago had proved him a capable publicist but whilst he was there other names crept up through the ranks to get the ear of Willie Hammerstein – fertile press agents such as Abe Levy, Ann Marble, Nellie Revell, John Pollock, Joe Flynn and the ubiquitous Morris Gest. This was a time when Hammerstein's flair for sensationalism, ably abetted by the above names, 'assured loyal patrons they need not leave their seats for a close-up of every headline and trend of the period. In truth, any Hammerstein bill was practically a living newspaper of the more sensational news items.'

Nottage's name is noticeable by its absence from this quote – according to his papers he was involved as deeply as he was able to be on the edges of Hammerstein's empire, despite his work for Evarts Friedman and his Salomé act being 'directly responsible for Hammerstein's famous publicity coup in getting Gertrude Hoffman arrested for lewdness'. Hoffman didn't know anything about the set-up, so she fought hard to defend herself. The ruthless Hammerstein – far more so than Nottage was prepared to be with his clients – sacrificed her career to make her famous by arranging, without her knowledge, to have her arrested for encouraging licentiousness, knowing that his notoriety as a producer would last even if Hoffman's fame flashed and faded. She was 'a sacrificial mutton dressed as seductive lamb', according to Nottage, who went on to comment, 'When I got back to New York, I got a meeting with Hammerstein and went over a lot of what I'd done in Chicago – he must have heard some of it from Friedman as well – I could see the excited look in his eye when I mentioned the Salomé act,' wrote Nottage in the notes for his unpublished autobiography. 'When I said I'd done everything short of getting her arrested he was ecstatic – and this was several months before Hoffman wound up in jail. I wish I'd had the nerve to get Martha arrested – things might have turned out so different. I guess that's a good reason not to fall for the charms of your clients; though that's not something I realized in the early days. I got some work with him, but it wasn't much more than bread and butter so I decided to go it alone.'

When Gertrude Hoffman was arrested in 1907, Willie Hammerstein asked Nottage, by then a press agent in his own right, to create more of a storm, along with Morris Gest and others in his publicity team. Nottage writes that he arranged for several of his actors to stir up trouble in the crowd, some of them supporting the policemen's actions, some of them braying for Hoffman to be released. He also paid them to act as stooges for letters he sent to the press. 'It was payback, of a small sort, for stealing my ideas,' wrote Nottage, 'but to survive you had to take what work you could get.'

This attitude is bolstered by a letter in Nottage's archive dated 1908 from a young girl called Helen Brown, who had been visiting Chicago with her family, thanking him sweetly for introducing her to lions. 'It was so nice to be able to touch the lions,' said the letter. 'They are so soft and lovely, it seems strange that when they grow up they will be big and dangerous. I found them very sweet and liked the way their tongues were rough like my friend Sarah's cat only very, very big.'

There is also a message from her mother thanking Nottage for the $25 fee and for giving her daughter a brief brush with fame.

Looking through the archive, I found reference to a stunt involving the release of a lion from its cage to drum up publicity for the circus, which had run into financial trouble in Chicago. According to the cuttings from the papers, which came from all over the USA, the lioness "escaped" (it was in fact released at Nottage's suggestion) just after its cubs were born and roamed around the city for several hours, while the cubs, which were in need of a motherly figure, were left to the tender care of the letter writer, who smiled winsomely for the cameras and provided an acre of coverage.

'Animals and children always rouse the public into waves of sickly sympathy,' wrote Nottage later in life, 'and I knew it was the perfect way to tap into their pockets. The circus went from a stumbling bum down to its last dollar to a sensational crowd puller who could easily afford my $200 fee.'

With this stunt, he essentially created the art of releasing animals and using the ensuing chaos to form a tidal wave of publicity, which harked back to Barnum's use of Jumbo the elephant. The only furrow Nottage's beasts ploughed were on the front pages, however. At the time, animal acts were all the rage in vaudeville – Charles Barnold and his drunken dog act had not long been lured away from Hammerstein by Klaw and Erlanger for the astonishing fee of $1,000 a week, the highest price paid for an animal act before 1907.

What Nottage did was take this enthusiasm and add a thrilling element of fear. It played perfectly with the news-reading public, who liked their animals safely humiliated on the stage and were prone to pay close attention if the beasts escaped or were said to have escaped. The use of Helen Brown, the innocent from Washington who kept the lion cubs happy whilst their mother stalked the streets of Chicago, was a masterstroke as it created waves of fear and sugary sentimentality from the audience. The animal stunt continued right up until the 1950s, used by everyone from Reichenbach to Jim Moran. Even the graffiti artist Banksy has got in on the game, painting an elephant pink and leaving it in a room in 2006. Animals never fail to get attention and the media are still hypnotized by any stunt involving them.

According to Nottage's rough archive, he kept in touch with the Brown family, who were based in Washington, and when Helen went on to fame and fortune as the actress Helen Hayes, he was clearly eager to try and capitalize on the fact that he had given her a first taste of fame. The fact that there's no mention of her response to his overtures suggests that she rejected him out of hand. Certainly, the drafts of letters that remain in his archive betray his desperation to attract a big star to his roster. It is also possible that her family kept him at bay, since his dealings with the young women on his roster was, by his own admission, not particularly healthy.

By the end of the first decade of the twentieth century films were rapidly growing up and it was the movies, ever more prevalently from 1910 onwards, that were drawing in the crowds. Vaudeville may have still commanded big stars like Douglas Fairbanks in 1911, but it wouldn't last much longer. Burlesque was on the way out and the age of the movie was dawning.

Early films were shot almost exclusively in and around New York and Long Island, but as demand expanded, the larger companies started moving to locations in Arizona and California so they could film during the winter months. In the early days there weren't many residents in Edendale, as the area that became Hollywood was known at the time, and land was expansive and inexpensive. In 1906, Hollywood was still little more than a large ranch. Rancho La Brea was bought by a millionaire Prohibitionist real estate developer named Horace Henderson Wilcox, with his wife Daeida, in 1886. They were religious fanatics and devised a grid-based community with room for a Methodist, Prohibitionist church on every block. Wilcox offered free land in Edendale to anyone who wanted to put a church up and as a consequence most residents were involved in some church or other. Alcohol was prohibited, as was gambling – even in people's homes – and any work outdoors on a Sunday was frowned upon.

This, then, was not the most likely of places to set up a Babylonian empire of dreams, but film makers were drawn by the empty space and excellent light and, once the movie industry became a success, it was inevitable that money would follow the movie makers out to the then desolate West Coast. The studios started to settle in the area in 1908, with the arrival of the Selig Polyscope Company, and between 1910 and 1913 numerous others followed, including D. W. Griffiths' Biograph Studio. 'By 1913, little happened during the day in Edendale that wasn't movie related. The once ghostly-quiet town had become busy with "movies".'*

In 1913, the Centaur Film Company decided it would relocate its entire operation to Hollywood, leaving the East Coast behind. It was swiftly followed by the Goldwyn-Lasky group, who came to film *The Squaw Man*, a Western that used real cowboys, including Hal Roach, and was Cecil B. DeMille's first Californian movie. *The Squaw Man* took two weeks to shoot, and was launched in New York on 14 February 1914. It astonished the assembled crowd of film distributors and theatre owners, among them Louis B. Mayer and Adolph Zukor. The film cost $47,000 to make and within three months it had taken $250,000 at the box office. In the following months 325 movies were shot in California and every major studio had relocated to Hollywood within the next two years.

The original locals in Hollywood were none too keen on their new neighbours, however, and took to posting signs in the hotel windows stating: 'No dogs! No Jews. No Actors!' or 'No dogs or Movie People Allowed!'† Directors took to carrying guns after being chased off land by armed locals intent on keeping moviemakers away from their farms. The locals may have been fascinated by the movies, but they didn't take kindly to outsiders and their degenerate ways. It was a situation that required good publicists, and it soon became necessary to manage the news as much as create it since by now the whole world was watching.

All the strays who had chanced upon the movie industry were

---

* E. J. Fleming, *The Fixers*, page 10

† Miriam Cooper, *Dark Lady of the Silents*, page 44

becoming hardened, hard-nosed professionals. Carl Laemmle, who had moved on from the Nickelodeon business to make his own films under the Universal Picture Company name, brought his wife's best friend's son, Irving Thalberg, into the business as a favour. Cecil B. DeMille started out as a stagehand, but he also acted off Broadway and played cornet in a vaudeville pit orchestra with Jesse Lasky, who later hired him as general manager of the Jesse L. Lasky Feature Play Company. Samuel Goldfish was a glove-maker who lost his job in 1913 and went straight into the movies, starting a film company with Lasky, his brother in law.

Adolph Zukor, who was deeply enamoured of European film, which he and partner Marcus Loew imported and distributed exclusively, founded the Famous Players Company in 1912. In 1916 he was the first man to initiate a merger, with Lasky's Feature Play Company. He also bought distributor Paramount Pictures Corporation and created Paramount Pictures.

This was the beginning of a frenzy of mergers. In the ten years between 1915 and 1925, the power in Hollywood shifted and changed regularly, in an echo of the way a film star could appear in the firmament and then be gone, snapping out of the public's affection in an instant. The Zukor–Lasky merger, for example, left Samuel Goldfish in the lurch, as he was in the midst of a divorce from Lasky's sister. He picked up another partner fairly quickly, however, in the shape of film distributor Edgar Selwyn. They formed Goldwyn Pictures, and Goldfish legally took the name Goldwyn as his own in 1918.

The movie industry was fairly intertwined and incestuous as nearly everyone knew each other from the early days. Nick and Joe Schenck, who started out owning drug stores, moved into the beer concession for an amusement park and made enough money to buy the park, were connected to Loew, who invested in their Paradise Park. In 1913, the Schencks went to work for Loew's chain of theatres, though they kept their parks.

Russian immigrant Louis B. Mayer started small, buying a disused burlesque hall near Boston and turning it into a movie theatre. Like others before him, he moved into the distribution business where he secured an exclusive contract to exhibit the first blockbuster movie, D. W. Griffiths' *Birth of a Nation*. It made him a millionaire and funded his move into making movies. Mayer started out with Metro Pictures and then, in 1918, moved to Hollywood and set up Louis B. Mayer Pictures Corporation. It was the perfect move, as he had a keen eye for what made a good movie – he had invested heavily in *The Squaw Man*. He also had the good fortune to hire Irving Thalberg – who was the man set to reshape the movie industry. Thalberg was short and vaguely effeminate, but notoriously hard-nosed. Screen tough guy Edward G. Robinson famously once fled a contract negotiation with Thalberg so he could throw up outside his office.*

Into this febrile world stepped Nottage, fighting to make an impression from as early as 1907. One of the early doyennes of Nottage's talent farm was a woman who had encumbered herself with the unfortunate stage name of Tara Tiplady. She was a writer who started out in showbiz to fund her art and her real name was Annette Westbay. After working a few successful stunts for Nottage, she was picked up by the Selig Polyscope company in early 1907 to make movies on account of her luminous, rather saintly good looks. What they failed to realize – and failed to ask Nottage, who knew her intimately – was that she couldn't keep out of trouble. Her saintly visage belied a far from saintly nature.

'Tiplady lived up to her stage name,' wrote Nottage, 'in that she could get a guy to tip his woman at the drop of a hat. She'd have her fun, then move on to the next stooge who looked like a cowboy. It still amazes me that she accepted my advances. It didn't last long – she got herself noticed through me, then she was off on the annual winter migration to the west coast with Selig to make movies.'

Selig soon found out what trouble she could get herself into as she slept her way through cast and crew. She was on a final warning from the studio when she got herself into a 'spot of bother' with a co-star named Rozbert, who was rather more keen on cooking than

---

* Roland Flamini, *Thalberg: The Last Tycoon and the World of MGM*

Tara would have liked. As Rozbert was cooking pancakes for himself, she insisted on performing oral sex on him. What was supposed to be a pleasurable event for the two of them ended in disaster as, in the heat of passion, Rozbert lost his grip on the pan and spilt boiling oil down Tara's back. She clenched her teeth around him and, in agony, he hit her over the head with the pan.

She was admitted to hospital with severe burns on her back and a broken cheekbone and was followed into the hospital shortly after by Rozbert, bent double in pain. At roughly the same time the publicist Maynard Nottage received a telegram from Selig to come to the LA County Hospital without delay. Luckily, Nottage was in Chicago at the time, which cut the travelling time considerably.

'The tone was insistent,' wrote Nottage, 'and as, despite her flaws, I still had a thing for Tara, I dropped everything and got the train over to Los Angeles, cooking up a few schemes as I travelled. It was a long journey and I had plenty of time to create a sensational press release that kept the prurient elements at bay.'

Tiplady was playing the part of the Virgin Mary in a film about the birth of Christ, and her reputation had to be whiter than white. Nottage admits that he had his 'work cut out to get a measure of this one'. He arrived at the LA County hospital just in time to stop Rozbert admitting the truth; the filmmakers had kept as tight a wrap on everything as they were able, but rumour was beginning to spill out. They had to keep a tight hand on the story as news of Tara's sexual shenanigans would have killed the film before it came out if they'd become widely known, especially in the Christian States, and a lot of money had been thrown into producing it.

Nottage arrived with a statement for the press stating that Tara Tiplady was suffering from concussion and a broken cheekbone after being struck by the donkey, which had been startled by a rattlesnake in the birth of Jesus scene. It also suggested that Rozbert, who was playing one of the three wise men, had gone to Tara's rescue and been kicked in the groin by the donkey. Nottage played the animal card again, telling the press that due to both actors' good Christian upbringings, the film would continue shooting with the donkey instead of having it shot.

The newspapers lapped up the story and gave it glorious headlines. People flocked to see the movie, now sadly lost, when it came out and Nottage even arranged for the donkey to do a tour of the country, making yet more money for the film and himself. Selig heaved a sigh of relief – a scandal had been averted and even turned to their advantage. 'It couldn't have been a more perfect play,' wrote Nottage. 'I made Tara appear virginal, Rozbert appear wise and gentlemanly and the donkey appeared to have been startled by the devil itself. The film stormed the religious market, who were delighted with the extra biblical impact I wove into the accident. It was a ropey film, but it didn't matter any more. I was in.'

Tara Tiplady may have been rescued by Nottage, but her career in the movies petered out not long afterwards, despite Nottage's mountain of belief in his powers and his best efforts on her behalf. She became a short-story writer and maintained contact with Nottage, grateful at least for saving her reputation. It was through that connection that she got work as a writer in Hollywood in 1926 on the Joan Crawford movie *The Boob*, the only surviving work of hers in a Hollywood she tried and failed to break into.

Nottage's cover-up was one of the first of its kind, though in later years it would become a routine matter for publicists to hide the excesses of their stars. This was the first slab laid on the road that would lead to the era of 'the Fixers', Eddie Mannix and the infamous Howard Strickling, the true master of the cover-up. Nottage was in at the beginning.

He was also in at the beginning of the rise of star power. In 1910 when the studios were just starting their mass exodus to California, Carl Laemmle, then the head of Independent Moving Pictures (IMP), turned his eyes towards The Biograph Girl and decided to woo her away from the rival studio.

Florence Lawrence had appeared in well over a hundred films for Biograph, but despite public demand for more information this highly popular star was known only as The Biograph Girl. The industry at that time recognized that the faces sold the movies but refused to put names to the faces in case they demanded more money. Laemmle promised Lawrence that if she joined him she would be known as Florence Lawrence – the IMP Girl. She agreed, and Laemmle organized an intricate stunt, much imitated later on. Lawrence was taken out of New York by Maynard Nottage, who was paid by Laemmle to look after her – 'I was under strict instructions not to try and seduce her, but there wasn't any chance of that,' wrote Nottage. Laemmle's publicity department then began planting stories about 'the missing star' in the press. A flurry of rumour and counter-rumour followed that bears all the hallmarks of a Nottage campaign, although the only archival evidence that he was involved is the passage quoted above. She was dying of a terminal illness, suggested one rumour. She had been kidnapped, insisted another. She was the victim of foul play, whispered yet another source. Later campaigns of a similar nature would see publicists finding nameless John or Jane Doe corpses and disingenuously suggesting to the appropriate sources that the corpse may actually belong to a famous star who had gone conveniently MINOA (missing in need of attention).

The story of the missing Biograph Girl went worldwide and Biograph were perplexed and very anxious. They, like the general public, had no idea where she was. Laemmle was ecstatic with the response and gleefully encouraged a story to be planted suggesting that she'd been killed in a car accident before presenting her at a press conference with her leading man in a new IMP film. She went on to make dozens of films for Laemmle, first as a contracted star and later as an independent producer and star.

The fallout from the incident altered the course of the industry enormously – Laemmle had essentially created the star system, with a small contribution from Nottage which he would attempt to trade on, unsuccessfully, for years afterwards. Stars now had to be named and the studios realized they had to prevent their biggest assets from being stolen in the same manner. As a result, iron-clad contracts were drawn up. It also became evident that publicity was an essential tool.

Nottage, though still working for vaudeville, now had semi-regular work for the blossoming movie business, opening up a whole new chapter for him. Success bolstered his confidence to an extraordinary degree. 'I felt like I was king of the world,' he wrote towards the end of his life. 'I felt I could do anything, make anyone, hide anybody's foibles or indiscretions. I felt indestructible.'

• Six •

DELIVERING THE SHOWMAN

It was said that a producer might slap his spouse, even abuse his children or scratch his best friend's eyes out, but he would never risk injury to his reputation by being called a bad showman.

Showmanship in the early 1900s was a thing of wonder, exemplified by the likes of Willie Hammerstein. He triumphed when he arranged the arrest of Gertrude Hoffman in 1907 for writhing, mildly by today's standards, on the boards for the wily old goat. The judge assisted Hammerstein at the box office by warning the dancer to wear ankle length tights and appointing an inspector to check her costume each day. Although Hammerstein took credit for the scam, the svengali behind it was another publicist whose name is replaced in Nottage's notes by curses and swear words. It prefigures Nottage's obsession with outdoing Reichenbach which blossomed from 1914 onwards and shows how obsessed he was with the idea of people copying him.

'Hammerstein I could understand,' he wrote, 'but this guy leeched everything and not one idea he had was actually his. I'd have killed him if I could.'

This attitude figures heavily in his notes. Any innovator will find that mimics spring up in his wake, but Nottage's reputation and innovation was subsumed by people like Morris Gest, who went on to be a theatre producer and powerful figure in the industry. History tends to be written by the winners, and Nottage was not a winner in this respect, however innovatory he may have been.

Harry Reichenbach was an altogether different kettle of fish. He had spent eighteen years building up his skills before he set up in his own right. From the age of twelve to thirty, he was learning on the road, and finally, in 1912, he was ready to take charge of his own destiny, a task that involved sending a telegram to Marcus Loew.

In the early 1900s, Marcus Loew was by far the most adventurous showman on Broadway. As early as 1902 he put a picture of himself on chewing gum wrappers along with a personal guarantee that those who presented it at any Loew house would get a five-cent rebate. To sell intermission lemonade, he would lure audiences to the rear of his American Roof Theatre, with its luxurious gardens complete with potted plants, running vines, bamboo arbour and a wooden deck for a view of the Hudson and New Jersey. Modern communicators might marvel at the ingenuity of this experiential marketing sold by the yard a century later.

All showmen shared a problem with Monday-night audiences and business, so much so that Loew got desperate and advertised that his theatre would give away one baby, absolutely free. The plan backfired, though, because he had no baby to give away and he was found out. Loew became obsessed with finding a blockbuster to play Mondays only. At the time Reynard was, without a doubt, the world's most famous illusionist. A telegram was transmitted to Paris where Reynard was performing, and in it Loew offered an eye-watering fee for the magician to play an exclusive set of shows at his theatre. At the same time, Harry Reichenbach and Reynard had reached a critical point in their relationship. Harry felt unloved by his client – all publicists, in time, become inflicted by this curse, until it becomes a seismic divide.

'When I'd get stories published that the Great Reynard had been decorated by the Sultan of Turkey, the Shah of Persia, the Kings of England and Spain, Reynard would tell my stories back to me of an evening,' wrote Harry in his autobiography. 'He described in detail how the Sultan had forced a medal on him and how the King of England had begged him to become a British subject so he could make him a duke. I remember the time, on our wide travels from Pierre to Pernambuco, and from Mexico to Australia, the only royalty we ever met were the king spiders of Bahia! It was me that he seemed to forget was the master of his image and adoration.'

The arrival of Loew's offer sent Harry into a spin of ecstasy; a run on Broadway with Reynard! The bliss was overwhelming. All Harry's plans rested on Reynard's acceptance of the generous contract. The Great Reynard, however, was not so thrilled. The city was too formidable a menace to his pride. Reynard was now established in Europe; he loved the culture, the climate and most importantly the adoration. Initially he mused on the offer, but he was too much in love with Europe, where he was the toast of the aristocratic salons. Why would he want to go back to America to play for the roughnecks that frequented Broadway? He was at the pinnacle of his career, the zenith of his ambition. Harry, on the other hand, could see an opportunity to make a triumphant return to the city he dreamed of owning, so he went to work trying to persuade the Austrian to go back across the Atlantic. After a week, Harry realized that Reynard wouldn't be swayed; his ship was docked in Europe and there he was going to stay.

Realizing that the magician was his key to unlocking Broadway, Harry did a bold and crazy thing: he left the performer, making excuses about a sick mother, and shipped himself back to the States, promising to be back within a month. His real intention was to meet Loew and strike a deal to deliver Reynard on a diamond-encrusted platter. Before he boarded the steamer, he cabled the entrepreneur, advising him that he was coming to New York at the behest of his client to strike a deal.

Loew received Reichenbach eagerly, unaware that the young cove had tried and failed to meet him before. Once inside the inner sanctum, with his best poker face, Harry told Loew of Reynard's refusal to return to the States in a deliberately detached manner. Loew upped his offer, believing Harry's news to be a ploy to get more money. Harry told him the man was beyond his reach. Reynard was richer than any performer and was in the winter of his career. He told Loew that Reynard had declared that he would retire from the rigours of the stage and set up home in Paris and would only come out of retirement to perform for crowned heads of state. Reichenbach was sly; he had researched Loew and knew he was a powerful, incisive man who never accepted a refusal on any of his offers. So he put forward a conspiracy and struck a bargain with the showman. If Harry could deliver Reynard for a final season in a Loew house, he would have to give the young publicist two shows to promote to prove his genius in the art. If Loew was suitably impressed with his endeavours, then a publicity contract for a year would be a just reward for Reynard's scalp. Loew looked down at the young man and laughed; he was impressed by Harry's chutzpah and manipulative genius. The mighty entertainment mogul thrust out his hand and the deal was struck, supported by the written contract Reichenbach had requested.

Wasting no time, Harry surreptitiously set to work on his plot to persuade Reynard to return. He had come up with a scheme that he was certain would persuade the magician to pack his props and medals and hot foot it back across the ocean. It was put into motion even before he boarded a ship back to Europe. He enlisted a number of friends to telegraph Reynard in his Parisian eyrie, telling him about a new magician who was about to take Broadway by storm and who had been booked by Loew. The telegrams were sent over a period of five days and all of them insinuated that the aspiring act had borrowed many of Reynard's stage tactics and was nothing more than a showy copy of the master. On his return to Paris at Loew's expense, Harry was confronted by Reynard clutching a sheaf of telegrams. Harry knew a thing or two about a performer's fragility, so it was no surprise that his plan had taken effect before his return.

Reynard stood before his publicist and confidant, a wounded and distraught man, tightly clutching the telegrams. Dramatically, and with rather a camp flourish, he threw the correspondence across the table, demanding to know who the charlatan masquerading as his successor was. Playing bewildered, Harry fingered the missives, attempting to calm the heated encounter. He claimed to be puzzled by the 'phoney, blaming his ignorance about the act on not being in contact with the world of showbusiness. He sought Reynard's sympathy; with only one day in New York he was not party to "circuit gossip".'

Reynard, in a paranoid fluster, was clearly unprepared to see his stature degraded by some cheap forgery and he implored his publicist and broker to wire Loew, accepting his offer. Harry, ever the tactician, counselled his client that perhaps it was time to hang up his stage costumes and enjoy the good life in Europe. Reynard's latent anger suddenly erupted, like a dormant volcano. He would return to Broadway! It is unclear whether Reynard ever found out that there were no impostors standing in the proverbial wings; Harry was far too smart to allow his charge to be bothered with the fake.

When they disembarked in New York six weeks later, Harry ensured there was a huge gathering of media and Loew's sycophants to meet Reynard as, ever the showman, he delivered up some astounding shows to crack the Monday night conundrum and make his producer a healthy return on his outlay.

Harry's ploy was straight out of the Doc's handbook on how to motivate difficult acts that had let their self-esteem get the better of their original character.

'Every morning Doc Crosby would give me a lesson in rectitude and honesty while I helped him prepare the bottles of medicine for his evening miracle cures. "Harry my boy," he'd begin, "remember that honesty is the best policy. Dr Crosby's Wonder Tonic and Immortal Beverage has been a standard product for over twenty years – and you know why? Because I've never adulterated it! I've always stuck honestly to the same formula – from sixty-five to ninety per cent water, a little perfume of camphor, a drop of corn whiskey and a touch of vegetable dye. So don't adulterate this priceless tonic by adding too much whiskey and too little water!" His aim in life was to get his miracle medicine down to such a fine point where it would be all water. "For nothing is purer than water!" he told me, drinking out of a whiskey bottle. "Water is nature's gift to man!" But at the evening show, he helped Nature along a little by planting a shillaber. This man volunteered to inform the populace that he had just moved to the town from Minonk, Illinois and was glad to let Doctor Crosby know that his mother was out of bed and well, though she had been laid up for five months until she took his wonder tonic. If the shillaber's story didn't sell out our stock of toilet water, we had a stunt to top it that never failed.'

Harry remained, throughout his life, a devotee of the outrageous hokum of the Doc. The showman grifter was an unapologetic character who proved on a daily basis that he had few scruples. His twisted logic and kaleidoscopic array of lies were not to be surpassed. Harry's observations had taught him that tricks and scams were everyday occurrences; the better they were, the quicker they would propel a sideshow through every hick town, sucking up the small change that was happily discarded by the poor rubes that couldn't see the sucker punch coming. The Doc was righteous and he lived by an uncompromising code, immoral but always riveting. Harry desperately wanted to move on, but he enlisted this elaborate chop logic and fake psychology to take his prize, reinventing it as a new language of publicity in a new epoch.

Harry's plan to return Reynard to New York came from the same school of confidence trickery. At this point in his career, Harry had few scruples.

Loew called in his contract with Reichenbach when the vacillating audiences began to tire of the act. After two months, it began to lose its lustre, and Loew threw down the gauntlet, demanding that Harry demonstrate his talent for creating publicity and challenging him to deliver a humbug to draw in the crowds.

The spark came a day later when, walking home, Harry saw a brownstone ablaze. Reichenbach witnessed the dramatic rescue of a little girl by a fireman and decided to use that event for his own purposes. He secretly arranged with the fireman to deliver one of Reynard's rings to the lost and found department of a newspaper and to report that the rescue of the child had been aided by a mysterious hero. The fireman, well oiled with cash, agreed. The newspaper, naturally, ran the story, describing the ring in detail. When the owner came forward to claim it, it was none other than Reichenbach's client, the Great Reynard. He became the toast of New York again, his mythical heroism re-engaging the public. However, the performer's ego had grown to untameable proportions and the duo finally split.

When Reynard retold the story of his heroism, he vividly described how he had thrown off his coat, dived into the Hudson and saved the drowning girl. 'But I could never understand,' he would add with an air of mystery, 'how that fireman fished my ring out from the bottom of the river!'

Unfortunately, although Loew thought Harry's stunt a stroke of genius, he lost interest in Reichenbach and broke the contract. It was a lesson that underlined the inconsistencies of producers and the door once again closed in Harry's face. He would need to find another hairpin to re-pick the lock.

Seven

THE PERILS OF PUBLICITY

Maynard Nottage may have got his name noticed by the movie industry with the Tara Tiplady affair, but his bread-and-butter work until 1913 was still rooted in vaudeville, burlesque and the New York scene. His list of clients was, on the whole, an ineffective collection of the odd and the useless, who he nevertheless toiled for endlessly. Though he dreamt of bigger and better things, all his potential stars ever brought him was enough money for a cold lunch. The trouble was that he got on too well with most of them, and the few who brought in decent money were either poached by other publicists or whisked off to the sort of dream factory in the Hollywood hills that Nottage wanted to create. Nottage was also hampered by a quick temper, a jealous nature and an inability to work well in a team. His habit of sleeping, or trying to sleep, with his female clients also didn't help his cause.

One such client was The Great Decantle, an exotic dancer and sword swallower who Nottage met at a party in 1909. The exotic temptress of self-proclaimed Arabic extraction had been booked to entertain guests with her python act, which stretched the bounds of taste somewhat further than the Salomé act. Maynard was smitten on first sight and pronounced that he would make her a household name.

'She was slinkier than the snakes she worked with,' Nottage wrote, 'and as agile as a monkey. What was there not to love? But besides that, it was just the sort of act that would astonish and outrage the crowds, who were tiring of cleaned-up, family friendly vaudeville and burlesque and wanted either the movies or a compulsive and thrilling show to keep them occupied.'

His strategy was to start her with a small part in a New York burlesque revue, by this time not the likeliest launch pad for universal fame. Nottage then hired a handsome waiter from a downtown Greek restaurant to pose as a fake sheikh to publicly woo Decantle. The waiter's first, and last, romantic deed was to buy a huge advertising site outside the theatre declaring his love for Decantle.

The poster, written in Arabic, begged her to accept the fake Sheik's invitation to dine with him, or so Nottage thought, but his stunt had been hijacked by Walt Simmons, a rival press agent, who had lost a client to Nottage the previous year and was out for revenge. Nottage doesn't explain how Simmons heard about the ruse, but Simmons paid the printer double to change the translation. As a result it went up with an outrageous slur on Decantle's character, suggesting the dancer's swallowing skills weren't limited to swords and thanking her for her athletic private performance.

Nottage had one stroke of luck though: one of the workers at the print shop was the brother of a client and tipped him off. A furious Nottage vowed to turn an apparent disaster to the advantage of his client, and instead of spiking the poster, he exposed the stunt himself, tipping off the newspapers that he had put the poster up but that his work had been spiked. He promptly made front-page news, guaranteeing further headlines when Decantle, at Nottage's own suggestion, announced plans to sue her publicist for negligence.

Jealous of all the attention Nottage was getting, Simmons confessed to the prank, guaranteeing himself a few vital column inches in the process. The New York press then gleefully ran an 'exclusive' about the rival publicists' feud, concluding that Walt Simmons was angry about Nottage trying to poach his roster of talent and wanted to teach the upstart a lesson. Decantle was so impressed with Simmons' bravado that she fired Nottage and hired him instead, and although he never made her a star, they fell in love and were married six months later. Despite failing to win her heart, Nottage saw an opportunity to get his own name into the papers again by agreeing to be the best man. After all, it was he who had brought them together. The happy couple went on to have three children after The Great Decantle hung up her python. They died together on 6 May 1937, victims of the Hindenburg airship disaster.

In 1911, Nottage recovered from his infatuation with The Great Decantle and fell in love with Bessie Button, but it was a whirlwind romance and both of them were young and foolish. Nottage was working for a small-time illusionist at the time. Bessie's first job in showbiz was as a knife-thrower's stooge, and a scar and a damaged ear proved that she had served her time, but by the time they met she had become a glamorous hoofer in a vaudeville show. Bessie became a secretive alcoholic after settling into married life and marriage didn't appear to suit her or Nottage. The marriage collapsed after the birth of their daughter in 1913 – the constant attentions of young actresses were too powerful a temptation for Nottage, who by that time was consumed by a state of such overwhelming self-belief he saw himself as a Zeus-like figure with the power to grant fame with a thunderbolt of inspired publicity.

Nottage wanted to create a famous name desperately. 'I had a roster of small-time talent to work with – all of whom were great at making a noise in a crowd. The few that had aspirations of greatness failed to live up to the challenge though – Tara Tiplady was a hopeless actress, The Great Decantle only really wanted to settle and get married. More and more, showbusiness was turning to movies and I didn't want to be left behind. I saw what the studios failed to see – that those luminous faces on the screen were going to be more lasting and more famous than the numerous acts on the stage whose talents would be eaten up by time. They'd be nothing more than names in a book 100 years down the line. But the filmmakers didn't recognize it – they still saw the movies as a quick buck, something that would please the crowds until something bigger and better came along. I tried to tell them, but Zukor wasn't interested, Loew wasn't interested. No one paid any attention except the actors themselves.'

Nottage met Charlie Chaplin and Arthur Stanley Jefferson, later known as Stan Laurel, when they toured America as part of the Fred Karno troupe between 1910 and 1912. 'They were hungry kids and they wanted to make a buck,' he wrote, despite being only a few years older than either of them. 'We talked a lot and I let rip my opinions about how the movies would be the biggest thing to hit America and how it would be the stars who drove the business. Chaplin was most receptive – he took my card. One of the best contacts I ever made, but I honestly didn't think he'd be back in the country again.'

Nottage would meet Chaplin again in 1914, when he was hired to promote the Chaplin movie *Laughing Gas*, but in 1912 he was still struggling to get a break in the industry. It was imperative that he did so – burlesque, dressed and undressed, was in decline, as was big-time vaudeville – although the smaller, more reasonably priced shows still flourished. Much of the decline is attributable to the marked increase in money and decadence – like a microcosm of the decline of Rome, the bigger the money and the extravaganza, the more the decline became a fall. Burlesque producer Al Reeves bought a car in 1912 which was facetiously described by *Variety* as a 'limousine built along the general lines of a Queen Anne cottage, with latticed windows and everything flossy except a tennis court in the front yard. It anchored in front of the Columbia Theatre about noon and was surrounded by a crowd all day.'

In 1911, Douglas Fairbanks left the legitimate stage, not yet for movies, but for vaudeville at $2,000 a week. Vaudeville struggled on for the next fifteen years or so, but it became more of a staging ground for the movies, which was the main cause of its decline. Anyone who made their name on the vaudeville stage tended to be snapped up by the film industry very quickly.

One of Nottage's more intriguing ideas at this time of change was an attempt to prop up The Casino in Brooklyn, a purveyor of burlesque that had been suffering a decline in interest.

'They were utterly desperate to make back some of the money they were forced to spend on acts, and they weren't getting close,' wrote Nottage, 'so I was drafted in to try and turn their fortunes around and give them a much needed shot of good publicity. There wasn't much I could do, given the fall off of interest in burlesque and the paucity of dollars, so I had a hard think and decided to offer the audiences, most of them immigrants, most of them poor, the sort of giveaway I thought they couldn't refuse. I went in with a proposal suggesting they raffle off boxes full of essential supplies to a few lucky audience members.'

The Casino ran with the idea, but found it couldn't afford to run with the sort of hampers Nottage had in mind, and instead they tried to give away coal, then hams, then a goat and finally, in desperation, a live horse. Someone suggested that a $100 reward for anyone who would take the burly show off the theatre's hands would be more helpful. 'The money ran out', wrote Nottage, 'and they failed to pay me, so I cut my losses and moved on. Luckily my name wasn't publicly attached to the failure.'

Things finally seemed to be looking up for Nottage when he was hired to promote *A Monkey Bite* for Pathé in 1912, in which people behave like apes after being bitten by wild monkeys. To push the film, Nottage added a young Californian called George Brocklet to his roster of actors and got him to pose as a man who thought he was turning into a monkey. He set up various photo calls in which Brocklet was examined and had his head measured by an 'eminent medical man'. In actual fact, said medical man was a quack in the pay of Nottage and he duly announced that Brocklet's 'arms had grown longer and his gait more bent' and that Brocklet appeared to be 'growing tall'.

This Barnumesque stunt was going well until an adhesive used to stick animal hair to Brocklet's torso caused a violent allergic reaction, resulting in a vicious rash that led to him being hospitalized. Despite Nottage's best efforts, the hospital couldn't be persuaded to keep quiet and the ruse was exposed, which of course gave the film even more publicity. Brocklet, however, had to be paid to disappear. He was only hired again in 1935 for a similar stunt for a French cosmetic product. This time the scam was a huge hit, especially when the tail of a large dog was grafted on to the actor's hindquarters, but it inflicted considerable damage to Brocklet's already unstable mental health. The long-suffering Brocklet went on to live in a small zoo in Belgium. The zoo's owner was an eccentric French aristocrat who had financed *A Monkey Bite* as well as being the director of the cosmetic company, but he 'shunned publicity although he was in awe of the processes behind it' and Nottage doesn't reveal his name. Brocklet died seven years later, having been crushed to death by a rhino, if Nottage is to be believed, and was laid to rest in Ghent.

Nottage, in a cruel, bitter humour at the time he documented the stunt in the early 1950s, was inclined to blame Brocklet for his own failures: 'His headstone should be etched with a simple inscription: George Brocklet, Monkey Man 1892–1942. If you pay peanuts, you get Brocklet.' Perhaps he was thinking of his own fate.

But in 1912 Nottage was in with the movies again just as they were moving their operations lock, stock and barrel to Hollywood. This was where the rot began, as his career took a downwards turn when he started to indulge in the excesses that led to his removal from the inner circle of showbiz power and towards the overwhelming bitterness that consumed the last years of his life.

• Eight •

SMALL STEPS FOR REICHENBACH, GIANT LEAPS FOR PUBLICITY

Harry Reichenbach built his notoriety and fortune through small steps, leaving a trail of stunts in his wake, then watching the press and public follow them out of the woods in eager partnership, like Hansel and Gretel leaving the witch behind and travelling off to help build Hollywood, the biggest gingerbread cottage of them all. Reichenbach's giant leap from freight-hopping carnival spieler and grifter, travelling America heating the feet of ducks to make them dance, to fêted Hollywood insider, retained by studios for $1,000 a week, was achieved through a combination of an imagination in overdrive, desire for money and relentless hard work.

His time with Reynard had showed Reichenbach the world and put him in touch with the movers and shakers of the nascent movie industry, so that he understood the mindset of people who were – or thought they were – stars. One can see echoes of Reynard's delusional state throughout the years in the fantasy worlds inhabited by Michael Jackson, Howard Hughes, superstar sports players and politicians, all of whom think they're above scrutiny. Self-belief and delusion is the volcanic core of the hubristic world of celebrity. Reynard also took Reichenbach to New York, and this is where he flourished: 'I tore up my guidebook, took a long walk and interviewed every policeman I could find. By the third day I was a thoroughbred New Yorker.' Reynard was not so enamoured with the city and fled to Europe, leaving Reichenbach in a city that perfectly combined the new and old worlds.

Not that it was easy to begin with. Reichenbach took a one-room office in the Putnam Building and painted 'Harry Reichenbach – Publicity' on the door. No one came. 'I spent much time getting about, becoming acquainted, picking up friends, but no business,' he wrote. 'I had to give up my room, but I wouldn't give up my office. It was hard to sleep on a desk, but I covered it with a newspaper and found myself on the front page.'

It was this sort of self-deprecating wit and his endless travels across America and around the world, often in reduced circumstances, that saw Reichenbach through some of his leanest times as he slowly made a name for himself in New York. Even Walter Kingsley, who was the biggest name in Broadway publicity at the time, was unable to find Reichenbach work. Despite both working in a field that engendered the sort of 'keen rivalry and aloofness' Nottage maintained whenever he and Reichenbach came into contact, Kingsley gave Reichenbach good counsel and friendship as well as the occasional beer; a testament to Reichenbach's charm as much as Kingsley's good nature. He talked 'in a casual, indifferent manner of the glittering stars, unique personalities, enchanting beauties who waited in his office pleading for notices, vying with each other to offer him checks'. Reichenbach, who was hustling small advertising jobs just to pay the $45 per month rent, must have salivated at the scent of money wafting from Kingsley.

Raised in poverty and trained on the carnival trail, he knew well enough how to follow an instinct, and when the first opportunity to make money presented itself in May 1913, Reichenbach jumped at it. He took work at a small art shop 'that had printed a lithograph of a nude girl standing in a quiet pool. The picture sold at ten cents apiece but nobody would buy it.' Reichenbach, who would be paid his month's rent if he sold 2,000 of them, fished around for ideas. Suddenly it occurred to him to introduce the 'immodest young maiden' to Anthony Comstock, who was at the time head of the Anti-Vice Society. If Reichenbach could get this 'arch-angel of virtue' to come down heavily against the picture, he reasoned that New

Yorkers would get excited by it merely as a counterbalance. Comstock was not easily roused into a state of ire, however, and 'refused to jump at the opportunity to be shocked'.

Reichenbach was not easily dissuaded and telephoned Comstock numerous times to protest against an extravagantly sized print of the picture that he'd installed in the shop window himself. Still Comstock maintained a dignified silence on the issue, so Reichenbach gathered together a team of protestors and pushed them, filled with manufactured outrage, in Comstock's direction. Then he visited Comstock personally. 'This picture is an outrage,' he declared with gusto. 'It's undermining the morals of our city's youth!' And he persuaded Comstock to come with him to the shop to see for himself.

The crowning glory of the stunt was a gaggle of youths leering, gawping and chuckling to themselves outside the shop. They had been hired by Reichenbach for the purpose at fifty cents apiece and were 'uttering expressions of unholy glee'.

'Comstock swallowed the scene and almost choked,' wrote Reichenbach. '"Remove that picture!" he fumed, and when the shopkeeper refused, the Anti-Vice Society appealed to the courts. This brought the picture into the newspapers and into fame.' Thanks to Reichenbach's scheming, a lithograph that had been rejected for a calendar became an overnight national issue, the subject of songs and jokes on vaudeville, eye-rolling denouncements from reformers and, as he had rightly guessed, a sell out. Reichenbach had only been commissioned to clear stock, and instead he'd created a runaway bestseller. The 2,000 copies sold out in moments and seven million more sold at a dollar each, making Reichenbach his $45 rent and the picture's creator a fortune.

The name of the lithograph was *September Morn*. As the title implies, it was a beautiful, innocent lithograph that hardly deserved the notoriety it received – even Reichenbach himself likened it to a picture of one's sister as a child in the family album. This didn't stop him exploiting it ruthlessly, though, sex being something that had always, and will always, sell. *September Morn* may not have made Reichenbach a fortune, but it made his reputation. For his next job – persuading the Postmaster General to ban *Three Weeks*, a book as innocent of perversion or depravity as *September Morn* – he was paid three months' rent. The book, whose only sex scene was faded out with asterisks, went through a similar period of protest and was banned from being carried by the postal service.

This trend continues to this day, from *Lady Chatterley* to Frankie Goes to Hollywood's 'Relax', Elvis Presley's licentious hip gyrations to Madonna's *Sex* book. More often than not, though, these products are ruthlessly exploited and less than pleasing aesthetically. Reichenbach, writing in his autobiography in 1931, notes this process, which has only intensified in the following seventy-five years: 'Many exploiters have since developed the superficial idea that any product which is suppressed or attacked automatically becomes a success,' he wrote. 'They have used this as a pretext to spread really bad stuff that deserved suppression and were disappointed when the public failed to support them. In the case of *September Morn* and *Three Weeks*, it was a laugh on the overzealous guardians of virtue and the whole American people joined in the jest.'

Harry Reichenbach was clever with money; he needed to be to stay ahead of the game in the rapidly changing world of showbiz. Past experience had taught him the value of cash and he translated this canny attitude into his bright new world. On the road with the carnival he had learned two lessons: the first was how to short change – 'Raise the booth as high as possible so the suckers couldn't see the change' – and the second was to spend months visiting innumerable towns doing basic homework. He would spend hours counting the empty stores, noting the days the local mills paid wages, which days were best for business and what locations were good for shows. Harry noted down all these facts and eventually collated a book of facts and figures that covered about 200 towns across America. Like a comedian who gathers all his best gags in one place, he hoarded this information like gold, and it proved as valuable – Reichenbach sold the information on to a number of carnivals and outdoor companies, including the Ringling Bros circus. Harry conducted a similar research exercise in New York and quickly discovered the pecking order amongst the producers and their respective businesses. He surmised which shows had worked and why, and rooted out the reasons some shows failed, using this careful analysis to make his publicity empire pre-eminent in a very short space of time. This strictly analytical approach quickly surpassed the more romantic methods of Maynard Nottage.

Reichenbach was tough opposition for Nottage, who was more sold on the lifestyle and had a rather more slapdash approach. 'Everywhere people clamoured to be fooled and it was gratifying to see how much they appreciated it when they were well fooled,' he said. Reichenbach on the other hand was more than a super showman and press agent extraordinaire; he attained his own measure of fame. Always thinking faster, probing deeper and adventuring further than those about him, Reichenbach carved himself a niche with stunts such as slapping an actress hard to make her crying-mad for an interview with a prominent journalist. Eventually Maynard Nottage, working several rungs down the New York showbiz ladder, was forced to recognize who the crowned publicity Tsar was, and he didn't like it one bit.

The front page, which had been Reichenbach's objective, became his stomping ground and he grew up with the emergent movie industry and its magnates. He worked like crazy to get in, finding Jesse Lasky and Adolph Zukor a number of possible stars – Douglas Fairbanks was one that they rejected, only to see him hired for $10,000 a week two years later in 1915. Reichenbach also claims to have discovered Clara Kimball Young. He worked as an office boy, a secretary and whatever else he could, all the while making sure the publicity went out and the people came to the films. Reichenbach's street savvy helped him enormously at this time, and he soon moved on to Metro for $300 a week, where he signed up Francis X. Bushman, who was already a star having worked with Vitagraph in 1915.

Bushman became a huge star with Reichenbach pushing him into the limelight. One publicity stunt he pulled was at a convention in San Fransisco where Bushman was due to be guest of honour. News came that Jesse Lasky had signed Geraldine Farrar and that she would be coming to the convention too. Not wishing to lose the limelight, Reichenbach paid a girl to take a flower box to Bushman's hotel and ask the clerk to deliver it. After she left, the package started to smoke and panic ensued. It was thrown in water, and when the bomb squad came to inspect it, they declared it would have atomized the hotel if it hadn't been soaked. A letter had come with the box and it read, 'Dear Francis, I have written you time and again but have received no reply. I love you still and when I read that you are dead I shall kill myself, too, that we may meet in heaven. Forever yours, L.M.'

The story took the front page for three days and Bushman was in the press continually. This was all timed to coincide with Farrar's arrival, which happened in a blaze of obscurity. The press was far too interested in Bushman's near-death experience. The story went around the world until it 'died of exposure' when it was revealed that the bomb was little more than 'scouring powder and a little sulphur', but by then the job was done. All that was needed to complete the obscuring of Lasky's star was a blackout. And Reichenbach managed this by switching off the lights at the movie convention ball where she was to be taken in on the arm of the mayor. The lights only came back on again once it was agreed that Farrar would take one mayoral arm and Bushman the other.

By hard work and ingenuity, Reichenbach became the ace of aces in his own realm and one of Broadway's most quoted raconteurs. He was a fixture in the New York Biograph Studio and the money he made from the movies was immense as he charged $1,200 a month in 1915 and was known to retain a financial interest in some of the movies he pushed. He was top of the publicity pile, and in an interview with *Motion Picture Magazine* in 1920 he boasted, 'I'll take an unknown girl, provided she is fairly attractive, and put her name in electric lights on Broadway in ten days at a star's salary . . . Pick out one of the smaller countries in Latin America and I'll change a government in five days . . . I'll make a handcuff king out of a man who can't even get out of his own nightshirt. Give me a young man who can wear pleated pants and in three weeks I'll make him the idol of American womanhood . . . I'll do all these things because I've already done them and can do them again!'

Such statements could be viewed as the ramblings of a certified lunatic, but this was the man whose miraculous scam campaigns made a huge impact on the world of movies, and so they were believed. Reichenbach was a deft and calculating exploiter, who helped to grease the wheels of the pre-war publicity machine with industrial quantities of banana oil. Prior to the golden age of the movies, Reichenbach's reputation was such that he even worked for the American war machine in 1917, but it was in the heady world of Hollywood that he made the biggest impact.

The greatest silent era stars – Mary Pickford, Gloria Swanson, Rudolph Valentino and Douglas Fairbanks – all had Harry to thank for their fame. Even the director Cecil B. DeMille enjoyed his council. RKO Pictures used Harry, as did Keith-Orpheum Theatres, and the FBO Company (Film Booker's Organization), which was owned by Joseph P. Kennedy. This was the smallest studio of the majors at the time, but it punched well above its weight thanks to Harry's creative publicity. Marcus Loew of Loew's Inc., the parent company of what eventually became Metro Goldwyn Mayer, was also a client, despite an earlier rejection. Loew was not a man to miss out on a publicity goldmine, and Reichenbach bore no grudges, providing the money was right. Metro Pictures Corporation, founded in late 1915 by Richard A. Rowland and Louis B. Mayer, knew Reichenbach well and gave him movies when their own in-house players failed to make the grade.

Indeed, when Mayer left this partnership in 1918 to start up his own production company, it was Reichenbach who decided that it should be called Louis B. Mayer Pictures. In 1920, Metro Pictures Corporation, which had at this point already acquired Goldwyn Pictures Corporation, was purchased by Loew, who merged the company with Mayer Pictures in 1924 to create Metro Goldwyn Mayer. Mayer then talked himself into the position of Vice President in Charge of Production, where Reichenbach worked in the background to hype the newly minted company. He was a huge presence over the whole industry, and his campaigns became legendary as he flitted between New York – his favoured home – and his offices in Hollywood.

Having travelled the country in all sorts of guises and all sorts of conditions, Reichenbach understood the human condition in the early years of the twentieth century. He was willing to talk to people, was interested in what made them tick and an expert at getting what he wanted from them by sleight of hand and lightning wit. Reichenbach knew that it wasn't enough to just 'stir up the prudes', he also resorted to using the outlandish and bizarre to attract attention to the things he promoted.

In 1917, Reichenbach's taste for the bizarre was brought to giddy life in the lobby of the Knickerbocker Hotel. Like many of his stunts, it was informed by his early life, in this case, his love of serialized stories. 'I remember one story in particular about a human ape out of the African jungle, who mixed among the people of a civilized community and learned the language and customs of men.'

Due to the poverty of the Reichenbach family, the instalments of this gripping tale stopped at the most exciting point as his mother tended to only be able to get old copies of the magazines from neighbours. Such was the nine-year-old Reichenbach's frustration at not being able to complete the story that his mother stopped supplying reading material altogether. He wasn't to learn the outcome of the tale until 24 years later, when it played a vital part in the establishment of his name and credentials as a publicity agent and formed the basis for one of his most enduring and anarchic stunts.

In the winter of 1917, Reichenbach met 'Smiling Billy' Parsons, a 'huge and genial Westerner' who had become fixated with the movie industry and raised money, by hook or by crook, from the cowhands and ranchers of Montana and Wyoming to make a movie. The film, which he produced for the then-extraordinary cost of $250,000, was called *Tarzan of the Apes*. At the preview, it was redubbed Tarzan of the Crêpes by the critics and was 'unanimously voted the worst mess of celluloid in moviedom'.

Smiling Billy had raised the money for the movie on the understanding that it would pay off the mortgages of the people who'd invested in it, and since this now seemed unlikely, Parsons became a large and tempting target for the group of gun-happy investors. Meeting Reichenbach, whose star was in the ascendant, was the perfect opportunity for both of them. Parsons, wrote Reichenbach, 'persuaded me to see the picture and see if anything could be done to salvage it'.

'For fifteen months he had kept it on a shelf, but his funds were down to gravel and even New York would soon be too small a place to hide in. As I sat in the projection room watching *Tarzan* a curious feeling of excitement gripped me. As a rule I seldom looked at the pictures I had to publicize for fear they would disillusion me and destroy the honest enthusiasm with which I could write about a picture I hadn't seen. But this time I was stirred to deep memories that harked back to the early story I had read in my childhood. A long interrupted dream was suddenly being continued.'

Reichenbach enthused wildly to Parsons, even offering to publicize the film on a commission-only basis rather than for a flat salary. He was so excited by the prospect of publicizing the film that he told Parsons, 'I'll accept fifteen per cent from all the money you make over fifty thousand dollars.' Parsons, mired in rejections from every distributor, insisted that Reichenbach take a salary of $100 a week, assuming that that was all he'd get from the movie. He didn't – couldn't – take into account the alchemical nature of Reichenbach's belief, but the whole of America would soon wake up to his ability to turn leaden material into box-office gold.

With no one willing to buy or rent the film, Reichenbach leased the Broadway Theatre from Carl Laemmle and handled everything himself. He had the jungle trees and foliage used as props in the movie transported from California to dress the Broadway Theatre so it looked like the African wilderness, then he placed a stuffed lion in the lobby and let apes loose in the theatre to swing from the trees. The coup de grâce, however, was taking Nottage's stunt with the lions in Chicago a decade earlier that necessary step further, by unleashing Prince Charley into the nation's conciousness via the front pages of the newspapers.

Prince Charley was a giant orangutan who, 'dressed in a neat-fitting tuxedo and high silk hat, entered the fashionable Knickerbocker Hotel on Saturday night when the lobby was aglitter with New York's elite'. His playful, screeched invitations to society's finest to join him in that great game of spinning in the revolving door of the hotel were met with pandemonium and, eventually, a police escort for Charley to the local night court on a charge of disorderly conduct.

The magistrate was 'inclined to fine him as a warning to all monkeys who paraded in tuxedos, but suspended sentence on the condition that the Jungle Prince would stick to coconuts and keep out of hotels. Prince Charley nodded penitently and started to eat his high hat.'

Prince Charley's arrival was also greeted with headlines like 'Simian Royalty Steps Out' and 'Jungle Prince Makes Society Debut'. He was the ape that made Reichenbach's name and brought him over $50,000 in commission, saved Billy Parsons from the wrath of the cowhands of Wyoming and made *Tarzan of the Apes* a worldwide triumph. The stories didn't note his quick return to the lobby of the Broadway Theatre.

'To me,' wrote Reichenbach, 'he has always been the human ape of the early Frank Reade, Jr. stories, projected into real life by an odd trick of chance. The idea that it would be possible for a monkey dressed in natty clothes to crash into society was something unusual, unbelievable, and when it happened it furnished front-page material. The fact that I had planted this episode and used it to promote the Tarzan picture, established more firmly in my mind that the whole difference between the things one dreamed about and reality was simply a matter of projection. Many publicity stunts that happened later on in my work took on this magic-lantern effect. An idea that would seem at first flush, extravagant and impossible, became by the proper projection into life, a big item of commanding news value.'

This is a perfect summation of Reichenbach's genius; he had an uncanny ability to make a reality out of the celluloid fantasies that abounded in Hollywood. Thanks to him, people got to smell and taste and feel the realities behind the fantasy. But Prince Charley was just the beginning, a mere messenger for the surprises and headline-grabbing stunts that would come from the anarchic Reichenbach stable.

Nine
LIONS AND LIONIZATION

As Reichenbach's confidence swelled, so did the grandeur of his stunts, in both imagination and execution. By 1919, with the war a slowly fading memory, he was approached to publicize *The Virgin of Stamboul*, the 'entirely original story of a Turkish maiden abducted by a villain . . . and rescued by a hero'. His intention was to transpose the world of the Arabian Nights to modern New York, 'the New York that people loved to think was a crystal city of diamonds transfigured out of the slums'.

Costume films were to the post-war silent movie industry what CGI is to Hollywood today – a high-risk, high-cost enterprise that often didn't earn back the cost of making them. Universal, who were producing the film, were worried that *The Virgin of Stamboul* would fall into this trap, lumbered as it was with high-cost stars in the shape of Priscilla Dean, Wallace Beery and Wheeler Oakman, plus the rigmarole of expensive costumes and sets.

Reichenbach's stunt took an awful lot of careful preparation. Given how much of the budget had been swallowed up just to make the 'dress parade' look right, Reichenbach was forced to look close to home to populate his Arabian Night: 'I took a trip to Little Turkey east of Chatham Square,' he wrote, 'and found that in the war of the tea-houses all the Turks had been routed by Greeks and Armenians. I befriended an Assyrian, Khalie Ossmun, who promised to dig up eight Turks and he did. They looked as if he had dug them out of sewers.'

The Turks were a mixed bunch including ex-dishwashers, lemonade sellers, pastry cooks and a scurrilous-looking scar-faced man, the sort who would normally inhabit the background of any Arabian Nights film as local colour. Reichenbach, in Fairy Godmother mode, transformed them on the spot. 'My Assyrian friend Khalie being the most intelligent and personable, I appointed him chief Sheik Ali Ben Mohammed, ruler of this motley band. The knife-scarred Turk whom we called "Goom" became lord high aide-de-camp and the white haired old mumbler I turned into the Grand Caliph Shafkrat. The pastry cook became his lordship, the Effendi Houssein, the two ex-dishwashers acquired the titles of Generals Hamedan and Rafkhat respectively and the lemonade peddlers became the grand eunuchs of the Sheik's harem, Jamil and Abdul Halsh.'

Having given them these grand titles, Reichenbach dispatched his rapidly less motley crew to a Turkish bath and completed the transformation by informing them that they were a high diplomatic body on a secret mission from the Levant. Then he dressed them in lavish splendour – pompoms, aigrets, sea-green trousers and gold-crested turbans – with the aid of a theatrical costumier. All went according to plan until it came to getting the group to behave in the manner befitting such an old-fashioned Middle Eastern court. America had worked too well on these immigrants and much of their culture was informed by the very industry Reichenbach was employing them to promote. Showbiz had created a nation. It didn't help that the image Reichenbach wished to create was based on an ancient formula that fell just the right side of cliché. However, nothing was going to stop Reichenbach in his tracks.

'I persuaded a friend of mine, Alexander Brown,' he wrote, 'who had spent many years in Constantinople as general representative of the American Licorice Company, to show them how to act with true Turkish elegance. For an entire week he drilled them in handling table service. He taught them to wear their decorations, how to salaam, and how the eunuchs were to taste all food before their masters would take the chance.'

A week was spent rehearsing the fake Sheik in his carefully concocted story and hurling questions at the Turks until they responded quite naturally with a simple, 'We cannot talk. You must ask the master.' The master was, of course, fully rehearsed in his speech and had been primed not to deviate from the script. Finally, they were ready to make a grand entrance into the heart of New York.

Reichenbach phoned the Hotel Majestic and declared in 'a tortured dialect' that he was part of a Turkish mission coming to America 'on a very secret importance'. He requested that the hotel reserve his party the best rooms and 'protect us please from the newspaper reporting'. Within two days, the party rolled up at the Majestic in regal fashion. At 4 p.m. that day they appeared in the hotel's tea rooms dressed to kill in extravagant clothing and behaving 'according to all the rules laid down by the American Licorice Company's manager'. The eunuchs played their part, scanning the room suspiciously, as if expecting cameras at every corner.

The hotel's press agent, O. O. McIntyre, tipped off the papers about the Turkish party's presence in the reticent manner of someone reluctantly spilling the beans on a matter of international significance. Reichenbach realized he'd pulled off the stunt when he crossed the lobby, and was told in confidential manner by a New York drama critic that this was understood to be a Turkish war mission. In an America rebuilding itself on the spice of Hollywood's visions after the Great War, anything glamorous and mysterious was received with open arms. By the evening the hotel was swamped with journalists, all busy reporting on the secret mission and describing the party's exquisite clothing in minute detail. 'Even the Prince of Wales's latest clothes were never more faithfully reported than these gaudy remnants of a Shubert flop,' gloated Reichenbach in *Phantom Fame*.

Then came the coup de grâce: Khalie Ossmun recited his rehearsed speech: 'Gentlemen, I come to this country, which to my desert-trained eye is like the heaven promised in the *Koran*, to seek the betrothed of my younger brother. She is Sari, so beautiful that in all Turkey there was none like her. She was known as the Virgin of Stamboul.' He followed this with a summary of the nine-reel movie Reichenbach was promoting, in which it was suggested that the virgin had fled to America pursuing an English-speaking lover, and 'the reporters swallowed every word avidly as news of the first magnitude'.

Everything was going beautifully until a newspaperman called Boyden Sparkes spotted a slightly soiled starched shirt cuff under one of the elaborate costumes. Suspicious of a hoax, Sparkes asked if the Sheik knew any Americans. Reichenbach had been ready for this and had primed the Sheik with a ready answer: 'I know your Mr Henry Morgenthau [who had been Ambassador to the Ottoman Empire during the First World War] very well. I am to have dinner with him.' Even this was prepared well – Reichenbach had checked with the great man's secretary and he was away that weekend, so would be unable to confirm or deny the story. Or so he thought.

Still suspicious, Sparkes called up Morgenthau, who turned out to be at home after all. Reichenbach fled, as did McIntyre, before the hawk-eyed journalist could accost either of them. The next day, two sets of reports came out: Sparkes' report and those of all the other journalists. Sparkes' report was as full and detailed as the others, but closed with the killer lines: 'Mr Morgenthau said Sheik Ben Mohamed was a blasted liar. Mr Morgenthau said more. He said the Sheik's costume was too good to be true. He made a solemn statement that he wasn't going to have the Sheik dine with him, and was unkind enough to call him a fake. But that won't interfere with the release of that thrilling picture, *The Virgin of Stamboul*.'

Reichenbach, however, had judged the mood of the American people far better than he could have dared hope. The incident had acquired a feeling of truth. It was too good to be true, perhaps, but also too good to be let go of. Reichenbach records it as one of those incidents that was considered to have been real even if it wasn't. Accordingly, the press continued to cover the Sheik's activities – two columns in every daily, newsreels of the Sheik posing in Central Park and a box at the Hippodrome Theatre; they 'even spread a carpet from the curb to the lobby that the holy feet of the dishwashers and lemonade peddlers should not touch unhallowed ground'.

Then, when Sari was 'found' at a rooming house a few days later, the newspapers swarmed again and were 'treated to a stirring Oriental scene' of an hysterical girl surrounded by the Sheik and his entourage, a physician jabbing a hypodermic needle relentlessly into the mattress as a nurse stood by and took notes. The man who found her was ceremoniously handed ten thousand-dollar bills by the Sheik – which he returned in private later – who then announced that his party was immensely grateful to the press and that they would be returning home on the White Star Line the following Saturday. The girl who played Sari was an accomplished actress, but she could speak neither Turkish nor French, so was kept well away from the press. 'We told them she was delirious,' wrote Reichenbach, 'but we made her sit up quietly in bed to get her picture taken. The press reported every detail faithfully to the end and *The Virgin of Stamboul* scored a record at the box office.'

This was an astonishingly successful campaign, despite the difficulties, but the best was yet to come. Reichenbach was as aware as Nottage of the use and importance of animals for attracting the attention of press and public, having brought Prince Charley the orangutan to the public's attention in 1917. But the fascination was more deep-rooted than that. 'Animals have been put to many uses,' Reichenbach wrote in *Phantom Fame*, 'from plowing the field to decorating the sofa, but my favourite use for them has been to make them break through the front page as they would through a circus hoop. One advantage is that in any press stunt animals never talk and are never suspected, but more than that, they hold a certain glamour for me since my days with the Mondy Circus. In fact, it was with Colonel Mondy that I learned the first daring steps in turning lions into headlines.'

Mondy knew no fear and once tried to stop two lions, which had broken the bounds of their cages to fight for the affections of a lioness, from tearing each other apart. He got into the cage to stop them and the lions turned their attentions on him instead. When the fire brigade came and turned their hoses on the lions, Mondy calmly repaired the cage before escaping. Mondy's fearlessness blinded him to the fact that others were more squeamish. He even planned to stage a wedding in the lions' den as a press stunt, but struggled to find willing participants. A poverty-stricken pair, sustained only by love, were finally induced to 'save the two dollars for a license and win a bedroom set besides, if they survived the ceremony'.

As a result, an awe of lions stayed with Reichenbach for life. Two decades later, in 1920, he found himself using a lion to promote *The Return of Tarzan*; it was, simply, a logical progression after Prince Charley the orangutan 'had made a hit of the first Tarzan Picture'. In the three years between the Tarzan movies that Reichenbach promoted, he had become a major player. Following *The Virgin of Stamboul*, he was employed by Universal at $1,000 per week to promote *Shipwrecked Among Cannibals*. The accompanying stunt, which should have revealed a collection of cannibals living in New York to the press, went wrong and failed to generate headlines, but it is more notable for Reichenbach's contract, which stipulated that 'no concrete plan of exploitation can be given here for this is largely a matter of inspiration and opportunity, but it is understood that Universal is engaging me upon the belief that unusual ideas and startling, sensational manifestations will be exercised to put the film over'.

That sort of freedom was rare then and even rarer now. Certainly it is the sort of free reign that Nottage envied but never achieved during his lifetime. It was this sort of freedom that allowed Reichenbach to pull off his greatest stunt. '*The Romance of Tarzan* had slipped in and out of New York unnoticed,' wrote Reichenbach, 'and without the aid of exploitation, it remained a permanent secret between the producer and the warehouse. Samuel Goldwyn, who took the third of the series, called *The Return of Tarzan*, didn't want this one to follow in the same hushed footsteps of the second. "Where is Prince Charley now?" he sighed regretfully as we watched the preview of the picture. I found that the last of the Tarzan pictures centred on a lion and that gave me a reminiscent thrill.'

He concocted an extraordinary plan; eight days before the movie opened he installed one of his actors – Greg Polar, who had started out as a fireman and got into the movie industry after allowing Reichenbach to use him as a stooge in the Great Reynard ring affair – disguised as an erratic-looking professor of music, at the exclusive Hotel Bellclaire in New York. The professor was primed to request a room on one of the lower floors since he needed his piano hoisted into his quarters. That afternoon, a huge piano box was lifted into his rooms and the professor settled in.

As is often the case with exclusive hotels, no one questioned the fact that the professor, who had been so insistent on having his piano with him, did not appear to be playing the instrument. Indeed, all that emanated from his rooms was an interesting smell. Still nothing was said and no one asked any questions at all. The next morning, untroubled by the staff for the whole night despite the increasing odour of animal leaking through the floorboards and under the door, the professor called for room service and a boy arrived to take his order. He claimed to have a delicate stomach, but asked for a vast quantity of meat.

The boy exclaimed in surprise, as Reichenbach had hoped he would, and the musician then invited him to see the reason he required so much meat: he had a lion in the room. Reichenbach had cunningly exploited the hotel's notorious willingness to accede to its guests' more curious demands. It's hard to imagine a hotel acting in the same politely unsuspicious manner today, except perhaps for the most insanely famous film stars, and that is thanks, in part, to Reichenbach's continuous and high-profile stuntsmanship in the early twentieth century.

Upon seeing the lion, which had yawned at him in an altogether too friendly fashion, the bellboy, unsurprisingly, fled to the management in a state of terror. The manager, an incurious and equable man by the name of Albert Flather, assumed that the panicking employee who arrived at his door talking incoherently about jungle animals was under the influence of illicit hooch, but the boy was so insistent that he went to take a look for himself.

One peek around the door was enough to put Flather in a lather and make him run from the room.

'And he didn't stop until he'd reached the Sixty-eighth Street police station,' wrote Reichenbach. 'There Flather gave the sergeant an incoherent story about about a crazy musician whose piano had turned into a lion. A policeman escorted Flather back to the hotel and together they entered the wild man's quarters. They found him and the lion sitting on the floor, chatting pleasantly. When the man asked a question, the lion answered with a roar. The officer felt lonesome and returned to the station for companionship. With drawn revolvers and followed by reporters and cameramen, the valiant detachment from the Sixty-eighth Street precinct finally arrived and tiptoed gingerly into the presence of the strange couple.

'"Hands up!" they commanded the lion and he turned playfully over on his back. "What's the meaning of this?" they asked the professor and he looked up into the inquisitive muzzles of their guns. He was persuaded to talk.

'"I bought Jim," he said, "from a circus when he was five days old and we've been pals ever since. He's just a big, overgrown kid. See?" And the strange man put his head in up to the neck between the ivory-shod jaws of the beast. The police stopped breathing until the man's head reappeared. Then he asked Jim to sit up, roll over, trot around and shake hands with the gentlemen of the force but they refused to believe he was different from other lions and kept him at target's length.

'"I've been reading a lot of stories,' explained the man, "about a boy born in South Africa who was kidnapped by an ape and who made a pet of a lion and a tiger. I'm on my way to the jungle just to see if I can't do what the boy did. I've made a lot of money out of the lumber business and can afford to get this thrill out of life. I've even changed my name to T. R. Zann to resemble that of the character in the book I'm telling you about, and I'm sailing next week on the Union Castle Line for the land where the lion is king."'

The hoax was a masterstroke on Reichenbach's part; the press lionized the story, featuring it on every front page of the morning papers in New York. The weekly newsreels picked up on it as well, adding further weight to the story's momentum. Before long, the story of T. R. Zann and his incongruous, hotel-bound lion friend had spread over the wires to the whole of America. Reichenbach gloated quietly and prepared the publicity machine for *The Return of Tarzan*. When the film's publicity finally appeared and the stunt became apparent, the newsmen, in the midst of a revelation of Damascene proportions, revelled in the hoax all over again, linking T. R. Zann of the Belleclaire Hotel with the Tarzan of the pictures.

'No animal ever worked so loyally to put over a publicity trick and at no time was I in danger that Jim would betray me by a single false move or word,' wrote Reichenbach. 'We polled over 25,000 columns in news stories and established the film as a national hit.' The lion was the property of Walter Beckwith, an animal trainer who had his animals quartered in Yonkers that Spring. He and Jim even appeared in person at the opening of the picture, adding further to the press's excitement.

Reichenbach married shortly after this, wooing his wife Lucinda by purchasing an expensive car to take her to see her hometown. When she asked how he could afford it, he told her to get in and took her on a tour of three producers' offices. At each office, he created a publicity campaign that paid him a vast sum of money – more than enough to pay for the car. In *Phantom Fame* he makes it sound as if it all happened in a flash, but there must have been some planning. Nonetheless, it impressed Lucinda enough to agree to marry him.

After they married, all they needed was a honeymoon, but Reichenbach, like many publicists after him, wasn't able to go off for long periods without working. In the end Carl Laemmle came up trumps – his movie *Outside the Law* had failed to get past the censor in Britain and he asked Reichenbach to rectify the situation, so Mr and Mrs Reichenbach packed their bags and saw the sights of England.

'Arriving in London,' wrote Reichenbach, 'I phoned T. P. O'Connor, chief of the British censors, whom I had met and introduced at several banquets in America. The great Tay Pay remembered me, invited me to tea, but it turned out to be a snuff-taking contest. After every sip of tea, Tay Pay offered me his snuffbox and out of politeness I took a pinch. When I left I was so snuff-drunk that I sneezed myself into the wrong cab and was followed back by the one I had taken out to his house and had to pay for both. But *Outside the Law* was passed by the liberal O'Connor and Lucinda and I could enjoy London at our leisure.'

Reichenbach's marriage continued in this mode, with Lucinda accepting the disappearances as long as the money came in. Such zealous work patterns have been a constant theme of a publicist's life ever since.

Reichenbach encountered numerous wannabe stars in his career, and many of them wanted some of his magic. One of the most notable was Rudolph Valentino, one of Hollywood's brightest, most short-lived stars, who Reichenbach discovered and helped in the early days, prior to his astronomical success.

'The bane of stars is their inflated ego,' wrote Reichenbach in *Phantom Fame*. 'Success fills them with such awe for themselves that they lose all sense of proportion and judgement. They walk on pedestals, sit on thrones and lie in state. The conceit with which they regard their every gesture and pose recalled to me the dictum of old "Jew" Murphy down on the circus lot that, "A bull is a helluva looking thing, but it must look good to a cow!"'

He met Valentino in the tearoom of the Alexander Hotel, Los Angeles, where the actor worked as a dancing partner for female patrons of the hotel. He was 'a hanger-on, one of the myriad hopefuls that one day dreamed to be used as an extra on the lots close by. I noticed him and he came over to greet me, anxious to introduce himself, saying he had heard a good deal about me. It happened that Clara Kimball Young needed a handsome young straight man in the *Eyes of Youth* – a sort of gigolo – and I told Herb Sanborn, her manager, to come and have a look at Valentino. At first Herb turned Rudolph down flat, for his left ear was cauliflowered, but after I convinced him that Rudolph didn't have to be photographed with a left profile, he agreed to take him on. Valentino never photographed with a left profile throughout his entire career on the screen.'

Some things never change, and this sort of ruse has become commonplace amongst stars. Short male leads find themselves soap-boxes to stand on when they kiss their leading ladies so that they can stoop when they kiss them and look more imposing, and make-up covers a myriad of sins and blemishes, both male and female. Everything in the world of movies is a long build-up to an illusion, paving the way to the prestige moment when the movie – with any luck – suspends the disbelief of the world.

'A month later, Valentino took some pictures and brought me the sun-proofs, asking me to get him some publicity,' wrote Reichenbach. '"But these are merely proofs," I told him. "You have to get real photos."

'"I can't. I haven't the money for that."

'"I'll take care of it for you," I told him.

'The next time I met him was during the Actors' Equity strike in Los Angeles. In spite of his opportunity with Young he had not clicked yet and I offered him $10 to go around and post notices of the strike.

'"O.K.," he said, eager to earn the $10.

'When I saw him again, he was a star. He had appeared in the *Four Horsemen of the Apocalypse* in 1919 and galloped in first.'

Years passed and Reichenbach's star rose almost as astonishingly quickly as Valentino's, though his ego – big as it was – did not increase at such an extraordinary rate. In 1925, Reichenbach was at the heart of the movie industry. His services were retained by Paramount, MGM and other studios and he was considered the ultimate publicity gun for hire. At Paramount he found himself placed in charge of the star's films and he was offered office space in their $1 million home at Marathon Street. It is here that his dictum on stardom, quoted above, comes into play.

'I went to the Astoria studio to meet my old friend Valentino whom I had actually given his first chance on the screen,' he wrote. 'His dressing room was locked and when I knocked, a valet appeared.

'"What do you want?" he asked.

'"Tell him Harry Reichenbach wants to see him."

'"Does Mr. Valentino know you?"

'"I think so. He borrowed two or three dollars at a time from me and knew to whom to bring them back!"

'The valet subsided into the dressing room and soon, returned.

'"Mr Valentino is resting just now. He's very tired. He suggested that you see Mrs. Valentino as she handles all his publicity matters."

'"I see. Well, you tell him that if *Mrs.* Valentino handles these matters, then let her call *Mrs.* Reichenbach."

'I returned to the Paramount offices and informed them that I would have nothing to do with Mrs. Valentino. I had heard a good deal about her and particularly her domination over Rudolph. The Paramount officials, however, told me that in their contract with Rudolph it was stipulated that either he or his wife would have to approve all advertising for his pictures. In that event there was nothing to do but prepare the copy and have Rudolph send someone to O.K. it. When Mrs. Valentino arrived I showed her the material I had prepared. She vetoed everything, saying she had the right to get up the copy.

'"Fine, then get it up," I told her.

'"But I don't know how."

'Then don't meddle in matters that you don't understand,' I cautioned her, but unfortunately for Valentino's career she ignored my advice. I firmly believe that Valentino's career was affected by her attitude. As Fay King aptly put it: "Rudolph Valentino left America the lover of all women and came back the slave of one."'

Stars, of whatever stripe and calibre, are prone to the ill effects of hubris, as are publicists who don't really know their job: the audience for *Monsieur Beaucaire*, for which 'the dictatorial madame' Mrs Valentino handled all publicity, was 80 per cent men when previously it had been comprised almost solely of lustful women. This picture proved a failure, as did the follow-up, *Sainted Devils*.

'In 1923, a thousand women swarmed around the Ritz-Carlton when I walked out of it with Rudolph Valentino,' wrote Reichenbach. 'But ten days before he died – he was eight years older then and already wore a wig – we went to see *George White's Scandals* and nobody knew he was in the theatre. In his case, his wife was an anti-alchemist changing gold to dross. She handled the selection of his stories, dominated him and the studio and inflated his ego to the breaking point.'

The marriage did not last long and ended in bitterness. When he died in 1926 of peritonitis – a complication after a perforated ulcer – he left her one dollar in his will, giving the rest of his money to her aunt, whom they both adored.

Reichenbach's way with money and his sharp, anarchic wit ensured that his star rose in the 1920s, to the point where he was fêted by

Photoplay magazine, which reserved most of its coverage for the stars of the day. By contrast, Nottage was struggling to make his way, lost in the fervour of self-satisfied belief that marked him as more of a wannabe star, unlike Reichenbach, who was paid a star's wage and, for the most part, kept himself out of the rigmarole of day-to-day decadence that marked the decline of the Golden Age of cinema.

• Ten •

THE SLIPPERY SLOPE

In the early days, when Nottage wanted to get legitimate movie work, he invited himself to all the key players' offices, but struggled to get a short meeting. He did, however, manage to corner one player. Nottage told Jesse Lasky that George Bernard Shaw was right when he said any man who pretends to be modest is a darn fool. 'No one is modest. I am the only publicist that can match Reichenbach and beat him at his own game.'

Reichenbach, it should be noted, gave off a distinct impression of an egotistical genius. Since all the playmakers were either clients or confidants, of course, he could afford to be blasé, but he was shrewd enough not to take his powerful position for granted.

Lasky, according to Nottage's notes, leaned back, took a long look at the pretender and said, 'Prove it. I will hand you an actress, and if you can make her famous I will give work. I won't pay you, and if you fail I never want to hear from you again. You can make up anything you please. I am partial to a degree of baloney.'

Nottage failed to impress Lasky that time – sadly, his notes do not detail how – but it's clear the challenge stung him and remained with him. One of Nottage's triumphs, which was clearly indebted to that encounter, was the launch of Theodosia Goodman, an actress he knew from New York in the early days of the twentieth century, as one of the first sex symbols of the movie era and the first fully fabricated star of the movies. Nottage immediately spotted the young actress's vampish potential beneath her meek demeanour and knew he could sell it, so he courted her relentlessly until she accepted him as her publicist. Nottage's labour on her behalf was a work of art and he summoned up a wonderfully exotic history for her from the depths of his imagination.

Working with Frank Powell at William Fox's Box Office Attractions studio, Nottage christened her Theda Bara, which was touted as an anagram for 'Arab death', despite the name being a reduction of her real name and her maternal grandfather's surname. They then dubbed her a 'vamp' because of 'her incongruous, vampirish persona, on and off screen' and conjured an Arabian past for her. Her first film as Theda Bara, *A Fool There Was*, was released in 1915, and Nottage persuaded the studio to make his faux history gospel and present her in flamboyant fur attire. It made her a star, and she was third only to Mary Pickford and Charlie Chaplin throughout the Great War in terms of star appeal. In many circles the campaign was credited solely to Powell, but Nottage's writings confirm that he was heavily involved.

Nottage continued to create a series of iconographic publicity shots of her throughout her short but meteoric career with Fox, dressing her in clothes that left less and less to the imagination – the sort of thing the Hays code obliterated when it came into effect in the 1930s. He had her photographed with skulls and snakes, wearing beaded, fringed clothing that looks ludicrous by current standards, but which were deliberately aimed to titillate and shock in those more impressionable days, for films such as *Cleopatra* and *Salome*. Nottage, like all great publicists, never let the facts stand in the way of a good story, and it was essential that he didn't. Theodosia Goodman of Cincinnati, Ohio's background was in fact deeply ordinary; she was a meek and prim, well-behaved young woman and the daughter of a milliner.

'It was all true at the time,' wrote Nottage in his notes. 'She became all that I made her and more. Audiences liked their girls to be exotic – a milliner's daughter from Ohio just wasn't going to cut the ice – the ice had to be melted in style. So I threw in a splash of Egyptian sun, made out that she was born to a French woman and an Italian man with bohemian leanings in the shadow of the Sphinx. I even had her talking about occultism in interviews, primed her properly to cause a stir. The ice became steam in minutes.

'She was even referenced in songs – one line particularly sticks in my mind: "I know things that Theda Bara's just startin' to learn / make my dresses from asbestos, I'm liable to burn". [The song was called 'Red Hot Hannah'.]. And it was all thanks to me – now I felt I could conquer the world. I was earning $600 a week working for Theda Bara and Fox. It wasn't as much as Reichenbach was earning, and believe me I kept as close an eye as I could on everything he did even though we only met occasionally, but it was enough.'

Theda, given her meek off-screen demeanour, found it difficult to keep up the hype, and although she enjoyed the fruits of Nottage's endeavours, her films only remained popular for a brief period. It didn't help that she was thirty years old when her first film came out – Hollywood was as unkind to women over a certain age then as it is now. When her contract was dropped by Fox in 1919, her film career was essentially over. She married director Charles Brabin in 1921 and made one more movie, Hal Roach's *Madame Mystery*, in 1926. 'Theda had a taste for performance,' wrote Nottage, as an appearance on Broadway the following year proved. Theda tried to reengage Nottage for her Broadway relaunch in *The Blue Flame*, but this time their working relationship was not successful. The public's tastes had moved on, as had Nottage's. Vamps were passé, and innocent virginal heroines were in vogue. Added to that, Charles Brabin did not appear keen for his wife to take the limelight again.

'My heart wasn't in promoting her,' wrote Nottage. 'Added to the fact that she was past her best years was the fact that any stunt I cooked up to promote the show was leaked to the press well in advance, losing all the impact it might have had. I suspect Brabin was responsible – can't prove it, but I'm certain. I'd say he wanted a respectable wife, a good Jewish milliner's daughter, to be a good Hollywood hostess for him and his friends. Ironic, given that he only met her thanks to my persuasive promotion and that I'm certain people only visited them because of the allure I created for her.'

Back in the post-war years, as Theda Bara's career snaked to a close, Hollywood was becoming a synonym of sin. As the Roaring Twenties began, Nottage played up his stable of clients to fit the cliché. It was easy to get banner headlines and equate his talent to sex, drugs and the movie lifestyle given that he was arranging house parties for a selection of the choicest starlets as well as the more predatory directors, producers and power brokers. Into this mix, Nottage added a selection of newspaper editors and policemen and a discreet photographer, which allowed him a measure of control over the eager young women in case they realized they were being used as high-class whores and tried to expose the ready supply of drugs and alcohol available. He never seems to have overplayed his hand and got a number of rising stars to come to his parties. All the same, he hated some of the more vulgar aspects of what he was doing and was prone to writing long, guilty letters to his father – never posted – decrying his shameful, lustful, sinful life.

The age was exuberant and consumed with the fire of money, lust, greed and decadence, and the making of films was supported by extravagant, unfettered publicity campaigns. Kenneth Anger called it a 'delirious decade of wonderful nonsense' where life increasingly became a tightrope as fears grew that the bottom was about to drop out of the market. Was it all about to disintegrate and would the riches suddenly end? Investors got nervous as the headlines became more sensational, and organized campaigns to halt the depravity gathered speed from the mid 1920s onwards as yet more people flocked to the picture palaces and more money filled the coffers of the astonished and delighted studios.

By 1920, Nottage was an itinerant publicist, vacillating between New York and Hollywood. Nottage managed to steal some business from his great rival Harry Reichenbach and his successful campaigns attracted those desperate for renown to his door. These campaigns included work for Louise Brooks, whom he promoted in 1922 when she joined the Denishawn Dance Company, and put in the way of movie directors long before her Broadway breakthrough, making her eventual ascension to movie stardom a surer thing. He also worked for former child star Dolores Costello (Drew Barrymore's grandmother), helping her get her first adult role in the 1923 film

The Glimpses of the Moon with a series of carefully placed adverts featuring her picture and a suggestive tag line. A corner of the office Nottage rented was given over to a huge leather Chesterfield, a precursor to the casting couch. One can only imagine a scene straight out of an early silent movie melodrama – the lunging publicist chasing the poor actresses as they deftly manoeuvred around his wiry frame.

Some might describe this new world as a Sodom and Gomorrah; certainly the growing industry was dusted with 'joy powder', as cocaine was known, and sexually transmitted diseases were rife. Many were lured into its unreality by myths of the lifestyle. The media had not yet uncovered the fat, corrupt underbelly of some of the cocaine- and drink-crazed lunatics that made up Nottage's clients list, but Nottage's notes suggest that many of his female clients were nothing less than a personal harem.

One client who escaped his clutches was Clara Bow. Nottage met Clara shortly after she won the Motion Picture Magazine's Fame and Fortune contest in 1921. Bow's prize was a part in a film, *Beyond the Rainbow*, and she was actively looking for representation to help get her name noticed and spawn more movie work. Nottage saw photographs of the sixteen-year-old Bow and decided he would like to work with her. 'She had a fragile quality about her,' he wrote, 'a haunted look that was instantly appealing. I could see that she would be famous and that she needed protection from Hollywood and the corrupting influence of stardom. I arranged a meeting with her, but she said I reminded her of her father and refused to work with me.'

This wasn't a surprising reaction, given that her father had raped her when she was fifteen. Bow and Nottage kept in touch, however, and he watched with despair as she lived up to his predictions, succumbing to drink, drugs and promiscuity. 'I could have made her a lasting star,' wrote Nottage. 'I could have kept her away from the booze and the dope and the men. She wouldn't have retired if I'd managed her – she'd still be famous today. We could have worked on her accent. Nobody thought of that before the advent of sound.' Lynda Fairweather remembers Nottage talking about Clara Bow. 'I think he was in love with her,' she told me. 'More than with many of the women he fell for. Her name came up on the occasions he spoke about the past at all. He was twenty years older than her, though. It wouldn't have worked.'

Nottage's protective attitude towards Clara Bow has a measure of nobility to it, but it seems to have been equally driven by desire. Certainly, there is a suggestion in his papers that he had invited Bow to some of the parties he hosted and may well have had compromising photographs of her somewhere – none survives in his archive but the hint of them does. He was torn between the necessities of making money and a deep love of his more often than not female clients, which veered between the Christian ideal of love and a more lustful version. With Clara Bow, he certainly seems to have regretted taking that measure of control over her and tried his best to make amends in later life.

Bow apparently wrote to Nottage in 1949 after being diagnosed as schizophrenic. Her letter doesn't survive, but Nottage quotes it. 'I wish I'd taken your offer, Maynard,' she apparently told him. 'You didn't have the breaks you could have had and I could have helped with that. What you did have – though I couldn't see it at the time – was a love of your clients over and above the call of duty. They were family to you, however awful and useless some of them were. I wish I'd joined that family – it was a mistake not to. Perhaps I wouldn't be in the state I am now if I'd let you represent me.'

Nottage's notes show that he was at the heart of some of the biggest stories of the early 1920s and the off-screen scandals that were beginning to plague Hollywood. He made a friend of Mabel Normand, the hugely popular comedienne, whom he met in 1914 through Fatty Arbuckle on the set of *In the Clutches of the Gang*, and he worked on her publicity on and off for ten years, though it seems the relationship went deeper than that. Certainly it was he who masterminded her anti-drugs stance, which 'deflected attention away from her habit of ingesting "joy powder" in enormous quantities like one of those mirrors the Greeks used to burn ships'.

Frustratingly, much of what Nottage wrote about Normand and her set of debauched friends is missing, presumably destroyed. That said, a few remarkable notes remain, which put Nottage right at the heart of one of Hollywood's great unsolved murders. Interest in the murder of William Desmond Taylor has increased as time has elapsed. On the morning of 2 February 1922, Taylor's body was found inside his bungalow at the Alvarado Court Apartments in the Westlake Park area of downtown Los Angeles (then a chic and affluent area). A group of people gathered inside and a man who identified himself as a doctor made a cursory examination of the body and declared the victim had died from either a heart attack or a stomach haemorrhage. Strangely, the doctor was never seen again.

Sometime later that day, doubts arose and the police turned the body over to reveal the forty-nine-year-old film director had been shot in the back. A sum of $5,000 in cash, which Taylor had shown to his accountant the day before, was missing and never accounted for. A string of celebrities and moving picture producers were linked to his death and questioned about their relationship to the deceased and their movements during the early hours of 2 February. Among them were Mabel Normand, Mary Miles Minter, Carl Stockdale, Mack Sennett (with whom Mabel Normand had had an affair), and Gareth Hughes. The case was never solved. Poor crime scene management and apparent corruption meant that much of the physical evidence was lost at the time, while the rest of it vanished over the years. No police files are known to remain. Various theories have been put forward over the intervening decades, but no hard evidence has ever been uncovered to link the crime to a particular individual.

It is apparent from his notes, however, that Maynard Nottage was one of the people summoned on the morning of 2 February. Mabel was a close friend of Taylor and was the last person to see him alive, fifteen minutes before he died. It is certain that Taylor was aware of her cocaine addiction and tried to help her fight it. What happened during the early hours of that day, and to the $5,000, remains a matter of speculation, but Normand's career never recovered from the scandal. The scant documentation linking Nottage to Normand and to a process of attention diversion certainly adds a new and unwholesome layer to the mystery surrounding Taylor's death. Added to that, he had worked with Mary Miles Minter whose affair with Taylor was revealed after the director's death. The resulting furore destroyed her career too.

Whether Nottage was involved in a cover-up or not, his career also suffered after the death of Taylor. It is possible that his arrogant disposition was augmented by cocaine use and that this was the point at which he really began to believe in his own myth. Either way, he never made it any bigger and a bitterness crept into his demeanour that never entirely left. A measure of desperation, misogyny and despair crept into his later work, something that's abundantly clear from his writings, even though he doesn't acknowledge it specifically, despite moments of self-awareness.

A case in point is the launch of a vaudeville show that he promoted in the early 1920s called *Jazz Nights*, which sensationally promised a peek at 'beautiful jazz babies, champagne baths, midnight revels, petting parties in the purple dawn'. The subsequent press communiqué was full of Nottage's trademark purple adjectives: 'neckers, white kisses, pleasure-mad daughters, sensation-craving mothers' and the like. Journalists, not yet attuned to blood-and-thunder leaders about depravity and keen for more long-running stories like the fall of Fatty Arbuckle and the death of William Desmond Taylor, talked about the show 'taking you completely out of yourself into a wonderful new world'.

Nottage created a nationwide promotional tour, which saw scantily clad women in cages positioned outside theatres that were running competitors' films and shows. Leaflets were handed out proclaiming, 'Out of the cage of everyday existence! If only for an afternoon or an evening – Escape!' In each town, Nottage threw a lavish party for local journalists, who enjoyed the revelry, which unsurprisingly curried enough favour to fill the pages of the newspapers with glowing reports about the show's visit.

Nottage's love of decadence was born of jealousy – he wanted the money that Reichenbach commanded but couldn't get it – and this was mostly due to the fact that he couldn't suppress the urge to tour. He didn't understand the great trick that Reichenbach had learned: that of getting the press to come to him. Reichenbach created great ideas and *they* brought the journalists and eager public flocking to him. Nottage was a great ideas man, but he couldn't get the chase out of his blood and always felt the need to take the story to the journalists. In the increasingly cutthroat world of showbiz publicity, this tendency lost him the cutting edge.

As did Nottage's way with alcohol. When Prohibition arrived in 1920, Nottage had stockpiled liquor and a healthy supply of stimulants. Each of Nottage's clients relied on him not only to keep them in print with the right stories, but to supply them with recreational materials: 'I had my own private play pens,' he boasted. Things became heavy when one of his clients, Art Acord, the horse-opera star, was driven to suicide by bad-booze insanity, while another client, western star Leo Maloney, died from overindulgence. According to Nottage, movie world gossips whispered his name as the reason for his client's addictive downfalls. 'They only talked about the bad times, never the good things I did for them,' he moaned, which suggests a certain drug-fuelled paranoia.

Nottage's parties were known as orgiastic Bacchanalian 'whoop it ups' characterized by nudity and riotous abandon. With an eye to sensationalism and an ear to mutterings, he used these occasions to attract prospective clients and feed interesting titbits to any hapless hacks who might have gone too far. Ironically, he wasn't trying to corrupt people's morals, since neither he nor the new consumers had yet been told that people's morals were that easily corruptible. It was left to the reformers to take that line.

After Taylor's death, Nottage kept an almost obsessive record of notes that linked many movie stars with debauchery and scandalous behaviour. The Hearst press had destroyed Fatty Arbuckle's career after he was accused of rape the year before, and Nottage, it seems, may have used the atmosphere of paranoia to instigate a whispering campaign against certain stars. There are a number of notes in his archive addressed to various journalists dated between 1922 and 1924 – not long after the Hays Office opened in fact – saying things like '[Barbara] La Marr's been seen with Captain Spaulding again' – a reference to a notorious Hollywood drug dealer who was immortalized in a Marx Brothers' song. It is not clear why he would have turned to this sort of gossip, but it would partly explain why he became isolated from a number of his friends in the business, since the appearance of these letters in his archive corresponds with the beginning of his decline. If such a campaign took place, he may have been forced into it by studio pressure: his way of accommodating the rise of authoritarian in-house publicists like Howard Strickling. There is no record of how he used these notes, or even if he did, but the fact that they are there at all is fascinating.

Harry Reichenbach remained unimpressed, however much Nottage tried to steal his thunder and his clients: 'I declare my progressive work as the screen's pre-eminent promotional model', boasted an advertisement that he placed in the trade paper, *Photoplay*. In many ways, it was. Nottage had the imaginative chops to rival Reichenbach, but having run from a strict, hard-working Methodist upbringing, he was too keen on having fun and living on the edge of the luxurious lap of showbiz to bite the hands that fed him. While Nottage wanted the money and lifestyle of his bigger clients, he didn't have the wherewithal to steady himself to the task. Reichenbach, on the other hand, wanted to work towards something better and insinuated himself into the workings of the studios. He wanted the money to make a lifestyle of his own and operated with an almost zenlike self-belief and control. By the mid 1920s, Nottage was no longer in charge of his destiny, whilst Reichenbach was up to his ears in work, stability and money.

• Eleven •

RADIO KILLED THE PUBLICITY STAR

Even as Nottage and Reichenbach were planning and executing their astonishing stunts in the early 1920s, their way of life was already ebbing away. Their way of working began its freefall into decline with the arrival of the first public radio station in 1921. By 1924 two and a half million radios had found their way into American homes and information was spreading too far and fast for the great imaginative stunts the early publicists thrived on. Added to that, airmail helped spread information rapidly across America. Barnum had had his trains, telegrams and newspapers, but that era was over and the speed of communication took an urgent step up.

Print journalism was also changing fast, with William Randolph Hearst creating the template for the new tabloid aesthetic. Hearst's approach, which had learned a good few lessons from the Barnum model, was typified by his attitude to the Spanish–American war in 1898 – he insisted he would supply the war if his artist would supply pictures, from Cuba, despite there being not even the slightest hint of a scuffle.

The apogee of his media-mogul-as-god complex was the creation of personality journalists, in the shape of the supremely queenly Louella Parsons, who moved to LA in 1925, having negotiated a deal with Hearst, who had fired her eight years before and was only just waking up to the possibility that movie stars and the pictures they appeared in were news. Parsons created a bond with a large number of stars and refused to write kindly things about people unless they sent her Christmas presents – Stan Laurel and Oliver Hardy never received a decent write-up from her because they refused to pander to her whims. Hearst built Parsons up as someone who integrated wholly and utterly with her subject matter. This was all done to help his mistress become a star – when Marion Davies arrived at MGM it was with a flurry of Hearst money and Parsons behind her. Parsons was under strict instructions to toe the MGM line and, as a consequence, many unlikely stories provided by the studio were printed as fact and many potential scandals disappeared in a puff of smoke.

The template was set in motion early on; Parsons became the main gossip writer for the papers within Hearst's empire, thanks to a story she *didn't* write – a rare and doubtless carefully calculated moment of silence in a career of sly nods and outright attacks on celebrities. In 1924, the director Thomas Ince died in suspicious circumstances aboard Hearst's yacht during a party. The official story was that Ince died of a heart attack, but rumours persisted that Hearst had shot him, either for making love to Marion Davies or by accident, mistaking him for Charlie Chaplin, who was rumoured to be sleeping with Davies and who was also on board at the time. One source from which no rumours sprang was Louella Parsons, who happened to be on board the yacht for the party even though she held a relatively lowly position in the Hearst empire at the time. The price of her silence was a huge promotion and the opening up of a whole new world of gossip journalism that up until then had been dominated by the gentler, more easily persuadable fanzines such as *Photoplay*.

Reichenbach, Nottage and their ilk's brand of publicity was often reliant on a glorious fantasy world that couldn't stand up to serious scrutiny and which suffered badly with Parsons' arrival. 'Louella Parsons was a two-legged earthquake,' wrote Nottage. 'She sank my corner of Hollywood slowly in the warm waters of the Pacific. I never could sell her a story – she wanted to know too much about it in advance and would never just take my word for it.'

Until these changes began to take place, it had been a simple case of creating the story – Nottage and Reichenbach presented people with grand ideas, fully-fledged figments of their imagination, and created the images the movie industry and newspapers thrived on. With the new, speedier world of radio and gossip journalism, which was invariably syndicated worldwide, like Louella Parsons' column in the *Los Angeles Examiner*, combined with a more commercially minded movie industry, there was less and less opportunity to be creative as people and organizations became involved in the star-making process.

An extraordinary number of disgruntled people were left by the wayside thanks to this new factory approach, and many of them resorted to feeding stories to the press, meaning that Louella Parsons and other, lesser gossip writers were constantly fed stories by people inside, and cast aside by, the industry.

When Marion Davies, who never became the star Hearst hoped she would, despite starring in a great many films, parted company with MGM a little over a decade later, so did Parsons. By that time Hedda Hopper had set up as Parsons' rival monarch of gossip, and MGM's publicity department came to an understanding with her instead.

With the new breed of journalism came a new understanding of how the system worked and a new understanding of the value of a story. Now the net and camera phones make everybody a part of the process, from reporting to publicizing, and in the 1920s it was the same sort of revolution, though on a lesser scale – the involvement of consumers in the lives of the stars was another deciding factor in the death of the silent era of publicity.

Respect was an essential commodity in the golden era of movie making – it was clear to the studios that it was necessary for their stars to be respected if the studios were to continue to make money from them, despite the almost constant philandering, drug abuse and free-thinking tendencies engendered by the end of the Great War and the glamour lent such louche behaviour by Prohibition.

William Hay, who had helped clean up baseball's shoddy image and corrupt ways, was employed in 1922 to begin the investigation into the movie industry that would lead to the Hays Code. Stunts that relied on flights of fancy and risked adverse publicity for the studios, who were rapidly coalescing into fully fledged businesses after their early boom-and-bust days, were not so easily tolerated. This new seriousness, and the money that surrounded it, meant that the press were quicker to expose a hoax. In effect, the creative impetus of publicists like Reichenbach and Nottage, and the licentious behaviour that went with it, was placed in a bell jar and the oxygen was slowly sucked out as the Twenties progressed.

The Hays Code had its beginnings in the conservative mores of America and was fuelled by a Christian right wing that still exerts an influence today. In 1915, the United States Supreme Court ruled that movies were not covered by the First Amendment and certain cities passed ordinances banning 'immoral' films. Studios, which had freely committed the most lavish lasciviousness manageable on celluloid with relative impunity, feared that they would become subject to state or federal regulation.

It is remarkable, given America's conservative nature, that it took so long for such regulations to fall into place, but the industry was forced to react after several shocking incidents that incensed the public and led, thanks to the uncontrolled way in which they spread through the press, to the end of the Reichenbach/Nottage era. One was the trial of Fatty Arbuckle for his alleged involvement in the death of actress Virgina Rappe at an orgiastic party in San Francisco in 1921; another was the murder in 1922 of William Desmond Taylor and subsequent revelations about the director's bisexuality. There were also the drug-related deaths throughout the 1920s of Wallace Reid, Olive Thomas, Barbara La Marr, Alma Rubens and others.

Without restrictions, film might never have become the force it is today as America would probably never have taken it so gratefully to its bosom. At the time, film was viewed by many as pornographic, a perception fuelled in the 1920s by an influx of so-called decadent post-war European influences. In the days before silicone enhancement and carefully controlled special effects, pornography was a great deal more real – to such an extent that sex films from the early days of Hollywood still have the power to shock, thanks to the coruscating air of truth that seeps from the celluloid. It is also certain that numerous film stars started out making pornographic films. A porn film allegedly starring Joan Crawford, for example, was carefully suppressed by MGM, with all copies hidden or destroyed and showings limited to select groups of MGM executives.

The star system that Reichenbach and, to a lesser extent, Nottage helped found, with the promotion of Francis X. Bushman, Rudolph Valentino, Theda Bara and others, was fuelled by sex and drugs, which were an essential aid to actors unused to the pressures of fame and a relentless production schedule. Hollywood, too, was driven by sex, drugs and the needs of its stars, as were innumerable executives, not to mention publicists such as Nottage, who craved the lifestyle they sold to the newspapers. Hollywood could no longer afford, however, to expose these relentless drives to a morally minded government and public in the manner of a slapdash flasher. The scandals that rocked Hollywood in the early to mid Twenties led to a tug of war between the studios and William Hays, who vowed to cast an air of moral authority over Hollywood. For some time he tugged with little success, despite the introduction of a 'Don'ts and Be Carefuls' list in 1927, but that was to change with the arrival of sound.

Radio, which had been becoming more prominent throughout the decade, spread like wildfire with the arrival of the National Broadcasting Company in New York in 1926. It reached the West Coast of America within months and suddenly everyone was able to hear the latest news instantaneously, putting the final nail in the early publicists' coffin.

Against this background, a new age of cinema had been emerging in the 1920s, as the small companies that littered Hollywood joined forces and loomed over their one-time rivals like King Kong. These mergers were born of necessity as well as of greed, since over the years many companies had overstretched themselves and started to fall apart, despite the astonishing amounts of money coming in. This had much to do with the fact that the stars had all the earning power – a state of affairs helped by Reichenbach and Nottage's careful early groundwork. The studios felt they needed to assert some control, especially in light of the death, drug addiction and sexual promiscuity that plagued the millionaires who starred in their movies.

Paramount came early to the table, born out of the Famous Players–Lasky merger with Samuel Goldwyn in 1916. Warner Brothers Incorporated was formed in 1923, and in 1924 MGM opened its doors, poaching Irving Thalberg from Universal, which remained at the fringes of the industry for some years, thanks to the absence of this tough negotiator and movie buff, as indeed did Columbia Pictures, though both managed to retain their independence.

MGM was the pre-eminent studio of the period, even though it nearly merged with William Fox's company – Fox later went on to form 20th Century Fox. The merger was stopped by Mayer for violating Federal antitrust laws; he called in some favours with friends in the Justice Department because he had no shares in the company and stood to make no money. A latecomer to the party was RKO Radio Pictures, who appeared on the scene at the same time as the talkies and never made a silent film.

These mergers made it easier for the studios to control the stars, as with less competition they could tie them in to long contracts more easily. This was done with a view to protecting the studios from the increasing sense of moral outrage sweeping the country and putting their profits at risk and stopping the stars from running amok, since many of them came from nothing to a state of such extraordinary wealth that they were unable to cope. They needed to be kept in line and have an eye kept on them. At the very least they needed their sexual shenanigans kept hidden from the press. But how could they do it? They needed publicists who understood the value of a story as well as the journalists, publicists who could adapt to the rise of new technologies with ease and who could ingratiate, bully, cajole, bribe and spin with the best of them. They needed fixers. And with the arrival of the Golden Age of cinema, that's just what they got.

• Twelve •

OF MICE AND ENDS

By the late 1920s, Nottage was attaining the air of a spent force and was much whispered against in the circles he moved in. The pressure of attempting to keep up with Reichenbach had exhausted him, as had his habit of dipping into the well of hard liquor he kept for his clients. It was this attachment to the old order of stardom and its decadent, attendant lifestyle that worked most against him. Nottage didn't just want to make money with creative ideas, he wanted to be the star of his own little world. In essence, he believed he was a star, though he was little known outside showbiz circles.

He may have looked a little like a seedier James Stewart, but he was never likely to achieve the same status. The role of a publicity agent was to turn dreams into reality, turn small, effete girls, through the alchemy of exposure and carefully invented stories, into sexual predators, and weak, pretty men into demi-gods; then watch as they came to believe the stories they'd been dressed in. Nottage barely recognized his peripheral role in the order of stardom right up to the end of his life, caught as he was in the belief that, because he had made actors like Theda Bara famous, he was famous too. Thanks to a combination of alcohol and arrogance, Nottage began to believe his own press – a state of mind that Reichenbach had noted in the Great Reynard years before. The only difference was that Nottage told these stories about himself, and the only people who believed them – or even listened – were some of his more hapless clients. The rest moved on, became famous, had their careers killed off by the end of silent movies or were stifled entirely by the Hays Code, which came into force in the 1930s and destroyed Nottage's career.

Throughout Prohibition, Nottage lived up to Oscar Wilde's famous aphorism: 'Work is the curse of the drinking classes.' He worked, certainly, but it was more towards achieving the state of alcoholic nirvana that his clients – and the clients he wished he had – reached. His drinking buddies included W. C. Fields, Al Jolson, and a cabal of actors, runners and producers. But a drinking buddy does not necessarily constitute a real friend, as a note at the bottom of an invite to the premiere of *The Jazz Singer*, released in 1927, suggests: 'Come if you must, Maynard,' it reads, 'but bring your work hat. If you can find it. If you can't find it, bring some booze. If there's no booze, don't bother.' He was downcast by his failure to achieve the giddy heights of notoriety and fiscal success that Reichenbach had managed and, as the Twenties drew to a close, along with his career, he became ever more desperate.

In 1928, Reichenbach was managing New York's Colony Theatre. He had moved back there for a change of scene and with the thought of moving into other strands of the movie industry. Nottage, 'scratching around for any work I could get – again', wrote, 'I went to see a film Reichenbach was pushing as the best thing since sliced bread, a rip off of a Buster Keaton movie starring a jug-eared mouse called *Steamboat Willie*, and I was shocked. It struck me that Reichenbach could make gold out of anything and I hated him all the more for it. I'd seen the beginnings of animation – I met Winsor McCay back before the Great War, when he was peddling Gertie the Dinosaur around the vaudeville circuit, and this tawdry mouse wasn't a patch on McCay's early phantasmagorical works.

'I guess I prefer *Steamboat Willie*, with the benefit of hindsight, to the sort of gooey dross that Walt Disney began to churn out later, but my opinion is colored by the way I felt the film echoed my life at that time. The mouse starts out in charge, but Captain Pete comes along and throws him off the bridge. The mouse rescues the girl and gets her to play music with the animals, performing all sorts of outrageous stunts like turning a goat into a phonograph machine, with his tail as the handle. All this disturbs the captain, so he sets him about peeling potatoes. For Captain Pete, read Reichenbach, the man who stole my thunder, took the clients I should have had, managed the theatres I should have been managing and didn't drink the drink I drank. Damn him.'

Whatever bitter spin Nottage may put on the movie, there is no doubt Reichenbach was again making a success of himself. In *Walt Disney: The Biography* (Arum, 2007), Neal Gabler says, '. . . Reichenbach, after years of representing a variety of film companies in promotional stunts, had become manager of the Colony Theatre on Broadway, the very place where Universal had hoped to screen [*Steamboat*] *Willie* before negotiations broke down. Ever since the recording session, Walt had been taking his print of *Willie* from distributor to distributor, sitting in the projection room while the cartoon was run and looking through the portholes to see the executives' reaction, only to be told they would be in touch if they were interested. Reichenbach happened to attend one of these screenings and was impressed enough to approach Walt about the possibility of showing *Willie* for two weeks at his theatre. When Walt fretted to Reichenbach, as he had to Universal, that the showing might harm his chances to land a distributor, Reichenbach told him that distributors never knew if a film was good until they heard the public and press response and he assured Walt that "they'll like it". Reichenbach offered him $500 for the run. Somewhat bravely by his own admission, Walt countered with $1,000 – "the highest price that anybody's ever paid up to that time for a cartoon on Broadway" – and Reichenbach, who obviously saw potential in *Willie*, agreed.'

His midas touch was as assured as ever: Reichenbach had spotted one of the biggest brands of the twentieth century and given it its first push on the road to success. Without the voice of his experience, it is quite possible that Mickey Mouse would not have found a footing in the world's collective consciousness at all.

Nottage's circumstances were much reduced, however, and the fact that he drank with the stars left them considerably less inclined to employ him. They knew that a publicist working on their behalf needed to maintain a clear head, a bit of distance and a clean, though cunning, reputation. All this was leaving Nottage, as were his beloved family of no-hope clients. A letter from one unnamed client, only the first page of which survives in his tatty archive, sums up this feeling, particularly amongst his female clients. 'My dear Maynard,' it reads, 'I suppose I have enjoyed our working relationship over the last eight years and I have certainly enjoyed the access to alcohol that didn't blind me – unlike Maureen, who got in too deep with the men from Chicago you introduced her too – though the numerous times you tried to seduce me in a drunken stupor didn't win you any favors. I forgave you that – I might even have succumbed if you'd tried me sober – but it's all the broken promises of stardom that have led me to find other representation.

'You were never going to make me famous by getting me to stand in crowds as a patsy, like this business was all still a carnival from before I was born, and the way you tried to get me to sleep with those dismissive actors who you'd known fifteen years ago, and who clearly didn't care to know you now, was little better than prostitution. Or it would have been if it had worked. All the same, I regret that our . . .'

The letter ends abruptly, and Nottage's career petered out in the same way, on a note of regret that would last him the rest of his life as he was reduced to taking nickel work to keep going. One of his last major jobs from that period was a commission to revive the fortunes of an almost bankrupt clothing manufacturer, Rutger Brothers from Arkansas. The Rutger brothers were sons of European dissidents who had arrived in America in the early 1900s. They had been manufacturers of high-quality Lederhosen, amongst other things, but these skills were far from useful in America, even amongst German refugees, who had struggled to adapt and become Americans rather than cling on to the traditions of their past. The Rutger family were desperate to be accepted, but hadn't a clue how to go about it, so, unable to afford anyone else, they hired Nottage. Relieved to get away from New York for a while, Nottage went south to work on the project and, having had a look at the religious make-up of Arkansas, decided that the best way to go was to play to the religious sympathies of the south. He came up with a "How to dress your preacher" competition, an audacious concept that melded the Hollywood approach with religious fervour in a way rarely seen until the relatively recent rise of the Church of Scientology.

Women from all over the state of Arkansas were invited to get together to talk about how best to dress their preacher in order to maximize church attendance and promote a desire to better understand the scriptures. Nottage paid passage down to Arkansas for one of the few remaining members of his cabal of hopeful actresses, a demure young woman called Jane Hathaway. He paid her to infiltrate the group and encourage the women to choose colours and fabric that already existed in the Rutger Brothers factory so they could win the competition. The result was a striking outfit consisting of black woollen crêpe trousers tucked into knee-high black leather boots, and completed with a black shirt sporting an armband depicting a scene from the Old Testament.

Unfortunately, Jane was not as demure as she looked, having developed a considerable fondness for, but no tolerance of, drinking, and she was discovered in a drinking den, talking about Nottage's plans while in the arms of a handsome Arkansas man who turned out to be a relative of one of the other competitors. With the ruse uncovered in such tawdry circumstances, the Rutger Brothers were disqualified. Nottage was relieved of his duties and nothing more came of the competition.

Nottage and Jane were able to escape back to New York on the next train, but the Rutger Brothers were ruined immediately. They sold their business for a knockdown price to one of their rivals and used the proceeds to return to Germany in 1929. According to Nottage, they took the idea for the resultant uniform with them and, ten years later, became one of the richest clothing manufacturers in Europe, creating a uniform for their country that would be remembered for decades to come.

All that, however, was of no use to Nottage – he had a lifestyle to maintain. His next step was to try to break into the Hearst empire, which he had supplied with stories on and off throughout his career.

William Randolph Hearst was the first of the great press lords, ruler of a $220,000,000 domain and inventor of tabloid journalism.

His family made its riches in the Nevada silver mines, and he used his fortune to acquire newspapers and 'make news'. The establishment of his empire provided the new breed of publicists, especially Reichenbach and Nottage, with a canvas on which to paint portraits of their clients. In truth, Hearst led the way with his own illustrative stunts, one of the most famous of which was to hire someone to jump into San Francisco Bay to see how long it took for City Emergency Services to respond.

Another of his more famous antics revolved around the Spanish–American War in 1898. He hired the famous artist Remington to go to Cuba and send back images relevant to the growing conflict there between Spain and the United States.

When Remington wired Hearst that there was nothing to draw, Hearst insisted that if Remington supplies the pictures, he would supply the war. He did, and in doing so, Hearst became immensely powerful behind the scene, with the open intention of making himself politically powerful too.

Significantly, he also became infatuated with the silent film star Marion Davies, and used his ownership of a Hollywood studio and chain of newspapers to boost her career. This infatuation with news creation and the manufacture of celebrity was important for the likes of Nottage and Reichenbach, who got involved in Hearst's empire in order to further their own aims. Hearst fuelled an appetite for popular journalism and the use of publicity. He had proved that they were symbiotic and that the average person on the street lapped it up, as they still do.

However, the new dependency on a publicity juggernaut created new, unfathomable abysses. The Hollywood industry press had awesome potency in the rigid self-centred movie-town commune. When you're trying and failing to get back up there, or when you're on a roll, booming and swimming in cash with all the trappings and not too much to dwell on, what do you actually think about? Your press persona, of course, or the acres of publicity that the producer or performer next door is harvesting. One picture, as some guru from East Hollywood once said, is worth a thousand words. Money is the life blood of the community, and publicity – or a lack of the right kind of publicity – goes right along with it. If you could deliver it, you had the best seat in the house and the juiciest clients, but if you failed or managed to mishandle a project, you were made to suffer.

Hollywood is self-absorbed and thin-skinned about the printed word. A good many publicists with an appreciable reputation, who make a great deal of money preying on this sensitivity, are frequently concerned about how they will be rewarded. This crosses a line because the masters expect too much for too little reward, and those that pushed the point became necessary irritations. If the stars of the trade were forcibly put on the spot, they would probably confess that they didn't deserve what they got. They were therefore markedly prickly about what was written about them.

Nottage was, of course, aware of this and tried his luck at getting back into Hearst's inner circle, which he had slipped in and out of over the years with stories about Tara Tiplady, Theda Bara and more. His mistake was to use a few illicit drinking sessions with Marion Davies and others as a basis for ingratiating himself with Hearst. 'He told me, in no uncertain terms, what he thought of my career prospects within the Hearst empire,' wrote Nottage years later. 'He would not be employing a man whose best years, he claimed, were twenty years in the past and who had anyway drunkenly propositioned the object of his affections in a speakeasy in Chicago. He even suggested that my main skill was "creating moonshine of the alcoholic variety rather than the sort that sold newspapers".'

It is certain that, after this failed attempt to get back into the big time, Nottage's star fell from the sky. Nottage clearly suspected Hearst's influence. A fragmentary note in his archive reads, 'I'm certain he gave me the Kane treatment – almost no-one I'd known in the years I'd worked in show business spoke to me after that.' This is a reference to Hearst's reaction to Orson Welles' masterpiece, *Citizen Kane*, which was loosely based on Hearst's life. Hearst disliked the movie so much that he and a number of his Hollywood friends persuaded many theatres to limit bookings of the movie, having failed to get it banned outright.

At the end of Prohibition and with the rise of the Hays Code, not only was Nottage out of step, he was out of favour. He was reduced to working the small-time jobs he'd begun with in the early days in between movies and vaudeville – nothing else would touch him. All the people he had worked with or known were either dead, drunk, jostled from the limelight by the rise of the talkies or refusing to talk to him. And to crown it all, in 1931 Reichenbach, his great rival and the one thing that had kept him focused on getting bigger and better work, died of cancer aged forty-nine.

The obituaries for Reichenbach were fulsome, as was the public praise of his peers – perhaps out of relief that the master stuntster was gone, an inverse of Gore Vidal's well-known aphorism, 'Every time a friend succeeds, I die a little.' Sometimes it's easy to praise, especially as the world he had inhabited was more or less a thing of the past by the time of his death.

Nottage greeted the news with both enthusiasm and regret: 'Everyone needs a nemesis, especially in showbiz,' he wrote. 'Reichenbach had kept me moving. With him gone there was nothing left to compete with. All the rules had changed. It was ironic, really, that it was throat cancer that killed him. His voice, which the cancer destroyed, was his weapon – his ability to woo anyone listening to him into believing what he said, however fanciful.

'I guess that for a while my upbringing returned with a vengeful streak – I spent a couple of years after Reichenbach died elated that he was dead, guilty for that elation and terrified that the wrath of God would descend on me in the same manner for all the terrible excesses I'd unleashed in the name of a good story. It left me in a state of indecision that crippled what chances I had of getting work even more – and the moralistic climate of the time was doing a good job of shutting me out. And in the meantime, all the young bucks in the new, hard-nosed, sharp suited world of publicity moved further and further away from anything I recognized and loved.'

Part Two:

THE FAME FACTORY

• • •

'Contained within fan worship is the potential for hatred and disdain, it's binary. The switch can be flipped at any time' DAVID GRITTEN *Daily Telegraph*

'Celebrity worship – and the moral-aesthetic-intellectual relativism it enshrines – is a symptom of cultural decline and confusion; time will tell how serious' *New Yorker*

• Thirteen •

CHANGE IN THE AIR

The advent of sound rang a death knell for the silent movie era. Talking pictures created a whole new level of perceived and potential obscenity, so it was decided that the Hays Office needed a sterner, more formal approach. A Production Code, more commonly known as the Hays Code, was written and adopted in 1930, although it took four years for it to be enforced. It offered three general principles to be adhered to: 1) no picture shall be produced that will lower the moral standards of those who see it. Hence the sympathy of the audience should never be thrown to the side of crime, wrongdoing, evil or sin; 2) Correct standards of life, subject only to the requirements of drama and entertainment, shall be presented; 3) Law, natural or human, shall not be ridiculed, nor shall sympathy be created for its violation. A series of related sub-clauses made it clear that such things as nudity and suggestive dancing – a bugbear of the moral majority since the Salomé dances – the ridicule of religion, the use of drugs, the consumption of alcohol – unless it was for the necessary propulsion of the plot – representations of inter-racial breeding and a great deal more besides were prohibited.

When the code was finally enforced in 1934, it was in many ways the saving of Hollywood, allowing time for the population of late 1950s and early 1960s America to catch up with 'Sin City's' liberal values. In the meantime, the industry resorted to a subtler, more artful means of putting across their message, and this filtered through to the publicists as well.

A new breed of operator was required to cope with these changing times, making the ramshackle circus hucksters and charming, inventive snake oil medicine men surplus to requirements. They were perceived to be as unreliable as the stars they promoted, something that may well have been true of Maynard Nottage, but was unfair to Harry Reichenbach. Put simply, the publicists who appeared born to their jobs were slowly being replaced by a new breed of media-savvy individuals from the newspaper age, who understood and could cope with the increasingly fast spin cycle of information, but at the expense of the joy that marked out the publicity campaigns of the movie industry's early years.

From the mid Twenties to the Fifties, a training period for publicists was instigated to wean out the more random elements and they were drilled in the process relentlessly. Nowadays, as in the early days when Reichenbach and Nottage were starting out, anyone can get involved, and as a consequence, PR people are taking chances with the medium, as the talent and power have shifted away from the executives.

At the time, the change was as remarkable and rapid as the one that's occurred recently with the rise of the internet and the broadband generation. The twenty-first-century media world is an echoing mass of information, slave to the 24/7 media agenda. Satellite and cable throb with ever more sensational stories about celebrities, whose lives are currency in an ever-competitive world. Only the constantly scrabbled-after scoop delivers readership in an ever-decreasing printed media world; the digital agenda throbs with excitement, taking every opportunity to nail a celebrity. The white noise created by thousands of publicists suggests we are living in an age of sophisticated media manipulation, and as a consequence the ghosts of publicity past can seem anachronistic in their often romantic attempts to publicize burgeoning talent and suppress the scandal that was, and probably always will be, a by-product of the heightened reality that showbusiness operates in. But then, in the media world, very few genuflect to the past – the zeitgeist is all. The issue is now, the news is now and the stomach of the beast needs constant enrichment. There's no time to consider, to sit back and reflect. It's all about the excitement that exists in the ephemeral present tense. Cinema, and other forms of entertainment, are constantly at risk from some grand new innovation, be it TV, the internet, a high moral climate, and canny publicists are always finding ways to breathe new life into tired genres – they are there to teach, sometimes literally, old dogs new tricks.

The late 1920s and early 1930s were the tail-spinning end of a very different world – the people in charge of the change had taken on the legacy of the vaudevillean publicists, the fledgling movie publicists, the personality hypesters, and refined their practices into shapes that are shadows of today's media world. They reacted to the mood of the time and regenerated the way the media thought and acted. Movies were big business, played by big characters, and the people involved in their creation were ruthless about making money. The idea of craft shops formulating mighty movies to entertain were, as today, informed by the need to see a return on the vast investments. The money flew into the box office, the profits were quick – even in the depression, when cuts had to be made – and the people connected with the big studios knew that. Without stars, the movies could not be made, but they were contracted, created, cosseted and controlled by the new breed of publicist, whose eye was on the effective running of the machine. This is not to suggest that they didn't make use of the methods used by the generation before them – they knew as well as Reichenbach the value of word of mouth and the purity of a great idea – the main difference was the measure of control the studios had. They needed it, as the stars and older publicists were ill-equipped to deal with the sudden changes brought about by the rise of the new communications empires. The newly combined studios took the work of people like Reichenbach and created a new pantheon of demi-gods. If religious and moral zeal was to suppress the bawdier elements of the movie industry, they would respond by creating a religion, of sorts, of their own. The family of screen gods at MGM, from Gable to Garland, would be built to appear as over-sized as their screen images.

By 1930 radio was massive. The National Broadcasting Company (NBC) and Columbia Broadcasting System (CBS), which had formed in the mid 1920s, were bringing news, stories and stars to the American people. Radio saved the careers of a select few vaudeville stars, whose circuit had been greatly reduced as the movies squeezed them out of theatres, and created new stars, but the most lasting effect of its arrival was that it created another breed of journalist. Radio made stories about the stars that much more human and immediate by linking them more directly into the public arena. As a consequence, as radio grew in terms of listenership, it became necessary to find stars who could stand up to the scrutiny. The rise of new and improved methods of communication may not have been as rapid and catch-all as today's new media, but the quality of the stars being presented was higher as there were fewer of them.

Today, in the effervescent world of TMZ, Popbitch and Holy Moly, camera phones and broadband, celebrity froths up like Andrews Liver Salts, leaving only a surfeit of scum behind. In the early days of the golden age of the movies, it was about glamour, a high, grand lifestyle and impeccable image-making that tolerated no bubble-pricking. The new breed of publicist had to appease the Hays Office and keep the orgiastic excesses of the stars – pushed as they were into the public eye with little experience of pressures or money – out of the eye of a more morally minded public than exists today. If the geese were to be allowed to keep laying golden eggs for their studio masters, they had to appear squeaky clean, something that had rarely happened in the early days. Then, as now, the media revelled in any evidence of wrongdoing. Then, however, the power shifted away from the stars and their freelance publicists towards the studios such as MGM, away from potential mayhem towards a slick, corporate, fixed approach.

So who were the new players? Who was drafted in to fix things for the studios? Who took on the legacy that Reichenbach and Nottage had forged? The influence of Barnum was now, of necessity, being reshaped, and the publicists were more ringmasters and horse trainers than circus barkers. They were at the heart of the industry, not on the outside, luring people in with grand stories, and the most influential amongst them were Eddie Mannix and Howard Strickling.

Eddie Mannix was born in 1891 in New Jersey and was a brutal and ruthless man with alleged mob connections, who rose to the heady heights of second in command to Louis B. Mayer at MGM. He first came to notice in 1911, when he started working as a carnival bouncer for the Schenck Brothers at New York's Paradise amusement park. Little else is known about his early days – he kept a great deal hidden – but he quickly became the Schencks' right-hand man, keeping them and their business interests out of trouble. His fortunes rose with the Schencks', and when they co-created MGM and needed someone to spy on Louis Mayer, whom Nick Schenck loathed, in the Los Angeles branch of the new conglomerate, Mannix was their most trusted choice.

Mannix had risen rapidly through the ranks from his early days as a bouncer and strong arm, watching the excesses of the publicity departments as the Schencks' entertainment empire expanded. Given his later careful management, one can only imagine the mixture of elation and frustration the wayward though successful antics of Reichenbach and Nottage must have left him with. He was eventually appointed financial comptroller of MGM and exerted a massive influence on the fate of the company and its stars.

Howard Strickling arrived in Hollywood in 1919 aged twenty-three and began working as an office boy for Metro. Within a year he was working for Goldwyn as a publicist and by 1924 he was working for Pete Smith's publicity agency and was highly respected in his field. Pete Smith was one of the few early-generation publicists who made the transition. He started out working for Famous Players–Lasky and succeeded thanks to a quick wit and caustic manner of delivery. 'I was glad when [Smith] went in to making movies,' wrote Nottage. 'I believed – foolishly as it turned out – that that would leave more room for me in the game.' He was a rival of both Nottage and Reichenbach, but by the early 1920s, Smith's agency was successfully representing several studios, directors and writers from its base in Los Angeles. Louis Mayer and Irving Thalberg approached him to work for the newly formed MGM in 1924 when their first choice, Howard Dietz, refused to leave New York.

Smith's readiness to use animals marked him out as a man of an earlier era, and his most famous stunt was to take MGM's Leo the Lion around the country by plane on a promotional tour. The stunt went wrong when the plane had to make a crash landing in Arizona, and the lion and crew were rescued by the Navy after Mayer's assistant, Ida Koverman, pulled a few strings with her ex-employer President Hoover. The plane had landed in the top of a tree, with the lion, snarling and not a little bewildered, still in its cage. Smith also tamed the animal instincts of his employers, writing letters and speeches for Mayer and easing him away from ad libbing in public. Mayer was notoriously rough hewn in speech and manners and, given that he was a very public figurehead, it was essential that he didn't startle the horses every time he made a speech. Smith was far more interested in writing for the screen than publicity, however, and after he fell ill he essentially let Strickling manoeuvre himself into a position of power.

Strickling was put in charge of the studio's publicity, leaving Smith free to create as he no longer had to deal with the day-to-day mechanics of the publicity business. Smith's creative streak paid off, as he ended up writing, producing and narrating 150 short films for MGM under the title *Pete Smith Specialities*, and even won two Oscars. He is probably the only publicist to have a star on the Hollywood Walk of Fame. It would appear that Mayer and Thalberg brought Smith to MGM as a way of getting his second-in-command, Strickling. If so, they certainly rewarded Smith well.

Strickling was the son of a grocer and brought the steady hand of a bookkeeper to the job, along with what later turned out to be a somewhat Machiavellian approach to the art of publicity. He formed a formidable team with Eddie Mannix and together they ruled the MGM roost for forty years. Both Strickling and Mannix appear in numerous star biographies, but their titles within the company are rarely mentioned. They appear in books solely in times of trouble for the stars, more often than not with a ready fix – in several senses of the word in the case of Judy Garland.

'I met Strickling in the early 30s,' wrote Nottage much later. 'He was a dour, dull man with no sense of the work I could do. I was desperate for some work in the industry – since Reichenbach died I was the only man who'd been in the publicity game since the beginning and knew the whole history of it. But he wasn't interested in history, didn't care about the roadshows, he'd forgotten vaudeville, and burly [burlesque] was a degenerate subculture from another life to him, fit only for historical films. He listened as I pitched him my ideas, didn't say a word. When I'd finished, he thanked me for coming and then showed me out. A couple of guys followed me, made sure I left the lot. I was never allowed back in.'

Although this is clearly the biased and subjective view of a deeply bitter man, it is true that there was no room for the messes and scrapes that Nottage got into at MGM. To them he was yesterday's man, despite the fact that his and Riechenbach's ideas would be recycled and adapted ad nauseam by the publicity department; it would all come under the watchful eye of Mannix and Strickling, who were on hand to arrange abortions, faux marriages and spells in rehab recast as glorious holidays with faked snaps to 'prove' it. The covert publicity practised by Strickling and Mannix would serve as a good model for a spy movie, covering up some of the most appalling and astonishing scandals.

Mannix and Strickling became immensely powerful at MGM in 1925, charged with selling the studio as a clean, wholesome dream factory, though that was far from the truth. The studio heads were smart cookies – they could see that they needed a large measure of professionalism, given that in the first year of production the twenty-six films the studio produced had made $5 million – $100 million in today's money – and they were making forty-six films in 1925. Situations were changing in the industry and hubris was growing amongst a number of the stars. With the arrival of Marion Davies, Hearst's mistress, at MGM came separate dressing rooms, and with separate dressing rooms came a lesser sense of camaraderie. It was this sense of family that helped keep respect, and it lasted until the 1950s.

Essentially, the Fixers created what is now known as brand management: they sold MGM, by hook or by crook, as a family of stars and star makers, and kept their stars firmly in line so the story held water. They courted journalists, policemen, politicians and mobsters and paid them so the fantasy would stay afloat. Egos and pay packets rose to galactic proportions in the 1930s, and in the depression audiences were far less inclined to like stars who openly revelled in their wealth and freedom. It is testament to Strickling and Mannix's skills that they managed to take the foundations laid by Reichenbach and Nottage and build an empire on them, using the talents born of the circus and applying a new, grim realism, like daub to the wattle of the fantastic.

Many of the new brand of publicists came to the movie industry from newspapers, because the studios required a sharper professional outlook – it was very much a case of poacher turning gamekeeper. Russell Birdwell, who left journalism to work for David O. Selznick, summed the process up in a typically succinct manner: 'Wherever ego, I go!' The same holds true today – many journalists are becoming publicists because the money is so much better. The rules of the game have changed, however, and in a slicker more professional world, the twenty-first century's new arrivals more often than not do not have the ability to become players, however many chances they are prepared to take. The circus life trained nascent publicists such as Reichenbach and Nottage in all the little foibles of humanity that were needed to make a good publicity stunt tick. They were well-defined characters, rounded individuals, defined by their struggle to get out of jobs as circus barkers and into the heady world of vaudeville and Hollywood. Howard Strickling understood the insanity of the human condition although, as the son of a grocer, his first frame of reference was money and making a profit. He may have become a fixer – a behind-the-scenes mogul – but it's clear from the stories he created in defence of the MGM dream factory that he understood how the public consciousness worked.

Not all the new breed of publicists were required to fix things, of course; the new publicity machine was as reliant as ever on a good, positive, entertaining story, be it a puff of delightful whimsy or a gleefully Hays Code-defying stunt. Men such as Pete Smith, Russell Birdwell and James Moran were still employed to create interest and excitement about the latest big thing, and to create the new big thing from sometimes less than stellar source material. The difference was that they operated from within the system rather than outside it, taking a wage rather than demanding a fee. The nature of publicity had changed because journalists wanted to break down taboos – they were no longer content to sit back and be spoon-fed in the manner of the fan magazines; they wanted to scoop out the best stories themselves. The studios, in a powerful, newly moneyed position, were, unsurprisingly, eager to prevent anything that undermined their power, such as the stars, from reaching the front page, so deals had to be made.

Nottage and Reichenbach had not been the deal-making types; they had grown up in a world where they were as notorious as the stars they promoted and where, more importantly, they controlled the content they created and fed it to journalists eager for any glamour they could find. With the arrival of radio and Louella Parsons and her ilk – all scratching away at the surface glamour of showbusiness – they were rendered unnecessary. The new publicists' personalities were, on the whole, subsumed by studio and client.

Perhaps the most influential figure of the new age was Russell Birdwell, who ran some of the most notable movie publicity campaigns of the golden age for the Selznick company. He was also responsible, in cahoots with Howard Strickling, for what is arguably the most influential publicity campaign of all time – the three-year campaign for *Gone with the Wind* – which began with a search for an actress to play Scarlett O'Hara well before a single frame of celluloid had been shot. Birdwell was also the first publicist to go it alone, leaving the Selznick nest in 1938 to set up an independent company that became the model for the modern PR company.

Joker in the pack, James Moran, was a different kettle of fish entirely, a phrase that would have tickled his questing, surrealist intellect to the point of finding out – for publicity purposes, of course – what a different kettle of fish looked like. Moran's stunts include leading a bull through a china shop to see if the phrase 'like a bull in a china shop' held true. As it turned out, the only person to break anything was the star whose career Moran was publicizing. Little survives to suggest what Nottage thought of Moran, but there is a scrawled note saying, 'Moran – a good egg!' Whether this refers to one of Moran's most famous stunts, involving hatching an ostrich egg over twenty days to promote a movie, or to an actual meeting is unclear, but it reinforces the fact that Moran was the most obvious successor to Nottage and Reichenbach's romantic brand of anarchy. He was certainly the antithesis of the studio-system publicist, though he worked for the studios for a while. Most of his stunts, however, were cooked up on his own, and he catered for a different brand of client.

Many people came to Hollywood to follow a dream, but it was a dark dream, darkened further by the Wall Street Crash in 1929 and the Great Depression that followed. By the 1930s the real powerbrokers were very much in the shadows. There was, and still is, a very dark, intense side to Hollywood, a hedonistic head-rush of money, power, sex, abuse and greed. Publicists created endless illusions to cloak this darkness, to make it seem funny and delightful and carefree. Through them, the studios sold the lifestyle like a pusher sells drugs, the aim being to make people feel they wanted, needed, couldn't live without the fame and success that, for example, Clark Gable or Myrna Loy achieved. The business fed on the need to attract people. Eager young women were continually optioned by the studios for six months on the promise of fame, only to suffer at the hands of rampant studio bosses and notorious sexaholics like Gable – the six-month option list at MGM might as well have been a roll-call in a brothel.

The publicists understood perfectly the processes and emotions that drove this, both the need for fame and the need for control, and they had done since the early days, but with the rise of the studio system they stood back; they didn't let the passions of fame and its trappings consume them. Pete Smith, making witty films that suited his temperament, was an exception. Jim Moran, maverick to the last, never fitted into the studio system because he had a tendency to turn the conversation to himself. Otherwise, none of them wanted to be in front of the camera. They could see the tensions and negative aspects

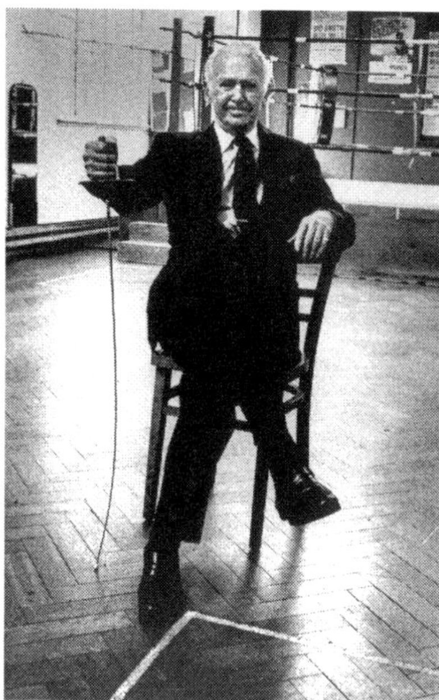

Above left Douglas Fairbanks giving fencing lessons in London for an early Borkowski publicity stunt – without his agreeing to this stunt, the author would never have discovered so much about the early days of publicity, as Fairbanks discussed all the greats he had worked with. (Harvey Mann) *Above right* Phineas Taylor Barnum, without whom modern PR would be a different beast entirely, with Commodore Nutt circa 1862. (Getty Images)

Harry Reichenbach (right) striking a deal with Alfred Hamburger, president of the Hamburger movie theatre circuit. Reichenbach pioneered the art of making himself look like an important businessman in print, understanding that this would by extension make his clients look more important. (Courtesy of the Chicago Historical Society)

A tattered print of this picture, taken in Chicago and showing Mary Miles Minter (wearing the light coloured dress) around the time of her first feature appearance in 1915, was part of Maynard Nottage's archive. Of the four unidentified men, it seems that the man behind her may well be Nottage. His association with Minter started early and lasted until her career fell apart in the wake of the William Desmond Taylor murder. (Courtesy of the Chicago Historical Society)

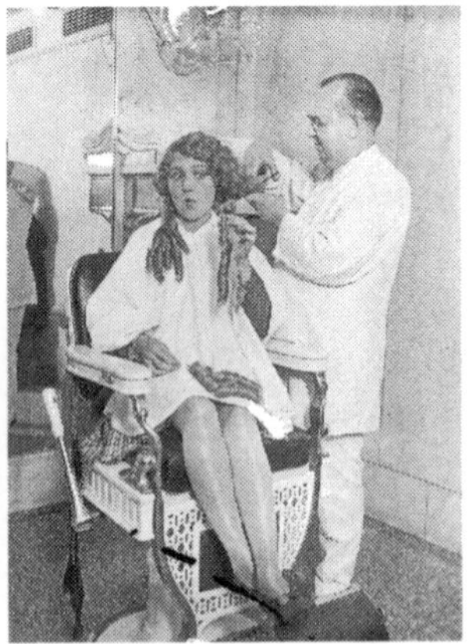

Above left A copy of this picture was also found in Nottage's archive and was his first foray into the type of publicity that has lead to reality TV shows, media sponsorship and the proliferation of competitions. The picture was used to promote a *Daily News* contest in which members of the public were invited to send in movie scripts and compete for cash prizes. The cook pictured, a Mrs Rose Cour, was one of his stable of aspiring actors. (Courtesy of the Chicago Historical Society)
Above right A portrait of Mary Pickford which appeared in *Photoplay* magazine. This is perhaps the first example of Harry Reichenbach using celebrity and a semi-cheesecake style to create a story from an unusual angle. (Courtesy of the Chicago Historical Society)

A copy of this picture was also found in Nottage's archive. It is unclear from his notes whether he organised this photo opportunity for cowboy-actor Tom Mix at Soldier Field in Chicago or if he felt that he was responsible for the genesis of such environmental shots which created touching public moments for stars and excellent news coverage. Certainly, he freely associates it with his idea to promote *The Great Train Robbery* in 1903 by taking a cowboy roadshow around the country. (Courtesy of the Chicago Historical Society)

Maynard Nottage's first vamp, Theda Bara, photographed in 1917 as part of the promotional campaign for *Cleopatra*, in which she starred. (Popperfoto/Getty Images)

Howard Dietz and Pete Smith, the engineers of early MGM publicity prior to the rise of the Fixers, photographed goofing around in the mid 1920s. (John Singer Collection/Corbis)

MGM's stars were expected from the off to pose for press-grabbing photographs. Here, MGM manages a double coup – gossip queen Louella Parsons is also in the photograph. The photo was taken to promote *Lights of Old Broadway* in 1925 and features, from left to right, stars Conrad Nagel and Marion Davies, director Monta Bell, Louella Parsons and Ramon Novarro, who just 'happened' to be there. (Bettmann/Corbis)

In death, it was easier to manage Rudolph Valentino's press image, as this photograph of his lavish funeral in 1926 shows. In life, Harry Reichenbach discovered that Valentino preferred to have his wife run his publicity, even though, with her careful management, the star's career became more that of a meteorite burning upon re-entry. (Bettmann/Corbis)

Right Johnny Weissmuller and Lupe Velez out their romance. (Getty Images)

A publicity shot of the Danish model turned actress Gwili Andre, taken in 1933 shortly before her movie career, which had begun mere months previously, began to falter. (Getty Images)

IDENTIFIED—Mrs. Gwili Cross, dead in fire, as she appeared years ago when she was a top model.

2-9-59

Victim of Fire Identified as Ex-Cover Girl

Mrs. Gwili Cross, 52, who died Thursday in a fire at her apartment at 2108-B Ocean Front, Venice, was identified yesterday as the former Gwili Andre, onetime top fashion model and candidate for Hollywood fame.

Gwili Andre came to Los Angeles in 1932 to try for a movie career after having been highly successful as a fashion photographers' model, first in her native Denmark and later in New York City. She appeared as a cover girl on many foreign and U.S. magazines and earned upward of $25,000 a year.

Signed by Selznick

She was signed by David O. Selznick to work in pictures for RKO-Radio but appeared in only three films.

In [illegible] a secret marriage to Stasch Mlotkowski, former Pacific Coast chess champion, was revealed when the model filed for a divorce in Reno.

She later was married to William Dallas Cross Jr. in Riverside. They were divorced 10 years ago and Cross has custody of a son, Lance, 14. Cross, a real estate developer, identified his former wife's body yesterday at the County Morgue.

Mrs. Cross was suffocated in the fire which apparently started in the bedroom of her apartment.

Below MGM did everything they could to protect one of their hottest stars, the original Platinum Blonde Jean Harlow, even to the point of covering up the facts behind her husband Paul Bern's death. Nothing could protect her from herself, however – she died in 1937, two years after this was taken, of kidney failure exacerbated by long term ill health and a hedonistic Hollywood lifestyle. (Getty Images) *Inset* The alleged suicide note of Paul Bern addressed to Jean Harlow, which was taken away from the scene by Louis Mayer and released as a suicide note by Howard Strickling. (Bettmann/Corbis)

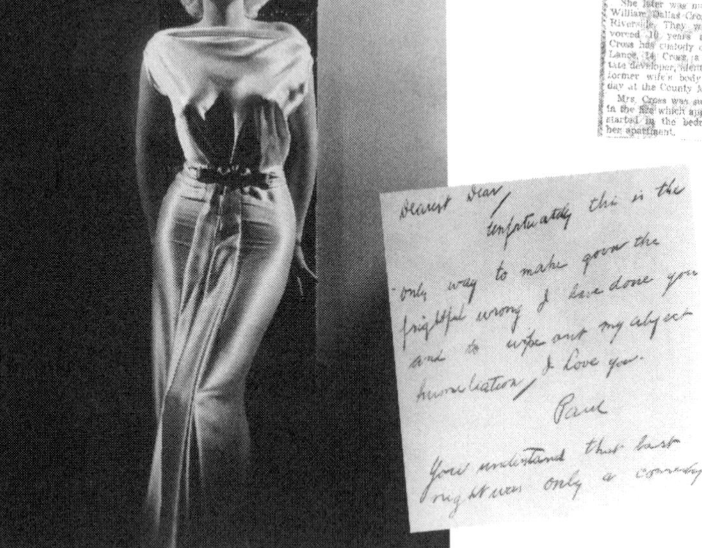

Dearest Dear,
Unfortunately this is the only way to make good the frightful wrong I have done you and to wipe out my abject humiliation, I Love you.
Paul
You understand that last night was only a comedy

A meeting of Hollywood moguls: Mary Pickford and Douglas Fairbanks, both of whom had Harry Reichenbach to thank for their early fame, joined the board of United Artists and here are recorded meeting with other moguls at the office of Samuel Goldwyn in 1936. Back row from left to right are Douglas Fairbanks Jr, Samuel Goldwyn, Jock Whitney, David Selznick, Jesse Lasky and Douglas Fairbanks Sr. Front row from left to right are Charlie Chaplin (also of United Artists), Walter Wanger and Roy Disney. Mary Pickford is seated at the front. (Bettmann/Corbis)

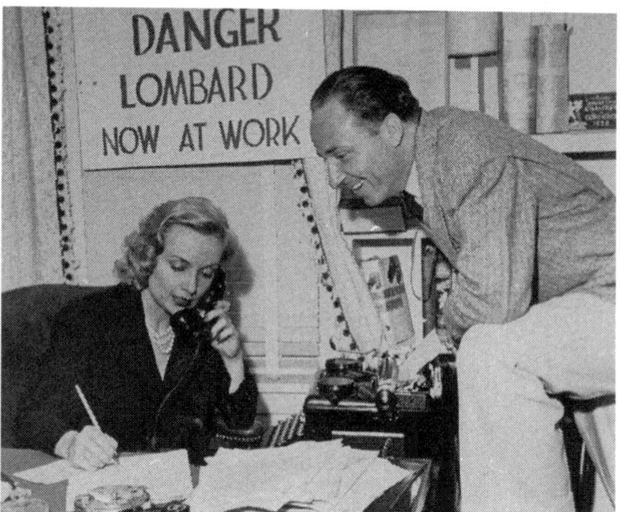

One of Russell Birdwell's early, subtle stunts for Selznick International was to announce that he was regularly working with screwball star Carole Lombard when she had time off from her busy movie career. It was a stunt that made Lombard appear human, Selznick International appear forward-thinking and Birdwell a happy man. Apparently Lombard would have made an excellent publicist in her own right. (*Time & Life* Pictures/Getty Images)

Jim Moran in 1938, discussing trained Alaskan fleas with Claudette Colbert at Paramount Studios. The fleas, he argued, would be ideal for movie work as the bright snow light they were used to had made them resistant to the harsh klieg lights. This was the maverick publicist's first major foray into Hollywood. (Bettmann/Corbis)

After the intense publicity of the search for Scarlett O'Hara, Vivien Leigh finally signs her contract for the role at Selznick International in Culver City. She is being watched by David O. Selznick and the already cast Leslie Howard (standing) and Olivia De Havilland. (Bettmann/Corbis)

that went with fame and they were very much control freaks, from Reichenbach to Mannix, whose title at MGM was financial comptroller, with the emphasis on control.

Publicity became a game of snakes and ladders, played by arch manipulators driven by money and an all-consuming attention to detail. There was no way that Nottage could have competed, since his cheerfully slapdash style was entirely at odds with the polish and detail that had become a requirement. The studio publicists operated with military precision; after all, they had studios full of people to organize. By 1928, MGM's publicity department alone employed 100 people. A Lone Star maverick like Nottage, who fed tasty figments of his imagination to the media, would have been seen through immediately in the glare of the shiny new MGM publicity model, which had less and less time for the fan magazines, whose softly, softly approach to the stars had dominated the early years of Reichenbach and Nottage's campaigns. By the 1930s even the fan magazines had to compete and Nottage's Hollywood fairytale was over; Louella Parsons would have called him Rumplestiltskin as soon as look at him and she would certainly have had no truck with the straw Nottage tried to spin into gold.

She and the rest of the savvy star-obsessed media were more concerned with the largesse of the studios. Huge budgets were put aside to keep journalists happy. There were trains full of booze as journalists crossing the country on press junkets became commonplace, and these were a particular success in the late Twenties, as the constant crossing of state lines made it easier to bypass Prohibition laws without having recourse to bribing the police. This was the nature of the deal: journalists were to be cosseted by the studios and fed exclusives, and they were to be paid well to prevent damaging stories leaking, as were any officials who got in the way.

The great skill of the publicist in this era was making journalists think they had the measure of power they craved when in fact they were simply desperate for access to be granted. The old days of presenting a story that journalists would flock to report were over. In the new millennium, this relationship has come full circle, and the media are much more aware of the nature of their relationship with the celebrities they report on and the publicists who manage them, while publicists have a measure of control unprecedented by any of their forerunners. This has created any number of hostilities and it's why many journalists are once again moving to the other side of the fence.

The publicists of the transitional days of publicity, when it became an industry, had learned their lessons well from the early days and, even in an era of control, with the moral authority of the Hays Code hanging over them like a many-pointed sword of Damocles, it's astonishing just how much they covered up and got away with. They used the Hays Code as a measure of what they could get away with in their promotional duties in much the same way as the creators of the screwball comedies that dominated the 1930s tested the Hays Code with a barrage of carefully written innuendo. They dealt with the golden age of cinema, with icons who have stood the test of time. As we will see, it is quite possible that stars such as Joan Crawford, Clark Gable, Carole Lombard, Tallulah Bankhead and Gary Cooper would never have had such a lasting impact had it not been for their publicists, those alchemists of celebrity who busily concocted fantasies and fallacies for the world to swallow.

• Fourteen •

THE RISE OF THE FIXERS

Howard Strickling and Eddie Mannix started their tenure as MGM's fixers as they meant to go on, massaging as best they could the tarnished reputation of Barbara La Marr, who had spiralled from a girl 'too beautiful to be left alone unattended in the big city' to the girl too addicted to drugs to function properly. She had come to Hollywood as a screenwriter, where she had been discovered by Louis B. Mayer and brought to Metro to star in movies like *The Three Musketeers* (1921) and *The Prisoner of Zenda* (1922), alongside the likes of Douglas Fairbanks and Ramon Novarro.

La Marr had started out wild, having worked in burlesque and as a call girl from an early age – essentially, she was a sexually precocious early runner in what became the Roaring Twenties, possessed of the same earthy beauty and vampish screen persona as Theda Bara. Unlike Bara, however, she was as vampish in real life as she was on screen, with an impressive appetite for men and recreational narcotics, as her famous, disingenuous quote for the press shows: she never slept for more than two hours a night because she 'didn't want to waste a single minute of [her] wonderful life sleeping'. This allegedly wonderful life included several brief marriages – her second husband, Lawrence Converse, was so smitten that he married her bigamously and reputedly beat his head so hard against the bars of his jail cell while moaning her name that he died of his injuries.

By 1925, La Marr had been inherited by MGM, but was not

working at anything like the rate she had in the early 1920s. Between 1921 and 1924 she made over thirty films, whereas between 1925 and 1926 – the last two years of her life – she made only three. She kept her supply of cocaine in a solid gold case shaped like a piano and apparently had a tunnel connecting her garage to her bedroom, so her lovers could gain access unseen. Such occupations kept her busy enough to be thoroughly unconcerned with movie making, and in such unchecked surroundings, cosseted by Mayer, who worshipped her, she let her habits spiral out of control to the point that, in late 1924, Mannix and Strickling had her committed to a sanitarium after she was found unconscious in her house. It was widely, and correctly, believed that she was killing herself with her lifestyle.

In November 1925, La Marr was arrested carrying forty cubes of morphine and was so frail from her drug addiction that prosecutors realized she wouldn't live to see trial. At MGM's suggestion, she was taken to her father's home to live out her final days, and Mannix and Strickling quickly set to work making use of her for publicity purposes. In the wake of the arrival of the Hays Office in 1922 and the fall-out of a series of scandals in the press, Mannix and Strickling couldn't allow one of their prize assets to appear flawed and unrepentant and, more pertinently, they couldn't allow anyone to point an accusatory finger at the studio for allowing her to get herself into such a state. According to E. J. Fleming in *The Fixers* they put her on a minor salary on the condition that she make regular appearances in the fan magazines, giving interviews about the dangers of drug abuse. On La Marr's death, in January 1926, her poor state of health was put down to 'vigorous dieting' and the coroner was persuaded to attribute her death to tuberculosis, a disease publicity agents often used to mask the effects of drug overdoses.

Drugs and sexuality were at the heart of most of the Mannix and Strickling fixes. In the 1920s they were still learning the game and hadn't quite mastered the requisite pressure they needed to apply to their stars to prevent the money drying up. They began picking people up on their behaviour, veering between Strickling's headmasterly, avuncular style and Mannix's tough-as-nails nasty-cop style, which seems to have been inherent in him from the start. Their double act was a careful and gentlemanly one, and they were well paid to maintain a code of silence and sense of blind loyalty to the studio that altered the face of publicity. Even though Mannix wasn't a publicist, he is included here simply because he was integral to the process of news suppression and star management that MGM developed. He and Strickling saw the tightrope being walked between the pitfalls of instant fame and the need for the studios to make money, so they worked unceasingly at bottling the genie of fame.

William Haines, the first openly homosexual movie star, caused them problems in 1926 because he simply would not cover up his sexuality. He had experimented with women, including brief flings with Barbara La Marr and Norma Shearer for example, but returned to his lover Ramon Novarro with a regularity that frustrated Mayer, a deep-rooted homophobe, and, by extension, Strickling and Howard Dietz, who had tried to match him with eligible women in Los Angeles and New York. When questioned by the press as to which women he was attracted to, Haines would routinely and mischievously name actresses in their fifties or those with equine features who were far removed from the glamorous women the MGM fixers tried to associate him with. By the time Elinor Glyn's famous *Photoplay* article about who in Hollywood had 'it' was published, giving rise to the Clara Bow It Girl phenomenon, rumours about Haines were spreading fast. Certainly Glyn decided that Haines didn't have 'it', even though his films had been hugely successful.

In 1926 Haines was rumoured to have been picked up for cottaging in a vice squad swoop, though Mannix and Strickling suppressed the story. It happened again in 1929, and the latter story never appeared in the press, although a number of autobiographies written after Haines's fall from stardom featured it. Despite refusing all attempts to hide his sexuality, Haines remained a huge star, and the money he made for MGM kept him his job, whatever Mayer's prejudices. But as magazines like *Photoplay* started to write stories suggesting that his childhood hobbies included making clothes for his dolls, it became apparent that something had to be done.

The publicity department's job often involved attempting to temper the dislikes and prejudices of Louis B. Mayer, but at times it was impossible to manage. Since Pete Smith was training Mayer in how to deal with the public, he became adept at dressing up his extreme reactions in polite language, but Mayer loathed John Gilbert, MGM's biggest star in the mid Twenties, infuriated by his many infidelities to his first wife, Leatrice Joy. In the end Mayer set out to destroy his career by hook or by crook, which surprised Strickling as it was entirely at odds with the studio's need to make money and the requirement that the Fixers sell MGM as a happy family. Strickling is quoted in *Dark Star: The Untold Story of the Meteoric Rise and Fall of the Legendary Silent Screen Star John Gilbert*, written by Gilbert's daughter Leatrice Gilbert Fountain, as follows: 'It was very strange, this thing between Mayer and Jack. Like he'd made up his mind to hate the guy from the first time he saw him. As far as I was concerned Mayer was way off base, but you couldn't tell him that. Anything good about Jack Gilbert, he didn't want to know. It was strange because Jack was always one of the good guys. Not that he wasn't a little eccentric, and temperamental sometimes, but all great actors are. But people now say that Jack was crazy. It's the damnedest thing, he was one of the most interesting guys out here and one of the best liked.'

The beginning of the end for Gilbert was the arrival of Greta Garbo in the USA at Mayer's invitation. She arrived late, because her director, Mauritz Stiller, delayed the journey. It gave Garbo time to lose weight, since Mayer had told her America didn't like fat girls, but left Mayer angry. She was kept in New York and left to stew – Howard Dietz, whose refusal to leave New York had cost him the top job at MGM's publicity department, was so unimpressed that he didn't even meet her off the boat. While she waited in New York, unable to work, an MGM photographer met her at a party and took a number of portraits, which he displayed in his studio window. This resulted in a frenzy of agents desperate to find out who she was, but Garbo wasn't to be found, having finally been summoned to LA. Given the journey time between New York and LA, however, by the time she arrived in September 1925 she was a celebrity.

Garbo and Gilbert were assigned to the film *Flesh and the Devil*, and an instant attraction was evident, both on and off screen. That chemistry, and the fact that this was the first film to show a kiss with parted lips, made it a huge success. Gilbert and Garbo became an inseparable item and were taken under Strickling's wing. The relationship was fraught at the best of times, but was made even more so by the relentless stream of press mileage Strickling extracted from it. It didn't help that Garbo agreed to marry Gilbert four times and cried off on each occasion. Mayer's loathing of Gilbert was exacerbated by an incident at one of these attempted weddings. In September 1926, Garbo again agreed to marry Gilbert in a double wedding with King Vidor and his fiancée, but once again she fled the scene on the morning of the wedding. According to Gilbert's daughter, in her autobiography, Mayer encountered a visibly unhappy Gilbert in the bathroom and offered the distraught actor the following, unhelpful words of comfort, which would have had Pete Smith hiding his head in his hands: 'What's the matter with you, Gilbert? Don't marry her. Just fuck her and forget about her!'

Gilbert reacted with a predictable air of wounded virility, attacking Mayer so violently that Mannix had to step in and break up the fight. Mayer's reaction was a promise to destroy Gilbert's career, however much money it might cost him, and that is exactly what he did. Mayer assigned him bomb after bomb until the chance came to finish him completely with the advent of sound. Admittedly, his campaign was aided by Gilbert himself, who insisted on pursuing the capricious Garbo to the point of obsession and began drinking himself into oblivion regularly. He even shot up the car of a young couple enjoying a romantic encounter until stopped by the police, who had to be paid off by Mannix.

Whatever sympathies Strickling may have had for Gilbert, or any other star in the MGM stable, he had to suppress them for the good of the studio, and since Mayer was one of the top executives, his word was law, even if it had to be rewritten by the press department on a regular basis.

In April 1927, Gilbert broke into Garbo's beachfront house and was arrested. This time, Mayer forbade Mannix and Strickling to intervene and the police arrested and jailed Gilbert for drunk and disorderly conduct. An MGM press release went out that failed to defend Gilbert and he was sentenced to ten days in prison.

This incident alone shows the power the Fixers had over their charges, by demonstrating what happened when they withheld their influence, but the fallout also allowed them more sway over Mayer and MGM, as Mayer's latest attempt to destroy Gilbert turned into a PR fiasco of epic proportions after news of his incarceration hit the headlines. If Cecil B. DeMille had organized it, it couldn't have been grander. According to E. J. Fleming, Gilbert's friends and drinking buddies turned up at the jail, as did numerous publicity-seeking actresses and thousands of Gilbert's fans, all keen to see their idol in reduced circumstances. Within a day and a half, Mannix and Strickling were buttering up their contacts to have Gilbert released and maintain the sense of family that was, on the surface at least, so essential to MGM's image.

In the end it was the advent of sound that killed off Gilbert's career, as it did for many stars. Marion Davies survived only because her appalling stutter disappeared when she memorized her lines, while Gloria Swanson hired a vocal coach – many Broadway actors made a fine living coaching silent movie stars in speech. Others, such as Karl Dane, who spoke no English, went from the very highest of the high life in the 1920s, with Rolls Royces and luxury houses in the 1920s, to selling hot dogs outside the Paramount lot by 1933. He committed suicide in 1934 after being spotted by a Paramount employee and his body would have gone unclaimed had Buster Keaton not appealed to Mannix's sense of the MGM family, forcing him to persuade the company to pay for his funeral.

With Gilbert, it was not that he had a terrible voice – he didn't – it was apparently the way he was recorded. His first talkie, *His Glorious Night*, was no great shakes as a film, but Mayer insisted that Gilbert be recorded *sans* bass, so his voice came out as a squeak, causing uproar and hilarity in the audience. Strickling was then allegedly instructed to leak stories to the press suggesting that Gilbert's voice was unsuitable. His image was in tatters and, while still living with Garbo, he watched as Strickling fed the press stories about their on/

off relationship, which did nothing to improve his temperament. Only a behind-the-scenes deal brokered by Nick Schenck, who had appointed himself president of the company after Marcus Loew's sudden death, kept him in work at MGM, taking a wage, but this was done behind Mayer's back and only infuriated him into giving Gilbert lesser and lesser films. Gilbert died of alcoholism in 1936.

Come 1928, Strickling was earning $250 per week and he and Mannix would sit in on every major MGM meeting. Strickling's pay cheque was nothing compared to the riches that had fallen into Reichenbach's lap a decade earlier, but that was a small price to pay for a steady income and a position that would last until retirement. It was a steadiness that came in stark contrast to the lives he was paid to manage, publicize and fix.

Joan Crawford was another problem Strickling and Mannix had to deal with. From 1928 onwards, hiding her proclivities needed a constant stream of creative thinking and bribery. She drunkenly ran a red light and knocked over a woman that year, then made matters worse by trying to bribe the traffic cop who arrived on the scene, before driving away. Arrested at her home, her first phone call was to Strickling, who allegedly turned up at the hospital bed of Crawford's victim with a roll of crisp notes amounting to $10,000 (around $300,000 in today's money). Unsurprisingly, the woman refused to press charges. This was a rare example of a Joan Crawford problem that didn't revolve around sex – she was rampantly bisexual and slept with a number of women, including Tallulah Bankhead, whilst married to Douglas Fairbanks Junior and, later, Franchot Tone. She also slept with most of her co-stars. Her marriage to Fairbanks was rumoured to be one of convenience, since Fairbanks was stony broke and Crawford's image needed a good reworking over as she'd been cited in a couple of divorce cases for alienation of affection.

The biggest Crawford problem for Mannix and Strickling was the need to cover up all traces of an alleged porn film made in New York while Crawford was still known as Billie Cassin, rumour of which was spreading through Hollywood like wildfire at the time. There is no concrete evidence that the film exists, but Fairbanks, according to *Confidential* magazine – a tabloid that was rapidly replacing the fan magazines in readers' affections – spent their honeymoon in Paris looking for a copy and Mannix later told friends that he'd arranged to purchase the negative. According to E. J. Fleming, Crawford's FBI file presents the hardest evidence that the film exists, since it states that 'a film of Crawford in compromising positions was circulated'. Add to that the fact that records of her arrest in Detroit for prostitution suddenly disappeared from J. Edgar Hoover's offices at around the time of the *Confidential* article and there's a certain inevitability about the film's existence. It is worth noting that Hoover and Mayer were friends.

With the advent of the 1930s, a huge increase in the quantity of films being made and the huge influx of stars this entailed, there were even more problems for Strickling and Mannix to deal with. Crawford was only the first in a long line of stars whose sexuality was papered over in the press thanks to them, and a great deal of work still remained to keep the image of MGM as family friendly as possible. In many ways, MGM was a family, but thanks to the publicity work of Strickling and Mannix it was, of necessity, a pretty incestuous one. The 1930s are recorded as a golden age for movies, and that is thanks to the publicists who kept the worst elements of their stars out of the public eye. Much that has come out about the stars of this era has been forgiven in hindsight, but there is little doubt that, without Strickling's assiduous publicity work and Mannix's strong-arm tactics on behalf of the studio, movies, celebrities and the publicity industry itself would be very different today.

• Fifteen •

A BIRD IN THE STUDIO

Russell Birdwell earned his reputation as one of the biggest stars of the new publicity era with a series of campaigns for Selznick International in the mid 1930s, before setting up an independent company that commanded the highest of fees. He was the antithesis of the stereotypical 'gladda-seeya' flack, described as 'a well-tailored, reserved man with a broker's moustache who carries his slim, well-conditioned physique with a military precision that makes him look ten years younger'. James Bacon, who inherited Birdwell's role as a star Hollywood reporter in the 1960s, saw him differently, describing him as 'the most flamboyant of the old-time movie press agents. He once was profiled in the *New Yorker* magazine. The *New Yorker* article noted that Birdwell had become more famous than his stunts. Next day, all his clients, who never had a *New Yorker* profile, fired him.' Birdwell was his own best publicist and was seldom shy about appearing in the media, unlike Harry Brand and Howard Strickling, but this cannot take away from his achievements in the industry.

Born in Texas in 1903, Birdwell was certainly old enough to remember Reichenbach and Nottage's wilder stunts and young enough not to be entirely in thrall to their reputation and influence. His ability to sell a story had its roots in his father's profession as an oil and real estate salesman and his sideline as a tent evangelist, 'an old fashioned hallelujah and hellfire shouter', as *Playboy* magazine put it in an interview with Birdwell in the early 1960s. Indeed, these dichotomous interests of his father's reflect the trajectory of Birdwell's career – from the evangelical zeal of the star-making process in the golden age of Hollywood to the more workmanlike, though rather more lucrative, process of selling corporations, countries and crowned heads of state in later life.

It certainly helped that Birdwell lived a Tom Sawyer life in the early days of the twentieth century, when he encountered his father and maternal grandfather engaged in a shoot-out over who was the best chilli cook – they only laid down their weapons to avoid catching Birdwell and his siblings with a stray shot – and he witnessed and wrote about several lynchings. Not only did he show writing ability from an early age, he was adept at working his way into a situation and telling clever stories to keep himself there. His father wanted him to be a criminal lawyer, so when he heard there was to be a murder trial in the county court, he absconded from school for three weeks so that he could study the oratory skills of the district attorney and the defence lawyer. He only got into the courtroom by claiming he was the sheriff's son.

At the age of ten, he took up a challenge laid down by the editor of *The American Boy* to come up with ideas of how a child could make money after school, each of which would be paid for by the magazine to the tune of $2. Several of his ideas, which he'd rigorously pre-tested, earned him the $2 fee, but he earned more from the pre-testing itself. He dried pecan nuts on the roof and stuffed birds, selling them to his neighbours, as well as skinning skunks and selling the pelts. That last scheme got him into trouble when a skin merchant told him he'd pay more for skunk pelts that had been neatly clubbed than shot full of holes. His father, according to *Playboy*, declared himself an expert on skunks thanks to his dealings with his father-in-law and told Birdwell that, while clubbing may be the best way to kill a skunk, he had to be very fast.

Birdwell's father died when he was twelve and the family moved to Dallas. Here he discovered a yearning to be a journalist, and approached the editors of various local papers, all of whom were wary of sending out 'a boy in short pants to cover stories'. Not to be dissuaded, Birdwell asked to be allowed to bring in stories instead.

'Bring me a good story and I'll print it,' said the editor. Birdwell insinuated himself into the local jails again by pretending to be the sheriff's son – this innate understanding that a good story can and should be used and reused served him well in later life too – there he wormed his way into the confidence of numerous men awaiting execution and came back with several exclusives, such as the man who went to his execution with a lucky rabbit's foot in his pocket, hoping for a reprieve, and the confession of another unlucky man, who confessed to his crimes and said he was sorry. This letter of confession was in Birdwell's own hand, a fact quickly spotted by the editor. Birdwell's admission of guilt in this instance goes a long way to explaining his success as a press agent: 'He asked me to write it for him,' he said. 'He said he felt too nervous to write it himself.' The stars he dealt with in the Hollywood system, with a few notable exceptions, were of far too nervous a disposition to create a life or confessional scenario for themselves. They lived their wholly created lives, in which every aspect of their persona had been polished by publicity men, all of which would have been entirely unsustainable without the gems of creative fiction often based only lightly on fact.

The initial product had to be good – there had to be a modicum of talent for the publicists to work with – but the stars were thoroughly reinvented before being unleashed on the public. They needed to be seen to make an effort with the media and the public and, given that Birdwell was a journalist at the height of Reichenbach and Nottage's powers, he would have been only too aware of the damage a story about sex and drugs would do. Birdwell understood the power of stories and the necessity of finding hooks and emotional connections for his clients, who would otherwise have become completely detached thanks to their overwhelming effulgence. There always had to be a spike of good or cheerful publicity about a client in a Birdwell campaign, be it a cover feature, a stunt, a new relationship, a new house or the fact that the star was being considered for a role or an Oscar. As Reichenbach found with the Great Reynard, there was always a risk of clients losing themselves in the hyperbole and believing what was written about them, but Birdwell was a journalist first and foremost, and he knew that the biggest stories were always the ones that gathered speed slowly, bit by bit. He would build up to a big campaign using word of mouth, creating little bursts of publicity that finally revealed themselves to be part of a grand campaign. His more emotional style was at odds with the clinical approach taken by the Fixers, who held things back. Birdwell threw everything at a story, even in his earliest days as a cub reporter.

Birdwell's perseverance in Dallas paid off. He got work as a part-time reporter for the *Dallas Dispatch* through school and afterwards went to the University of Texas. He only stayed a year, but managed to write and produce a play called *And Don't Forget It* while he was there. It is likely that it wouldn't have lived up to its title and been entirely forgotten had it not engendered Birdwell's first recorded publicity stunt. The play was awful – even the cast thought so – so Birdwell bought up all the eggs from markets near the university and egged his own actors from the gallery, 'a publicity gesture which made the play a box-office success'.

After quitting college, Birdwell got work as the police reporter on the *Houston Post*, where he became a local expert on the Ku Klux Klan, having made friends with victims of the KKK's tar and feather campaigns. He kept a tub of gasoline, the quickest and least painful system for removing tar and feathers, on hand at all times and would extract scoops from grateful, immersed victims.

In 1921, he headed for Hollywood and made a beeline for the offices of the *Los Angeles Times*, where he mistook the city editor for an office boy yet still managed to find employment. It's likely that his aggressive approach to coverage of the police night court in Houston got him the job. He spent the next thirteen years covering the sex scandals, unsolved murders, orgies and dope parties that were erupting like minor volcanoes throughout Hollywood. Birdwell said, 'I had been assigned to the first Hollywood beat, the beat which was to become the most famous in the world . . . Hallett Abend, city editor of the *Los Angeles Times*, had assigned me to this unique news route because I wore patent leather shoes in the day time and had a complete suit.' He was the star reporter for the paper, but never earned more than $45 per week and, with a young son and daughter to feed, he was forced to write for pulp magazines and ghost write movie-star confessionals to keep his head above water. In this way he found himself at the heart of the Hollywood game in both a predatory and defensive position and he soon got to know all the major players and build strong relationships with them.

Birdwell wasn't content with the money and would regularly quit the paper to direct movies for $1,250 per week, write a syndicated Hollywood column, or work for Hearst's *New York Daily Mirror*, where he scooped the story of Lindbergh's takeoff for Paris. Over a half million copies of the paper carrying his page-one story announcing the takeoff were sold. Hearst had an interest in transatlantic flight and had funded an unsuccessful attempt. Aware of the public's interest as much as his publisher's, Birdwell carefully staged a photograph showing crowds waving Lindbergh farewell and splashed it across the front page quicker than any of their competitors. He also wrote theatre reviews for the *New York Telegram*, amongst other jobs.

By his own account, he worked for twenty-three newspapers in twenty years, but the thrill of the scoop kept pulling him back to LA and Hollywood and, in 1935, he found himself back on the *Los Angeles Times* on $45 per week again. It wouldn't last long; David O. Selznick, who had just set up an independent studio in Culver City, wooed Birdwell away from the front page with the offer of a $250-per-week position as the studio's press agent, an astronomical fee that was steady and guaranteed, so long as he kept coming up with the goods. Selznick told him, 'You are eminently qualified for the job I have to offer to you – director of all advertising and publicity for Selznick International Pictures.' He was told to be 'daring but never sensational for the sake of sensationalism,' and given the former office of Joseph P. Kennedy (from his Gloria Swanson days).

It was a match made in heaven; Birdwell's imaginative streak was allowed to run riot concocting lavish campaigns for Selznick's equally lavish productions. Birdwell was immediately drafted in to promote *Little Lord Fauntleroy*, the first film from the Selznick stable. He tackled the job with élan and ambition, taking a simple idea that Reichenbach or Nottage would have been proud of and adding a machine-age twist. His idea was to paint 'David O. Selznick's Production of the immortal Little Lord Fauntleroy will have its world premiere on [such-and-such a date at such-and-such a theatre]' in massive letters on one of the highways in Culver City, near to Selznick's studio, then pay someone to photograph the graffiti from an aeroplane. Unfortunately, as with the murderer's confession in Birdwell's own hand, he had overreached himself. The words had been painted along several miles of pristine highway, and it wasn't safe to take the plane high enough to capture the image in a single shot. It could have ended his career if it hadn't been for the fact that Birdwell spotted people bent over in the street, peering at the letters and trying to work out what they said.

'The sign began at the edge of Los Angeles,' said Birdwell in a series of interviews published in the *Hollywood Reporter* in 1965, 'and ended at the entrance to the MGM studios. Newspapers, magazines, syndicates and photographers, both from the foreign and domestic media rushed to Culver City to investigate the calls flooding the press switchboards. Indignant MGM officials wryly commented the sign could at least have ended somewhere short of the front door to their studio. Baffled City Fathers rushed to the archives of ordinances but could not discover any legislation that outlawed the sign that was making news around the world. Unable to photograph the sign in its entirety the photographers came up with a solution. They posed all the Selznick International stars alongside various letters contained within the five-and-a-half mile advertisement.'

It's the sort of stunt that still gets reused today – publicists promoting the 2007 release of *The Simpsons Movie* in Britain painted a huge Homer Simpson on the side of the hill next to the Cerne Abbas giant, generating worldwide interest in the movie and proving that nothing is original; the greatest knack a flack can learn is how to raise the bar higher with every stunt. With a single stroke, *Little Lord Fauntleroy* left the realms of mere moviedom and became an event, making Birdwell, or Bird as he was known, an established name. Selznick was certainly happy and inscribed the following on the invitational programme, 'For Russell Reichenbach, Menace, Madman, and Master of his racket – with appreciation and admiration of DOS.'

Another of Birdwell's early major assignments for Selznick was the promotion of *Nothing Sacred*, a screwball comedy starring Carole Lombard, who was something of a muse to Birdwell during his Selznick years. The film, an entertaining satire on the dangers of the Reichenbach model of publicity, which features a girl who pretends to be dying of radium poisoning and comes to national attention thanks to a ruthless newspaper man, offered little for a publicist to get his teeth into in these more careful times. Nottage or Reichenbach would most likely have paid an actress to pretend she was dying and set her loose in New York to see what the press would make of it, while subtly inserting references to the forthcoming film throughout the stunt, which would become crystal clear once the movie opened. Birdwell didn't have the licence to be quite that daring, thanks to the careful ministrations of Louella Parsons et al., so instead he latched on to a brief moment in the film in which the supposedly terminal heroine is being fêted with a grand show that features numerous famous women from history, including Lady Godiva. His idea, which was equally daring given the mores of the day and the Hays Code – which the stunt was clearly designed to stretch the boundaries of – was to parade the actress playing Godiva on horseback through the streets of downtown San Francisco to mark the spurious 900th anniversary of Godiva's infamous gallop through Coventry. No one, not even Louella Parsons, could challenge the veracity of the date, as no one is sure when it happened, or indeed if it happened.

As soon as Birdwell announced his intention to have Dorothy Fargo, who played Godiva, and her horse Penelope parade through the streets, the police, appalled – publicly at least – at the idea of a naked woman displaying herself in such a fashion on their patch, forbade the ride on the grounds that horse-drawn vehicles were illegal. Birdwell responded that Lady Godiva was no vehicle and sent Dorothy Fargo out, apparently dressed only in a wig that reached to her hips, carrying a banner that read, 'Nothing is Sacred'. The ride caused a sensation, drawing huge crowds of prurient press and public. The police, however, failed to cooperate in the hoped-for manner and the ride went ahead uninterrupted.

Birdwell understood the machinations of Louella Parsons and her rival gossip columnist Hedda Hopper. He once advised Selznick that his share of the cost of building a new projection room for Parsons, who was still taking bungs every Christmas to ensure her goodwill, would be $35,000 – a princely sum in those days – and Selznick paid his dues. Birdwell understood because he had worked in her shadow a decade before and he knew what made her tick. As a consequence, they did not get on.

He also clearly understood the global implications of his work and made it clear that he was prepared to operate far beyond the realms of Parsons in seeking out good publicity, which must have aggravated her. As proof of his extravagant reach, Bird even managed to draw the British royal family into his stunts, indirectly anyway. While *The Prisoner of Zenda* was being filmed, George VI was crowned king. Birdwell corralled the numerous British members of the cast into hosting a noisy and, of course, very public coronation party, and he also drew the Duke and Duchess of Windsor into his web of publicity intrigue when *The Garden of Allah* (1936) was being remade by Selznick International.

'Marlene Dietrich and Charles Boyer – among the most sought-after stars of that time – agreed to do the picture before reading a word,' wrote Birdwell in the *Hollywood Reporter* in 1965. 'About this time I felt I should come up with a publicity idea or two before DOS beat me to it and set the theme for the entire campaign. I hurried to my office and put in a long distance call to Robert Hichens [the author of the novel on which the film was based] in Luxor, Egypt, on the border of the Garden of Allah. In vain I tried to interview him but he was more interested – some $225 worth of Selznick's long distance money – in the Southern Californian weather than he was in discussing the production.

'Robert Hichens told me of his arthritis, his rheumatic condition and why he always lived in the heart of the hottest countries he could find, and the best, so far, was the Garden of Allah area. Suddenly I got through to him. Recalling that [King Edward VIII] had on the night before abdicated . . . I asked Mr Hichens if he would cable [him] and, upon his marriage to Mrs Wallis Simpson, invite them to spend their honeymoon in the Garden of Allah.' When the Windsors accepted the invite, Birdwell gleefully announced through the London press that they would be visiting the Garden of Allah.

Bird came up with another stunt for the film, which involved putting on a Christmas Eve cocktail party in his home at the end of June – 'an idea to be followed later by someone writing a song called 'Christmas in July' – and covering the house with fir trees, decorations and all the usual Christmas trimmings. 'Christmas in June is as colourful as The Garden of Allah,' read the invites. It was left to the neighbours to call the press, and even the police, but the story still went around the world, with photographs and full credit to Selznick.

Despite turning gamekeeper when he joined Selznick International, Birdwell retained his journalistic ear for a quote throughout his career and often put it to use. One such exploitation of a chance snippet was for an off-the-cuff comment from Carole Lombard about taxes. He had something of an affinity with Lombard anyway; one of his early stunts to get her name in the papers involved installing her as head of publicity at Selznick International for a day. The mayor of Culver City appointed her honorary mayor for the same day and she promptly declared that the following Wednesday would be a holiday. Consequently, nobody turned up to work at the Selznick lot that day and Selznick, true to his prickly reputation, complained that the stunt had cost him $50,000, which was the daily cost of *Made for Each Other*, the Lombard vehicle the stunt was designed to promote. Birdwell, back from a day of lawn-mowing, retorted that they'd got at least that in free publicity. Selznick was forced to agree.

Birdwell's relationship with Lombard ran deeper than that, however: 'Carole used to be my assistant,' Birdwell said. 'When she wasn't acting, she'd check in at 9am and work all day. She was born to be a champion in all departments, including my kind of work, and she, too, suggested many an idea for which, over the years I have undeservedly been given the credit. Often she confessed to me she liked the strategy and the creativity of our work more than that of her own.'

The chance snippet from Lombard that Birdwell exploited was her reaction to a director paid $7,000 per week, who complained about the amount of income tax he had to pay. Lombard, unusually for a woman in full command of her wit, remained silent during this whinge, but as soon as the director left, she exploded into a tantrum that ended with her announcing to Birdwell that she was proud and happy to pay the full tax on her income, at that time an astonishing $150,000 per picture. Birdwell's ears pricked up: no one earning that much money had ever made such a statement before, and given that this was the tail end of the Great Depression, Bird phoned the wire services and asked Lombard to repeat her statement to all and sundry. Her patriotic and altruistic sentiments made the front pages of virtually every paper in America.

Bird also chanced to hear Franklin D. Roosevelt commenting on Janet Gaynor, another Selznick star, when he accompanied her to the White House, where she was to be thanked for her charity work. 'Why, she's as cute as a button,' gushed FDR – the first time an American President had ever been caught acting like a movie fan. The compliment shot around the world's press thanks to Birdwell pushing it to the assembled press.

One area that Birdwell found difficult was operating as a cover-up merchant, since it was hard to take the journalist out of the publicist. New, small studios like Selznick International didn't have as much to lose as MGM and were freer to flout the rules a little. Birdwell brought to the profession a love of stories and an ability to place them on the wire and in the papers as well as the networks he had built up in his journalistic career. He surrounded everyone he worked with, from Selznick to Carole Lombard, with spikes of publicity. There is no doubt that he had learned from Strickling, but there is no escaping that he had a little of the early publicists' joie de vivre too.

The biggest and most spectacular campaign that Birdwell undertook for Selznick was the four-year promotion for *Gone With the Wind*. It book-ended his time with the studio – from the moment he came on board it consumed him, and it was also the cause of his eventual departure. Before he left Selznick to set up on his own, he had helped create the template for the movie-as-spectacle publicity engine that spawned an entire sub-genre of collectable movie ephemera and created a career model for himself that allowed him to command astonishing fees, but he was not the only publicist stretching his creative muscles within the confines of the movie industry.

• Sixteen •

THE 20TH CENTURY FOX BRAND

Another major player in the newly reborn publicity industry was the appositely named Harry Brand. Born in New York in 1896, Brand, his parents and three brothers moved to Los Angeles when he was a young boy. He broke his left leg at the age of six, but it wasn't set correctly, so he walked with a bad limp and was in pain for the rest of his life. He was an avid sports fan, as is often the case when one can't compete oneself, and he became a sportswriter and later sports editor of the *Los Angeles Express*. Politics interested him, so he quit sports journalism to work as secretary to the Los Angeles mayor, Arthur Snyder, holding that post for three years. For Brand, politics was to be a lifelong fascination – in and out of the studio – and one he would later share with his wife.

He arrived on the Hollywood scene when the promise of a higher salary drew him to begin working in publicity for Warner Brothers. This was a short-term post and he was quickly lured away from Warner by Joseph M. Schenck and his independent production company where he produced two films, though he found the confines of the publicity department more to his liking. Brand landed on his feet, looking after early clients such as Fatty Arbuckle and Buster Keaton in the late teens and early twenties of the twentieth century. This was the end of the Reichenbach and Nottage era, the point where things began to change, and Brand was in at the beginning of the publicity industry's rebirth. He may even have been partly responsible for one of the defining moments of the end of the Reichenbach era. Certainly, James Bacon has insisted that it was Brand who urged Arbuckle to give the ill-fated party in San Francisco that resulted in three trials for murder and the snuffing out of Arbuckle's star. Whether or not he encouraged Arbuckle's redoubtable party spirit, Brand certainly cut his teeth in the industry by dealing with the ensuing crisis.

In 1922, Brand banded together with a group of other press agents to form the WAMPAS (Western Association of Motion Picture Advertisers), a social and professional organization. The men met every week for dinner and threw an annual ball, the WAMPAS Frolic, to select the WAMPAS Baby Stars of the Year, who included Clara Bow in 1924 and Fay Wray in 1926. Among the association's members were Pete Smith and Howard Strickling.

It's not the sort of social occasion one can imagine Nottage and Reichenbach indulging in and, as such, marks the gentrification of the publicity industry. There may well have been a fair measure of professional jealousy amongst those involved in WAMPAS – it would be surprising if there weren't – but it would not, in these more refined circumstances, have had any of the Tom and Jerry edge to it that Nottage's professional stalking of Reichenbach took on.

As early as 1923, Brand was sending press releases to Louella Parsons, then a columnist for the *Los Angeles Morning Telegraph*. One was about his purchase of an automobile, still a novelty in LA. In the release he said he had gained 'the distinction of being the only man in the picture industry with sole and indisputable title to the vehicle in which he rides'. There was a noticeable trend amongst the early publicity agents to make themselves part of the story, which only began to vanish with Howard Strickling, but in this instance, Brand's self-publicity is as indicative of his desire to make the industry more respectable as it is to make a name for himself.

Nineteen thirty-three was a good year for Harry Brand: he married Sybil Morris, the daughter of a well-known Los Angeles family and, with the amalgamation of Twentieth Century and Fox studios, he finally found himself in a position of power, just as the WAMPAS frolics were coming to an end, shut down by the studios because they were too independent. Brand's early boss, Darryl F. Zanuck, joined forces with Joe Schenck to form Twentieth Century, adding Fox in 1935. Brand was given the job of Head of Publicity at one of the most iconic studios to emerge from Golden Era Hollywood. As Harrison Carroll announced, 'One of Hollywood's best loved figures, Harry Brand, has been appointed to head the publicity department for the combined Fox-Twentieth Century productions. Harry has been with Joseph M. Schenck for twelve years and he can write his own ticket with newspaper and fan magazine correspondents.'

Brand may have been at the top of his game, but in time his wife became even more famous than her husband, at least in Los Angeles. As Sybil Brand, she was one of the most prominent philanthropists and civic workers in Southern California. Her pet project was the new Motion Picture Relief Fund for retired showbiz professionals, but she devoted even more volunteer time to raising money to help female prisoners. The Sybil Brand Institute for Women was named after her in 1963 in recognition of her efforts, which raised the $8 million dollars necessary to build it.

Working with Darryl Zanuck had its ups and downs. Notoriously tyrannical, Zanuck didn't share decision-making at all and wasn't widely liked. Brand, in the publicity department, was forced to play nice cop to Zanuck's nasty cop, sometimes mediating battles between the combative studio head and his stars. Nonetheless, the gregarious Brand enjoyed the larger studio setting and became fast friends with many of his clients. The early years had him mapping star-building campaigns for Shirley Temple, Alice Faye, Ronald Colman, Rita Hayworth and dozens more, and he also supervised the careers of Marilyn Monroe, Betty Grable, Barbara Stanwyck, Victor Mature and Don Ameche.

The art of the publicist in such star-building campaigns was to take the star in question through an initiation process of lunches and launches, glamorous photo shoots and interviews with fan magazines, priming and preparing them with salient quotes and witty asides that suggested a knowledge deeper than they already had, be it of sex or politics. The main thing was the *suggestion* of sex, in as unadulterated a form as the Hays Code would allow. Brand trained his charges to exude an air of innuendo and coquettishness, dressed up sublimely by stylists. Indicative of the publicist's influence is the insurance by Fox studios of Betty Grable's legs for $1 million, a stunt that guaranteed headlines and encourage interest in the iconic photographs of her that kept American soldiers' minds off the horrors of World War Two.

The prime objective was to make the leading ladies of the day seem a little more like the girl next door – the average man would then feel like he had a chance with her, whereas an intensely glamorized superstar with no grounding in reality would only attract the same. This was particularly important during the Great Depression, when the divide between the wealth of the movie star and the poverty of the general public was so extreme, but the attitude prevailed for years afterwards. Nowadays anyone can become a star if they work at it, but then the attitude was that you could become a star if you were discovered, and consequently many biographies of starlets exist, stating that they were found working as waitresses in cocktail bars or leaning over cars in tight dresses in car parks. Jean Harlow was discovered on the Fox lot in exactly that way, although she didn't take the offer of work seriously at first and had to be pushed to go back by her mother. There was an innocence and sensuality about the stories created then which have been lost today – everything is much more blatant now that there's no threat of moral censure. A perfect summation of this stylish approach is the moment that Marilyn Monroe, when asked what she wore in bed, replied 'Chanel No. 5'; a knowing but innocent quip, rumoured to be supplied by Harry Brand's team, and ideally suited to the mouth of Monroe as she was perceived by the public.

Monroe first came to public attention as a pin-up girl and she had also done a nude photo shoot. This ran counter to the prevailing morality of the time, but Fox got around it neatly by knowingly acknowledging her overt, soon-to-be-iconic sexuality. They put it about that Monroe would 'look good even in a potato sack', and to push the point further, they bought a clean potato sack and dressed her in it, draping the material suggestively, though not revealing too much. The resulting photo went worldwide.

It wasn't all about sex, however; an example of positive star-building *sans* a lubricious coating of sex can be found in the story of Shirley Temple's Hawaiian holiday. Her parents called Brand, saying they were going on holiday to Hawaii and did he know anyone who could show them around. He naturally promised that he would. Temple's parents had kept her away from the more extreme trappings of fame but Brand knew a good way of getting headlines when he saw one, so instead of simply arranging for a friendly guide, which is no doubt what the family wanted, he persuaded the Hawaiian authorities to give all of Honolulu's schoolchildren the day off in order to greet Shirley Temple at the airport, thereby guaranteeing headlines about Temple's star power.

Time magazine ran a feature on Brand and Birdwell in late 1940, which clearly portrays their influence: 'Harry and Russell have since grown into the foremost trumpeters of Hollywood's bizarre and boisterous activities,' it reads. 'They are publicity men. It is their job to keep the world aware of movies, beglamored about movie stars, and thus herd in admissions to the box office.

'. . . Harry, Russell & Co. have done the job so well that Hollywood is now considered the third largest news source in the U. S. More than 400 reporters, from matter-of-fact A. P. to Paul-Prying fan magazines, now scavenge Hollywood for tidbits to feed millions of readers. To keep them happy, Hollywood studios maintain vast publicity departments filled with smooth-writing ex-reporters, quick-smiling "contact men," expert photographers, menial flunkeys.

'Lots of people can run a publicity department, but it takes a peculiar man to think up ideas . . . Harry and Russell are primarily idea men – each with a different approach.'

Alice Faye wrote of her alliance with Brand: 'I'd read stories about Alice Faye in the papers – stories the studio publicity department had planted – and I would wonder who that girl was. It didn't sound like anybody I knew.' But the stories were 'harmless and silly', and gave the shy star something to discuss with the ever-present reporters and gossip columnists. She liked Brand, describing him as a 'low-key man who rarely let the substantial pressures of his work bother him'.

James Bacon tells of a conversation with Brand about those years, discussing one of his best-known publicity tricks. The opera star

Lawrence Tibbett had just been signed by Fox: 'Harry sent one of his publicity guys over to Grauman's Chinese with an enormous counter,' wrote Bacon. 'His job – count how many women went to the ladies room during the Tibbett picture.' A mere thirty-four women made use of the facilities during Tibbett's debut, so Brand announced that Tibbett would never make it as a major star. 'Valentino used to make 200 girls pee an hour,' he pronounced. He was right, too. After only a few films, Tibbett returned to the opera. Brand's dismissive attitude shows a hard edge under the genial surface. He was well aware of the need to keep finding clay that he and the studio could mould, and if a potential star couldn't cut the mustard, they were summarily dismissed. Tibbett appeared in the first film made by the newly amalgamated 20th Century Fox in 1935, called *Metropolitan*, and it was a flop. He was a fine singer, but he wasn't pleasing the all-important female audience who read the fan magazines and the tabloids that followed them.

A significant part of a press agent's job was to be a suppress agent, as stars found it easier and easier to get into trouble. Keeping the studio's young and often marginally civilized charges out of trouble was a job in itself, especially as, by the 1930s, bisexuality was common practice in Hollywood, and a career could be destroyed if it became public. Brand worked unceasingly to toughen up the images of Tyrone Power, Robert Taylor and Cesar Romero. At the start of Tyrone Power's career, Brand exaggerated his height a little, writing that he was a 6 ft-tall, handsome youth. In reality, he was closer to 5 ft 8in, according to one biographer. There is also a story, written by Power's confidential secretary Bill Gallagher in *Screen Stars* in 1947, some years after the event described, about a trip he, Power, Cesar Romero and Jim Denton took to South America in Power's plane. It's full of the usual hunting, shooting and fishing exploits that follow many of the male movie stars of the thirties who needed a tougher image to accompany their screen roles – Gary Cooper used to go off on well-publicized jaunts, often in the company of Ernest Hemingway. What's interesting is the way the article throws in Jim Denton: 'Jim Denton, a member of Harry Brand's powerful publicity machine at 20th Century Fox, surprised at nothing, said he'd go. Jim's known

Ty since the handsome youngster first walked into the studio from New York. And Jim will tell you that he also recalls when Ty was sent to Director Sidney Lanfield for a role in *Sing Baby Sing*. Lanfield literally threw Ty off the set. "I want an actor, not a baby," Lanfield said. "This Power kid has no future." Three months later, Ty made his debut in a small role in *Girls' Dormitory* and immediately aroused public interest.'

One can see the long fingers of 'Harry Brand's powerful publicity machine at 20th Century Fox' at work in this – his man is off with the stars making sure there are plenty of stories circulating about their macho exploits and the image of Power as a 'baby' is dismissed for good.

Alice Faye wrote, 'The studios protected the stars they had under contract. They carefully monitored publicity.' It didn't hurt that Brand's wife was tight with the police and that his brother had become a judge. As A. C. Lyles has said, 'It wasn't that the studios did anything illegal. They didn't pay bribes. They just used friendship when they needed some help.'

Prevention was essential in the 1930s and 1940s. Birdwell pushed David O. Selznick into contributing to the Louella Parsons Christmas slush fund in an effort to keep the Selznick stars out of the grubbier end of the gossip market. Brand's most public coup of this kind was to arrange the provision of office space to the powerful and vituperative Walter Winchell, who, along with Parsons, had created the gossip column in the early 1920s. Winchell was notorious for his savagery and inventiveness, so Brand's quid-pro-quo approach offered insurance against unforeseen attacks on Fox's stable of stars.

As with Birdwell, the secret to Brand's success was his public personality. He was known for his camaraderie and his ability to get along with everyone, whilst remaining, a *Variety* writer noted, 'Always interested in the problems of others, even those who were not particularly close friends, Brand would go to bat for them, whether they were office boys, secretaries or the most high. His unselfishness was genuine; on several occasions when he had been offered a raise he asked that it be given to members of his staff.'

His sense of humour was warm and good-spirited and he greeted everyone he met with an egalitarian geniality. He could disarm a reporter asking a difficult question with a jocular aside along the lines of 'Before I tell ya – did ya ever hear the one about . . . ?' He had the soul of a comedian but without the dark undercurrent. 'Harry Brand, whose province is 20th Century-Fox,' wrote *Time* magazine in 1940, 'takes things easier [than Birdwell], but his results are as good. First he pampers the press into pliability with his genial hand-pumping personality; then he showers them with copy and stills of the forthcoming production. Thanks to Brand – and to the Fox commissary pressroom, where the food is the best of any studio in town – Fox is the most popular studio in Hollywood with reporters. Harry's office is always open to them; his invariable procedure is to crack a few jokes, pat them on the back, roar: "You're my pal. Let me know if there's anything I can do for you." When the time arrives for the correspondents to do something for Harry, they find it easy to reciprocate.'

Like most publicists, he was often glued to the telephone. Every day he called most of his close friends. Apparently, visitors to his office were occasionally forced to phone him from the next room just to get his attention. Brand's friendships transcended disciplines. His close friends included Presidents Truman and Nixon, several California governors, Supreme Court Chief Justice Earl Warren and scores of famous writers. He knew all the major political players in Southern California on a first-name basis.

Brand's most iconic publicity stunt took place in the 1950s, when he was credited with engineering Marilyn Monroe's famous New York street scene photo shoot, where she stood over an air grille while publicizing *The Seven Year Itch*. It might have been the wind from the subway train passing underneath that blew Monroe's skirt over her head, or it could have been gusts of enthusiasm from Fox's publicity department; certainly the crowd – informed of the stunt in advance by Brand's department – were so noisy that the scene had to be shot without sound, which was dubbed in later. It remains one of the best known and loved images in cinema publicity history, but at the time many people thought that flashing Monroe's legs in this manner was a vulgar stunt that may have been the final blow to the fraught marriage between Monroe and then-husband Joe DiMaggio, who objected vigorously to her pubic hair being flashed to the assembled crowd and soon afterwards filed for divorce. That's as maybe, but it also marked the beginning of the end for the Hays Code, given how openly it flaunted Monroe's sexuality. Brand played both sides of the fence on the matter, putting out a release attributing the Monroe/DiMaggio split to 'the incompatibility resulting from the conflicting demands of their careers'. Of course this was merely a public nicety as DiMaggio had retired, so his career had no demands.

Brand's own retirement in 1962 may have been hastened by a severe economic downturn for 20th Century Fox, which coincided with the making of the extravagantly expensive Elizabeth Taylor vehicle, *Cleopatra*. His once huge department was cut almost in half. The studio, recognizing his early power and influence, gave him an office on the lot, where he reported for duty four days a week. On Thursday he would return to his Palm Springs home, some two hours outside Los Angeles, only to drive back to LA on Monday morning. Unable to pull himself out of the heady world he had inhabited for so many years, he maintained this schedule until illness caught up with him.

Harry Brand died in 1989, atypically for the industry, a relatively happy man, although his retirement years spent in his special office on the Fox lot would suggest a sense of loss. Ironically, he requested that there be no service to comfort his legion of friends and admirers, asking instead that donations be made to the Motion Picture Country House and Hospital. It was a gesture typical of a generous man. Before his death, the *Beverly Hills Courier* had written, 'Despite the important role he has played in building and maintaining the industry, Harry Brand is a kind and gentle person. There is no one nicer in the industry, no one more widely beloved.' Nottage would have been amazed.

Seventeen

THE QUESTING WIT OF JAMES MORAN

As the darker arts of MGM's publicity department were being put into practice, one of the publicity world's most maverick, creative and surrealist forces was beginning to make a name for himself. Born in 1907 to an attorney for the US Agriculture Department, Jim Moran grew up in Woodstock, Virginia. His three brothers took respectable jobs, but the restraint of small-town life left Moran with itchy feet. 'I could have come home after murdering the President of the United States,' he once said, 'and it could have been on the radio and all over the newspapers, and nobody would have ever mentioned it to me.' Consequently, he developed the habit of making himself the centre of attention to prevent the ennui of Woodstock life from overwhelming him, a habit that translated perfectly onto a wider stage when he reached adulthood.

Jim Moran was a large man with a penchant for wearing a big beard – unconventional in clean-cut mid-century America – and a fez. He was one of the biggest personalities in an industry rife with larger-than-life characters, so much so that his personality wound its way inextricably into many of his stunts. Moran's range of interests was enormous – he learned the classical guitar as a teenager and continued to study it throughout his life under Sophocles Pappas – but a normal schooling wasn't one of them. He spent his summers while at school working in the wheat and oil fields, loading ships and even down the zinc mines, and he declined a college career on the basis that he probably knew most of the answers already. In 1925, Moran got a job in advertising at the *Washington Daily News* and shortly after became a cub reporter. He was no Birdwell, however, and lasted less than two years in journalism. 'I'm strictly an oral writer,' he said in an interview in the *Saturday Evening Post* in 1949. 'Trying to put a story down on paper with a typewriter just paralyzes me.' He married his childhood sweetheart in 1929, but the marriage ended in divorce in 1931. Like his hometown and his straight jobs, marriage seems to have been too much of a cage for Moran.

Moran's first break came in 1935, while he was selling radios in Washington DC. He read about a Dr William Mann, the director of the Washington Zoo, who was leaving for Sumatra and Borneo on a hunt for new animals. According to the press he was especially keen to find a male orangutan, so Moran found a recording studio and made a recording of himself howling and yodelling in orangutanish fashion. Then he contacted the papers and sold them a story about how he'd captured the voice of a female orangutan in full mating cry, which he proposed to donate to the Mann expedition so they could play it in the jungle and lure the restless and horny male orangutans from their bachelor pads in the trees. The papers revelled in the story and it led to a flurry of publicity for the recording studio. Through it, Moran met a man who owned a canary that could, so the owner claimed, sing 'Yankee Doodle'. Moran promptly arranged some radio concerts for the canary, named Pete, with the US Navy Band and booked him into a New York nightclub. Pete, apparently, shed his feathers two days before the shows, which according to Moran, led the bird into a severe depression that prevented it from singing 'Yankee Doodle' – or anything else, for that matter – even when its feathers grew back. This didn't stop articles on the luckless Pete appearing, though, which gave Moran ample mention and led a New York dairy to contact him, desperate to get a mention in the papers.

Moran's first reaction was to test the nursery rhyme 'Hey Diddle Diddle' and get a cow to jump over the moon – he was as fond of a good animal stunt as Reichenbach or Nottage had been – but he swiftly rejected the idea as too impracticable and too expensive, so he turned his mind to other ditties. Eventually he happened upon a famous jingle by Gelett Burgess that included the line, 'I never saw a purple cow.'

Moran immediately hoofed it up to the dairy in New York and took possession of the most sedate-looking cow he could find and dyed it purple, except for the hooves, which were painted silver. Moran then gathered the cow and a herd of journalists and took them all to the hotel where Burgess was staying. He made a phone call from the hotel lobby and told Burgess, 'It's important, sir, that I see you in the lobby!' Burgess's reaction upon seeing the cow he swore he'd never see was a very satisfying, 'My God!' On seeing Burgess's expression, the journalists went into overdrive, interviewing him and relentlessly photographing him from every angle with the cow – in the bleak days of the Great Depression, this sort of fodder was ideal for cheering up the nation. Moran gleefully told all and sundry where he'd acquired the cow and the dairy was awash with publicity and the milk of human interest.

It's an early example of the direction Moran's brand of publicity stunt took, and he was wont, throughout his career, to pick up on some hoary old truism or cliché and push it to illogical and often wonderful extremes. Whilst falling squarely into Barnum-esque territory, Moran's approach has a more philosophical, questing nature that would soon see him at odds with the system that MGM and Russell Birdwell had put in place. Put simply, Moran was dangerously witty and prone to letting the story outweigh the person he was publicizing.

Moran's wit had always had an unblemished directness – while selling magazine subscriptions door to door, he used to pitch to the householders with the modest and blunt, 'I am not working my way through college. I am doing this because I like money.' He also sold radiator covers door to door to wealthy ladies in Washington. He had printed a set of engraved cards with his name and a swish Park Lane address, which usually got him through the door, then by the time they discovered he was selling radiator covers, they'd fallen for his hypnotic voice and mannerisms. His was a gentler, more philosophical brand of ballyhoo, but with examples such as Reichenbach fresh in his mind, it's little wonder he ambled into the world of publicity.

He followed the purple cow with another bovine stunt, this time in aid of bandleader Fred Waring's career. Given that Moran had contacts with the New York dairy, he could presumably easily get his hands on a docile bull, but what is amazing is that he managed to persuade Plummer's, an upmarket shop selling fine chinaware on Fifth Avenue, to let him take the bull, and Fred Waring, on a tour of the premises to test what a bull in a china shop was really likely to do. One can only assume that the bull, led around by Moran and Waring, had been drugged, despite assurances from the Jersey Breeders Association that it was a serene bull, as it broke nothing. Great play was made in the next day's papers about the fact that Waring had smashed $40 worth of china after bumping into a shelf, possibly jostled into it by the twelve reporters, twenty photographers and seven newsreel cameramen present.

Moran, who prior to this moment had been a specialist in aviation, newspaper advertising, lecturing on sightseeing buses, giving guitar lessons and distributing magazines door to door, had arrived.

His next venture was one of his most remarkable. His ear, ever attuned to the word on the street, caught on a couple of salesmen discussing their work and complaining that one job had turned out to be as 'hard as selling an icebox to an Eskimo'. Moran's brain lit up with the possibilities this simple phrase had triggered and made his way to NBC, where he talked them into advancing him $300 for three broadcasts from Alaska. He followed this with a visit to an airline, which he persuaded to give him free passage to Alaska in exchange for mentioning them in any press he garnered for the trip. Then he talked to the National Association of Ice Advertisers, who were keen to promote the sales of cake ice and who gave him a refrigerator and promised him $2,500 if he managed to do what he proposed and sell an icebox to a Eskimo.

On arriving in Alaska, he eventually found himself a willing Eskimo, a man who spoke no English but who nonetheless purchased the refrigerator for $100, two fox furs and a piece of ivory. It's not surprising that Moran managed it – his powers of persuasion were firing on all cylinders – but what is astonishing is the complexity of the stunt and the amount of people he managed to help, please, amuse and inform in one fell swoop. Not least of these was himself; knowing that he was going to be the focus of a great deal of attention on his return, thanks to his broadcasts and a raft of press coverage, Moran took the process several stages further. First he took two fleas from the back of the husky dog that belonged to the proud owner of the refrigerator and put them in a matchbox to take home, then he had 300 pounds of ice hacked out of an ancient glacier, which he took to Hollywood.

His first stop, on arrival in California, was at Paramount Studios. He had read before leaving Alaska that Paramount were casting for fleas, so he touted his fleas as snow-blind and therefore able to resist the glare of klieg lights, which were so bright they'd been known to blind actors. 'They are trained Eskimo fleas,' he said. 'Most Eskimos, who have nothing to do during the long northern winter, spend months training fleas. The best trained fleas are Eskimo fleas, as anybody in the flea business knows.'

Paramount liked the spiel and paid him $750 to talk up the fleas, which would be used to crawl up the back of Claudette Colbert in her next extravaganza, which was coming soon from the Paramount lot. Unsurprisingly Claudette Colbert reacted with indignation to the idea of a pair of fleas crawling up her back, snow-blind or otherwise, and a story was sown in the press, worth $750 of any studio's money.

Moran then sold 10 pounds of his precious glacier ice – 'the oldest, coldest, slickest ice in existence' – to the press agent for Dorothy Lamour for $500. This too became a newsworthy story, providing the sort of coverage a star could get for $500 with a good press agent. The rest of the ice he sold to ice dealers, who proudly displayed it in their windows with a note, no doubt suggested by Moran, proclaiming it was ice from the same glacier that Dorothy Lamour had bought and, despite it being formed naturally 100,000 years ago in Alaska, their ice was purer by far. Laboratory tests, it was claimed, proved it.

Moran had got himself noticed in the giddy circles of Hollywood, but his brand of publicity, smacking as it did of Reichenbach, Nottage and the irresponsible early days of publicity, was not hugely in favour in the movie industry, which was, in the late 1930s, determinedly slick and very cautious. Moran therefore determined to sell himself further and came up with another offering: to find out how long, exactly, it took to find a needle in a haystack, on the understanding that crooner Rudy Vallee would pay him $500 per week to do so. The fee was not just for Moran's time spent searching, it also paid for regular appearances on Vallee's radio show, discussing the nature of the search. 'My gimmick,' he said, 'was that the English language is full of double talk. "As hard as finding a needle in a haystack." How hard is it exactly? I'd find out once and for all.'

Vallee took the bait, so Moran erected a twelve-foot high haystack in the centre of Washington DC and persuaded the head of the Board of Trade to place a marked needle carefully inside it. Moran, dressed for the occasion in an aviation suit tight enough to keep out particles of straw, a miner's hat, a dust respirator and a pair of swimming goggles, dived in and started burrowing around for the needle. 'The thing wasn't as simple as it seemed,' he told the *Saturday Evening Post* in 1949. 'I mean, if you're looking for a large needle in a small haystack, it's easier than looking for a small needle in a large haystack. See? Well, we did research on haystacks all over the farm belt and came up with the average-size haystack. Then we asked the needle companies to give us needle lengths, and the needle we used was an average needle.'

Despite this careful, if playful, planning, it took Moran eighty-two hours to find the needle. The matter might have been more swiftly resolved had passers-by not kept throwing other needles into the haystack. He did, however, make sure money was made from these meddlesome jokers: straws from the stack were sold at ten cents a straw and came packaged in an envelope bearing the message, 'Moran Needle-Hunting Expedition: This envelope contains one genuine bona fide straw from the Moran Haystack, situated on the corner of Connecticut Avenue and N Street, Northwest, in Washington, D.C., the Nation's Capital. This straw has been carefully inspected and closely scrutinized by Mr Moran personally. He does aver, attest, affirm and pronounce this straw to be free and devoid of any needle whatsoever. (signed) Jim Moran.'

Another fine example of his bizarre wit, edged with a keen eye for subtly promoting the product he was engaged to sell, was the commission, in the late 1930s, to promote optical glass. Moran travelled to Boston and placed an advert in the *Boston Herald*, which read, 'Wanted 12 Unemployed Men. Pay $4 a day. Two must be nearsighted, two farsighted, two with normal vision. Two bright-eyed, two bleary-eyed, one with pink eye, one with cross-eyes.'

Several hundred unemployed men with eyes in varying stages of dysfunction appeared at his hotel, accompanied by some farsighted reporters who smelled a story. Moran wasn't about to give them one, though, not yet. He simply said he was making 'a historical experiment'. He picked his twelve men and dressed six as redcoats and six in colonial costumes. Arming them with muskets and himself with a sword, he drilled them as if they were soldiers on Boston Common.

After the drilling was over, Moran revealed his plan to the press. He was going to recreate the Battle of Bunker Hill, a famous skirmish in the American war of Independence. 'I'm going to prove that Colonel Prescott's command, "Don't fire until you see the whites of their eyes", was probably the stupidest command in the history of warfare,' said Moran. 'I mean a nearsighted soldier would see a bleary-eyed redcoat much later than a farsighted man would spot a bright-eyed guy, and so all of Prescott's men would have been firing at different times if they had taken his order literally.'

Moran claimed his theory was entirely vindicated in the ensuing battle, which was chaotic in the extreme. The bright-eyed redcoats were spotted by farsighted colonials at 75 feet, the colonial soldiers with normal vision fired at 50 feet and 'the nearsighted minute men would have been slaughtered as they never saw the bleary-eyed redcoats until it was too late'. The press revelled in the story and some barely even noticed the plug Moran subtly inserted at the end, though they all printed it: 'That would never have happened if they had modern eyeglasses in those days.'

Moran was far from the ideal of the MGM-style studio publicist. His approach to work was, even in the early days, to make as much money as possible and retire to spend it before going out to work again. It is not surprising, therefore, that his second marriage, undertaken in 1934, dissolved in 1942 because his wife, who had doubtless been charmed initially by his winning intellect, ready humour and persuasive manner, succumbed to fury at his uneven lifestyle and wayward approach to finances. The divorce left him shell-shocked and distraught, so he moved to Hollywood. One of the first things he did there was to rent a house in Culver City and sublet some of the rooms to aspiring starlets. There is a certain amount of coyness about what went on there, and in an interview with *Playboy* it is suggested that Moran carefully, playfully avoided the subject of those starlets, while according to the *Saturday Evening Post*, he maintained order like a Sorority house mother. Whatever the truth, this was not an auspicious start to a career in Hollywood, being the sort of living arrangement that Nottage, in particular, would have adored. The past meant little in Hollywood, but the people who mattered had long memories.

Eighteen

FIRST STEPS ON THE ROAD TO CHANGE

Henry Rogers, whose company, Rogers & Cowan, was to change the course of public relations entirely at the beginning of the television age in the 1950s, arrived in the public relations business in 1935 aged twenty-one. He was too young, therefore, to remember much, if any, of the stunts and campaigns of the early days of PR and walked into the golden age of Hollywood with a fresh perspective on the machinations of the industry, by then more influenced by the careful management of Strickling, Birdwell and Harry Brand than by the inventions and snowball nature of Reichenbach and Nottage's stunts. There was more to Rogers than that, however – he was younger than his peers and much more adept and eager to insinuate himself into every level of the Hollywood life. It must have helped that he looked a little like Gary Cooper, only without the intensity, and he remained throughout his working life a dapper and amenable man, willing to work his way into the affections of everyone, from his clients to journalists such as Louella Parson and Hedda Hopper, large corporations and the public at large.

Rogers, like many other flacks before him, worked his way up through the industry; the difference was that he was actively gathering the scruffy tail ends of it in his wake and folding them up into a neat pile, smoothing out the creases wherever he went. He trod a middle path, neither melting into the foreground like his fellow independents Jim Moran, Maynard Nottage, Russell Birdwell and Harry Reichenbach, nor scuttling to the edge of the studio web and staying out of sight like Howard Strickling. By the time Rogers & Cowan was at the height of its powers in the early 1960s, he was a recognizable figure on the Hollywood scene, but one known mostly to insiders and journalists. The public didn't know much about him, but they knew his work intimately. Only on one occasion did he poke his head far above the parapet, and that was to take a stand against the McCarthy witch hunts.

Like Strickling, Rogers came from a retailing background. His father ran a dry goods store in New Jersey and Rogers, due to inherit the business, was sent to study at the Wharton School of Finance and Commerce at the University of Pennsylvania in Philadelphia. The depression forced him home as his father's business began to struggle, and in 1934 he enrolled in Commerce night classes in New York, working in the store five days a week. Even this didn't save his father's business, though, and he went bankrupt in October 1934, like many small businesses at the tail end of the depression. In desperation, the family moved to Los Angeles, to join Rogers' older sister, who had moved there with her husband in 1932.

Desperation forced inventiveness on Rogers, and he quit his degree in commerce and fished around for jobs, eventually getting himself hired as an office boy in a PR company run by Grace Nolan, where his sister worked as a secretary. He was twenty at the time, and $5 a week was a good wage to be earning. Rogers' early responsibilities included collecting the clippings from the papers featuring Nolan's clients and driving her press releases to the movie columnists at the *Times*, the *Herald*, the *Express*, the *Post* and the *Daily News*, as well as the *Hollywood Citizen-News*.

'During the day, in addition to my messenger chores, I was teaching myself to write publicity copy,' wrote Rogers in his autobiography. 'It came easily to me. When I was in high school, I was a member of the press club and reported Irvington High School athletic events to the *Irvington Herald*. At college I prepped for the *Daily Pennsylvanian*, the university's newspaper. It was not difficult for me to adapt my reportorial style to Hollywood gossip columns and movie trade papers. It was a far cry from the dry goods business, and it was readily apparent that Hollywood held something more for me than had Irvington.'

Rogers did well enough in his first three months to warrant a raise from $5 to $12 per week and for the business to catch hold of him like a virus. He very quickly decided that a business that allowed him to meet stars like Cesar Romero after only a few months of work was for him. He was swayed by many events, as it would appear Grace Nolan intended – according to Rogers' account, at least, she eased him into situations where he would meet more and more stars and people who were important to the movie industry.

One such situation was the time that Nolan asked Rogers to accompany her aunt, Grace Kingsley, who had just retired as movie critic and columnist for the *Los Angeles Times*, to the Guy Lombardo opening at the Coconut Grove in the Ambassador Hotel. Lombardo was a bandleader who specialized in romantic popular music and was one of the biggest acts of the time. Kingsley was still working freelance for the *Times*, and so received invitations to the big events, and the Lombardo opening was the biggest that year, a social gathering of heavenly magnitude. Rogers jumped at the chance to accompany Grace and wrote of it in his autobiography with the glow of a man possessed by the possible proximity of celebrity.

'I was almost twenty-one years old and I was being shown to a ringside table, one of the best in the house. Grace Kingsley still commanded respect among the head waiters who remembered her in her days of fame and glory. If I was a "nobody" then, they were truly the most beautiful young people in the world of that day. Tom Brown, Anita Louise, Patricia Ellis and Johnny Downs are the names I remember. I was introduced as "Henry Rogers, my niece Grace Nolan's new business associate."'

Rogers acquired a taste for the high life from such encounters, although he was astute enough to realize that he was just one of a long line of young men who had been asked to accompany Grace Kingsley to such functions. Proof of that came swiftly too – Nolan, for all her priming, did not take kindly to mistakes. One Saturday afternoon, on returning home, Rogers discovered that he had not left the keys to her car in the vehicle after doing his Saturday morning press-release run to the papers, but instead still had them in his pocket. Nolan had, as a consequence, missed an appointment with a client in Santa Monica. 'She was furious and I was fired,' he wrote, summing up neatly the peremptory nature of the industry's attitude to failure.

Rogers was not disheartened however; he had had a taste of the publicity industry and he definitely wanted more. 'My resolve to become a Hollywood press agent was stronger than ever,' he wrote. 'Easier said than done. It was the Depression, I had just turned twenty-one and my only job experience was that of office boy. There were six well-established Hollywood publicity firms at the time and when I approached each of them for a job I was turned down. I was not very impressive in an interview, owing to a speech defect I had had since the age of five. I stuttered badly. Both in high school and college my grades did not reflect my IQ.'

Despite sympathy for his stutter, which was, he claimed, born of being a left-handed child forced to write with his right hand, no jobs were forthcoming, so Rogers decided to go into business himself. He approached his father for a loan of $500 to start up in business, a sum that he had carefully worked out would keep him going for half a year if he continued to live at home – long enough, he hoped, to establish a business. His father, understandably, was concerned – not only did he not believe that anyone would pay his son, or anyone for that matter, to get their names in the newspapers, he was worried that his son's stutter, which intensified on the telephone, would hinder his ability to conduct business. Rogers told his father that all he could do was try. 'I'm n-n-not going to s-s-sit home and worry about it all m-m-my life,' he said. 'I'll just have to f-f-fight it through.' His father wrote the cheque and he was in business.

Rogers rented a room with another press agent, Hal Weiner, on Hollywood Boulevard and placed an advert in *Daily Variety* and the *Hollywood Reporter*. Then he waited. And waited. And waited. After a few days of nail-biting and phone watching, a call came through from Joe Fine, the advertising director of *Daily Variety*, who Rogers had dealt with when he took out the ad; he announced he had a client for Rogers. It was the dance team of Kirby and De Gage, who had just appeared in a Warner Brothers musical. They were not a big draw, but they were determined to become one, so they wanted a press agent to push them. They agreed to pay Rogers $15 a week to get their names placed in the trades and gossip columns, so that casting directors would look on them in a warmer light.

Being young and naïve, Rogers got down to work and placed them wherever he could, cashing in on the fact that he was remembered from the press-release delivery rounds he used to do for Grace Nolan. Three weeks went by and still he hadn't seen any money. His father, ever the businessman, brought him up on this, worried that it would be the undoing of his investment. Rogers remembers him saying, 'I don't know anything about your business, but I do know human nature. Your clients will never get round to paying you unless you keep after them.' He then proposed to go with Rogers to the Agua Caliente Hotel, where Kirby and De Gage were dancing after the film had wrapped. It was fortuitous that the family went en masse as this one occasion washed away all objections to Rogers' choice of career. Not only did the dancers smile at Rogers when they saw him from the stage, they offered up the money they owed him without a word passing his lips.

The dancers did not last long as clients, but they gave Rogers the start he needed, and by 1937, the year he married, he was earning $75 a week representing actors, actresses, nightclubs and restaurants. Slowly his fees started creeping up from $10–15 per client per week to $25–35 and eventually $50 a week. He was operating in the Nottage end of the market – one client promised to pay him $15 a week when he was working and $10 when he wasn't. 'The trouble was that he never worked, so he never paid me,' wrote Rogers. His stutter was holding him back, and if it hadn't been for a chance encounter with Rita Hayworth, it's possible that Rogers would have vanished from the annals of history as completely as Nottage did. The difference was that Rogers only really suffered from a stutter; he would have made a good life for himself outside the movie industry, unlike Nottage, who suffered and stewed until the end of his life.

Rogers met Rita Hayworth by chance at a ten-cent poker game he was regularly involved in when business was slow. It was the perfect place to meet people – Hollywood, for most stars, is one big gamble, a risk waiting to pay off. Rogers, by then twenty-five years old, was affability personified and, in social circumstances, far less impeded by his stutter. So when Hayworth, who was nineteen, joined the game with her husband Eddie Judson, he must have charmed them considerably. Hayworth and Judson were an ambitious couple, she for herself and he, intensely, on her behalf. However, her option with Columbia was nearly up and Hayworth hadn't been made as much use of as either of them would have liked. They needed a press agent if they were to raise Hayworth's profile, and they thought back to the personable, ambitious press agent they'd met playing poker.

They needed someone at the start of his game – there was no way they could afford a more established independent publicist's fees – and they needed to strike a deal. Rogers was the perfect man: he agreed to take 5 per cent of her income – which was $300 a week at the time – in exchange for his services for three years. She had just finished filming Howard Hawks' *Only Angels Have Wings* with Cary Grant, but her role was small and there seemed little that would come from it in terms of publicity or furtherance of Hayworth's career. Judson, Hayworth and Rogers put their heads together and decided they had to do something big, something thrilling and audacious. The discussion stalled there until, in a quiet moment, Judson began to discuss Hayworth's wardrobe and expand on the idea that a dramatic range of clothing was a large part of an actress's allure.

At this point, Rogers came up with an idea – a risky one that harked back to the early days of Nottage and Reichenbach – and he went to Gene Herrick, the West Coast editor of *Look* magazine, with his idea.

'"Gene," I said, "I have a very exciting idea for you. Rita Hayworth—"

'"Who?" he asked.

'"Rita Hayworth", I continued, "is an actress at Columbia who receives a salary of £15,000 a year. She spends every cent of it on clothes. She is comparatively unknown here in Hollywood, and yet her wardrobe ranks beyond that of any of the big stars. Her wardrobe is fabulous because she feels that being well dressed is one of the most important things a girl can do in her struggle to become a big star. Interestingly enough, her wardrobe is already gaining recognition because she has just won an award." '

At this point, Rogers presented the intrigued editor with a telegram, addressed to Hayworth, signed by the entirely fictional Jackson Carberry, president of the Fashion Couturiers Association of America. The telegram, written by Rogers, said that Carole Lombard had just been voted the best dressed on-screen actress and that Rita Hayworth had been voted the best dressed off-screen actress. He pushed it as an excellent feature for an upcoming issue of *Look*: a beautiful girl so eager to be a star that she already had the wardrobe of an established screen goddess.

The whole spiel was, of course, a tissue of lies – Hayworth was not paying Rogers in underwear every week, otherwise he wouldn't have been doing the job and standing in the offices of *Look*. She did not even have much of a fabulous wardrobe beyond what a woman earning $300 a week would have in order to keep up with fashion. It was a big risk for Rogers to take, but the worst that could have happened is that he'd have been thrown out of the office, leaving him free to try and persuade someone else. It's remarkable, though, given how much had changed in the PR world since the mid 1920s, that Herrick didn't check up on Rogers' story. One can only assume that the aura of respectability that people such as Strickling had brought to the profession served Rogers in his one old-fashioned, deliciously mendacious stunt. In short, Herrick loved the idea; it may even be that he loved it so much he didn't care to discover its veracity. Instead, he assigned his top photographer to shoot her for a feature.

Rogers was astonished and delighted, but quickly realized that he now had to rustle up a wardrobe every bit as fabulous as he had made it out to be. He and Judson spent many hours begging and borrowing clothes from speciality shops, department stores and designers. The fabulous wardrobe of fiction became a reality in a matter of days, and when the photographer arrived, he was enamoured enough of his subject to shoot hundreds of photographs, including the one that went on the cover of *Look*, a famous shot of Hayworth with her hair in Spanish style and her shoulders bared as she struck a flamenco pose. The shoot was an enormous success and when it was printed it became a wildfire phenomenon throughout Hollywood. Suddenly Rita Hayworth's name and picture was all over town, Columbia picked up her option and she was on her way to becoming a major star.

To achieve this, Rogers courted *Daily Variety* and the *Hollywood Reporter* with ideas he'd cooked up with Hayworth and Judson, as well as wooing Louella Parsons and the other columnists with more and more stories about Hayworth. They snapped them up like fish after live bait until finally Rogers found himself reeling in a shark: *Life* magazine wanted to talk to Hayworth and took the provocative, bed-bound photograph that made her a pin-up girl for the American army. Sadly, after the three years were up, Hayworth decided not to renew the contract, leaving Rogers, by his own admission, rather bitter. It was an early taste of the disappointment many publicists feel when their clients desert them. It can seem like a familial relationship, but at the end of the day it's a business arrangement between publicist and client, and if the client finds something better, financially or otherwise, they're going to move on with little more than a 'thanks for the memories'.

In his autobiography Rogers refuses to accept that he made Hayworth a star – he states simply that he just started the ball rolling – and is gracious enough to admit that he felt hurt at the time. Nottage, on the other hand, would have been spitting blood and teeth at such a memory, but Rogers acknowledges that without Hayworth he would not have achieved anything like as much as he did. 'I became associated with a Hollywood phenomenon,' he wrote. 'Suddenly people knew who I was. Suddenly the name Henry Rogers became recognized. Maybe it would have happened without her. I'll never know. I do know that Rita Hayworth made me a star.'

One thing that was clear to Rogers was the urgent need for new clients. Luckily for him, his association with Hayworth put him in the way of Claudette Colbert, then the highest-paid actress in Hollywood, and his career soon took an urgent, more frenetic turn.

Nineteen

OVER THE RAINBOW

If the names of Howard Strickling and Eddie Mannix are familiar today, it may be because they have been prominently featured in recent exposés about the Golden Age of Hollywood and in the movie *Hollywoodland*, which examines their final fix. They were involved in covering up some of the major scandals of the day and created a hermetically sealed existence for the MGM family. In *The Fixers* E. J. Fleming quotes Strickling: 'We did everything for them. There were no agents, personal press agents, business managers or answering services in those days. All these services were furnished by the MGM publicity department; no other studio did it quite the way we did. We told stars what they could say and what they couldn't, and they did what we said because they knew we knew best. When things went wrong, we had a way of covering up for them, too.'

This hermetically sealed existence certainly helped keep the peccadilloes of the stars under wraps, but it also helped create them. The opening years of the 1930s were the beginning of a twenty-year golden age, and most of the stars we think of as legends were under contract to MGM. Two of the biggest films of the decade had an MGM stamp – *Gone With the Wind* and *The Wizard of Oz*. For the former, Birdwell took care of the Selznick end, as the next chapter details, and Strickling handled MGM's part, and with these two dynamos on board, the film's success was guaranteed.

The Wizard of Oz was meant to be as big as *Gone With the Wind*

– and it has certainly become that over time – but it started out as something of a failure, given that its budget was enormous for the time. Strickling sent out a thirty-two-page press release about the film with exaggerated numbers, intending to wow moviegoers with its grandiosity. He claimed there were 9,200 actors (actually there were less than 600) and breathlessly added, 'as many as 350 huge lights were used on a single set, generating enough electricity to light 550 five-room houses with two 60-watt globes in each room'. This, at the end of the Great Depression, should have awed the public into appreciating the magic that only Hollywood could create, and to some extent it did, but it was only on re-release at the end of the 1940s, when its whimsical, loving look at an old America, utterly changed by World War Two, hit a new, nostalgic chord, that it took off and became the Christmas favourite it is today. What it certainly *did* achieve was the launch of its star, Judy Garland, who was one of the most fixed of the MGM stable of demi-gods.

The Wizard of Oz serves as an excellent analogy for the world MGM created in the early Thirties, thanks to the assiduous work of Howard Strickling, who finally became head of publicity in 1931. People such as Joan Crawford, Clark Gable and Judy Garland were literally carried over the rainbow into a technicolour world beyond the ken of the stark, sepia realities of financial recession and the steady stalk towards war. The MGM publicity machine created a beautiful prison, filled with fabulous characters, and Howard Strickling's role in the MGM Oz was Scarecrow to the collective Dorothy of the stars he worked with. The scene from the film where the Scarecrow offers Dorothy directions by pointing every which way at once pretty well sums up how Strickling managed the press, while Mayer, Mannix and Thalberg flitted between the roles of Cowardly Lion and Wicked Witch of the West with alarming regularity. MGM was not as clear-cut and simple a place as Oz, which is saying something, given the dream-like set of rules Oz operated on, but it was just as much of a fantasy world.

Fabricated biographies were the norm. Mickey Rooney, who eventually penned his own story, wrote of 'a studio biography that had little or nothing to do with reality. Instead of collecting blondes, brunettes and redheads, they had me collecting stamps, coins and matchboxes. My favorite author, according to this studio fantasy, was Eugene O'Neill. That would have implied that I read books. But I didn't read books. I barely read the plays I starred in.'

Katharine Hepburn used to say that Strickling was one of the reasons she signed with MGM. 'Strick took his work very seriously, shuffling promotional schedules as well as the personal lives of as many as fifteen top MGM stars at once – from train schedules to restaurant reservations.'

Joan Crawford told author Roy Newquist, 'I really knew I was a star when Mayer ordered the publicity department to get me into every fan magazine and gossip column and to make sure I dated the right men and to accompany my every personal appearance and make sure I said the right things.' She later added, 'I adored Howard Strickling . . . and if Mayer did put us under lock and key, Howard was an adorable guard.'

There was much to guard in the 1930s; as the takings increased and the stars grew more stellar, the number of trade magazines and gossip sheets increased exponentially – the *Hollywood Reporter*, for example, was founded in 1930 – and the quality of intrigue became more and more astonishing.

Nineteen thirty was the year Marlene Dietrich arrived in Hollywood, and the MGM machine worked hard to keep her away from Greta Garbo, knowing of both stars' lesbian tendencies. According to E. J. Fleming Mannix had strangled a relationship between Garbo and Fifi D'Orsay by telling Garbo that D'Orsay had blabbed to the press – a fiercely private Garbo never spoke to D'Orsay again, so never learned the truth. Mannix also prevented Mayer from suing Lon Chaney's estate for a $50,000 advance awarded to him while he was terminally ill. Mannix's opinion was that it would cost a great deal more than $50k in lost revenue and bad publicity if Mayer were to sue the grieving family of one of their recently departed stars.

In 1931, William Haines got himself into serious trouble. He had, for several years, been one of MGM's biggest stars, but was unpopular with Mayer because he was homosexual. Not only that, he was open about it, and a big enough star to flout the morality clauses in his contract with little fear of a backlash. In 1930, however, his films started to take less money and rumours began to fly. The next year, by his own admission, he was arrested for having sex with a sailor. That no record of the incident exists other than his admission is testament to the work of Mannix and Strickling, but, as E. J. Fleming reveals in *The Fixers*, his wages were slashed by more than half and his name was plunged below the title in publicity. Haines maintained a close friendship with Irving Thalberg, which meant that he was spared being fired for flouting Mannix and Strickling's careful attempts to suppress his proclivities, but in 1930 his salary was finally slashed by an aggrieved Mayer and in 1933 he was dropped – one of the first sacrifices of the new publicity era and a salient warning to others who were unwilling to toe the studio line. It didn't help that the director F. W. Murnau had died in March that year in a car accident – his young houseboy had been driving while Murnau fellated him. Only eleven people turned up to his funeral.

No less troublesome for the studio was the relationship between Johnny Weissmuller of *Tarzan* fame and Lupe Velez, the Mexican Spitfire. Velez had already had an intense affair with Gary Cooper, which ended with her shooting at him as he caught a train to get away from her. Her relationship with Weissmuller was no less fiery, and it proved almost impossible for Strickling to keep their violent excesses out of the papers. His only major success with the couple was in getting Bobbe Arnst, Weismuller's wife, to quietly go away $10,000 better off, as MGM considered that both Weismuller and Velez's stars would be tarnished if she were branded a home-wrecker. Velez and Weissmuller married in 1933 and stayed together for five tempestuous years. During this time Strickling paid out countless times to make photographs of Velez's naked crotch go away – she was prone to drinking, then dancing wildly at parties with her skirt raised. Nowadays, of course, this is a popular sport, with numerous celebrities being photographed getting out of cars without knickers; I'm sure there are publicists out there who wish they had Strickling's measure of control over their clients.

Even in death Velez was difficult to manage; in 1944 she committed suicide by swallowing a large number of pills, but instead of sending her into a peaceful final sleep, it upset her stomach, and while running to the lavatory to expel the contents of her stomach, she tripped and fell headfirst into the bowl, breaking her neck. Strickling's press release, unable to deny the fact that she had taken her own life, instead cast her as a woman finally at peace, who had taken to her bed as the pills worked through her and who was found in a relaxed state, looking beautiful and possessed of a beatific smile.

One of Strickling's favourite clients was undoubtedly Clark Gable, who told Ava Gardner, 'If it hadn't been for Howard, I'd probably still be driving a truck.' In later years, Strickling admitted to being closer to some than others, especially Robert Taylor, Jean Harlow and Norma Shearer. Shearer, of course, was married to Irving Thalberg, with whom Louis Mayer had an intense rivalry, despite having at first hired, encouraged and mentored him. Mayer was a populist through and through while Thalberg leaned more towards movies as art; he was also friendly with most of the actors Mayer loathed. Ever the masterful politician, Strickling moved easily between the two men, perhaps helping their alliance last as long as it did, truncated only by Thalberg's sudden death in the mid 1930s.

Gable had arrived in Hollywood in the mid 1920s with an acting tutor, Josephine Dillon, who became his wife. He promptly left her for another woman more likely to further his career, and proceeded to move through women, invariably older and richer than him, at a rate of knots, eager to find someone who could make him a star. He apparently even had a brief fling with William Haines during the mid 1920s. He was discovered by MGM in 1930, despite resistance to his jug ears. Mayer's assistant Ida Koverman, an ever-present force at the studio until the death of the studio system who spotted many stars, saw beyond the ears. Along with director Lionel Barrymore, Koverman pushed him on Thalberg, who gave in after initial resistance, hired him and handed him over to Strickling. The first thing Strickling did was make Gable ditch the expensive 'actorly' clothes Gable's various mistresses had dressed him in and turn him into a manly man, dressed in hunting clothes. The following years were spent covering up affairs, pregnancies, drinking binges and accidents.

Protecting the stars from their peccadilloes was absolutely necessary, and not only for economic reasons. Every contract contained a morals clause: 'the artist agrees to conduct himself with due regard to public convention . . . he will not do or commit any act or thing that will tend to degrade him in society or bring him into public hatred, contempt, scorn or ridicule, or that will tend to shock, insult or offend the community or ridicule public morals . . .' The general public were prone to throwing their hands up in despair at depraved behaviour – today, a veneer of post-modern cynicism lies behind the outrage aroused by stars sleeping around, with true repulsion reserved, on the whole, only for murder, paedophilia and, in Britain at least, being too successful. Back in the 1930s, shock was a more liberally applied phenomenon and MGM needed to keep its nose clean. The stars were told, 'If you get into trouble, don't call the police. Don't call the hospital. Don't call your lawyer. Call Howard.' The lesson of what happened after John Gilbert's arrest had been learned.

However much the stars were expected and desired to conform to the MGM norm, they didn't. Money and fame erased morals as easily as chalk from a board and Strickling was called on more and more as the decade wore on. It was imperative that they remained clean – movies were the major method of escape for a nation bewildered by the Wall Street crash. Democracy and capitalism were in question on a worldwide scale, the American way of life seemed to be slipping out of control, and the stars were required to be a paradigm in a crazy world; it could not be known how little control they had.

Despite the more human and ultimately forgivable shenanigans the fixers covered up, the dark side of the bright and blinding world that was MGM stardom was never too deeply hidden. So it was that in 1932 Strickling and Mannix found themselves engaged in the biggest cover-up of their early Hollywood careers.

The cover-up involved Jean Harlow, who had wandered on to the Fox lot wearing a short skirt a few years earlier, while giving a friend a lift to an audition. In 1932, although she had been one of the most bankable stars in Hollywood for a few years, her career was in the doldrums. All this despite her joyfully naïve approach to sexuality, which as a young girl starting out in the movies bordered on that of

Adam and Eve prior to their expulsion from Paradise. In one Laurel and Hardy film, the first take of a scene, where her skirt was caught in the door of a car by Stan Laurel, reduced the set to chaos when it was revealed that she was wearing no underwear. Asked by her co-star in *The Public Enemy*, James Cagney, how she got her nipples so erect, she replied without shame that she iced them. She was no great shakes as an actress, but the camera had a tendency to put anyone who stood next to Harlow in the shade – Clara Bow noticed this early, during filming for 1929's *The Saturday Night Kid*.

Harlow bounced around studios and boyfriends for a while, appearing in Frank Capra's *Gallagher* at Columbia, at which point a Columbia publicity man coined a new nickname for her: the Platinum Blonde. This epithet rocketed her to enormous fame and even became the name of the film she was appearing in as Capra and the publicity team felt it would be best to capitalize on her fame. From that point on, Harlow could have had the pick of any man she wanted, but she astonished everyone in Hollywood by dating and then marrying the director Paul Bern, who was forty-five, short, bald and determined to get Harlow to MGM. He eventually persuaded Thalberg to sign her up in March 1932 after a lull in her career.

The relationship was not out of character for Bern who had doted on numerous women who were, to put it politely, easy of virtue. One such was Barbara La Marr, whom he doted on to the point of buying her a wedding ring for husband number five and attempting suicide when she refused to marry him after that marriage fell apart. He pursued numerous other actresses across Hollywood before he met 'Baby' Harlow – the only difference this time was that his infatuation was reciprocated. They married in July 1932 and appeared to be blissfully happy. Both Bern and Harlow were well-loved in Hollywood, but by September of that year, following the influence of Strickling and Mannix, the relationship between the forty-five-year-old Bern and the twenty-one-year-old Harlow, which appears on close inspection to have been guilelessly loving, had been spun into a disturbing, claustrophobic relationship that Harlow conducted with a Machiavellian contempt for the devoted Bern.

On 5 September 1932 a call came through to Strickling from

Harlow, urging him to come to her house as Bern was dead. Strickling turned up with a posse of MGM management, including Thalberg and Mannix, and an MGM photographer, Virgil Apger, to find Bern's body in a state of advanced rigor mortis. What they all knew, as, it became apparent, did Harlow, was that Bern was still, to all intents and purposes, married to an actress called Dorothy Millette, whom he had met in 1911 and lived with for nearly a decade. They also knew that Millette had visited Bern that weekend. She was his common-law wife when he married Harlow, and despite not being a *legal* impediment to their nuptials, had her existence become public knowledge the moral outcry would have obliterated not only Harlow's career but also MGM's reputation. Strickling and Mannix knew this, so within seconds of arriving at the murder scene they put into motion a plan to deflect attention away from Harlow and MGM by suggesting Bern had committed suicide. A suicide would allow Harlow to be the innocent victim of a selfish and unconcerned husband. More importantly, it would cover up the fact that she had married a man whose common-law wife had killed him in a fit of rage. Strickling took Harlow to her mother's house and later claimed she had been with her mother all along, thus extracting her from any implication in her husband's death.

A note, found by Mayer in Bern's visitors book, which contained messages from friends like Gary Cooper, Irving Thalberg and Lupe Velez, was used to mark Bern's death as a suicide. It read, 'Dearest Dear, Unfortuately (sic) this is the only way to make good the frightful wrong I have done you and wipe out my abject humiliation. I love you. Paul. You understand that last night was "only a comedy . . ." ' This was used as the cornerstone of the suicide story, which suggested that Bern had sexual problems and had beaten Harlow, then killed himself in shame. Strickling quickly put together a story that suggested Bern was a sexual deviant who was unable to perform. Friends and acquaintances of Bern's were drafted in by Strickling and Mannix to make comments suggesting that Bern was suicidal – easy to do, given what happened with Barbara La Marr. Given the short amount of time they had to concoct such a story, numerous discrepancies appeared at an early stage, such as the fact that neighbours saw a veiled woman arrive on the night of Bern's death and had heard loud arguments the night Bern died. But the police, more than likely thanks to MGM's constant wooing, ignored them all.

Strickling recruited Adela Rogers St John, whose husband had shared a house with Bern years before, to spread the word about Bern's impotence and genital deformity – a partial and useful truth – roping in the conveniently dead La Marr by saying that she'd told Adela the reason she never married Bern was because of this. Later Adela told friends that Harlow had been at the house when Bern died, but had that been the case, Millette, who was very unstable, having been abandoned in an apartment in the Algonquin hotel by Bern over a decade before, would probably have killed her too. Even the maid was recruited to claim that Bern had told her that 'Baby' was still a virgin the morning after the wedding – something that Bern, or anyone in the same position, would have been highly unlikely to do.

Mannix and his good friend the DA, Buron Fitts, choreographed the inquest so that Bern's brother didn't appear and none of the witnesses who saw Millette at the house testified. The man who shined Bern's shoes claimed that he'd talked to him about suicide and that he carried a gun at all times. Bern's family, initially furious at the flurry of defamation, were most likely bought off, as his brother Henry went from outrage to silence as soon as he arrived in LA and met with Strickling. Doctors were also persuaded to claim that Bern had been depressed, and guns were placed in his house that he would not have kept. A photograph of Apger's shows Bern's hands empty, yet a police detective claims to have pried a gun from his fingers. Only Harlow refused to smear her husband, but the police ignored that too.

Even Bern's funeral was treated as a circus and his coffin lid was raised for the congregation to take a 'last look'. Harlow was horrified and burst into tears, as did Irving Thalberg, who had been very close to Bern. Clark Gable fled the chapel and Jack Gilbert threw up. Afterwards, a number of reporters who had picked up on Henry Bern's comment prior to his sudden, bought silence that his brother had been 'morally married', discovered evidence of Dorothy Millette, registered at the Algonquin hotel as Mrs Paul Bern. She had vanished, however, and was found a week later, washed up dead on the shores of the Sacramento River.

The truth died with Dorothy Millette and Strickling managed her death with his usual aplomb, paying for a funeral and headstone and informing the press, almost certainly untruthfully, that Harlow had insisted on paying for everything. Strickling, aided by Mannix and the rest of the MGM management – even Thalberg, though he apparently only joined in after Mayer swore to kill him if he didn't – spun a web of confusion around the simple fact that Millette, distraught that Bern was clearly never coming back to her, had killed him in a moment of despair and jealousy, then killed herself. It's perfectly possible that even the note used as the cornerstone of Strickling's carefully woven story was a forgery – Mayer didn't show it to Strickling immediately and only kept it because it was strange. It certainly doesn't read like the last words of a man bent on killing himself.

Gerald Clarke, the biographer of Judy Garland and other Hollywood legends, has written, 'Between them, Howard Strickling . . . and Whitey Hendry, the studio's police chief, could grease enough important palms to fix almost anything. No less a figure than Los Angeles' top prosecutor, District Attorney Buron Fitts himself, was on the take. Metro was, or so it seemed, omnipotent.' The power that Strickling and Mannix had amassed was extraordinary. The campaign to smear Bern and preserve the career of Jean Harlow had drawn in an enormous number of people from across Hollywood: David O. Selznick and Jack Gilbert – both close friends of Bern's – offering scripted quotes, most likely concocted by Strickling; the press, which suggested that Bern would have considered suicide in the right circumstances; the DA and the coroner's office. Despite the insinuations bandied about, nothing ever tarnished the Platinum Blonde; she retained public sympathy throughout her short life, while Paul Bern, a much-loved director who had been friends with most of Hollywood, had his reputation utterly destroyed. It was the star that mattered; a director could be easily replaced.

The Strickling who could assist in such a cover-up, even to the point of suggesting suicide as a deflection, seems a far cry from the Strickling who Katharine Hepburn claimed as the reason for signing with MGM, but they're not so far removed. Both sides of the man are about strict loyalty to the company and a determination to help MGM make money, even at the expense of friendship if needs be. Pointing the finger at Bern not only cleared Harlow of any possible involvement, but Bern's alleged reason for suicide – despair at his sexual inadequacy – was a massive boost to her allure. After all, how could any man satisfy such a woman?

• Twenty •

BIRD ON THE WING

Gone With the Wind was one of the most spectacular films of the Golden Age of Hollywood and was blessed with one of the most astonishing build-ups in publicity history. It was almost the first thing that Russell Birdwell got his teeth into, embarked upon just as the campaign for *Little Lord Fauntleroy* got under way, and it marked his time with Selznick International to perfection; he left just before the movie opened in 1939. The film's place in the history of the publicity industry cannot be over-emphasized as it was the model everyone looked to. Birdwell's campaign differed from anything that Reichenbach or Nottage would have concocted in that it was fed by his early days as a reporter and pulp writer – the stories he concocted and presented in an inimitably personal style to every editor he could lay his hands on sprang from a well of reality. All the fantastical elements were so carefully woven into this, and so well backed up with evidence and quotes, that the media could not fail to be seduced by them.

Gone With the Wind had not been published when Selznick optioned it, so even the buying of the film rights was used as a story to attract attention. Selznick, so the story ran, had read the proofs of Margaret Mitchell's book and become very excited by its epic potential. He was warned off buying the rights by friends and advisers on the grounds that a film set in the south, describing the Civil War – still at that time within living memory and a risky proposition in a country recovering from the ravages of severe economic depression – was taboo.

However, Selznick believed in the book, and was backed up in his belief by John Hay Whitney and by his brother Myron Selznick, the agent responsible for brokering deals that saw stars' pay packets skyrocket in the Twenties and Thirties. In the end he made Mitchell an offer of $50,000 for the rights. The director and producer Mervyn LeRoy, who launched Edward G. Robinson's career with *Little Caesar*, as well as discovering Clark Gable, Lana Turner and Robert Mitchum, promptly put in a bid of $55,000, but Mitchell, who seems to have been swayed by Selznick's belief in the book, went with the lower offer. He later felt guilty about getting the rights for such a knock-down price and sent Mitchell a cheque for a further $50,000, but even this may be a carefully structured piece of propaganda from Birdwell, as it's unclear whether the cheque was sent a few weeks after or when Selznick was winding up his company in 1942.

Selznick and Birdwell immediately went into overdrive to promote the movie and push its epic nature into the public consciousness. Even before Birdwell had read the proofs – 'It'll take me more than a month to read this!' he told Selznick – the determined producer began pushing an agenda for the film which was still four years away from release. 'There is only one person who can play Rhett Butler and that is Clark Gable,' Selznick told Birdwell. 'Why don't you put out a story, start some sort of rumour, that Clark Gable is going to be Rhett Butler?'

'With the book unpublished,' wrote Birdwell in one of his *Hollywood Reporter* articles from the mid 1960s, 'the press didn't know what I was talking about. Nevertheless, they carried a few items that Clark Gable was up for the role of Rhett Butler.' That was just the beginning; the really epic nature of the campaign began in earnest after the book was published. By then it was already receiving considerable notice, thanks to the association of Gable's name with the film, but it would become one of the most talked about book and movie projects thanks largely to the campaign to find an actress to play Scarlett O'Hara.

The search for Scarlett had its roots in a similar stunt to find an actor to play Tom Sawyer. When Mark Twain's classic was being cast, Selznick had seen any number of Hollywood actors and deemed none of them suitable for the role of Tom, so he and Birdwell cooked up a nationwide search for the ideal unknown Tom Sawyer. Fifty talent scouts were brought in to look for suitable juvenile actors across the USA, and in less than three months Tommy Kelly, the son of a church janitor in the New York Bronx, was cast.

'Nationwide searches for potential stars were then, as now, always a suspect press agent device for obtaining free space,' wrote Birdwell in the *Hollywood Reporter* in 1965, 'but [this] search was looked upon as being legitimate and [the] nationwide campaign was to pay off and once again pre-sell a motion picture before it even went to camera.' The publicity for *The Adventures of Tom Sawyer* was helped considerably by the family of Tommy Kelly, who loudly insisted on sharing one room at the hotel they were booked into and, to the assembled press's even greater joy, made the beds themselves. 'I've been taking care of our house for more than thirty years,' Mrs Kelly was reported as saying, 'and I'm not going to have some maid coming in doing it for me now.'

Such searches still go on, the search for the actor to play Harry Potter being a notable recent example. The casting net that caught Daniel Radcliffe intensified the already fervent interest in the movie version of *Harry Potter and the Philosopher's Stone* in the early part of the new millennium. Yet nothing before or since has matched the search for Scarlett O'Hara, a quest that involved 1,500 screen tests and tens of thousands of press releases finding their way to the news desks and editors of the international press, all generated by Bird and his office. One hundred and fifty talent scouts were employed to 'scour the nation and the world' for Scarlett. The search turned up all sorts of surprises; among the huge number of women seen for the role, a handful of them went on to later success and some even got parts in *Gone With the Wind*, though not as Scarlett.

'Thousands upon thousands of women were interviewed,' wrote Birdwell, 'hundreds were tested. Margaret Tallichet, Paulette Goddard, Frances Dee and a few others were in the back of Mr Selznick's mind in the event he did not find an unknown.

'A New York hat model, Edythe Marriner, was flown out and tested. Although she didn't get the part she went on to become Susan Hayward, the brilliant screen star.

'A pretty little girl in Atlanta, Georgia, Mary Anderson, sent a photograph of herself to me, along with a letter explaining she was working as an usherette in a theatre. Selznick gave me permission to fly her to Hollywood. She was immediately signed for the picture – not for the role of Scarlett but for one of the other important parts – and she went on to become a big star at 20th Century Fox Studio, then on to Broadway stardom . . .

'More than five or six of the hundreds of girls tested either were given jobs in *Gone With the Wind* or later went on to become stars on their own.'

Added to that, a number of stars were keen to get in on the action and land the role, despite not being the unknown Selznick was after. 'The biggest stars were fighting for the part,' said Birdwell. 'Norma Shearer, Miriam Hopkins, Tallulah Bankhead . . . Carole Lombard used to say: "I'm the only broad in town who doesn't want it." '

Selznick's ambition and Birdwell's canny puffing of the necessity of Gable in the Rhett Butler role led to the film being produced in association with MGM. Irving Thalberg, displaying a rare lapse in judgement, had initially passed up on any involvement with the movie, telling Mayer that 'no Civil War movie ever made a dime'. Given that Gable was contracted to MGM, however, Selznick needed to strike a deal if he was to get him and, since Bird had been assiduously promulgating the absolute impossibility of anyone but Gable playing Rhett Butler, it would have meant a huge loss of face to cast anyone else in the role. The publicity that Birdwell had planted grew vigorously enough in the fertile soil of gossip, and by the time Selznick went back to MGM to negotiate a deal, *Gone With the Wind* no longer seemed such an unlikely proposition. Always able to scent a winner, Mayer offered Gable's participation in return for distribution rights and half the profits from the movie. It was an astute move, given that it became the highest-grossing movie of all time and, allowing for inflation, has held that title ever since. The deal also gave Birdwell access to the might of the MGM publicity department and Howard Strickling, and between them they made sure the campaign was inescapable. *Gone With the Wind* was burned into the minds, retinas and ears of the general public two years before it was released.

The search for an unknown to play the role of Scarlett went on for nearly three years, and still no one proved satisfactory to the perfectionist Selznick. Birdwell claims that he gave up and started filming using a double, saying the schedule was rearranged to film scenes where the real actors didn't have to be seen in order to buy a few weeks' grace while the search continued.

Another part of the deal with MGM allowed Selznick access to the MGM lots, which allowed the scenery to reach epic proportions. In apparent despair, Selznick began filming the burning of Atlanta, and Mayer had given him permission to dispose of a huge number of sets that dated back to the early part of the silent era; it was an appropriate sacrifice given that *Gone With the Wind* changed the scale and nature of movie-making considerably, making a necessary break from the past.

'It was to be a mighty conflagration,' wrote Bird, 'one in which Rhett Butler and Scarlett O'Hara were driving through the fire in a horse-drawn buggy. Doubles were used.

'DOS and I agreed we would not tip off the press that *Gone With the Wind* was going to get underway. Instead, hopefully, the tremendous fire would cause callers to telephone the police department and the press. We would have waiting at the scene of the fire some forty telephones so that if the press did show up and did treat the matter as a breaking news story all of the facilities of communication would be at their command.

'The fire was raging over more than twenty-five acres when the press and police arrived. Newspaper reporters flocked to the telephones to dictate stories that made page one the following day.'

Birdwell's machinations worked a treat, but there was a surprise in store more spectacular than the massive conflagration. Selznick's mother, Florence, and his brother Myron were due at the shoot to help him celebrate the film's launch, and Myron turned up with Laurence Olivier and his actress girlfriend.

'As DOS excitedly was explaining the action to his mother,' wrote Bird, 'Myron kept tugging at DOS's coat tails, saying, "I have brought Scarlett O'Hara along with me . . ." ' He kept pointing to Laurence Olivier's girlfriend. Selznick apparently tried to humour his brother, but Myron became insistent: ' "This is Scarlett O'Hara," he said. "She has the sixteen-inch waist, the green eyes and the experience to play Scarlett." '

She was, of course, Vivien Leigh, whose star was rising in Britain but who was virtually unknown in America at the time. Myron Selznick was evangelical in his zeal, telling his brother that she wasn't even his client and that he'd only just met her. Myron was so determinedly enthusiastic on Leigh's behalf that a screen test, filmed by George Cukor, was arranged in December 1938, more out of family affection than anything else. 'The rest is motion picture history,' as Birdwell put it.

It's a beautiful story, cyclical and clinical in its perfection. The set burns down, the crew have given up on finding some perfect unknown actress and then, phoenix-like, Scarlett flickers into life among the flames, not quite unknown, but not a famous American star. Birdwell understood the power of a good story. He learned early on that it was the story – the spark of an idea – that drove all aspects of the movie industry, from the publicity department upwards. It was this that kept him close in spirit to Reichenbach and Nottage, even if his practices were more methodical. Bird was so enamoured of stories that he even hired an ex-FBI man to guard the ideas and stories due to be used by Selznick for his films. Selznick was mortified when Birdwell first leaked this nugget of information to the press, but it received so much positive attention that he was forced to accept it.

The official line on the casting of Scarlett O'Hara, and a story reiterated relentlessly by Bird and others, suggests that Vivien Leigh just happened to arrive on set with Laurence Olivier in late 1938 and was thrown into the role. However, it would appear that Selznick had been considering Leigh for the role of Scarlett since February, when he saw her in *Fire Over England* and *A Yank at Oxford*. She had also apparently put her name forward for consideration. By the summer Selznick was negotiating with Alexander Korda, to whom

Leigh was under contract, for her services. Her agent in Britain also worked for Myron Selznick and Birdwell represented him too. The meeting at the burning of Atlanta was, then, arranged purely for publicity reasons and is testimony to the epic nature of Birdwell's publicity.

Such a complex, carefully woven stunt certainly fitted in with the modus operandi that Bird was given by Selznick when he arrived at the studio in 1935. 'I don't want any press agentry,' Selznick told him. 'I want imagination, but it must be accurate and true and possess a quality that will match the product we hopefully will produce. You may be daring but never sensational for the sake of sensationalism; I trust you will bring innovations into the field of publicity and advertising. You will become involved in a work which I have always enjoyed and one of which my father was the master showman. If my path had not led me into production, I would have become a publicity director and public relations counsellor.'

Selznick and Birdwell were prone to keeping and creating secrets. An element of mystery, of secrecy, was essential to the process of promoting the movies the Selznick studio produced. 'We kept all stills [for *Gone With the Wind*] under lock and key,' wrote Bird, 'save a few which, at the strategic moment, were hidden in areas where we hoped someone would find them.

'Vance King . . . found and "stole" the first photographs from *GWTW* and they first appeared in the *Motion Picture Herald* and *Motion Picture Daily*, thus letting multiple thousands of exhibitors get a peek at Vivien Leigh . . .'

Not only did they stage manage the search for Scarlett and her discovery, they also created a fashion for merchandizing that has persisted and multiplied to this day. Before the movie went out, the wedding dress that Scarlett O'Hara was to wear appeared in shop windows and throughout the press. Bird's idea was to have the dress become an object of desire across America prior to the film's arrival – not only would it lead to a rash of purchases, it would spread the all-important word of mouth on *Gone With the Wind* even further than it had already gone. Birdwell struck deals with department stores from Dallas to Boston and sat back contentedly as the appearance of the dress did just what he'd hoped. It's clear now that he was one of the early pioneers in high-end movie marketing, which has become an essential part of the industry. Since *Star Wars*, merchandise and memorabilia have come to be almost as important to financial movie-making success as box-office takings.

The premiere of the film was turned into a publicity opportunity of a less-than-usual sort, for the time at least. Selznick had taken 150 tickets for the best seats and 'forgotten' to give them out. 'My staff and I,' wrote Birdwell, 'went out on Wilshire Boulevard and flagged down autos, pedestrians and truck drivers and said, "You are invited to the world premiere of *Gone With the Wind*".' It became the biggest grossing picture of all time, and Bird was inviting to the premiere the exact people who would make it such a phenomenon.

By the time *Gone With the Wind* was finally filming, Bird was ready to move on to bigger things. His worth to Selznick had been amply proved – he had masterminded a most spectacular, far-reaching publicity campaign that lasted three years and had carefully and quietly promoted a wealth of other films and stars. The dapper, well-spoken gentleman of the publicity industry was ready for more independence and more money.

Life magazine called him 'perhaps the ablest and certainly the best known publicist in Hollywood' at the time he left Selznick in 1938, and he was reportedly inundated with offers of work from other studios, as well as rejecting a five-year contract to stay with Selznick International. Bird wanted to set up an international publicity agency and would let nothing stand in his way. He did not leave on bad terms with Selznick, though, who was one of the first clients to sign up for Bird's new, independent company. Selznick was prepared to pay the extra money necessary to retain Bird's services, even as one of a string of clients. Bird had proved beyond doubt that he could keep many irons in the fire without losing sight of his individual clients' goals and was even prepared to juggle them occasionally if the client demanded it.

Bird's new company charged enormous fees – $25,000 upfront would buy an individual Birdwell's services for one year, while $50,000 would buy a business, corporation or city his services. It is a measure of the respect he held throughout the industry that he could command such high fees, but even more telling is the fact that he claims never to have solicited work; initially all the stars he dealt with came to him from the Selznick years, while the rest sought him out because of his reputation. One of the first people to do so after *Gone With the Wind* was the reclusive director and billionaire Howard Hughes.

'At the supper party [after the premiere of *Gone With the Wind*], a skinny chap came up to me and he had on little tails that he must have had in high school,' Bird remembered. 'He said, "I'd like to see you two months from now". I said, "That would be fine" and continued talking to my clients. I think it was Norma Shearer who said, "Do you know who that is? That's Howard Hughes."

'Two months later my secretary came in and said, "There's a man outside who can't talk . . . he has to see you."

' "Send him in."

'This man put a note down on my desk. It said "Mr Hughes will see you tomorrow at 3.00". I wrote "3 p.m.?" The man wrote "3 a.m.". I wrote "OK" and he left. Next day he came back and handed me a note that said "Have confirmed appointment".'

Such eccentricities were par for the course with Hughes, whose foibles and reclusive nature became the stuff of Hollywood legend towards the end of his life. Eccentricity aside, Hughes had a keen eye for stars and had identified Birdwell as a rising one. He had a film that he wanted to make, and he wanted an extraordinary campaign for it.

'I am making a picture called *The Outlaw*,' he told Birdwell. 'Can you put on another *Gone With the Wind* campaign for me?'

'No,' replied Birdwell, 'but maybe I can put on an original *Outlaw* campaign.'

The answer pleased Hughes and the campaign for *The Outlaw* got underway in 1940. At the time, Birdwell was also working for Alexander Korda and numerous others, but it is the creation of Jane Russell that is his most memorable work of the period immediately following *Gone With the Wind*. Bird's legend has it that she was discovered by Hughes working in his dentist's office as a part-time receptionist making \$37.50 a week. For \$50 per week she was put under contract and assigned to *The Outlaw*. It is one of those stories, common at the time, that are designed to make the star all that much more accessible to the film-going public and something the actress herself has since laughed off as hype. Regardless, since no one had heard of Jane Russell, Birdwell worked to ensure her name was ubiquitous by the time *The Outlaw* was released.

'I'd been to all the newspapers and magazines with the *Cinderella* story,' he said, '[but] nobody was interested. They couldn't use it.'

So Bird took a careful look at the movie and noticed a scene where Russell and Jack Bhetel were together in a barn. His brain went through the associative ticks that make a good publicist: they're in a barn, a barn is synonymous in the public's mind with hay; Russell was a pretty, busty girl; what do most people want to do with pretty, busty girls in hay? Bird was on a roll with the hay, so he called up the photographer George Hurrell.

'When you think of Gable you get a picture in your mind; Sophia Loren, a picture,' he said later. 'Not five hundred pictures, a picture. That was what I was after. I said to Hurrell, "What would you charge me to shoot this girl from 1 p.m. to 8 p.m. – you don't answer the telephone, you just shoot and shoot?" He said \$500. '"No, that wasn't what I had in mind." "Too much?" "No, not enough. I'll pay you \$3,000 plus all costs. I'm going to deliver this girl and a load of hay and you just shoot." He must have shot thousands of snaps. I took one.'

Bird went to *Life* magazine with this one picture and they took it enthusiastically. But the promotion of Jane Russell was far from over. Birdwell had sent his assistant, Dale Armstrong, up to Santa Barbara with Jane and K. T. Stevens, with instructions to photograph them among the oil fields. By this time, America was involved in the Second World War, and Birdwell's justification that the oil fields were merely an interesting background must be taken with a slight pinch of salt, as the area was a target for enemy action. What happened next, however, could not have been more perfect for Bird's ambitions.

'[Dale] telephoned me and said, "I hope you'll believe me. A Japanese submarine has just surfaced off Santa Barbara and has shelled our two clients."

'"I believe you implicitly," I said. "How close was it?"

'"The fragments fell about thirty yards away. I am now making photographs of the girls holding the shell fragments. If memory serves, this is the first enemy shell to fall on continental U.S. [soil] since revolutionary days."'

Birdwell immediately asked if Armstrong could back up this statement and how he was so certain that the submarine was Japanese; it turned out that his assistant was an old Navy man and had seen the Rising Sun on the sub as it surfaced. With that knowledge in hand, Bird immediately called the newspapers, the wire services and the trade papers, all the while keeping Armstrong on the line. They believed the story implicitly, except for Arthur Unger of *Variety*, who thought the story so outlandish he assumed that Bird had flipped and told him so with a tone of gracious apology. Within minutes, however, the War Office confirmed the shelling and 'Jane Russell and K. T. Stevens were on the front pages of every paper in the country – page one. Across America in half an hour'.

'I had a 60 by 40 blow up of the Jane Russell hay picture – thousands were sent all over the world. She replaced Betty Grable as the number one pin up. I took [this] big blow up and got a sick looking G.I. to pose with it plastered on his barracks wall. He was sitting there looking at Jane and knitting. He had a sweater for her half finished. This picture went all over the world.'

His mission to make Jane Russell the most recognized woman in the world was an unmitigated success, thanks to her ample bosom, a look in her eye that smacked of a blend of innocent experience and insouciant cynicism and the sort of 'who the hell are you?' pout that was guaranteed to get any woman-starved G.I. hot very far beneath the collar. Bird then turned his hand to promoting the actual movie, which, for its time, was rather racy, with an especially notorious scene in which Jane Russell's character strips off and gets into bed with Billy the Kid to keep him warm when he's ill.

It was a simple matter to promote the film after the Johnston office ordered that 102 cuts be made to the picture, mostly to remove what was perceived as major over-exposure of Russell's bosom. Bird went back into Hays-baiting mode and, with a piece of inspired pedantry cooked up by Bird and Hughes, broke the argument against the movie into pieces. Hughes refused to make any cuts and was bullishly determined to release the movie under his own steam, so Birdwell went and represented him at a meeting of the Producers' Association in New York.

The ruse was simple and involved proving that less of Jane, in proportion to her size, was revealed to the lustful public than of any other star of the early 1940s. 'We had exhibits,' said Bird later on, '8 by 10s of every star in town. It was the greatest display of mammary glands in the history of the universe. And these tired old men saw it. We hired the top mathematician at Columbia University and he showed up . . . and measured each girl. And we proved that, in relationship to her size, less of Jane was exposed than any other star in the business.'

It was simple, it was humorous and it worked as the number of requested cuts was reduced to two. Hughes, however, wouldn't countenance even two cuts to his movie, and Bird responded by announcing it to the press and on billboards as 'the picture that couldn't be stopped'. It was released in the end in 1943 – two years after the film's completion – and only to a limited audience, as many towns banned it. Bird also spread the word about a special bra that Hughes had designed to hold Russell's irrepressible bosom in place; in hindsight, this was almost definitely a publicity ruse, and Russell says, in her autobiography, that she never wore it as it was a poor fit. The making of the bra alone though was enough for Bird to capitalize on.

The Outlaw only achieved general release in 1946, but thanks to Bird, Jane Russell was a major star well before then. By 1946, the Forces sweetheart was itching to cut her teeth on other films, as she had made nothing apart from *The Outlaw* and only had one year left of her seven-year contract with Hughes. The film cost a fortune to make, thanks to delays releasing it and battles over scripts, but it became a slow-burning hit and had taken $17 million by the early 1960s.

*

Bird had a way with starlets and their creation. He turned Anne Baxter, already an established name, into a major star by getting her to smoke big black cigars for a photo shoot, got Zsa Zsa Gabor no end of publicity by persuading her to cover up one of her much commented upon eyes with an eye-patch, boosted Marlene Dietrich's flagging career by pushing her into taking a part in one of her biggest hits, *Destry Rides Again*, despite her unwillingness, and got Vanessa Brown reams of copy by persuading her to refuse to perform at an atomic testing camp in Nevada in case it affected her fertility. He also resurrected Loretta Young's career with a premiere of one of her movies in Salt Lake City, home to the Mormons. Young was a descendant of Brigham Young, the founder of the church, and Bird persuaded a large number of Mormons, all called Young, to meet her off the train as a beloved relative, a stunt that got her career rolling again.

His magic didn't always work, however. Toni Seven, who he engineered into a public strip poker game along with a number of other actresses, in order to raise awareness for a drive to collect clothing for victims of the war in Europe, didn't want the stardom. And Diane Hartman, who paid for his services for a twenty-four-hour period in the early 1960s and received an extraordinary amount of interest after he placed an advert in the Hollywood trade papers, only ended up with a career in nightclubs – steady work and worth the investment, but nothing like as stellar as Bird's other promotions of nubile flesh.

Starlets were far from the only interest of Birdwell's World Publicity Agency – he dabbled in politics as well. One of his less successful ventures into the political arena was a bid to make the ex-King Carol II of Romania a palatable guest of the United States of America in the early 1940s. The ex-king, an ageing playboy, had fled the Romanian throne as the war in Europe hotted up and was living in Mexico City. He employed Birdwell to bring him in from the cold and sell him as an anti-fascist, a patriot and a leader in exile in the mould of de Gaulle. There were excellent incentives for this – $80 million of Romanian money had been frozen by America to prevent the Nazis getting hold of it, and Carol was eager to reclaim control of it by forming a government in exile. Such acceptance would possibly also have allowed him to reclaim his throne when the war ended.

The trouble was the ex-king's record of anti-fascism could be described, politely, as patchy at best. He had acquiesced all too often with Hitler, only to make some minor act of rebellion at a later date, which was relatively inconsequential in the scheme of things. Eventually, having dribbled much of his power away, he was of no use to Hitler, so he fled with his mistress, Elena Lupescu, to Mexico, where he set himself up as a force against fascism.

Essentially, Birdwell had his work cut out trying to make Carol II of Romania palatable to the American people. He did his best, writing royal proclamations declaring that Carol was the first monarch to openly fight fascism, that he hadn't fled Romania until gunfire was turned his way and that he was a 'good King', but this was all too much for certain newspapers, *PM* being one of the most prominent, who went out of their way to debunk Birdwell's positive propaganda. The *Daily Mirror* in London was the most vocally dismissive, suggesting that Carol's attempt to rally the Romanian people to fight fascism was 'a call to action piped on a rusty tin whistle by a fool suffering from moral asthma. His long distance patriotism and his record of double dealing with the Nazis make him an object of derision in the eyes of all combatants.'

Birdwell's efforts to sell a new seriousness in the ex-king came under a lot of fire from all fronts, but his winning way with a press story seems to have won the attention of Roosevelt. In an interview in 1968 he reminisced, 'Finally FDR did invite him. I remember we drank many toasts that night. But an addendum arrived. He was to come without Mme. Lupescu. And, of course, he would not. I enjoyed that account. He was a great fellow. I enjoyed writing royal proclamations.' But enjoyment wasn't enough: ex-King Carol clearly didn't want to fight fascism or reclaim his throne enough. However much Bird tried to rebrand him, however much he thought he was a great guy, Carol of Romania remained the dissolute playboy that the press had dismissed him as, which no amount of kind thoughts or carefully crafted press releases could alter.

Birdwell may have been happiest promoting kings and starlets, movies and plays, but his money came just as regularly from corporate sources and sometimes from film directing and writing books and plays. He wasn't content to settle in just one field; indeed, his life's work proves that he was determined to mine as many veins of creativity as possible. But he always came back to publicity work, even in his final years, when he wrote a play about a PR man, which Bird swore was not autobiographical. One of the best examples of his corporate work is the account, taken on in 1958, to promote men's hats, which had slumped in sales by the mid to late 1950s. Bird determined to at least go and buy a hat if he was going to promote them and he took with him two of his female assistants, Joanne Howell and Midge Hamilton.

Bird, who hadn't worn a hat for twenty years, erred on the side of caution and bought a good Texan Stetson, just like his father and grandfather had worn. His assistants, however, gleefully tried on men's hats elsewhere in the store and caused outrage amongst the shop workers. He picked his assistants with a good eye – Midge Hamilton approached him wearing a straw hat at a rakish angle, pursued by a pained-looking shop assistant, and suggested that instead of selling the hats to men, who had been refusing to buy them in ever-increasing numbers, they should try selling men's hats to women, as they obviously suited them.

Bird thought it was a great idea, but if the pained expressions in the shop were anything to go by, one can imagine the expressions of the hat manufacturers, whose staid attitude had been partly responsible for the decline in sales. However, by the end of the year, there was little for them to complain about: Princess Margaret, a nonconformist by Royal standards, had turned up to Ascot in a men's hat, models were wearing them on the catwalk and the hat warehouses were emptied.

That was the first hurdle – the next was to get men buying hats again. He solved the problem with some sneaky psychology. A column, written five years previously in a Dallas paper, had suggested that only homosexuals went hatless. 'Real' men wore Stetsons or helmets or crowns – hats of any sort were to be seen as a sign of virility, according to the psychologist's research. Bird pushed this out in the general direction of insecure men everywhere and it worked like a charm; thousands of men rushed to their hat shops, desperate to prove they were heterosexual.

Despite the financial allure of the corporate world, Bird always returned to the movies, which had been his first interest. In 1960, he undertook one of his more memorable campaigns in the pages of *Life* magazine, and like any good Bird stunt, it grew far beyond that. Just prior to the Democratic Convention in 1960, an advert that read like an editorial piece appeared on page one of the magazine. It was entitled 'There Were No Ghost Writers at the Alamo, by Russell Birdwell'. The copy asked if the reader would ever truly know the man they elected president, given that all his speeches were ghost written and these ghost writers would design his delivery and stage every last detail of his public life.

The article then launched into a piece of carefully worded nostalgia, saying that in 1836, the Americans who lived at the time of the siege of the Alamo would have felt free to speak their minds as well as offering a history lesson on the Alamo itself. It was all very bold and noble and patriotic in a backward-looking sort of way, as many of the best Westerns were, but not until the last lines was it revealed that this was a piece of ballyhoo designed to promulgate John Wayne's new movie, *The Alamo*. If anyone missed the point at the end of the article, a flap on the opposite page concealed a picture of the Texan fort and bold text stating that the movie's world premiere would be happening in October.

The advert cost $152,000 but a couple of days later it was earning back every penny for the film company, when Senator Jack Kennedy was asked in a live TV interview if he had considered the possibility that Birdwell's advert was a veiled plug for Lyndon Johnson, who was his chief rival for the presidential nomination. Kennedy, looking astonished, paused before saying, 'No, I didn't read that into it. I thought it was a plug for the picture.' It doesn't take much to work out that the influence of Birdwell was at play behind the question; it had to be. Not only was Bird well-connected, he was sharp enough to know that getting the charismatic presidential candidate to mention the movie was far and away the best free plug the movie could get. He was still playing politics, but this time with a slightly classier brand of playboy.

It's also worth noting that *Life* magazine's advertising team had Bird's *Alamo* advert printed on vellum and distributed amongst rich potential clients, using it as proof of the power of *Life* as an advertising medium.

Russell Birdwell was a different sort of publicist to Henry Rogers, who was moving more and more into the corporate world of publicity and whose business borders with the advertising world and Madison Avenue were becoming more and more blurred by the late 1950s. Bird was never likely to play the corporate game and seems to have seen the writing on the wall for his brand of publicity early on. He also saw the burnout inherent in the industry and how it had consumed Nottage and his entire legacy and continues to affect publicists to this day. In the end he carefully withdrew and left the PR industry in the hands of Rogers and his partner Warren Cowan.

• Twenty-One •

THE PURSUIT OF RESPECTABILITY

Henry Rogers' stammer was an impediment to business, but he was determined not to let that get in the way of making a name for himself. Thanks to Rita Hayworth, Rogers was a name to be conjured with in 1940s Hollywood, but such conjurations did not – and do not – last long in the PR business if the name disappears from the consciousness of potential clients for more than a few weeks. A star can wait it out, disappear for a year or so and, if they are effulgent enough in the public consciousness, come out from behind the clouds and shine just as brightly, if not even more so. A slack flack whose name disappears will not return so easily, and Nottage is a prime example of this. So Rogers went into overdrive to get more names on his roster of clients.

Rogers' start with Hayworth was a fortuitous one, but playing ten-cent poker with the more established stars was not an option. Rogers had to find other ways of getting to them, so he refined his games of chance and played them instead on the doorsteps of agents, business managers and lawyers who dealt with the stars, taking a grassroots approach to finding out who needed new representation. 'I learned that one contact opened the door to the next,' he wrote in his autobiography. 'One agent, if he liked me and respected me, would introduce me to his friend, the business manager, whose office was down the hall. So it was that Rita Hayworth's agent, Tom Somlyo, introduced me to Claudette Colbert's agent, Charles Wendling, who also happened to be her brother.'

This meeting happened at a fortuitous time for Rogers: Colbert was just about to shoot *Boom Town* for MGM, to whom she'd been loaned by Paramount. She had won the Oscar for *It Happened One Night* in 1934, starring opposite Clark Gable, and had had considerable success in the following years, but she was concerned that *Boom Town*, which also starred MGM stalwarts Gable, Hedy Lamarr and Spencer Tracy, wouldn't generate her much publicity. She believed, probably quite accurately, that Strickling's publicity team at MGM would concentrate its efforts on their in-house stars and would not spend much time or effort promoting her. It was enough of a cause for concern that she discussed it with Wendling, who agreed that it was a potential problem. He then remembered meeting Rogers a few weeks earlier and discussed him with Colbert. She had heard of him, thanks to his campaign on Hayworth's behalf, and agreed to a meeting.

Rogers received an invite to Colbert's home, a stylish and tasteful place designed by William Haines, now safely out of MGM's hair and lavishing his flair for interior decoration on the homes of stars who had come up through the Hollywood ranks with and after him. Rogers was much at ease in such lavish, gracious surroundings – these were the sort of luxurious homes and circles he aimed to be moving in if he played his cards right, and ever since the poker game with Rita Hayworth he'd been playing exceptionally well. Even his stutter dried up when Colbert received him. It helped that she made it clear she'd heard good reports of him, and he'd also done plenty of research among journalist friends so he knew what would tick the right boxes for this rather retiring star.

Asked what he thought he could do on her behalf, he told her that she'd received little publicity since her Oscar win for *It Happened One Night* because she had, simply, not actively sought it out.

'You have allowed yourself the luxury of doing without publicity,' he said. 'The press is interested in Claudette Colbert. They just won't exert any great effort to knock down your door, because everyone else is knocking down their door. If you are interested and will cooperate, you will get as much publicity in connection with *Boom Town* as will Clark Gable, Spencer Tracy and Hedy Lamarr.'

Colbert, who had also done her research, sprang on this. 'When you say "cooperate",' she fired back, 'you don't mean that you're going to ask me to pose in my bed in a black and white satin nightgown with my boobs hanging out?'

Rogers, of course, knew that one could not treat two diametrically opposed stars the same and, no doubt with a quick glance at the tasteful surroundings, assured her that she was a lady and would be treated as such. He then outlined his plan to set up an interview with Louella Parsons, as long as Colbert didn't mind going out to meet the grand dame of gossip on her turf. Colbert had been interviewed by Parsons before and didn't mind, especially as Parsons was notorious for taking a few drinks and leaving the actual interview to her assistants, Dorothy Manners or Ruth Waterbury. He also listed a range of magazines, from movie magazines to *Life* and women's magazines, as well as newspapers, news services and other necessary outlets he would contact to arrange interviews. He promised column inches on a regular basis, glamorous photo shoots and all the usual apparel that attended a major star's publicity campaigns in 1940.

Within an hour of the meeting ending, Charles Wendling was in touch. Colbert was impressed. What was Rogers' fee?

'It was an important moment for me,' wrote Rogers. 'At the time Rita Hayworth was paying me a fee of $20 a week which was 5 per cent of her salary. Most of the other clients were paying $25 a week. Some were paying $35. I knew that Claudette Colbert was the highest-paid actress in the world. This was my big chance to increase my fees, set a new plateau. How high could I go? I gulped. "My fee is $100 a week," I said. There must have been a quaver in my voice. Charlie knew that that was much more than other clients were paying at the time. He also knew, though, that if his sister paid more than other clients, she would get more of my time. He was right.'

Not only that, but working for Claudette Colbert opened up a great number of other doors for Rogers. Wendling worked in a theatrical agency for Charles K. Feldman, who had also noticed Rogers. Feldman liked what he was doing for Colbert – who, Rogers noted, was one of Feldman's 'favourite clients' – and consequently Rogers was noticed by a great number of other agents and business managers. It helped that someone was willing to pay him $100 a week – for a press agent starting out in 1940, this was a solid platform from which to announce he had arrived at genuinely respectability. Within a few years, Marlene Dietrich, Maureen O'Hara, Dick Powell and Anne Baxter were also on Rogers' books.

It was respectability that Rogers craved. The whimsical stunts of Harry Reichenbach and Jim Moran, and the seamy desperation to clone a star's lifestyle like Nottage were not for him. Rogers wanted to be a captain of the new industry and command the sort of campaigns Russell Birdwell had masterminded. Unlike Birdwell, he wanted to be as much behind the headlines as Strickling was, but he didn't aspire to the same Machiavellian grandeur that was necessitated by the power struggles at MGM.

'The publicity business did not command a great deal of respect in those days,' he wrote. 'With a few exceptions the practitioners were a seedy lot. The few exceptions were Margaret Ettinger and Helen Ferguson. Margaret Ettinger had status and social position. It helped that she was Louella Parsons' cousin. Helen Ferguson had been a silent movie star, and, as such, had established personal relationships with many important film personalities . . . How was I ever going to break into that exalted company? First of all, I was not the same as the seedy practitioners of my craft. I looked for more in life and wanted more out of it. I liked the heady atmosphere of success. If I wanted to be successful, I knew that I would have to move up the social ladder as well as the business ladder.'

Rogers' great brainstorm was to realize that if he was to succeed more wholly as a publicist he would have to move up the social ladder, thoroughly greased though it was for publicists and press agents by the backhanders of the MGM publicity department and the wayward antics of the early renegade publicists, and become an establishment fixture, able to converse wittily and easily with the brightest and best-paid in the Hollywood firmament, rather than just being obsessed with the minutiae of the business. His wife, Rosalind, was an active cohort in this enterprise, and between them they wooed their way into the middle and upper echelons of Hollywood high society, climbing to the point where he was rubbing shoulders with lawyers, agents, business managers, producers, directors and studio executives – all the 'service' people who made the business run smoothly. He treated the publicity game as a business and treated business as a long, careful game of Monopoly.

This is not something Maynard Nottage could have done, nor Harry Reichenbach, as their travelling backgrounds simply weren't compatible with such company, however quick their wits or high their aspirations. Jim Moran, anarchic to the last, shied away from these circles instinctively, as the Asshole of the Year award he sent to the studio executives proved. Russell Birdwell was the most closely akin to Rogers in aspiration, but even he only raised his game by demanding a high fee and the subsequent respect it accorded in the business world. Henry Rogers changed the nature of the publicity industry by demanding it be recognized as a viable and respectable business. To do so, he hosted parties for his clients, put himself into the social whirl of Hollywood and made sure he was well read enough to be able to talk anything but shop when he was out on the town.

'I began to take my place as one of those "service" people in the movie industry who became accepted on the social as well as the business level,' wrote Rogers. 'The advantages of this were obvious. As a social equal I conducted my business on a higher level than a social "unequal". Take two young men with equal talent, drive and ambition. The young man who operates on the same social level as the people he hopes will some day be his peers has a decided edge over the other young man who returns right home in the evening. The young man who has entertained or been entertained by the prospective client the night before is treated with just a little more respect at the next morning's meeting than the other young man who stayed at home and mowed his lawn.'

It was a profoundly wise business decision, but it took a measure of the joy out of the publicity industry and made it ever more difficult for people like Jim Moran to operate. Perversely, however, Maynard Nottage had a degree of barbed respect for Rogers, as one hastily scribbled note, clearly a partial draft of a lost letter, in his archive shows: 'I wish I'd followed the Henry Rogers route and sucked up to all the suits back when I had a chance. I don't like the man, but has he ever made a business of publicity! Rogers and Cowan roll along at a pace unimagined when I was starting out, sucking up all the stars and business that come their way and even finding time to take an occasional moral stance in the immoral world of movie publicity. The only sad thing is they don't use enough animals, but a company that puts so much emphasis on seeping useful and interesting information out to the papers from the standpoint of truth and openness doesn't have room for crazy stunts involving animals or a few well placed outrageous lies. I miss those days of lions and tigers and bears and beautiful lies . . . but at least there's still Moran with his Ostrich and his bulls and his owls. Crazy guy. You have to love him.'

Beautiful lies were anathema to Rogers, however. He loathed the trivia that passed for publicity puffs in the papers, taking exception in his autobiography to stories like 'Loretta Young has built a new rose garden and spends her days off from the studio pruning her roses' or 'Tyrone Power is taking fencing lessons'.

'I felt that if a client paid me a fee I should be able to accomplish something for him besides just getting his name into print with no purpose,' he wrote. 'I decided to break the rules. I decided that if I was going to represent an actor, it was my responsibility to impress the top film executives, producers and directors in the business with the talent, the glamour and the box office appeal of my client. I was not concerned about reaching the moviegoer in Cleveland. If I could impress the industry to the extent that it would give my clients better roles and higher salaries, then I didn't have to worry about the moviegoer in Cleveland.'

To this end, he started persuading his clients that it was not imperative to just appear in print; he took his love of conversing and social climbing to another level and told them that it was what was said in the articles that mattered. It mattered who they talked to and who took the pictures, it mattered that they had something interesting to say and that it furthered their ability to climb to the top of the heap. It was an ethos that had been there at the beginning of his career – his one beautiful lie about Rita Hayworth's wardrobe had changed the studio's perceptions of her star quality immediately. Joan

Crawford hired Rogers because she was considered box-office poison. Claudette Colbert didn't want to be outshined. Maureen O'Hara hired him because she felt that RKO weren't giving her the roles she deserved. Henry Rogers' mission was to reverse that decline, and he was certain that placing stories in the press about Loretta Young's rose garden would not help her career. It would be interesting to know what Rogers would make of today's system, where Britney Spears, for example, can be routinely lambasted by the press, be caught on camera shaving her head and attacking cars with an umbrella and come away a bigger name than ever before. He would have no doubt loathed the whole paparazzi parade of vulgarity and knicker shots – today's stars are simply not the sort of people he would want to socialize or associate with.

Each of his star clients had problems that concerned the industry rather than the public, and he persuaded them that he was the man to communicate to the studios their value and worth in bold messages that eschewed the usual round of nonsense and instead offered substance. To do this he needed to establish a relationship with the major columnists, whose egos were of gargantuan proportions thanks to the flattery and bribery campaigns conducted by the major studios. Louella Parsons, Hedda Hopper, Sheila Graham and the other gossip queens and kings were still in the exalted position of being able to make or break a career with the stroke of a pen – a nasty story could finish a star while a flattering one could make them shine that much brighter.

To get attention for his clients, many of whom did not yet warrant notice from the likes of Louella Parsons, he began representing the nightclubs and restaurants the stars frequented. It was a good source of income, but more importantly it gave Rogers a place to network at a discount, his belief being that pleasure led to better business. These places allowed him to court the columnists too, and he established relationships with them all by firing off titbits of trivia about who was out with whom at what restaurants. It plugged the client's establishment and kept his name in the sights of the columnists long before he met many of them. This became an overwhelming aim of Rogers' business operation and by 1945 he was in a strong enough position to bring Warren Cowan into the company as a partner, with the express intention of getting Cowan to court the columnists whilst Rogers got on with expanding other areas of business. With Cowan on board, the company – now named Rogers & Cowan – really set about changing the perception and modus operandi of movie PR for ever.

• Twenty-Two •

WARNER'S WORLD

Press agents proliferated in Hollywood throughout the 1930s and 1940s, spurred on by the success of Russell Birdwell, Harry Brand and Howard Strickling. Stars wanted and needed an agent to deal with the press for them in order to mould their profiles into new and more interesting shapes. The press agents were more often than not ex-journalists who had, like Birdwell, flown the investigative coop in search of better pay. Some, like Birdwell for his books and films, even had their own press agents or, like Moran, were their own press agents.

More and more independent publicity offices sprang up during the build-up to war, following Bird's flight from the Selznick nest. Ezra Goodman was one such free-ranging flack; in the late 1930s he worked out of New York for independents like Leo Guild, who specialized in ingenious Reichenbach-style stunts. One such stunt was to promote a Warner film, *The Luck of the Irish*, which he did by planting a four-leaf clover in a crack in the pavement in front of the Broadway theatre in which the film was playing and arranging for the lucky charm to be found by a convenient passer-by, to the sound of much ballyhoo in the press. Guild followed this with a bill introduced to the New York State legislature requesting that the legal age of consent be reduced from eighteen to seventeen – all to promote the release, by Paramount, of the film *Seventeen*.

Goodman's next assignment with Guild was to create Michael

Mordkin Jr. a profile as a Broadway personality, as he had enough money to play with and a more than passing interest in showbiz circles. Mordkin was a successful printing salesman, but not the most inspiring man, so Goodman and Guild simply threw monthly parties in his penthouse apartment. 'The parties were an instantaneous hit,' wrote Goodman in his book *The Fifty-Year Decline and Fall of Hollywood*. 'Mordkin was an excellent host and, since he apparently did not want anything of his guests, he got a flood of publicity from the press, who found him thoroughly likeable and ingratiating.'

The first party was in honour of *Low Man on a Totem Pole*, a book by the humorist H. Allen Smith. People, many of them subjects of the book, came from all over the country to attend the party, which ran for several days. Mordkin rapidly became the Broadway character he had so desired to be without a great deal of effort: 'No one ever bothered to ask anything much about him,' wrote Goodman. 'It was sufficient that he was such an open-handed and magnanimous host.'

Goodman and Guild's next stunt was to take the Mordkin model – promoting someone with very little to go on – a logical leap further: they invented a playboy and created a life for him, which they delightedly announced in exciting serialized form to the press. The playboy, who Goodman coyly called X, hailed from Chicago and was an immediate hit in New York when he flew in and started accompanying unwitting young women to parties at all the hottest New York nightspots. 'In due course, gossip-column items about this non-existent playboy began to appear in all sorts of journalistic pillars,' wrote Goodman. 'We had X escorting young ladies from the stage and screen to El Morocco, the Stork Club and 21 . . . We even had him spiritedly dunking himself in the fountain in front of the Plaza Hotel.'

It was the sort of stunt that Reichenbach and Nottage would have loved, but they'd have found a convenient patsy to play the part of the playboy. What Goodman was doing was using the mythical X as a testing ground for later work. Nothing was tied into him – X did not mark the spot for any movie or brand. Goodman and Guild brought X to an untimely end when, as a result of the unquestioning stream of publicity he was getting, journalists finally decided it was time to interview the man they were writing about. 'We figured we had proved our publicistic point and that there might be complications if we pursued this gambit any further,' wrote Goodman.

Another Broadway press agent, Jack Tirman, pulled a similar stunt while promoting a Manhattan nightclub. The line-up was lousy, so Tirman simply created an exotic dance duo to star at the venue and managed to insert plenty of publicity for them in the press. A Broadway columnist reviewed the show but, fortunately for Tirman, it would appear he didn't watch the show before writing his review, because instead of lambasting the establishment for falsely advertising a dance duo, he gave the hapless dancers, who for obvious reasons hadn't put a foot wrong, a stinking review. Tirman, despite having got away with the lie, was mortified that his invented dancers had been outed as just not good enough, so replaced them with another, better, equally imaginary troupe of dancers.

Having cut his teeth in the independent world of Broadway publicity, Goodman moved on to Hollywood to work for Warner Brothers in the early 1940s. Like all publicists, he went where the money was steadiest and the stars most profligate. His immediate boss was Charles Einfeld, who was as much 'a merchandiser of photoplays' as a press agent. Einfeld was an executive in charge of advertising and publicity. A good part of his time at Warner Brothers was spent supervising advertising in Manhattan, where he was born and went to school and college. Einfeld kept his finger deep in the publicity pie; he took the press junket to dizzying new heights and originated the out-of-town premiere in the early 1930s. 'With the U. S. deep in depression,' wrote *Time* magazine in 1940, 'Einfeld loaded his *42nd Street* Special with a bevy of the prettiest girls he could find, swept them across the country with 28 stops. Incidentally, the trip plugged Southern California's climate and General Electric's products (he fed his beauties from an electrically equipped kitchen, tanned them under a G. E. sun lamp set up in a Malibu Beach wagon).'

Einfeld also sent press and press agents to Dodge City to promote the film of the same name. Under his regime, Ben Cohn had the freedom to promote a film called *Juarez* as follows: 'A guy jumped into a cab in New York City. "Take me to Juarez," he said. He was a night worker and he fell asleep. When he woke up the cab driver told him, "We're in Philadelphia. We ought to make Juarez, Mexico in four days." There was an argument. Two cops jailed them both. It hit page one of every paper.'

In 1940, Charlie Einfeld set out on the 'junket to end junkets'. 'He loaded 250 big stars, small stars and reporters on a "glamour train",' wrote *Time*, 'toted them off on a four-day trip to Santa Fe, N. Mex. for the world premiere of *Santa Fe Trail*. Since the train arrived on Friday 13th, he adopted a hard-luck motif. Invitations were attached to rabbits' feet and read: "The date is Friday 13th, and the place is Santa Fe. Here you'll find at the end of the trail the start of a perfect day." At Albuquerque it was planned to have a black cat appear on the train: an over-zealous assistant turned up with four. When the train pulled into Santa Fe a blizzard was in progress. The shivering crowd of 2,000 who met the train couldn't hear a word the stars said, as the sound system went haywire. The altitude speedily knocked out 75-year-old May Robson, who had to be removed to lower surroundings. And Olivia de Havilland, leading lady of the film, doubled up with appendicitis, had to be flown back to Hollywood. It all added up to 150,000 words of copy filed from his press car in 24 hours. Charlie was well satisfied.'

Goodman worked all the jobs you could get in the Warner Brothers office. Like Pete Smith had for Mayer a decade or so before, he ghost wrote for Jack Warner, under the beady eye of Einfeld who, when asked if it wouldn't be easier if Goodman went direct to Warner for directions, said in a severe tone, 'I can tell it to you better.' He wrote articles for *The Nation* discussing Hollywood war films, making specific reference to Warner films; the articles were assiduously recycled throughout the press by Einfeld, earning the movies yet more publicity. He also became the point of contact in the publicity department for the wayward but highly bankable Errol Flynn, who was in permanent conflict with all of the Warner Brothers management, from Jack Warner on down, due to Goodman bravely offering Flynn some constructive criticism on his thinly veiled autobiographical novel, published in 1946, which was a far cry from the celebrity novels of today in that a) it was written by Flynn and b) it was pretty good. Goodman was, as a result of his honesty with the notoriously difficult star, the only member of the publicity department who could negotiate press interviews with Flynn as well as negotiating him out of sticky situations.

Flynn was known to deliberately get sick just at the start of filming his latest project for Warner Brothers. A lothario through and through, he disappeared during filming of *Edge of Darkness*, only to be found in the arms of a woman who the suppress agents whisked one way whilst Flynn returned to the shoot. Money, inevitably, changed hands in exchange for silence.

The art of the publicist was as arcane at Warner Brothers as it was at MGM. They had a fictional woman by the name of Mary Doss, supposedly a sugar heiress, who they tied to the name of any actor they decided needed a boost of masculinity. One luckless actor, by the name of George Tobias, was presented in the gossips as having been seen dancing cheek to cheek with Doss. Either Tobias was stupid or the flacks were careful not to let out the truth about Doss's lack of corporeality, as Goodman remembers the actor marching into the publicity department 'angrily waving the clipping and shouting, "Don't tie me up with that dame! She's a tramp! She goes out with everybody!" '

Like Strickling at MGM, the Warner Brothers flacks developed favourites amongst the stars they dealt with. Goodman was potently enamoured of the devil-may-care attitude of Errol Flynn and charmed by the eccentricities of Ida Lupino, who once regaled him with the tale of her father's ghost coming back and crowning her husband with a cocktail shaker. Gig Young was every flack's favourite, however, mostly because he agreed to join any publicist who asked for lunch, which meant they could sign for it, since they were in the company of one of the studio's stars. Young agreed to confirm at all times that he had eaten lunch with a member of the publicity team, even if he hadn't, and as a consequence he received a lot of special favours from the team that other, more aloof stars would never have got. Young was drafted during the Second World War, however, when the publicists had to find other ways to supplement their diets.

Warner's, like all studios, was ever eager for publicity for its stars, while other publicity for the company, be it for producers or publicists, was frowned upon – this was reserved for Jack Warner. Goodman wrote an article praising Henry Blanke, the producer of *The Treasure of the Sierra Madre* and *The Maltese Falcon*, and after inspection by the publicity director, the piece swiftly vanished. Warner's had more difficulty restraining Jerry Wald, a writer turned producer who could well have been a publicist – for himself at least – given the number of 'exclusives' he offered Hollywood columnists. 'Wald became a gadfly in the publicity department's operation since he was probably a more enterprising and energetic press agent than any publicist at the studio,' wrote Goodman. 'He always gave the press top priority, even though he might be in the midst of a fire, flood or story conference. This talent ultimately helped carry him far in Hollywood.'

Warner Brothers' publicity department knew a thing or two about gadflies – they were one of only a few studios to employ Jim Moran, who was rapidly turning into more of a philosopher than a publicist, in their publicity office in 1945. His 'Eureka' moments tended not to fit in with the tone and mood of a major studio, however – to promote *The Lost Weekend*, a Billy Wilder film about an alcoholic on a bender, he chose to get a hoot owl drunk in order to test the simile 'as drunk as a hoot owl'. This brand of sharp-witted surrealism was out of place in a determinedly professional studio like Warner Brothers, where the stunt had to tie in to the product or the star as tightly as possible and wasn't allowed to spill out in random directions, however exciting they might promise to be.

Twenty-Three

CHANGING HORSES IN MIDSTREAM

Jim Moran's last act of ballyhoo for the Warner Brothers studio, before they set him loose, was to ruminate on the meat shortage engendered by the Second World War. He ruminated and reposed, thought long and hard and eventually came up with the idea of crossing a turkey with a centipede in order to provide the hungry of America with enough turkey drumsticks to last several lifetimes. Not content with waiting for a willing biologist to ascertain whether or not a turkey and a centipede would make a suitable genetic match, Moran got the props department to rustle up a model of the proposed beast in plaster and posed a number of tasty starlets around it as it was carefully carved for a photo shoot.

Warner Brothers didn't dispense with his services immediately; they assigned him to press/star liaison duties when interviews were taking place. This tended to end in disaster, at least from the studio's point of view, as Moran would often lose patience with the direction of the conversation and swing it round to himself instead.

If Moran wasn't fitting into the studio system, he was weaving himself into Hollywood with aplomb. Thanks to his excellent guitar playing, he joined the Beverly Hills No Refund Philharmonic Orchestra, which featured Harpo Marx on harp, Ben Hecht and Jack Benny on violin, Benny Goodman on clarinet and Orson Welles on drums – exalted company and a great point of contact, even if the fortnightly meetings were only to rehearse Ravel's *Bolero* and 'Stars and Stripes Forever'.

Moran also became well known in Hollywood circles as a guest cook, taking over the kitchens of a friend's house and preparing dinner where he specialized in Chinese food and curries. Moran's Washington days continued to bring forth surprises; he was approached by publicists representing the Republican Party, who were keen to oust Roosevelt in the 1944 election. FDR was running for an unprecedented fourth term, despite long-term serious illness. It had been said by many Democrats that, given the ongoing war, it would be inadvisable to change horses in midstream – in other words FDR should stay in power. This was grist to Moran's mill, so he took the job and steamed off to Reno, Nevada, carrying with him an Uncle Sam costume. When he got there, he hired a couple of horses and announced that he, Jim Moran, was going to change horses in midstream just to prove to the politicians and the voters that it could be done. A ream of photographers were on hand to snap away, and photographs of Moran achieving the feat the Democrats recommended against were splashed all over the press. This didn't help the Republicans one bit, though, and FDR was re-elected, only to die in 1945.

The stunt may not have helped the Republicans, but it was a defining metaphor for Moran's career, since he constantly switched jobs in midstream as the river of the publicity industry flowed beneath him. Moran was always keener to prick at society's norms than have a steady career, which was anathema to the studio system that rejected him, and to Nottage, whom he most closely resembled. Unlike Nottage, Moran never ran dry of ideas and didn't noticeably give in to the rampant bitterness that marked the last thirty years of Nottage's life. Moran always had something to move on to and he had an interesting enough life to promote to its own ends.

In 1946, after the studios declined to work with him on more than a freelance basis, Moran found himself employed to promote a hair tonic called Three Out of Five. To do so, he created an abstract artwork from enchilada sauce and nail polish, which he entitled 'Three Out of Five' and submitted, via avant-garde composer George Antheil, to the Art Association under the pseudonym Naromji, supposedly a shy Persian painter. The Art Association, to Moran's glee, was deeply impressed by the painting and chose it as one of twenty works that they would display. He sat idle for a week, gloating about this coup, and then tipped off a journalist at United Press in Los Angeles, who did an interview that went out across the wire service. 'Abstract art makes me wanna tear my hair out,' Moran said in the interview, 'so I figured the name of a remedy for bald heads would be an appropriate title for this painting.' The resulting hoo-ha demoralized the art world of LA, but Moran came out of it better off in more ways than one. When the picture was returned to him, he sold it for $750. 'It was the best work of my non-objective painting period,' he later said.

Moran was quite capable of shocking merely for effect; he once sat on the train to New York from Hollywood reading a completely blank book just to see what his fellow passengers would do. He said that this was to keep people from talking to him on a long journey when he was tired, but it's more likely he wanted to keep people talking *about* him. He also stashed money above the doors of restaurants, nightclubs and other venues around LA and, with the calm air of a master prestidigitator, would reach up and bring down a handful of coins 'just to astound people'.

The house he rented in Hollywood was, at one point, in serious need of external decoration, though the landlord refused to do anything about it. Moran simply painted an expletive in ten-foot-high letters on the side of the building and alerted the landlord to an act of wanton vandalism that had occurred at the house – it was quickly repainted.

Moran also set up his own awards system in 1945, as a reaction to the proliferation of awards in Hollywood. His 'statuettes' consisted of dried pigs' anuses laid delicately on velvet cushions and housed in jewelled boxes, which were sent to the heads of all the studios, from Louis B. Mayer to Jack Warner, with a note congratulating them on winning the Moran Asshole of the Year award. This behaviour goes some way towards explaining his lack of popularity at the studios, especially the ones run by kosher Jews! It is one of those awards that could stand to be revived in the ossified world of celebrity award standoff we find ourselves in today, though it is possibly no longer outrageous enough. The modern press would love it, then not be able to print it. Moran, swiftly sucked in and spat out again by the studio system, at least got some fun out of the process.

One of his more convoluted stunts took place around the time Saud El Saud, the crown prince of Saudi Arabia, visited Hollywood in 1947. Moran called together a collection of friends in the Hollywood press and told them he intended to reveal that the whole of Hollywood was a community of fakes and pretenders and that that was what one had to be to get ahead in the industry. He said that he intended to prove this by dressing as Saud El Saud and going to Ciro's nightclub to see how the clientele, the nightclub and the rest of Hollywood reacted to his presence. The press, delighted, followed him and his retinue of unemployed actors to the nightclub, all of them dressed in outfits from a costume company, echoing the stunts Nottage and Reichenbach used to pull thirty years earlier.

'I had on dark glasses which corrected my blue eyes,' said Moran. 'I had a great stain job – not the ordinary Hollywood make-up job. It lasted for three to four months afterwards. I really looked like Saud El Saud . . . My men all had jewelled scimitars and all the paraphernalia, like knives and guns. And I had a real Arab, an actor, in American business clothes with me to throw them off the trail. He looked like an American businessman of Arab descent.'

The phony party was serenaded with the Saudi national anthem by the house band, and waiters threw themselves at Moran's party, taking them to the best table in the house.

'The way I got attention was I sent a note to the bandleader requesting him to play a number, "Begin the Beguine", and afterwards I sent him a gift, one amethyst, beautifully cut. It cost $30. And I left a few minutes after I sent it. No one there was clever enough to appraise the stone. I pre-fed it by that device. That was what made the jewel thing so successful.'

By 'jewel thing', Moran meant the moment that he accidentally-on-purpose dropped a chamois bag of excellently crafted but utterly fake emeralds, rubies and diamonds as he left the building. A member of his retinue was primed to rush back and start to gather the escaping gems, only to be waved on in grand fashion by Moran, as if the last thing a Saudi king-in-waiting should do was stoop to gather a few measly jewels that had fallen from his pocket. Ciro's nightclub swiftly descended into chaos, with everyone from the band to the waiters, the busboys to the customers fighting on the dance floor to scrabble up one of the abandoned gems. In the following day's papers, the press gleefully described the swift and implacable suckering that had been pulled on the nightclub and its customers. They subscribed wholly to Moran's pre-stunt ballyhoo, not realizing until it was far too late that Moran intended them to be the suckers as much as anyone else – he was being paid to promote Ciro's and the only person who had been in the know was the club's boss, Herman Hover. It was a delirious example of a double bluff and one that Hollywood correspondent James Bacon was dragged into. In 1973, writing an article on a sex manual written by Moran, Bacon conveniently forgets that the press were equal victims of Moran's sense of the absurd.

Moran's interests were wide-ranging and erudite; he was fascinated by everything from philosophy to kite flying, politics to the guitar, and his fascinations invariably wound their way into his stunts. An early stunt that might have been involved both politics and music. While living in Washington, Moran owned a convertible car, which he claims the Democratic party asked to borrow for the inauguration parade of FDR when he won his first term in office in the early 1930s. Had it not rained, Moran claimed, he would have flashed, at an opportune moment during the parade, the following sign: 'See Moran for guitar lessons'. Another delightful failure from the Moran stable, and one that proved his desire to confound people en masse, was the instance when he persuaded a convention of magicians that he had come up with the greatest card trick of all time. He was invited to demonstrate this astonishing trick so, wearing a turban, he lodged himself behind a screen at the convention. Then he called for a sealed box containing packs of playing cards to be brought on stage. Three volunteers were called upon; one to choose a deck, one to open the pack and one to cut the pack.

Moran then requested that the volunteer concentrate on the card he'd chosen from the virgin deck and, after a short pause, announced that it was the six of diamonds. It wasn't the six of diamonds. 'But,' he said later, 'if it had been, those magicians would still be talking about it!'

It was Moran's fascination with kite flying that proved to be one of his most glorious failed stunts however. Many of his stunts did not take off and he would always claim that they would have been his best, but in this instance it's the truth. It began with a rant to friends about the abominable state of employment for midgets. 'During a war,' he would say, '[midgets] can work in aircraft factories, riveting in tight, crammed quarters, but in peacetime all they can be is freaks.'

He then endeavoured to find work for the midgets as advertising blimps. To this end, he devised a series of enormous kites, and tested them over a field in New Jersey with midget passengers strapped to them by a harness. The first design had a tendency to spin and Moran declared, 'If there's one thing I can't stand, it's a spinning midget.' Then he quickly designed rudders for the midgets to wear. These worked a treat, and the midgets were spin-free and ready to go into action as miniature Goodyear blimps. Moran proposed flying them over New York's Central Park holding up their banners. He had insured the lives of his advertising team for a fortune and believed that he had all bases covered. However, he hadn't counted upon intervention from New York's finest, a representative of which accosted him as he was preparing to launch his first intrepid kite-bound midget.

'What law am I breaking?' queried Moran in an injured tone as the policeman threatened to arrest him. The policeman, whose priorities were as deliciously skewed as one might hope, told him, 'You can't fly no midget on no kite in Central Park. Suppose one fell off? He might hit a ball-player, facrissake.' Not for him the health and safety issues that would impede such a stunt today – just don't risk a sportsman. It says a lot about the persuasiveness of Moran's personality that he manoeuvred the midgets into agreeing to fly the kites in the first place, but there was no escaping a stubborn, outraged sports fanatic of a policeman. Moran's frustration echoed round the world when, finally accepting that the police would brook no argument, he turned to the journalist and declared, 'It's a sad day for American capitalism if a man can't fly a midget over New York.'

Moran was positively Barnum-esque in his enthusiasm for midgets and animals and surrounded himself with as many trappings of circus promotion as possible, but he always had proof at hand, even for his more outrageous claims. Once, when asked by a late-night radio show presenter what he was up to, Moran replied that he had bought a Japanese midget submarine and was currently having a midget employee learn how to make it do a loop the loop underwater in a secret location off the Florida Keys. The presenter, Barry Gray, laughed and asked him what he was really doing, assuming Moran's ballyhoo extended only as far as his mouth, whereupon Moran produced an envelope and invited Gray to read it aloud. It was an insurance policy issued by Lloyd's of London insuring the life of a midget by the name of Morris MacAfie against any accident involving looping the loop in a Japanese midget submarine.

It was animals that obsessed Moran most, knowing that they were a constant source of inspiration and silent witnesses to the art of ballyhoo, as they had been since Barnum's day. He kept an owl for some time, so that he could prove to visitors that the phrase 'wise as an owl' was bunkum, which he did by jumping up and down in front of the owl, uttering dire imprecations at it and calling it every name under the sun. The owl, used to this, would blink and hoot in a distracted manner, entirely unfazed. He also publicized a play called *The Matchmaker* by rigging a taxi so that it would appear to be driven by a monkey while Moran controlled the vehicle from the back seat. A sign on the cab read, 'I am driving my master to see *The Matchmaker*.' During the World Fair in 1939, Moran tried to persuade the organizers to put in a huge tank containing whales, which they could then sell advertising space on. They might have taken him seriously had he not added that the best way to dispose of the aquarium and its contents afterwards would be to have a mass fish fry for New York.

His most spectacular animal stunt was for a book and film called *The Egg and I*, during which he became a father. Moran's idea was to hatch an ostrich egg so, with an aplomb that would have impressed Heath Robinson, he built a contraption that allowed him to sit on and incubate the egg without damaging it and even allowed him to sleep with his posterior resting gently on the egg. Dressed in a costume that included a good number of feathers, he sat on the egg for nineteen days, four hours and thirty-two minutes until it hatched, with occasional breaks when the sun came out strongly enough for the egg to remain warm of its own accord. His ostrich offspring was then sequestered in a zoo, only to be harked back to fifteen or so years later, when Moran was asked to promote a play called *Fanny*, which was running into trouble on Broadway. Moran announced on a chat show that his ostrich had become a father, making Moran a grandfather. When asked what the name of his feathered grandchild was, he told the host its name was Fanny.

Moran moved away from Hollywood shortly after the birth of his ostrich son in 1949, and his methods of working changed, too. He took more corporate work, more theatre work and started to write books, from children's books to sex manuals and musicals. In the 1960s he even recorded a spoken word album, became more involved in broadcasting and appeared on chat shows. Slowly but surely his publicity work declined, in quantity if not in quality. He remained an inveterate prankster, and in 1959 he opened an embassy for the fictitious Duchy of Grand Fenwick and installed himself in Washington as the country's ambassador on behalf of the British comedy *The Mouse That Roared*, a film about the smallest country in the world, which invades America by accident. Moran, or to give him his official title, Viscount James Stirling Moran, remembers it as follows: 'I had beautiful uniforms. I had them made. I had four different uniforms, one naval, one military and two nondescript. One was white, one pale blue, one dark and one black. They were elaborate and exquisitely done. I headquartered at the Shoreham. I drove around in a Mercedes Benz. I was there for two weeks. It ended up with a party for 250 people at the Shoreham and we showed the picture. It was not a hoax as such, but everyone went along with it. It got a lot of space. I was retained by Columbia Pictures and they think it made this picture.'

Moran's slow decline into chat-show land coincided perfectly with the rise of publicists like Henry Rogers and Warren Cowan, whose slick professionalism and hard-nosed attitude rode them through the end of the studio system into the TV age that dawned in the 1950s. If Moran wasn't ideally suited to the studio system, which at least saw fit to accommodate his situationist brand of ballyhoo occasionally, he was anathema to the Rogers & Cowan brand of PR, which has evolved into the modern business we're familiar with today. In their world, there was simply no room for his twisted, risky exhibitionism.

One of his friends, quoted in the *Saturday Evening Post* in 1949, said of Moran, 'He's a puzzling person. Not very warm, but quite passionate. Terribly honest in some ways about facing up to the realities of life, and yet you can never be sure when he's telling the truth. With Jim, the boundary line between what's real and what's imaginary is vague.'

This sums up Moran to a tee and also goes some way towards explaining why he vanished from the scene at retirement age; he was the most exquisite prankster, but he couldn't let anyone get too close to him. His aloofness, it would appear, drove them away. He didn't want for female companionship at the height of his powers, but he couldn't hold on to it – he pushed away three wives and his ostrich son was hardly a companion for old age. Moran lived only so long as his stunts did, and when the work dried up in the early 1970s he disappeared, living out his final years in seclusion. One can only hope that a man who gave so much insane pleasure to countless people throughout his life wasn't bitter and distraught, as Nottage and others became. Certainly he had less to feel betrayed about than Nottage; his masterwork was himself and all the wild inventiveness he threw into the publicity industry deserves to be remembered.

Twenty-Four

MORE FIXES THAN THERE ARE IN HEAVEN

It's not surprising that the 1930s and 1940s supplied Strickling with a series of indiscretions that needed to be covered up. After all, most of the stars of the day were undereducated, extremely popular and ludicrously rich. Many of them hadn't learned to set standards for themselves or say no to opportunity. Such were the challenges for the publicity department.

Clark Gable was the most bankable of MGM's stars in the 1930s, but he was also one of Howard Strickling's biggest headaches. Strickling dosed this with the aspirin of friendship: despite his Machiavellian approach to keeping the stars' noses clean, he maintained a strong bond with quite a number of them. Gable maintained a close affinity with Eddie Mannix as well. It's quite possible, given his habit of finding and maintaining bonds with people who could help his career, that Gable's attitudes were mercenary; certainly he chose to befriend the two people who could help him most.

Strickling maintained a tough line with Gable, regardless of friendship. He forced the new MGM star to divorce Josephine Dillon and marry wealthy divorcee Ria Langham, whom he had left Dillon for. On his arrival in Hollywood, Gable had promptly launched into a string of affairs and early conquests included his co-star Joan Crawford and columnist Adela Rogers St John. According to E. J. Fleming rumours persist that St John bore a child by Gable in the early 1930s, the veracity of which she coyly deflected by saying, 'What woman would deny that Clark Gable was the father of her child?' But she was a company woman, a friend of MGM to the core and also of Strickling for many years, thanks to the fact that her husband had once shared digs with Strickling. More of a problem was Gable's affair with Joan Crawford, which was, in the end, the cause of his unwanted marriage to Ria Langham.

Langham was so distraught that she approached Mayer's assistant, Ida Koverman, who had arranged for Gable to be hired when Irving Thalberg and others couldn't see beyond his jug ears (which were subsequently pinned back for every movie he appeared in). Langham told Koverman that she and Gable were not legally married, despite living together, and that she was prepared to take the story to the press and expose all of Gable's sexual foibles. Strickling was called in like a shot.

He and Thalberg called in Gable and threatened to invoke the moral turpitude clause in his contract if he didn't divorce Dillon and marry Langham. Gable, who had promised Crawford he would marry her, sacrificed that for the sake of his career with barely a whisper. He dutifully tied the knot with Langham, but the situation was complicated considerably by Joan Crawford's pregnancy. Strickling arranged for an abortion, despite uncertainty as to the paternity of the baby. Crawford later claimed it was almost certainly Gable's child, but at the time she told her husband, Douglas Fairbanks, that she had slipped during filming and lost it. Marriage and abortions didn't stop Gable and Crawford from seeing one another, however, and both reacted mulishly to attempts to separate them.

After Crawford took very vocal offence to Gable not being cast in *Letty Lynton*, it took the combined weight of Strickling, Mannix and Thalberg to insist that, for the good of MGM's image, they must stop seeing one another or be fired. This was a combination of people that would brook no argument and their intervention to protect MGM put a stop to the public nature of the affair, if not the stars' regular meetings for sex. After the filming of *Letty Lynton* was over, Crawford and Fairbanks were packed off by Mayer on an enforced second honeymoon. They were seen off by a huge, Strickling-organized parade of police cars and well-wishers escorting the couple to the pier.

Meanwhile, Gable and Langham were ordered on a press tour of America in order to announce their marriage as publicly as possible. At every town, Strickling's influence was felt via local agents, who rounded up a posse of reporters and photographers to plaster the 'happy couple' all over the papers and magazines. Gable was then ordered into a series of B movies as punishment for his behaviour. Seething about a marriage he didn't want and having to separate from Crawford, Gable did what any over-indulged red-blooded male would do: he had another affair designed to further his career, this time with Marion Davies, whose affair with Hearst was no longer sexual, given that he was sixty-five. MGM were furious, and when Gable asked for a pay rise they offered him a paltry $1,250 per week. Gable got Davies to persuade Hearst to apply pressure on his behalf, and in the end he got $2,000 per week, though he could have earned much more had it not been for his sexual addictions.

There were plenty of other problems for the MGM publicity department to deal with. Spencer Tracy was a high-maintenance star because of his alcoholism. More than once, Strickling sent a specially formed Tracy Squad, created in 1935 when Tracy was first signed to MGM, to bail him out or pay off a hotelier whose room Tracy had destroyed. There was a lot to cover up with Tracy; not only was he a lifelong violent alcoholic who reserved his rumpled charm almost entirely for the silver screen, he was almost as rampant and destructive a sex fiend as Gable. As E. J. Fleming reveals in *The Fixers*, Tracy is even alleged to have had an affair with Judy Garland when she was fourteen years old.

Judy Garland was another difficult entry in the Strickling suppression casebook. A child star on the vaudeville circuit as part of a sister-act singing troupe, Garland arrived in Hollywood in the early 1930s and, on attracting the attention of MGM, became one of its most bankable stars. But, as is often the case, her early fame came at a price. She had arrived at the age of twelve, a cute girl replete with puppy fat, but as her star grew her body found it hard to catch up.

As she developed, she was required to stay thin, but hormones are not something even MGM at the height of its powers could dictate to. Strickling did his best, ordering that Garland be fed a diet of soup and cottage cheese so she wouldn't become fat as she moved out of the cute phase of adolescence to become a fully functioning adult. For her defining early role as Dorothy, in *The Wizard of Oz*, a sixteen-year-old Garland was forced to have her rapidly developing breasts trussed up painfully so that she would appear to be a younger girl.

She was also forced to take a heady cocktail of drugs to keep her working. She was given Benzedrine, Phenobarbital and Seconal to keep her going and sleeping pills to knock her out at night; her amphetamine addiction was second to none come 1940 and Strickling kept her on a diet of pills, supplemented by therapy to keep her spiky, self-destructive temperament in check. It's bitterly ironic, given that the MGM model of publicity was born to put an end to the self-destructive tendencies of major stars and the chaos they wrought for their financial backers, that the only way they could mould Judy Garland into the sort of star they wanted her to be was to inflict on her the lifestyle they had suppressed in others for nearly two decades. She was far from stable in the first place, and by the end of her life she was a wreck, made paranoid by MGM's spying and addled from the doping they'd inflicted on her. That she had an addictive personality and would quite possibly have taken to drugs regardless does not excuse their behaviour, nor does the fact that the side effects of many of the drugs she was on were not then known. The studio wanted a perfect star, and it fell to Strickling to manage the maintenance of that illusion, with tacit approval from on high.

Garland became obsessed with the bandleader Artie Shaw, who was a known wife-beater and twice divorced. In desperation, her mother asked Strickling to intervene. He did so by assigning one of his publicity team, Betty Asher, to her as confidante and spy. Part of Strickling's regime at MGM was to get his team of publicists to insinuate themselves into the lives of their star charges as completely as possible, and Betty Asher did this with alacrity, having worked previously with Lana Turner. She became utterly indispensable to Garland, a confidante, best friend, valet and even, apparently, lover, but she was also sleeping with Mannix and reporting every move Garland made to him and Strickling. E. J. Fleming writes that Mickey Rooney, who was astute enough to keep his publicist cohort, Les Peterson, at arm's length, despite recognizing his embedded flack as 'vice president in charge of Mickey Rooney', warned Garland about Asher's double nature, but she wouldn't listen and only discovered years later that Asher had been under strict instructions to keep her charge in check at all times, diverting her away from troublesome relationships.

In the end, Garland was spared the untender ministrations of Artie Shaw by Lana Turner. Whether Betty Asher pushed her previous charge towards Shaw at Strickling's instruction is a matter for speculation. Certainly it would have killed two birds with one stone; Turner was notorious for her rampant sexuality and for sleeping with any man she could lay her hands on, while Garland was a fragile individual, partly because of her personality but largely thanks to the deleterious effects of the drugs she was being fed by Strickling's team.

She was distraught at the news of Turner and Shaw's marriage in 1940 and immediately started dating Shaw's best friend. However, Betty Asher had also slept with Shaw, ensuring she had all angles effectively covered. The Turner/Shaw marriage lasted less than three months; Turner threw him out but found herself pregnant. An abortion was arranged by Mannix, who had had to work very hard to prevent Mayer firing her. The costs of Turner's 'publicity tour' to Hawaii to have the abortion, accompanied by her mother and Betty Asher, came to $500, which Mannix then deducted from her wages.

In his biography of Judy Garland, Gerald Frank outlined the damage inflicted by the studio on the young girl. The worst, he thought, was the degree of protection they gave her, almost to the point of enabling. 'Judy Garland could not suffer so much as a pimple without an MGM magician on hand to make it vanish. In fact, MGM had a magical answer for everything, and none of it realistic. Adolescence is a preparation for life, a learning to cope; this preparation and this training to cope were denied Judy.'

Everyone under contract lived in the cocoon, and when they were released, life was harsh. Lana Turner told a friend, 'I didn't know how to make a hotel or airline reservation. For a long time I waited for my limousine that never came to pick me up. I was an orphan. MGM prepared us for stardom but not for life.'

Lena Horne told Ava Gardner, 'MGM created a certain name, but they didn't prepare you for real life. I mean, who do you say [call] when Howard Strickling wasn't around and you had to get an abortion?' Joan Crawford recalled a conversation with Robert Taylor. She asked him how he was doing and he replied, 'Fine, except that now I have to make up my own mind about things and nobody ever taught me how.'

When Ava Gardner first walked onto the lot in 1941, every robust male was on the scent. Mickey Rooney, perhaps her unlikeliest suitor, wouldn't give up. When he called Hedda Hopper to say they were engaged, she called Strickling to confirm. When he went to talk to Rooney, he admitted it was true but became defensive. Rooney didn't see what his personal life had to do with his commitment to MGM. Strickling enlightened him and insisted the matter be discussed with Mayer. Pulling out his usual repertoire of guilt, anger, threats and tears, Mayer lost to his newly valuable commodity Rooney, who had just scored big with the Andy Hardy films.

Since Mayer couldn't destroy the marriage, he sought to control it. One of Strickling's employees went on the honeymoon and followed the couple (almost) everywhere. When the short marriage broke up, so did Rooney. He was in the Army and went AWOL. Strickling kept it out of the papers, along with Gardner's concurrent affair with Howard Hughes. In spite of his interference Gardner had nothing but respect for Strickling. Indeed, Strickling was well-liked by his charges, in part because he dispatched his often Machiavellian duties with compassion and empathy. He did his work in the manner a good butcher would, swiftly and efficiently, knowing that if he treated people with a careful, authoritarian kindness, they would respect him, making it less likely that he'd have to involve Mannix or any of the harder-nosed MGM management. Strickling was not a despot, he was cool and clear-headed and recognized the parts played by everyone in the MGM stable. When Marie Dressler was dying in 1934, he kept up a steady stream of stories about her upcoming projects, which boosted her spirits, and she was sufficiently touched by the gesture to will her Oscar to him.

So convincing were his stories that often the stars themselves believed the hokum. In her autobiography, Myrna Loy wrote of a day on the set of *Test Pilot*. She was supposed to be trapped in a burning plane and Clark Gable was to rescue her: 'Supposedly, the controlled fire went wrong at this point, but Clark kept coming and yanked me out as the plane burst into flames. Ten seconds later, according to news reports, I might have burned to death. That incident received enormous coverage, but it could have been publicity . . . I don't recall feeling extreme heat or anything. I can't honestly say if Clark really saved me or not.'

Child star Elizabeth Taylor was seldom subjected to reality outside the MGM lot. According to Neal Gabler, 'The studio arranged everything from her first dates to her first wedding, so that the fiction on screen seamlessly extended into her life.' Taylor reflected, 'I liked playing the role of a young woman in love.' Gabler suggests this lack of contact with reality may be the reason for her dramatic personal life as well. She learned the lessons well. 'I am my own commodity,' she has said.

It is hard to ascertain what Strickling truly thought of the moral turpitude surrounding him, which he either covered up or distracted the public's attention away from, since he went to his grave without giving more than hints of his true feelings. Even his expression of surprise at Louis Mayer's hounding of John Gilbert was carefully couched in diplomatic language. He was a professional through and through – if you'd cut him in half, it wouldn't have been surprising to find MGM written all the way through him like a stick of rock. Nothing was given away. Strickling knew only too well that if he were to open his mouth without thinking the artifice on which MGM was built would have come tumbling down around his ears, taking the power and stability he had built up with it.

According to E. J. Fleming, English-born actor Lionel Atwill, best known for his villainous turns in Universal horror films, was renowned for throwing orgiastic invitation-only parties where the guests swiftly removed all their clothes after a formal dinner. The guest list regularly included Clark Gable, Joan Crawford, Marlene Dietrich and many more – even Mannix was reputed to have attended. Partners were assigned by Atwill according to sexual preference and he'd then go around the house in a voyeuristic frenzy. The Christmas 1940 party featured a selection of underage girls, however, and one, a sixteen-year-old runaway named Sylvia, became pregnant and took the matter to the police. Given that the age of consent in California at the time was eighteen, this was a matter of statutory rape and Atwill was held responsible. Atwill was found innocent at the trial in 1941, though he was convicted of perjury in October 1942 after admitting he had lied. It took all of Strickling's powers to persuade the authorities not to investigate his parties after that, and Sylvia was sent home with a wad of cash in her pocket.

Around this time, Spencer Tracy had begun an affair with Ingrid Bergman which was causing considerable ructions as he'd stolen her away from his friend Victor Fleming. The affair was nipped in the bud by Mannix after Bergman's husband approached Louis B. Mayer. Mannix threatened to fire Tracy if he didn't comply, while Strickling told the press that Tracy had been 'mentoring' Bergman and even arranged a hokey photo opportunity of the two sharing an ice cream to back up the story. After this Tracy started what was to become a thirty-year affair with Katharine Hepburn at the expense of his relationship with his wife and deaf son. Strickling took great pains to cover up the affair. He had two stars to protect, both troublesome – Tracy because of his drinking and womanizing, Hepburn because of her left-wing (by American standards) political stance and spiky demeanour. But Strickling also took care of Tracy's wife, even accompanying her to his funeral. This was after Strickling's tenure at MGM had ended and was surely as much about friendship as protecting the company's image.

Lana Turner cropped up in yet another imbroglio during the filming of *Johnny Eager* in 1941, when she set her sights, unsurprisingly, on her co-star Robert Taylor. What was a little more surprising is that he seems to have reciprocated, given that he was reputedly a bisexual man in a lavender marriage to Barbara Stanwyck, who bullied him. At this point, Turner seems to have lost interest, but

Stanwyck lost her composure and tried to kill herself by slitting her wrists. Taylor found her and got her to the hospital, but not before he had called in Strickling, who told the press that she had suffered cuts while trying to shut a stubborn window that had broken.

The aftermath of the Taylor affair barely put a crimp in Turner's stride and she was soon linked to another married co-star, Clark Gable. The womanizing Clark Gable had been tamed – slightly – by marriage to Carole Lombard in March 1939. His divorce from Ria Langham was precipitated by an affair with Loretta Young, who gave birth to a child as a consequence, though thanks to Strickling's careful ministrations her disappearance in her third trimester was put down to a long holiday. Soon afterwards, Gable met the smart-talking, much-loved Lombard, and for once he married a woman he actually loved. The couple were a suppress agent's dream – hopelessly and clearly devoted to each other, they called one another Ma and Pa and lived blissfully in Lombard's house. This didn't stop Gable from sleeping around, though the urge appeared to have receded somewhat and his indiscretions certainly became more discreet.

The gossip columnists were usually kept at bay by the veneer of domestic bliss, but when Gable allegedly took up with Lana Turner while filming *Somewhere I'll Find You*, having worked together on *Honky Tonk* in 1941, his marriage to Lombard erupted into fighting. This wasn't helped by some rather gloating press releases from Strickling for *Honky Tonk*, praising the onscreen fireworks between two 'powerful sex symbols'. Consequently, Lombard took to visiting the set of *Somewhere I'll Find You*, and threatening to kick Turner and Gable 'in the ass', betraying the sort of feistiness Russell Birdwell so much admired in her. In the end she was barred from the set.

Louella Parsons, who was fond of Lombard – it's hard to find anyone who wasn't – was offended by the thought of Turner, a notorious star climber, sleeping with Gable. According to E. J. Fleming she called Strickling and ordered him to tell Lana to lay off. Strickling told her, 'Louella, this is the first time I've heard of it. Lana's just a kid. Let me check on it.' Turner ran off shortly afterwards with Artie Shaw, but Gable and Lombard never got a chance to make up. Lombard went off to a bond-rally fundraising trip for the American war effort while filming was underway and, overwhelmed with jealousy, cut short her trip to return and make sure that nothing was going on between Gable and Turner. On 16 January 1942 she boarded a flight home, alerting Strickling, who got the press out in force to meet her plane and escort her back to her husband. The plane never made it, straying seven miles off course and crashing into a mountain.

One of Strickling's assistants was told about the accident and called Strickling and Mannix. A plane was chartered to fly to the crash site near Las Vegas, where, so the story goes, one of Lombard's earrings was found and given to Gable. Gable was inconsolable, bordering on suicidal, and decided that the only way to mask his grief was to join the war effort and fight in Europe.

Despite being distraught for his friend's loss, Strickling had no qualms about exploiting Gable's war career to boost MGM's publicity machine. Although Strickling led a crisis-based professional life, his most difficult moments were likely those following the death of Carole Lombard, particularly as one of his best press agents, Otto Winkler, also died in the crash. For years Strickling apparently felt guilty, thinking it should have been him on that plane.

Gable came back from war a hero but he remained an unhappy man who turned more and more to drink. One night he was involved in a one-car accident on Sunset Boulevard. One version suggests that he killed a woman while another states that he killed a tree. Whatever the truth of it, thanks to Strickling, Gable was hustled off to a private hospital and it never made the papers. Covering up such incidents is what Stricking was paid to do, but his relationship with Gable shows that he genuinely cared about many of the stars whose lives he stage-managed. He resumed his friendship with Gable, and the two men would often speak of Lombard, whose death marked a downturn in the star's career from which he never fully recovered.

Twenty-Five

ROGERS & COWAN: THE EVOLVING LANGUAGE OF SHOWBIZ

With the formation of Rogers & Cowan in 1945, the industry began to change very swiftly. Between them, Rogers and Cowan got all the gossip columnists onside, with the exception of Hedda Hopper, who fell out with them spectacularly over a perceived insult in 1946. Rogers had assiduously built a relationship with Hopper in the early days, but it fell victim to her rivalry with Louella Parsons. Parsons broke the story that Joan Crawford was to divorce Phillip Terry, scooping Hopper. Crawford was, at that time, a client of Rogers', and Hopper assumed that he had tipped her off. It was, in fact, one of Parsons' assistants, Ruth Waterbury, who was a close friend of Crawford's, but Rogers protected his client and lost the company's relationship with Hopper.

Hopper aside, Rogers and Cowan worked hard at maintaining a good relationship with Parsons and Sheila Graham. 'One of our clients was opening in a play at the Biltmore Theatre in downtown Los Angeles,' Rogers remembered. 'A kind word from Louella Parsons would move mountains. Warren and I invited her to go to dinner with us and then to the theatre opening afterwards. She accepted and at dinner we all had a few drinks. Shortly after the curtain went up, I heard a strange noise close to me in the hushed theatre. Roz was on my right, Louella on my left and Warren on her left. I looked over and there were Louella and Warren, both fast asleep – and snoring! I reached across Louella and poked Warren. He opened his eyes, became aware of what had happened and gently awakened Queen Louella. The same thing happened three times during the course of the evening. After the curtain went down on the last act, we all went backstage. Louella embraced our beaming client and cooed, "Darling you were just wonderful. You gave a superb performance." Two days later [she] ran two paragraphs in her column in which she extolled the performance of our client in glowing terms, even though she had slept through a good deal of it. Why was she so kind? She liked Warren and she liked me. She had had a pleasant evening. She neither liked nor disliked our client. She was not a theatre reviewer. Her integrity could not be questioned. It was just a kind gesture.'

A kind gesture from Louella Parsons as a favour to a pair of PR agents? Maynard Nottage would have spat with envy at the possibility if he'd known about it, but his career had been over for fifteen years by this point and the industry that was built on the bones of his and Reichenbach's work was changing beyond recognition.

Rogers also took Sheilah Graham out for regular dinners; she was third in the pecking order of gossip queens and would use his connections at swanky restaurants mercilessly in order to network, table-hopping back and forth between Bogart, Lana Turner and whoever else was eating out that night, yet always returning to Rogers for his news. 'What did I get out of all this?' he wrote. 'I had the number three columnist 100 per cent on my side and in those days that counted for a lot.' Graham's column was widely syndicated and 'it was the rare Rogers & Cowan client who didn't make [her] column'.

To have these columnists onside made an enormous difference, and it helped particularly with the Oscar campaign that Rogers & Cowan cooked up for Joan Crawford's Oscar nomination for *Mildred Pierce*, which was released in 1945. Rogers and Jerry Wald, producer of *Mildred Pierce* and a former flack and gossip columnist, planted a story with Hedda Hopper – prior to her feud with Rogers & Cowan – that Crawford's performance, which was barely in the can, was already attracting talk of an Oscar nomination. Wald insisted that Rogers call Hopper and tell her he'd been raving about Crawford's performance and was insistent that it was worthy of an Academy nomination. Rogers claims to have been sceptical, as was Hopper, but the story ran anyway. Crawford was similarly sceptical, but Rogers fired off on a tangent that became the basis for every film's and star's Oscar campaign to follow.

He argued that the Oscars were little more than a popularity contest, that he was certain he could get other columnists to join in now that Hopper had nailed Rogers' colours to the mast in her column and that word of mouth would make Crawford a dead certainty. 'I'm confident that people in our business can be influenced by what they read and what they hear,' he told her. 'Word of mouth is just as important as the printed word. You have a tremendous advantage. You have cultivated the press all these years and they love you. They are all indignant about the way you were treated at MGM, and they are already caught up with the idea that you are going to be a bigger star here at Warner Brothers than you ever were before.'

Crawford's immediate concern was that if it was discovered her press agent had been plugging her for an award, she would be a laughing stock. Rogers insisted that it wouldn't get out because everyone knew the studio believed in her and would be backing her in a campaign for *Mildred Pierce*. She asked if he was going to work with the studio, and he said he wasn't as that would guarantee the story blew up in her face. 'I want everyone here at the studio to think that the publicity is spontaneous, not instigated by me,' he said, 'and I want to generate enough enthusiasm for you right here so that you will pick up the majority of the Warner votes.'

Crawford didn't believe it would work, but she gave him the go-ahead and Rogers went into overdrive, placing careful stories in the press, who reacted as he'd hoped. Crawford's career may have been in the doldrums the year before, but the press still loved her. This novel whispering campaign took on such an intensity that even the producer, Hal Wallis, was taken in by it and started talking about casting Crawford in his next film. He asked Wald if it were true that she was that good. Wald, inwardly gloating, said it was true and asked Wallis where he'd heard it. Wallis wasn't sure – proof positive that Rogers' whispering campaign was a success; it was the 1940s equivalent of a viral campaign that spread without anyone ever knowing the source.

The campaign lasted six months and Warner Brothers suddenly found themselves in the happy position of having a film on their hands that seemed much more important than they had first suspected; they were so cheered by this that they started advertising it much earlier than normal. The film opened to huge audiences and excellent reviews, both for the film in general and Crawford in particular. Warner Brothers, delighted to have got one over on MGM and Louis Mayer, who had labelled Crawford box-office poison, finally went all out with their own Oscar campaign, which Rogers backed up with continued word-of-mouth pressure.

The Oscar voting system has remained pretty much unchanged since 1936, being a form of proportional representation. Each voter is given a ballot that asks them for their top five choices in the relevant categories; the ballots are then sorted by the first choice and further refined over a series of counts until the winners are announced. Joan Crawford, thanks to a stellar performance, and Rogers' equally stellar campaign to resuscitate her image, won the Best Actress Oscar in 1945, the only one of her career.

Rogers and Cowan, unlike Nottage, didn't want to live their lives like the stars; they wanted to live their lives surrounded by the stars, making money from and for them – the two being inextricably linked, even at the worst of times. They lived a life of keeping up with the Joneses, only on a grand scale. It was an extreme version of the American Dream, aspirational and humane in the way a Frank Capra movie tended to be, freed from the early days of Hollywood and its old-world decadence.

Rogers & Cowan was the public relations face of Hollywood from the late 1940s onwards – safe hands who rarely stepped over the bounds of decency – but this was a time when the perception of what was decent was shifting; the Hays Code was disintegrating under the sustained pressure of public interest in racier films that represented life more accurately than the code's restrictions allowed and a new threat to what Hollywood could and couldn't do was rearing its head. The Hays Code was becoming more and more of an irrelevance as the moral spectrum shifted after the Second World War and politicians began fixing their sights on communism in general and its influence on the movie industry in particular instead. The House Un-American Activities Committee was putting the industry under a spotlight more intense than any it had been under since the days of Fatty Arbuckle and Charlie Chaplin.

In 1947 the committee held a series of hearings to discover the extent of alleged communist propaganda and influence in Hollywood. Forty-three professionals, many of them screenwriters and directors known to have had links with the American Communist Party, were called to give evidence in front of the House Un-American Activities Committee. Ten refused, and after conviction on contempt of Congress charges, the 'Hollywood Ten' were blacklisted by the industry. The process snowballed in the years that followed, and more than 300 people, from directors to radio commentators, actors to screenwriters, were boycotted by the studios before the process came to a halt. Charlie Chaplin ended up leaving the USA to find work, while others wrote under pseudonyms or the names of colleagues. Only about 10 per cent succeeded in rebuilding careers within the entertainment industry.

'It was a time when Hollywood had become increasingly apprehensive about the political pressures that were being put on movie creators,' wrote Rogers. 'Washington . . . was directing its attention to Communist influences in the motion picture industry. The time had come to fight back, and although I was concerned about being tainted with the Red brush, I volunteered my services [to the Committee for the First Amendment].'

The Committee for the First Amendment was founded in 1947 by directors John Huston, William Wyler and the writer/director Philip Dunne. Their ethos was simple; it was the constitutional right of the movie industry to be allowed freedom of expression and, as Rogers wrote in his press release, 'to set arbitrary standards of Americanism is in itself disloyal to both the spirit and the letter of the constitution'. Rogers was invited to join because he was 'politically sympathetic' and because they knew they'd need good PR to counter the waves of hysteria running through society about Reds under the bed, not to mention lurking in the studios of Hollywood. He and a great number of other sympathetic Hollywood faces confronted the House Un-American Activities Committee and created a wave of favourable opinion. Humphrey Bogart, Gene Kelly and Danny Kaye were among those who attended, but Rogers' coup was to persuade them to let the less-volatile voices speak – the stars were the bait to draw in the press, and they then deferred to the founders of the Committee for the First Amendment when the time came to speak.

It was a triumph of public-minded publicity – conducted for no fee – and a long-term strategy that paid off very well for Rogers & Cowan when the witch-hunts finally ceased in the late 1950s. In the short term, as Rogers wryly notes, it would cause enmity. 'I felt that I had to walk away from the warm fire of security', he wrote, 'and take sides in a cold war.'

That cold war broke out again in the early 1950s when Rogers put his neck on the line for the writer and producer of *High Noon* Carl Foreman. Foreman was just finishing *High Noon* in May 1951 when he was served a subpoena to appear before McCarthy's House Un-American Activities Committee in the second wave of investigations, which gave rise to Arthur Miller's play *The Crucible*, ostensibly about the Salem Witch Trials but also a strong commentary on the paranoia flooding Hollywood at the time. Foreman refused to cooperate and was blacklisted.

Determined to fight back, he contacted Rogers & Cowan and asked them to write him a press release. He told them he was being bought out of the company he had worked with and wanted to put his side of the story and not allow his former partner, Stanley Kramer, to 'double cross him again'. Rogers put out a press release stating as much, and it was followed shortly after by a request from Foreman to announce that he was setting up in business with Gary Cooper, *High Noon*'s star. This was big news as Cooper was notoriously ultra-conservative and had previously stood before the House Un-American Activities Committee as a friendly witness, although in such

Louella Parsons made her career as the pre-eminent Hollywood gossip journalist work by ensuring that she kept the stars close and grateful. Here, she has persuaded Cary Grant – who had much to hide from gossips, given his homosexuality – to buy her lunch in 1945. (Bettmann/Corbis)

Another example of Louella Parsons' influence. Frank and Nancy Sinatra, Howard Strickling and Greer Garson chat at a testimonial dinner for the queen of Hollywood gossip in 1948. (*Time & Life* Pictures/Getty Images)

To counter the furore over Marilyn Monroe's early nude photoshoot, Harry Brand, who ran 20th Century Fox's publicity department, instructed his team to come up with a neat solution. They decided that she 'would even look good in a potato sack' and this photograph, from 1952, is the evidence. (Bettmann/Corbis)

Betty Grable's legs, insured for $1 million and seen to best effect in this classic pin-up shot, not only launched a million soldiers' fantasies but also a vast number of copycat publicity stunts by everyone from Russell Birdwell to Jay Bernstein. (Getty Images)

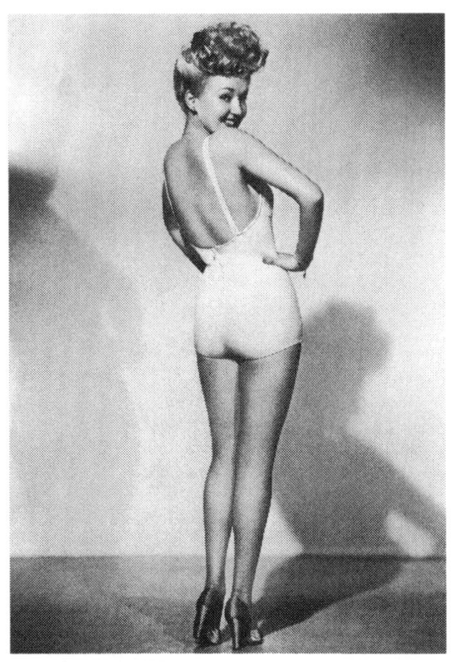

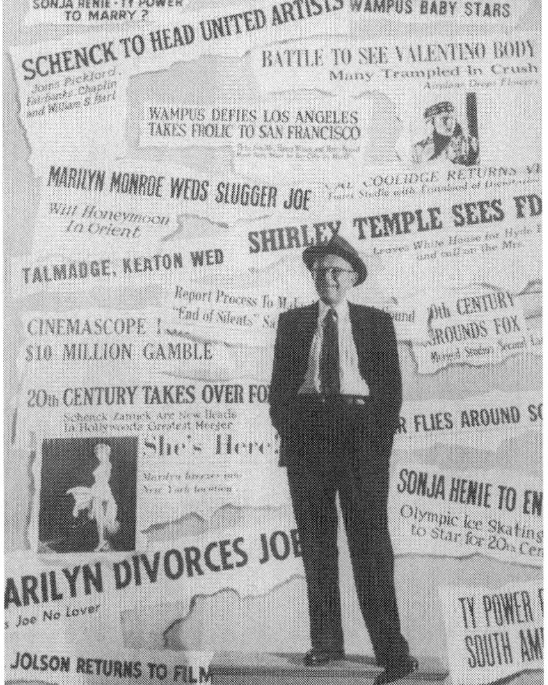

20th Century Fox's publicity supremo Harry Brand in 1956, backed by some of his biggest headlines. (*Time & Life* Pictures/Getty Images)

Jim Moran's best-known stunt. To promote the movie version of *The Egg and I*, he sat on an ostrich egg for nearly twenty days, hatched the egg and adopted the chick. Even the ostriches look impressed. (*Time & Life* Pictures/Getty Images)

Even Jim Moran's failed stunts made headlines. To promote a breakfast food, Moran decided that he would fly midgets on giant kites over Central Park in New York. He was prevented from doing so by police concerned that falling midgets might injure a ball-player in the park – a case of skewed priorities if ever there was one. (*Park East* magazine)

Left Uberagent Freddie Fields in his early days as Vice President of the Music Corporation of America, with his new bride, singer Polly Bergen, in 1956. (Bettmann/Corbis); *Below* The client who made Henry Rogers' name. He met Rita Hayworth and her husband at a poker game and she, eager to get a break, hired him, also eager to get a break, to manage her publicity. It paid off in spades for them both. (Underwood & Underwood/Corbis)

Below Howard Strickling's duties went far beyond that of mere publicist. Here, he escorts Spencer Tracy's widow from the star's funeral in 1967. Although the studio era had been dead for a decade or more and Strickling was retired, he still came out to help protect the good name of MGM's stars and keep the peace between Tracy's widow, the press and Tracy's longtime mistress Katharine Hepburn. (Bettmann/ Corbis)

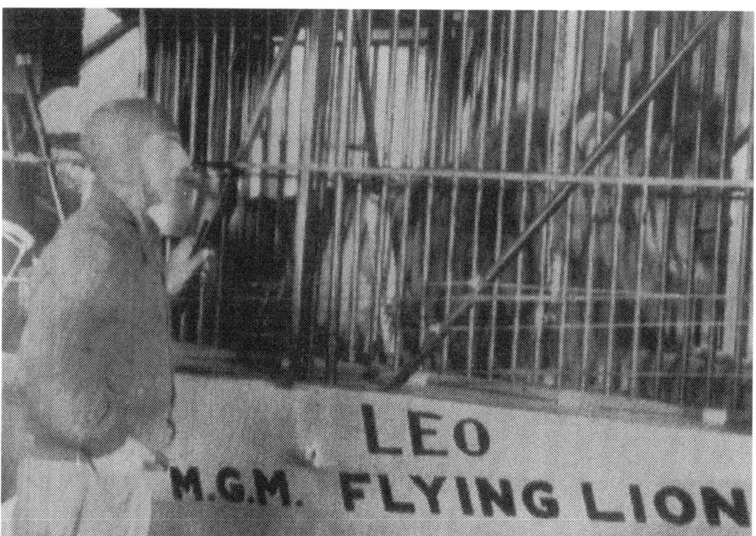

One of Pete Smith's early stunts was to fly Leo the MGM Lion around the country for publicity purposes. Here, the pilot is preparing his feline passenger for flight. It is not known if this is the flight that crashed. (The Academy of Motion Picture Arts and Sciences)

The MGM exploitation department: Frank Whitbeck, Si Scadler, Andy Hervey, and some of the unit reporters, publicists and photographers – the men in charge of polishing the final product. (The Academy of Motion Picture Arts and Sciences)

These screaming girls at a Frank Sinatra concert in 1944 were set off like dominos by a few girls, who had been paid and trained to scream by Sinatra's publicist George Evans. (Bettmann/Corbis)

Marty Weiser's most infamous stunt – a drive-in premiere of Mel Brooks' *Blazing Saddles* for people on horseback only. (Warner Brothers)

Maverick modern publicist Jay Bernstein, escorting his biggest star, Farah Fawcett, away from her stint of jury service in Beverly Hills in 2005, a year before his death. (Getty Images)

Pat Kingsley learned the art of publicity at Rogers & Cowan in the early 1960s and went on to become one of the most powerful publicists of modern Hollywood. Here she keeps a careful watch on her client Tom Cruise and his then-girlfriend Penelope Cruz at the premiere of *The Last Samurai*. (WireImage)

Bryan Lourd, Stan Rosenfield and one of his biggest clients, George Clooney, at the 78th Annual Academy Awards in 2006. (WireImage)

a vague and even-handedly good-natured fashion that he helped no one and had no one blacklisted. Apparently Foreman had impressed him when they made *High Noon* and Cooper felt the committee had overstepped the mark. Rogers offered to take a role in Foreman's company in lieu of fees: 'What's good enough for Gary Cooper is good enough for me,' he said. Foreman was cautious, saying it was a risk, but Rogers insisted.

Anti-communist hysteria was now at fever pitch, however, and conservative members of the Hollywood community were well organized. Hedda Hopper, who had regularly offered up names to be considered by the committee in the press, dropped her long-standing silent hostilities with Rogers and escalated to open warfare, insisting that she would have him driven from the business. Rogers' mother-in-law received calls from friends saying they didn't realize that Henry was a commie; John Wayne called to warn him off and journalist Jimmie Fidler threatened to expose him as a 'commie sympathizer'. Then Carl Foreman called and said that Gary Cooper had been forced to withdraw his name from the company, despite his 'high regard' for the filmmaker, leaving sights firmly set on Rogers & Cowan. John Wayne rounded up the Motion Picture Alliance for the Preservation of American Ideals and they bore down on Rogers & Cowan with all the weight they could muster, trying to bring down the business. In the end it was Foreman who stopped it; he met with Wayne and asked that the heat be taken off Rogers & Cowan and directed solely at him.

'There are times when personal considerations outweigh sound business judgements,' wrote Rogers, although he admitted that he too, like Gary Cooper, would have backed out if the pressure had become too great. But this, nonetheless, was another marked change in the publicity industry; conscience, when it mattered, outweighed money, and although Carl Foreman spared Rogers the really tough decisions by taking the fight away from his company, the stand he took was more than had been done before. Indeed, some publicists had been actively involved in tipping off the committee. Rogers & Cowan made the publicity industry respectable. Where before it had been anarchic or simply money-oriented, they smoothed the chaos into a sleek business model and allowed room for conscience to breathe.

Despite Rogers' insistence that he and Warren Cowan were 'showmen', they weren't. They were the spiritual grandchildren of showmen, grown up in a business that had polished away the last traces of the carnival. They had few of the latitudes that the barkers at circuses had had and they had insinuated themselves into the suited-and-booted business world with aplomb, winning friends and influencing people. It is ironic that, in the wake of Carl Foreman's blacklisting and Henry Rogers' involvement with him, the film that won the Oscar in 1952 was *The Greatest Show on Earth*, a lavish but empty spectacle movie from Cecil B. DeMille based in the Barnum and Bailey circus. It has been widely panned as one of the worst ever Oscar winners, and given that its competition was *High Noon* and *Singin' in the Rain*, it's not surprising. It would be intriguing to know what Barnum, the spiritual founder of PR and the fame factory it engendered, would have made of Rogers & Cowan's quiet and careful manoeuvring, of Joseph McCarthy and of the film *The Greatest Show on Earth*. In all cases, it's easy to suspect that he would have called for more elephants.

Rogers & Cowan still spoke the language of showmanship, but that language had been evolving continually since MGM opened its doors in the mid 1920s. By the mid 1950s television altered the vocabulary of showbusiness entirely, and Rogers & Cowan were perfectly adapted to speak it and threw themselves into it with fervour.

Twenty-Six

TO TELEVISION . . . AND BEYOND!

By 1952, Rogers & Cowan was the biggest fish in the small pond of the Hollywood publicity industry, and the movie industry was changing around them rapidly. In 1948, the outcome of the Hollywood Antitrust Case dealt a crippling blow to the studios and the way they operated. The movie industry had been created by men who owned theatres as a way of creating content to draw in audiences, and as these businesses had coalesced into the huge studios that ruled the Golden Age of Hollywood, they had retained those theatres since it was convenient to have places where the studios' films were guaranteed to be shown. The ruling of the Antitrust Case prevented the studios from holding a monopoly on the production and distribution of their films, opening up the industry to independent producers, distributors and theatres. The vast profits that *Gone With the Wind* made were a thing of the past and it became a scrap to get financial backing and attention. Added to that, ticket sales declined, especially with the arrival of television, which by the end of the 1950s was rapidly replacing cinema as the people's entertainment medium of choice.

As the studios faltered and failed, Rogers & Cowan picked up the dissatisfied and disillusioned stars who became fed up with being squeezed into the studio brand and instead modelled them into brands in their own right, independent of the needs of the money makers at MGM, Warner Brothers and 20th Century Fox. The company's independent spirit was exemplified by Rogers' willingness to stand against the McCarthy witch hunts and his and Warren Cowan's eagerness to explore new avenues for the company. They had spotted the zeitgeist and the stars were eager to join them.

Television was the obvious furrow to plough. Just as radio and the wire service had destroyed the ability of Reichenbach, Nottage and their peers to put across their anarchic stunts to a willing audience in the early 1920s, engendering the rise of the studio system, so TV and the Hollywood Antitrust Case crippled and consumed the studio system's methods, thus destroying the carefully aggregated protectionist PR the studios had once been able to afford. There was, therefore, a distinct gap in the market that nobody was filling in the early 1950s.

'If my experiences with Rita Hayworth from 1939 to 1942 had taught me that you could get lucky with your timing in launching a successful public relations campaign,' wrote Rogers, 'by the early 1950s I realized that we had to stay ahead of the rapidly changing climate of the public relations business if we were to stay on top of it. David Susskind once said to me, "In the business you are in, Henry, you better keep running faster and faster because your competitors will always be barking at your heels."

'I was determined that Rogers & Cowan would continue to grow and that television would be the next mountain to climb. We began to plan a strategy for breaking in. We knew we could do it: after all, in catching the attention of the public, a television show struck us as being no different than a movie, and we were considered experts at conducting publicity campaigns for motion pictures.'

Successful television shows in the 1950s were all sponsored by a single advertiser whose names were built into the show's title: the Colgate Comedy Hour, the Philco Playhouse and the Bell Telephone Hour being prime examples. It was common knowledge that a successful show increased sales in the sponsor's product and it was a formula that had been well developed throughout the 1930s and 40s on radio shows and had transferred seamlessly to television, improving on the formula in as much as the audience could see the product in question. Radio shows had employed publicity companies to attract audiences, but since radio was New York-based, few of the big Hollywood companies had become involved, as they were too busy building up a movie-based clientele.

'We were convinced that publicity campaigns on the shows, conceived and executed by us, could definitely influence television-viewing habits,' wrote Rogers. 'We were convinced that a publicity blitzkrieg could get audiences to tune in to a particular television program. Here was our great opportunity. We would try and convince advertisers, Philco, Bell, Ford etc., that if they engaged us to conduct publicity campaigns on the shows they sponsored, they could get higher ratings, and consequently enjoy increased sales for their products.'

Setting Warren Cowan the task of taking care of the Hollywood part of the business, Rogers set his sights on TV and began researching the best ways to break in to the new market. The first step was to open an office in New York, which was where the right people were. Then Rogers would need to approach the advertising agencies to get to the big sponsors of TV shows because 'the advertising agencies recommended to their clients that they buy certain television programs. They then supervised the production of those programs, and prepared the commercial messages that appeared intermittently throughout the program. Most of them did not have publicity or public relations departments. They felt that publicity . . . was the responsibility of the network . . . The agencies were specialists in advertising, not in show business publicity.'

The way of reaching the advertising agenies turned out to be blindingly obvious – Rogers simply followed the same path he had used to get an interview with Claudette Colbert: he talked to the Hollywood agents who knew what Rogers & Cowan were capable of, and asked who they recommended he approach. The Hollywood agencies, such as William Morris and the Music Corporation of America, were responsible for selling show formats and their stars to networks such as NBC and CBS, but sometimes they would bypass the networks and go straight to the advertising agencies to sell a show which they had developed for the stars they represented.

Rogers approached George Gruskin, a friend at the William Morris

Agency, and pitched the idea. Gruskin was intrigued and told him it was a 'wide-open field for you' and that he was surprised no one had thought of it before. He put Rogers in touch with Terry Clyne, head of television for the Milton Biow Agency, whose main client was Procter & Gamble, then the biggest advertiser in television, saying, 'You might as well start right at the top.'

There was, of course, nowhere else that Rogers would rather have started, his ambitions being what they were, especially given Rogers & Cowan's pre-eminence in the Hollywood publicity industry. He met with Clyne and expounded his theory for the future of television. '[I] told him my theory that television was show business, that show business had long recognized the advantages of aggressive publicity campaigns, and that I was convinced that if we could sell the television advertiser on the idea of a publicity campaign, conducted by show business experts, it would make a huge impact: a televison program backed up by a Rogers & Cowan creative publicity campaign had the opportunity to attract a larger audience than a television program which depended solely on the routine publicity which emanated from the network press information departments or ad agency publicity departments.'

Clyne was intrigued and set up a meeting with Bill Craig, second in command of television advertising at Procter & Gamble. Craig was also interested in the proposal and invited Rogers to meet his boss, Gail Smith. For this meeting, Rogers did his homework assiduously and was able to suggest that if they took up the model of publicity he proposed, they would not only increase the number of viewers but lessen the cost of reaching those viewers: 'the savings could be substantial – so substantial in fact that they could purchase additional advertising time for the same amount of dollars that they were spending now.'

It was hypothesis, of course, but Rogers' arguments were persuasive in a way that Nottage or Reichenbach could never have managed. Rogers took care of the pennies, while they had chased after dollar signs and glory. That's not to say that Rogers wasn't interested in the big pay or the glory, just that his approach was careful, measured and, ultimately, that much more successful. Successful enough for him to be invited back to prepare a full proposal, certainly, which went very well.

Procter & Gamble loved the proposal and agreed to it, but to Rogers' surprise – and obvious dismay – it was only the beginning. Television was a very different world from the movie industry, where if a studio or star accepted the publicity firm's proposal, that was that and the job was started. With TV in its early days, the advertiser may well love the idea, but all that meant was that they were prepared to let the publicity agency pitch it to their advertising agencies and the rounds of pitching started all over again. It was a bureaucratic headache of epic proportions and took up a great deal of Rogers' time, but with Warren Cowan on board, heading up the Hollywood division, he had the time to spare. He may have called the process 'madness', but said, 'I have no alternative. I must go along. I'm certainly not going to stop now.'

This determination paid off in spades. Despite a return of Rogers' stutter, he got the contract, got his foot in the door of television before any of his rivals and became instrumental in the changing nature of the publicity industry. Rogers' summation of this change is simple: 'Dog food and movie stars are much alike because they are both products in need of exposure.' It is this shift in perception that marks the change. In the early days of the star system, the stars were opalescent and godlike and had to do very little to be noticed and written about; a publicity agent need only come up with a glorious flight of fancy for it to be pounced upon and published. With the rise of rapid communications killing off the ability to lie so freely, that sheen was tarnished. The studio system arose to counter scandal and make money, and its PR model adapted to the changing speed of communication. MGM and other studios became brands that needed protection and the stars were bound in to that branding. Publicity, aside from the philosophical ramblings of Jim Moran, was as much about damage limitation as it was about promotion. With the arrival of TV and the slow disintegration of the studio system, the stars were let loose to fend for themselves. Given that so many people had bought in to the Hollywood dream of a fame factory, where you just had to be young, beautiful and/or charismatic to make a name for yourself, publicists were suddenly necessary to sort the wheat from the chaff.

Stars, and would-be stars, did all sorts of things to gain notice amongst their rivals and packaged themselves in as many new, shiny and exciting ways as possible. Not all were as cynical as this might make them sound: Danny Kaye became a goodwill ambassador for UNICEF, as did Audrey Hepburn (both were clients of Rogers & Cowan, whose charitable and philanthropic ventures were numerous). Cynical or not, such unselfish ventures gave them essential exposure. The publicity industry became a complicated ballet of negotiating TV space for what the TV shows wanted to discuss and who they wanted to discuss it with and what the clients wanted; a 'constant contest between us and the talent coordinators,' as Rogers put it.

Getting TV space for products was equally difficult. A producer would ask why the client didn't just buy advertising space, but the client 'hopes that his public relations firm can be creative enough to get coverage for the product within the editorial content of the show'. Such advertorials have become an essential component of daytime television; every fashion parade on *This Morning* or book club on *Richard & Judy* or *Oprah* can trace itself back to a PR agency pushing their client's products and, thanks to the more subliminal effect of a presenter talking about it, it can have a more profound impact on the consumer psyche, even now, when the routines and machinations are so well known.

All this can be traced back to the pioneering work of Rogers & Cowan who, to get Jockey International's jogging clothes well and truly plugged on *The Dinah Shore Show* in 1978 – and, importantly, give the producers a cheaper show – 'put together a segment for the show which would include a jogging expert and a number of important personalities who would be willing to jog', which meant that the programme would then also run a fashion show of Jockey's jogging wares and 'mention would be made a number of times that the clothes being shown were designed and manufactured by Jockey'.

Joanne Woodward was brought in. She was being mentioned in the press in relation to the Emmys for a TV film about a marathon runner and she was also a Rogers & Cowan client; it was a perfect match. Other star clients from the company's books were brought in, as was James Fixx, author of *The Complete Book of Running*, as a credible expert. 'When it was all over,' wrote Rogers, 'everyone's needs had been satisfied. Stars had been promoted, Jockey's clothing had been gushed over, Jim Fixx was fixed in America's consciousness as a fitness expert, the show producers had more time on their hands to research other stories for the show and Rogers & Cowan had woven together all aspects of their business in one successful story.'

They also proved, on Johnny Carson's *Tonight Show* in the early 1970s, that the American Telephone and Telegraph Company was an equal opportunities employer by getting a woman who climbed telegraph poles to fix the lines to appear on the show. She was, of course, young, pretty and eloquent and she taught Carson how to climb a telegraph pole. Carson was primed to mug to the camera as if to say, 'Why is this happening to me,' and to try and refuse to climb the pole, which had been set up in-studio, while the AT&T woman calmly told him to stop being a coward and get on with it, eventually resorting to pushing him up the pole. Carson then interviewed her and closed with the killer question the whole show had been leading up to, 'And how does your salary compare with your male counterparts?' It was, she said, exactly the same, just as Rogers & Cowan had hoped she would.

'Our print campaign, I felt, was not nearly so effective,' wrote Rogers. 'You can read an article in the newspaper that says AT&T is an Equal Opportunities Employer, but it will never make the same impact on you as will the sight of a pretty young girl talking to Johnny Carson on *The Tonight Show*.'

Product publicity wasn't just restricted to placing stories on TV shows, however; like Russell Birdwell, Rogers & Cowan pushed from all angles, scouring the papers for possible ideas. Perhaps the best example was their plan to promote Hidden Treasures bras, which came about after reading that a Miami telephone company had complained about female employees stealing $10 rolls of quarters by stuffing them in their bras. Rogers & Cowan employed a well-endowed aspiring actress to go to Miami and, with attendant press snapping away, explain to the boss of the telephone company how, if he were to give all of his female employees a Hidden Treasures bra, his problems would be solved. She would give a display of how well fitting and snug the bra was in public by attempting to insert a $10 roll of quarters into the one she was wearing. It all went according to plan – the press loved the idea, the modesty of the actress was assured and Hidden Treasures manufacturers Peter Pan were delighted. Even the boss of the telephone company, told that a representative of the company was coming to talk to him, thought it might be a good idea . . . until the day of the stunt, that is, when he saw the press filling the lobby of his offices and hid himself away, refusing to speak to the curvaceous beauty. The assembled journalists were not about to be put off a story they liked, however, and the story ran across America anyway.

From the cottage industry of the early years to the slick operation of the studio system to Rogers & Cowan's multinational, multitasking outlook, the fame game has always run like a production line. The products, be they canned soup or pop stars, art or actors, are carefully processed. The only difference being that the actors and pop stars can be processed at a place of their choosing. The fame industry is a factory and, like all good businessmen, the managers keep a careful eye on the future. When asked who his favourite client was, Warren Cowan simply said, 'The next one!'

Twenty-Seven

THE FINAL FIX

Throughout the 1950s, while Rogers & Cowan were clawing their way to the top of the pile, MGM, the behemoth of the earlier epoch of PR, was spluttering asthmatically to a halt. Strickling and Mannix were still there in the background, doing what they did best, but there seemed to be less and less to fix in the 1950s, as many of the stars had left or were in the process of leaving and more austere times, financially speaking, led to a somewhat less hedonistic lifestyle. Strickling and Mannix now took care of the major stars only, and there was little left of the galactic ambitions that typified early MGM. On the whole, the publicity department publicized movies and little else was needed of them.

It wasn't just that the stars of MGM's heyday were wearing out or revealing their shimmering glamour to be little more than tinfoil and careful lighting, the founding fathers of MGM were also out of touch and soon to be out of work. Louis B. Mayer, tenacious to the last, survived for a time after much of his power was given over to Dore Schary in 1948. The two argued continually after Schary took up his post. Schary, who was responsible for taming the wilder excesses of MGM and for refusing percentages in films to stars – which made sure that Clark Gable quit the company, taking only his affair with Grace Kelly as a reminder of studio life – was the polar opposite of Mayer, who clung to the old ways of doing things, right down to the shouting matches, the bullying and the belief that nothing could or should change.

In 1951, Mayer, who rightly believed that Nick Schenck had brought in Schary to undermine him, finally forced Schenck to choose between them. Mayer was gone within the week. Nick Schenck may well have seen that MGM needed to progress and move onwards, beyond Louis Mayer at least, but he too clung on to the Golden Age maxim of 'more stars than there are in heaven' and resolutely failed to acknowledge the rise of television and the need to cut corners economically. This meant that he too was moved aside unceremoniously a couple of years later, to be replaced, in the typically cyclical, incestuous manner of Hollywood, by Arthur Loew, the son of Marcus Loew, whom Schenck had replaced in the late 1920s.

Nor were the stars immune from the chop; Schary was not a man to put up with the worst excesses of 1930s hangovers like Clark Gable, Spencer Tracy, Lana Turner and Judy Garland. By 1954, Spencer Tracy no longer had an MGM Tracy Squad to follow him around, and fell into a terminal decline, beginning in 1951, around the time his long-term mistress Katharine Hepburn was finding her feet again with films like *The African Queen*. MGM kept him propped up as long as they could, because he was a relentless hit at the box office, but by 1954 enough was nearly enough. Despite remaining married to his wife, Tracy had been seeing Hepburn for years. Then in 1954 he took up with Grace Kelly – as had many, many other men; she was the female equivalent of Clark Gable, sleeping with absolutely anyone who might further her career.

Hepburn was far from impressed with this dalliance and, after the death of Tracy's surrogate mother Constance Collier in 1955, she left him to grieve alone and took a trip to Australia. Tracy saw this as punishment for his affair and reacted in the only way he knew how, disappearing inside a bottle. His dependence on alcohol and Dexedrine had left him in a parlous physical state, and this bender left his career in a similar position. He was meant to be filming *Tribute to a Bad Man* on location, but instead he disappeared for eight days. The director, Robert Wise, who had spent three careful months building an elaborate set in the mountains for filming, called Howard Strickling. Strickling, knowing the only way to get to Tracy now, called

Hepburn in Australia and asked her to talk him back on to the set. Tracy returned, but came with a set of such unreasonable demands that Wise had to call MGM and ask them to get rid of Tracy after only four days of filming, which in reality amounted to two days, because Tracy would only work for half of each day. Strickling was despatched to mediate, but the meetings went so badly that he eventually fired Tracy from MGM in a hotel room in Colorado, twenty years after the actor had arrived at the studio, trouble following in his wake even then.

MGM also fired Judy Garland, who had come to the studio a chubby, cute child star and left it a neurotic wreck, thanks in no small part to the drug addiction Strickling and the studio encouraged, all in the name of keeping her perfect and pristine and star-like, when Garland, left to herself, would most likely have tended towards the matronly. The potent cocktail of pills Garland was taking, some designed to make her work and others to bring her down again when she needed to rest, had ironically destroyed her desire and ability to work at all, so MGM simply ditched her in the summer of 1950, aged twenty-eight. What they hadn't expected was a wave of public sympathy for Garland, nor that she would make an attempt on her life. After a dismal meeting with her ex-husband Vincente Minnelli and various advisors, Garland retreated to the bathroom and smashed a mirror. She then used one of the shards to slice at her neck before she was found by Minnelli and rushed to hospital. According to E. J. Fleming, Strickling tried to pass it off as a minor incident, drafting in Hedda Hopper to dismiss the neck wound as a minor scratch, but less biddable journalists unwilling to cave in to the studio's demands soon got hold of the story and filled the front pages with news that Garland had just survived a suicide attempt.

Garland remained secluded for the best part of a year and Mannix, aware that public opinion was very much on her side, postponed her removal from MGM's books for many months. By the time she recovered, the company that had made and broken her had excised her completely. In 1953, she made *A Star is Born* for Warner Brothers on the understanding that she would sing at Jack Warner's daughter's birthday. The movie flopped and she didn't work again until 1958. Like Tracy, she died in the late 1960s, hollowed out and destroyed by the fame factory.

Strickling and Mannix were also involved in glossing over Lana Turner's suicide attempt in 1952. Intriguingly, Strickling used the same story – that Turner had slipped in the shower and cut her arm on glass as she fell – that he had used for Barbara Stanwyck a decade earlier. It seems that as the studio system ran out of steam, so did his deluge of ingenious ideas. In 1958, Strickling also made sure that Turner got sympathetic press in the wake of the killing of her mobster lover, Johnny Stompanato, by her daughter, Cheryl Crane, after a raging argument in which Stompanato threatened to kill both of them after Turner attended the Academy Awards without him. This was despite the fact that Turner was no longer under contract to MGM and was indicative of the change in the air, and particularly of the power of television, which had proved to be a profitable market for old Hollywood films. In effect, MGM and Strickling were protecting the back catalogue that went with Turner.

At that time, Strickling and Mannix were in virtual retirement. The studio system was little more than a memory, independent publicists were moving into new territories and the stars had more power at their disposal. But there was one last fix to be done, and this time it directly affected the Fixers themselves.

The circumstances for this fix were a long time in the making. In 1951, Toni Mannix met George Reeves, a handsome man who'd had a run of bad luck with his career. He had appeared in *Gone With the Wind* as one of the Tarleton brothers, who courted Scarlett O'Hara in the opening scenes, but he had failed to capitalize on the film's success, despite his good looks and imposing physical presence, and had struggled throughout the 1940s. Toni Mannix, an ex-Ziegfield Folly dancer, had been engaged in an affair with Eddie Mannix since the 1930s and, after the death of his wife Bernice in a suspicious car crash in 1937, they lived together as man and wife, although there is no definite proof that they ever married. All the same, Toni was commonly referred to as Mrs Mannix. Eddie was in his late fifties in 1951, and in poor health, suffering from heart trouble. He also maintained a Japanese mistress. So Toni, taken with Reeves, used all the money and influence available to her – which was a great deal, thanks to her Mannix association – to win him, with Eddie's tacit approval.

In 1951, Reeves' luck began to change – not only was he seen around town on the arm of a rich, powerful and attractive woman, but he finally got a part, as Superman in the television serial *The Adventures of Superman*. Reeves is on record as thinking little of the *Superman* serial and films, but all the same, regular work was a boost for the actor. According to E. J. Fleming, there has been speculation that Mannix, at Toni's insistence, helped him get the part. Certainly Mannix approved of Toni and Reeves' 'affair' and went out with them and his Japanese mistress on double dates from a very early stage in the relationship, as well as welcoming Reeves in the house and attending mass with them. However, given that Reeves was six foot two inches tall and well built, it's just as likely that he got the job on his own merits. That said, Mannix's money bought Reeves a house shortly after his relationship with Toni began.

The easy-going, decidedly public approach of Toni and Reeves shocked many in Hollywood, who didn't know of Eddie Mannix's approval. Part of this was to do with Mannix preparing for his eventual death, which, given that his heart was thoroughly diseased, was likely to happen at any point. He wanted Toni to be well cared for, and Reeves seemed the man to do it.

By 1959, when Reeves and Toni had been together for over seven years, *Superman* was an international phenomenon and Reeves a huge star, albeit for that one iconic character. Reeves was typically irritated, as many actors are, by becoming typecast, but the show had started out on a shoestring and, against all expectations, especially those of its star, become an astonishingly massive success. When the show went national in 1953, Kellogg's paid well in excess of $1,000,000 to sponsor 100 episodes of the show, guaranteeing its appearance for another four years – a marker of just how sensible Rogers & Cowan had been in making overtures to television. Then suddenly, much to the surprise of many of his friends, George Reeves apparently committed suicide, just as *Superman* was about to be re-commissioned for a new series in the wake of an enormously successful five-year run.

What happened to Reeves was the final nail in the coffin for that era, hammered home by Howard Strickling, whose influence is palpable in the confused testimonials that surround Reeves' death. Despite the official pronouncement of suicide, it is still unclear what exactly happened to him.

The filming schedule for *Superman* was gruelling: Reeves' muscle-bound costume comprised of a number of weights stitched into the padding, amounting to about 15 extra pounds which he had to lug around all day; he was injured falling from the wire that allowed him to fly; the twenty-six episodes were filmed continually. He needed the physique of a gymnast to keep up with it. To begin with he was very trim, but the hard-drinking high lifestyle he and Toni led soon began to take its toll. He earned a lot of money – $55,000 a year plus merchandise royalties – but he was accustomed to the water-through-fingers approach to money that Toni could afford to take. All the while, he also tried to maintain a movie career, but with only limited success. Certainly, Reeves landed a part in *From Here to Eternity*, but a (most likely apocryphal) story suggests that his part was cut thanks to the preview audience yelling, 'It's Superman!' every time he appeared on screen. It may not be true, but it illustrates the way he had become indelibly associated with the Superman brand and become unable to establish *himself* as a brand, and it was to establish such freedoms for themselves that actors, in the wake of the studio system's disintegration, found their way to the doors of Rogers & Cowan. Reeves was not successful at establishing a career as a star without wearing underpants over his clothes, but he did find himself adept at directing – some of the best *Superman* episodes from the 1957 season were directed by him.

When Reeves and Toni Mannix first met, she had been a seductive, young-looking forty-six-year-old and he a handsome, trim thirty-five-year-old. According to E. J. Fleming she had wryly taken to calling him 'the boy' when they met, and the name stuck. But by 1958, the epithet seemed more desperate – Toni had become more matronly, and though she was still attractive, she was a shadow of the glamour goddess she had once been. Reeves, at forty-two, had fame, wealth and an itch to be taken seriously. What's more, when his mother met Toni it had gone disastrously wrong: Toni wore tight trousers and was excessively affectionate in front of Reeves' disapproving mother, who was dangling a million-dollar inheritance in front of Reeves, who was always desperate for money despite Toni's largesse. Sex, which the relationship had been founded on, was no longer much of a pleasure for him. Toni had assumed that she and Reeves would marry after Eddie Mannix's death, but Mannix – a tough old carnival bouncer to the last – had survived several heart attacks and showed no signs of going anywhere. So Reeves, 'boy' to the last, weighed down with boredom on all fronts, went off to New York on promotional duties and came back in love with Leonore Lemmon, a brash, nymphomaniac thirty-eight-year-old socialite and party girl. During his two-week visit they were rarely apart, and shortly after returning to Los Angeles, he announced they were engaged.

This came as rather a shock to his friends and Hollywood acquaintances, who had gradually come to accept his relationship with Toni Mannix. Reeves was an immensely likeable man, given to wanton acts of charity with his and Toni's money, so to do something this crass and wilful was out of character, but boredom can take people that way and encourage risks.

And a risk it most certainly was. Reeves would surely have heard rumours of Eddie Mannix's tough and sometimes sordid past, which had seen his first wife die in a suspicious car crash, numerous girlfriends beaten and a history of resolving problems as brutally and efficiently as possible. He would have seen first-hand the power of the studios at their height, given that he had started out in films in the late 1930s, at the very apex of the MGM dream factory and Mannix's power. Even though Reeves had never actually drawn a cheque from MGM, Mannix was well known within the industry. Someone must have told Reeves how things might turn out if he stepped out of line with Toni. Even in his late sixties, officially retired from MGM and weak of heart, Eddie Mannix was a force to be reckoned with, and even if he was content to see his wife have an affair with Reeves, he wasn't likely to stand by and see her hurt. In late 1958, the car Reeves was driving was nearly pushed off the road into a ravine by a truck, in a manner eerily similar to the way Bernice Mannix died years before. This came on top of an earlier instance, where his car had been sandwiched between two trucks and he had escaped only by braking hard. Added to that, a black Sedan attempted to run Reeves down outside the house Toni had bought him. It's difficult to imagine that these incidents were accidents, coming as they did so close together, and certainly Reeves, who wasn't working at the time, reacted by descending into a stiffer-than-usual round of drinking and partying, most likely worrying about Eddie Mannix's reputation.

Reeves was essentially stalked by Toni Mannix after he broke off the relationship; she was seen outside the house numerous times and she seemed to be aggrieved enough to do something in her own right. She also made numerous harassing phone calls, which she could easily deny to the police, because there is evidence that she got one of the house staff to make the calls thirty or forty times a day. Reeves complained to the police, which brought the problem into the public arena, something that was guaranteed to offend Eddie Mannix, that doyen of secrecy. Toni asked Strickling, by then retired, to mount a media campaign to help her get Reeves back, and pestered other friends to help as well. It also seems likely that she was behind the kidnapping of his dog – apparently it was a loyal beast and would not have left the seat of Reeves' car, where he had left it to nip into a shop, unless someone it knew well had enticed it away. A number of Toni's friends apparently heard a small dog barking when they phoned her, but she dismissed any questions, claiming it was a neighbour's animal making the noise.

It became increasingly clear that someone wanted Reeves dead. His new car had its brakes cut – it ploughed into a lamppost and he got away, miraculously, with only a few injuries, despite having been hurled through the windscreen.

On top of all this, or perhaps because of it, Reeves' relationship with Lemmon was fading fast – it was a whirl of parties that she instigated in the house that Toni Mannix was still paying the bills for, and though Reeves' friends had come regularly at first, they started to weary of the parties, which were all Lemmon knew how to do, and instead they became filled with strangers, something that unsettled Reeves no end. There is considerable confusion as to whether he intended to marry Lemmon at all. And then on 16 June 1959, he apparently put a bullet in his head while three guests and Lemmon sat drinking below.

The police were called by one of the guests, Bill Bliss, who neither Reeves nor Lemmon knew, at 1.30 a.m., and they arrived half an hour later to find an appalling scene in the bedroom. The police remarked that if this was a suicide, the bullet had taken a very odd trajectory and noted that the Luger was suspiciously clean. They also noted that although the five people in the house were drunk, they all told the same story – that around midnight, Carol Von Ronkle had turned up with Bill Bliss after Lemmon had come downstairs for a drink because she couldn't sleep. Apparently, while doing this, she turned on the porch light, which was the signal for a party at the house. It was then that Von Ronkle and Bliss turned up, waking Robert Condon, who was staying at the house. The four began drinking and Reeves, awoken and suffering a blinding headache, came downstairs and berated them. Lemmon apparently told him to apologize and go back upstairs, which he did, and as soon as he left the room, she allegedly suggested he was going to shoot himself. A rustling was heard, and she said that he was now getting the gun, then shots were fired and Bill Bliss was ordered upstairs to investigate. As revealed in *The Fixers*, all four said that he came back down the stairs shouting, 'My friend is dead! My friend is dead!' They also all asserted that he had killed himself because of the typecasting that had come about as a result of his Superman fame.

The police, not knowing that Bliss was virtually unknown to Reeves, took all of this at face value and interviewed the four together, rather than separately, despite the fact that they were all drunk. Even fingerprints weren't taken. The coroner was no better – only two photos were taken, of the bullet's entry and exit point, while the body was given only a cursory examination, the wounds were sewn shut and the body was washed without tests being made for traces of gunpowder on the hands.

Bearing in mind that Toni Mannix, despite not being so much as mentioned as a possible reason for Reeves' depression, was at the heart of Reeves' alleged suicide, it is impossible not to draw comparisons to another great cover-up, that of the murder of Paul Bern nearly thirty years earlier, which had been staged by Howard Strickling and Eddie Mannix. Unlike Bern's death, however, this story got out of hand, especially as numerous friends of Reeves contested the story Lemmon and the three houseguests had given. It didn't help that Reeves' will left everything to Toni Mannix, as was only right, given that she had paid for pretty much everything. Strickling quickly concocted a story stating that she and Reeves had worked together on various charities and that she intended to use the monies to further that work, but things were complicated by Lemmon, who was caught at the house by the agent Art Weissman stealing $4,000 worth of travellers cheques and washing the bloody sheets. Weissman had put the blame on Toni from the beginning. Fearful that Weissman would report her and implicate her in Reeves' murder, rumour of which was spreading rapidly in the wake of widespread disbelief, Lemmon ran to the papers and gave an interview denying that she had forecast Reeves' death.

Rumours that Reeves had been killed by a jealous woman spread in the wake of Lemmon's assertion in the same interview that she and Reeves had been 'harassed by the wife of a studio executive', and the mystery surrounding the alleged suicide deepened with every new revelation. Strickling's powers of control and persuasion were not as great as they had been without the full might of MGM behind him and he relied, successfully given the mystery that still surrounds the case, on old contacts and friends.

A second autopsy stated that there were no powder burns on Reeves' head and that the wound was likely to have been made by a shot fired from a small distance. The photos from the first autopsy disappeared shortly afterwards. Bruises on Reeves' body suggest there was a struggle beforehand, and his personal trainer stated that there had been no bruises on Reeves' body earlier that day. Reeves' mother,

Helen Bessolo, took Reeves' body to Chicago for a third, independent autopsy, but the body was too decomposed to reveal anything new by that time. Apparently the LA police gave one of the doctors a number to call if his findings differed in any way from previous autopsies. When the findings were inconclusive and the number was called, a voice simply said, 'That's good news.' It was apparently the private number for the LA chief of police.

Inconsistencies abounded; Reeves came downstairs on the night of his death at 12.30 a.m. Police were not called until 1.30 a.m. Lemmon suggests that Von Ronkle and Bliss arrived at midnight, but then says that she was very surprised to see Bliss on the doorstep, making no mention of Von Ronkle at all. The fact that she was having an affair with Robert Condon would suggest that she was upstairs with him, in bed. Bliss had never met Reeves, but he was sent upstairs to check on him after shots were fired and came back saying, 'My friend is dead.' Then there is the fact that they must have waited forty-five minutes before calling the police. On top of this, Reeves' friends refuted the suggestion that he was depressed – in fact he was keen to get back to the new season being planned – and although he was annoyed by the situation with Toni he wasn't downcast about it. Reeves had planned to go to the graduation of a friend's son; he had bought $4,000 worth of travellers cheques for a trip to Spain; he had signed on for a movie early in 1959 and he was excited about taking part in an exhibition boxing match – he was an ex-boxer – with Archie Moore. As regards typecasting, it is most likely that Reeves was disappointed, having wanted a film career as spectacular as Gable's, but the fame and money from *Superman* had its compensations.

It is possible that Reeves killed himself, but the more one looks at the affair, the more unlikely that seems. Helen Bessolo, Reeves' mother, brought in a detective agency and the lawyer Jerry Giesler, who had defended Lana Turner's daughter Cheryl Crane the year before. Giesler, a powerful man in Hollywood law, soon backed off, despite having told the press that there were some strange and 'phony' aspects to the case. This is a man who represented the notorious gangster Bugsy Siegel and handled scandals involving Errol Flynn and

Charlie Chaplin, yet he quit the case, telling Bessolo there were too many dangerous people involved. He knew Mannix and Strickling well.

If it wasn't suicide, it was either Leonore Lemmon or someone else on behalf of Eddie and/or Toni Mannix who killed him. Lemmon had a fiery temper and knew about guns. Eddie Mannix was certainly angry – the car accidents were quite possibly warnings – but if he'd wanted Reeves dead, his connections would have ensured it would happen much sooner. Toni was hysterical and had to be sedated and kept under lock and key after Reeves' death. All three could either have done it or had it done, and the truth will never likely be known. Regardless of who did it, one thing is certain; the only fingerprints that one can easily discern are those of Howard Strickling and Eddie Mannix, protecting as best they could, for the final time, the image of MGM, the dying embers of the studio system and the peace of Toni Mannix.

The press releases issued immediately following Reeves' death bear Strickling and Mannix's hallmarks, in that they echoed the Paul Bern case so spookily, as does the fact that two additional bullet holes in the floor were covered by a rug, the police chief and Giesler both backed off, the coroner filed an incomplete report and Toni was kept in seclusion, sedated, having made one hysterical phone call to a friend only two and a half hours after the police arrived on the scene claiming that Reeves had been murdered.

The studio system was at an end and it was up to agents like Freddie Fields and the publicists under the wing of Rogers & Cowan and other independent PR groups to look after the messes made by the stars. The stars themselves had at last broken free of the constraints of the studio and were making their own way in Hollywood, tied to nothing but their egos and the people hired to fan them and make sure that reality lived up to their raging self-belief. Within four years Mannix was dead. On his retirement, Howard Strickling moved further and further away from Hollywood, taking all his secrets with him to his death, in relative obscurity, in 1982.

The circumstances surrounding Reeves' death have become notorious again in recent years in the aftermath of the film *Hollywoodland*, starring Ben Affleck, but even with the freedom that such faction allows, the film fudges the issue of what happened to Reeves, suggesting a number of causes of death without ever stating an outright opinion. It gently glosses over the parts played by Strickling and Eddie Mannix in covering up the truth, but then it can do little else; Hollywood looks after its own.

Part Three

THE FAME FORMULA

• • •

'The egos of the famous are pumped up and distorted by the adoration heaped upon them, then made paranoid and neurotic by the constant attention and scrutiny'
NOAM CHOMSKY, *Manufacturing Consent*

'Our age has produced a new kind of eminence . . . This new kind of eminence is "celebrity" and has been fabricated to satisfy our exaggerated expectations of human greatness. The hero was distinguished by his achievement; the celebrity by his image or trademark. The hero created himself; the media creates the celebrity. The celebrity is always a contemporary. Folklore, sacred texts and history books make the hero but the celebrity is the creature of gossip, of magazines, newspapers and the ephemeral images of the movie and television screen. Celebrities are differentiated mainly by trivia of personality. Entertainers are best qualified to become celebrities because they are skilled in the marginal differentiation of their personalities. Anyone can become a celebrity if only he can get into the news and stay there'
DANIEL BOORSTIN, *The Image: A Guide to Pseudo-events in America*

Twenty-Eight

WARREN COWAN AND THE OSCARS

This book started as a journey, a delve into the heart of PR. It's not exactly a Conradian heart of darkness, more a heart in several sections, each one carefully secreted in different locations and, to analyse the whole, one must address the various riddles put forward by the people involved in a business that runs on secrecy and subterfuge, despite living squarely in the foreground.

PR people, unless they are wild cards like Jim Moran, tend to keep their stories very close to their chests. The old guard, like Howard Strickling and Henry Rogers, had a litany of secrets that could have blown the lid off the rather sanctified image of some of Hollywood's early stars had they chosen to – Strickling joked about writing a book that would do just that, but in the end he took his secrets to the grave. Rogers' autobiography, whilst revealing, could have said a great deal more than it did. Such careful flacks do not divulge anything if they can possibly help it. Under their hats, secreted in the back pockets of their brains, is an endless seam of stories that could destroy the reputations of their ex-clients, and themselves for that matter, for good.

The people discussed in this section learned from these past masters and have kept a great deal to themselves. More often than not they have their stories planned and plotted – some, like Warren Cowan, claim to have books they're working on, while others are simply masters at setting the agenda to what they wish to speak about. This is the legacy of MGM and Rogers & Cowan; a culture of strict secrecy on behalf of the client is maintained at all times, even after that client has left for newer pastures and better-looking PR. Unless they happen to have really upset you, that is.

I was fortunate to have a well-known insider, Steve Jaffe, who was willing to introduce me to those modern greats of PR who were willing to speak. It helped, in some cases, that I was a member of the same club, and hindered in others. Steve's witty, insightful and very occasionally caustic asides gave me a breadth of understanding of the industry that would otherwise have taken months to acquire.

It is unsurprising that some of the great and the good of PR declined to be interviewed; the field is so stretched and full of competitors that it can be seen as risky to let one's guard down. Those flacks that have conglomerated, joined forces and bought each other out, such as Pat Kingsley, are in a position of enormous strength, which they do not want to jeopardize. The independents, rattling at the bars of fame's cage, are struggling to find a place in a viciously competitive world, and though they tend to be more willing to speak, they too can be cagey.

The business may have its roots in the itinerant carnival barkers and snake oil medicine men, the Sons of Barnum, but it has become a profession, staffed by college graduates who do not necessarily have the wherewithal to make the sort of instinctive choices that Harry Reichenbach or Maynard Nottage made. Both types have guarded their secrets as carefully and closely as the Magic Circle would their tricks. Some lesser stories will always leak out, but the greatest secrets tend to remain locked away for ever.

The journey detailed in this book has taken me to the publicists whose blip on the radar was clearest and strongest, the publicists whose influence was most profound. The people I spoke to whilst I was in Los Angeles are at the apogee of their profession and it was a great honour to talk to them. There are many more flacks out there, a lot of whom have done remarkable things within the industry, and there are more still who have done a passable job. The line of descent I have followed – from the early inventors of Hollywood to today's astonishingly powerful not-quite-secret cabal of power publicists and refiners of the game – takes in the people I think have had the biggest influence on the industry and on me. They are the architects of the modern incarnation of celebrity.

Hollywood is, without question, a fame factory and every factory needs a formula to succeed. Publicists, be they press agents or public relations gurus, are the gatekeepers of that factory, guarding its formula often to the death.

Warren Cowan was the quieter man in the Rogers & Cowan partnership, quieter but arguably more influential. He is responsible for many of the benevolent clichés of Hollywood that appear to have been there for years but only really came into existence after he joined forces with Henry Rogers in the 1940s. He oversaw the entertainment wing of Rogers & Cowan, while Rogers moved further into corporate publicity and television.

Cowan was born in New York in 1924 and, fortuitously for someone who rose to his position, went to school with Army Archerd, who became a renowned *Variety* columnist. He studied at UCLA and then worked in publicity for an outfit that was prone to celebrating wildly when they got a good piece in Walter Winchell's column. It gave him a taste of what publicity was about and – after a stint in the Air Force fighting in the Second World War – what he and Henry Rogers could make it.

Rogers hired him in 1945 because he recognized in Cowan an excellent ideas man who was clearly willing to go beyond what had gone before and use publicity to *build* careers rather than just putting ego-boosting puff pieces in the papers or suppressing the wayward tendencies of stars. Alongside Rogers, he wooed journalists relentlessly, and when the studio system finally broke down in the mid 1950s, leaving the columnists without any source of in-house gossip, their company was perfectly placed to represent the newly freed stars.

He rode the knife-edge between publicity's inventive old school and corporate modernity with a suavity and élan that many of his contemporaries could not manage, and he is, together with Rogers, entirely responsible for the rise in importance of the Oscars. In the late 1950s, when Rogers was pursuing television and corporate clients, Cowan took on the stars. He even filched Danny Kaye from

Rogers – much to Rogers' personal regret – because Cowan was interested in the same things as Kaye, like baseball.

Cowan's professed interest is 'creating news', but that news does not include himself. *He* was not news because he didn't want to detract attention from his clients; he didn't have the sort of need that Jim Moran did, like a junkie pursuing a fix, to exercise his wit in public. He is a wary man, not given to exposing himself to public appraisal – certainly he wasn't willing to be interviewed for this book, although that may have more to do with the fact that he is apparently preparing a book of his own – and direct quotes from him in the media are a rare commodity. He has been described as a seducer and cajoler, a man loyal to his clients to the point of invisibility. Unlike Strickling, or even some of his protégés, he encourages talent and hides the worst stories without making excessive demands on the press. He can afford to do this; he has had little to do with fomenting celebrity and a lot to do with nurturing talent. He has represented Frank Sinatra, Kirk Douglas, Elizabeth Taylor, Paul Newman, Warren Beatty, the Beatles, Audrey Hepburn, Michael Jackson, Dean Martin and Kareem Abdul-Jabbar. Even now, in his eighties, he represents a huge roster of Hollywood's older, more established fraternity, including Aaron Spelling, Debbie Reynolds, Polly Bergen and David Hasselhoff – although, given the latter's recent travails in the press, that may no longer be the case.

On the whole Cowan rose through the gentlemanly generation of publicists, before there was strident competition, men who had control over the job rather than letting it take control of them. He was, and remains, a humble but powerful force to be reckoned with, a consummate professional who has held on to his clients thanks to the discreet nature of his operation. This is perhaps another reason why he was uncomfortable talking to me. He got into the publicity game when there was enough business for everyone, and has presided over a rapidly changing era, training a generation of flacks who have had to fight for business as more and more people have become involved in PR – a fact that is partly attributable to the respectable veneer Rogers & Cowan gave the business.

The Academy Awards are an ideal illustration of what he achieved.

The Oscars are the longest-lasting Hollywood publicity stunt and the most visible. Begun in 1928, they were initially used to promote current films as much as to honour the industry's best and brightest. But thanks to Rogers, and particularly Warren Cowan, the Oscar ceremony, and the build-up to it, has become a publicity juggernaut in its own right. Approximately one sixth of the world's population watches the ceremony each year, lost in the carefully orchestrated glitz of it all. That translates to a lot of dollars spent at the multiplex. With the exception of *Crash* – already out of the movie theatres by the time its award was announced – the last Best Picture winner not to gross more than $75 million at the domestic box office was *The Last Emperor* in 1987. That said, it made $31 million after its nomination was announced.

What Rogers & Cowan started with the long, slow build-up for Joan Crawford's role in *Mildred Pierce* the year Cowan arrived at the firm became an art form by the late 1950s. It didn't always work, but was successful enough to be ripe for imitation. Thanks to Cowan's careful behind-the-scenes plotting – he has rarely publicized which clients he works with to avoid the studios and journalists reacting to stories with a weary 'Oh, Warren Cowan planted that one' – by the 1960s the buzz build-up to the Oscars was a masterpiece of Machiavellian publicity manoeuvring, with vast flocks of flacks working themselves into the ground to get the stars, the films and the directors mentioned in any and every relevant media outlet. Warren Cowan was the Prince presiding over all this. In 1964, he represented all five nominees for the Academy Award for Best Actress; Patricia Neal won for *Hud*, pipping Leslie Caron, Shirley MacLaine, Rachel Roberts and Natalie Wood to the post. It was a feat achievable only by a man who keeps himself out of the press's way, so as not to colour the end result he's building up to, and who has a vast army of flacks working for him, seeding the names of his stars in the fallow pastures of tomorrow's news.

It doesn't require a journey to the heart of Hollywood to notice the effects of the Oscar campaign, that great PR institution that rules the fortunes of the movie world. The Oscar ceremony was created as a way of promoting the movies by the Academy of Motion Picture

Arts and Sciences in 1928. Two hundred and fifty people attended the black tie banquet for the first ceremony in May 1929 at the Hotel Roosevelt, but it didn't really come to life as a promotional tool until Rogers & Cowan got involved. The Oscars have become, in the hands of the endless array of flacks who have followed in Rogers & Cowan's footsteps, an international multi-ringed circus of the gaudiest proportions. Phineas Barnum would be proud of the enterprising zeal and self-approbating hoo-ha that attends each year's awards season, and thanks to it, careers are made or broken.

According to Warren Cowan, the template for the Oscar ceremony was created by director Howard Hughes on 24 May 1930. That year, he launched the film *Hell's Angels*, and instead of the usual premiere, which had, until that point, been relatively run-of-the-mill, he decided the opening night would feature klieg lights, a red carpet and all the stars in the Hollywood galaxy, in an attempt to woo and excite as many press and people as possible about the film, and it worked. He invited all the stars he could get hold of to come and parade themselves in front of Grauman's Chinese Theatre, where the film was showing, and they duly did. All the stars and makers of the film attended, as well as Charlie Chaplin, with his girlfriend Georgia Hale, Buster Keaton, Dolores del Rio, Norma Talmadge, Mary Pickford and Douglas Fairbanks. These elements have been at the heart of the Oscar ceremony ever since and are essential to the inner workings of Oscar publicity. A scribbled note in Nottage's papers suggests he was convinced that Hughes had stolen the idea from him, but there is nothing to support this statement, which was written towards the end of his life, at the height of his bitterness towards the industry.

In the 1950s, NBC used to televise the New York Easter Parade, a less gaudy version of the Thanksgiving Day parade at which the city's social elite would parade around town in the latest fashions, and Cowan has gone on the record as saying that he used to push for clients to be interviewed live on that show – the Oscar carpet is a grander extension of that television-age logic. The Oscars were televised for the first time in 1953 and got more viewers than the Superbowl.

Hughes's template remains in place to this day, unchanged but for the number of flacks running down the carpet ahead of the stars they handle, alerting the media to who is coming and what exactly they have done to deserve their place on the red carpet in a tux or impossibly glamorous designer dress, and today the ceremony and its build-up is followed by one billion people around the world.

The Oscars are a source of essential exposure for a vast number of people – from the stars and everyone else involved in the movies to the dress designers, press, jewellers, caterers and anyone else who can persuade a star to talk about their product, charity, or whatever they want to get mentioned. Everyone makes a killing at the Oscars. For a newly minted star, the Oscars are a time to revel in their new-found status and hopefully charm the millions of people watching live around the world. For an older, more established star, it is a time to grit one's teeth, get out there and press flesh, while being thankful for the continued attention from the world's media and attentive public.

One of the reasons the ceremony is so well attended by the stars is that it's perfectly orchestrated – all the companies involved in the spectacular work together in ways otherwise unimaginable in a competitive town like LA. No paparazzi are allowed within shooting distance of the carpet, and while some of the assembled media may ask the occasional difficult question, it's highly unlikely – after all, they want to be invited back the following year.

The carpet itself goes down on the Thursday before the show, which takes place on a Sunday. From that point on the carpet is a hive of activity. There are even occasional interviews conducted on it prior to the day itself, but as they tend to bring less exposure, most are arranged for the day. At 2.30 p.m. on the day of the awards, people start arriving. All but the most established stars are encouraged, if not forced, by their publicists to turn up as early as possible to guarantee coverage. Some bigger stars may try to sneak in around the back, but on the whole the publicists get their clients out in the limelight without too much fuss.

Any fuss is reserved for behind the scenes, the six-month build-up to the ceremony, the campaigns that Rogers & Cowan create and refine for the stars and the movies or the process of wooing and schmoozing the Academy members. Unlike the high-gloss world of the awards ceremony, this is a murkier, harsher world of in-fighting, aggressive campaigning and duels fought with wads of cash and advertising. In the years since Rogers & Cowan created their whispering campaign for Joan Crawford's role in *Mildred Pierce*, everyone has got in on the action and blood pressure runs high over hotly contested films.

'The Academy Awards are more of a popularity contest than a talent contest,' wrote Henry Rogers in his autobiography *Walking the Tightrope*. 'If you have five brilliant actresses, each of whom has given a brilliant performance in a brilliant motion picture, how does the Academy voter decide who he will vote for?

'Whether Hollywood likes to face up to it or not, the voter casts his ballot emotionally and not critically. Unable to decide which performance he feels is the best, he allows his emotions to take over – he has no choice. So it comes down to a number of emotional and sometimes practical considerations, none of which have to do with the quality of the performance which is being judged.'

The publicity generated influences that emotional decision, but only so far. One of Cowan's innovations when Rogers & Cowan were campaigning for Rosalind Russell to win an Oscar in 1947, backfired spectacularly. Cowan's idea was to establish odds in Las Vegas and fix them so that Russell came out the front-runner. He and Rogers put out a lot of press releases to that effect, easing Russell into the lead position in the publicity stakes. The trouble was that Academy voters, when polled about who they'd voted for, said Rosalind Russell simply because they didn't want to appear out of step with the run of positive publicity building behind the actress – they wanted to be on the winning team – but in fact they had voted for Loretta Young. 'They had actually voted for Loretta Young,' wrote Rogers, 'because they felt that she deserved the award more than the other candidates.'

There is little doubt that Cowan learned from these experiences; his campaigns became more and more careful and his publicists' fingers stretched out to find every available pie in the Oscar campaigns that followed. Over-confidently overreaching, as had happened with Rosalind Russell, became, on the whole, a thing of the past. Under Cowan's tutelage, the Oscars have become *the* place for fresh-faced young flacks to cut their teeth. As more and more people were made members of the Academy, particularly after the Oscars were moved to Mann's Chinese Theatre, away from its beginnings as an exclusive dinner date with prizes thrown in for good measure, so the publicists' power base has expanded. Changes in technology have assisted this increase in power. Publicity in the build-up to the Oscars is now as carefully managed as a covert CIA operation, and any stunt must not show the hand of the publicist behind it. Academy voters are carefully collected and encouraged to see the films in question, celebrities who may be willing to mention the film are targeted and the jungle-drum network of gossip and word of mouth is employed unceasingly.

In the late 1990s, this hot-blooded tendency reached fever pitch in a war of words between the Miramax and DreamWorks studios over the latter's *Saving Private Ryan* and the former's *Shakespeare in Love* and *Life is Beautiful*. There's a great deal to be made from an Oscar nomination, as a win can add in excess of $40 million to the box office takings for a movie, so it's understandable that tensions run high, but the war of deep pockets and trade ads is rarely allowed to spill out onto the pages of the national press. In this case, however, it did, partly because the studios had tangled the previous year over spending on *American Beauty* and *The Cider House Rules*. Part of the trouble is that Miramax, one of the most successful independent studios in Hollywood, presided over by the bullish Harvey Weinstein, is a PR dream come true – nearly everything they touched for a number of years turned to box office gold, and this was, in no small part, thanks to the team of publicists they kept on board, as well as the quality of the films.

The trouble began when a rumour surfaced in the press that Miramax publicists were collaring critics and bending their ears over the relative merits of *Saving Private Ryan*. The suggestion was that these flacks had gone around telling anyone who would listen that the film was 'twenty minutes of extraordinary pyrotechnics foll-owed by an overlong and conventional war film'. Weinstein strongly denied this and hit back by saying that such a suggestion was 'an assault on his patriotism' and that people were trying to spoil his friendship with Steven Spielberg. *Saving Private Ryan* started life as a hot Oscar contender, only to have its hopes scuppered by Miramax's cappuccino-froth romp *Shakespeare in Love*, which was backed by a double-espresso-strength publicity campaign featuring contributions from Warren Cowan, Dick Guttman, Gerry Pam and Murray Weissman, all Academy members of a certain age with a huge range of contacts within the Academy.

Every Oscar contender since Joan Crawford has been backed by a rugged and determined publicity campaign of some sort or other, whether subtle or otherwise. Films are promoted relentlessly in the trade papers with adverts, which are universally acknowledged as the best way to keep the movie in question in the voters' eye. More and more in this celebrity-obsessed age the other awards ceremonies, such as the Golden Globes and even the Baftas, are playing their part, as stars pop out of the woodwork in the company of their publicists to press flesh and bask in the warm afterglow of parties and lights. Also essential is the ability of a publicist to get the star or movie a cover story in as many magazines and papers as possible. *Broadcast News*, which was nominated for several Oscars at the 1988 award ceremony, was noticeably pushed into the Academy's consciousness by one magazine using it as the cover image for a story about the changing face of television news, giving the film, which satirized the mass layoffs at CBS News in 1984, a new spin as a socially relevant film. Equally important is getting voters to see the movie in question, which was much more difficult prior to the invention of the video cassette. Until the Academy changed the rules, studios were prone to sending out their Oscar contenders in the flashiest packaging possible. Now a simple, plain box is all that's allowed.

Miramax's campaign proves that the Oscars remain an important part of Cowan's working pattern, and in 1997 Cowan introduced Roberto Benigni, who had just directed and starred in the Holocaust comedy, *Life is Beautiful*, to the Hollywood cognoscenti. Benigni was little known in Hollywood; he had appeared in cult films by Jim Jarmusch, but not much else, although he was a huge star in Italy. As the nomination deadline for the Oscars drew near, Cowan introduced the Italian director to Hollywood's most influential tastemakers, all of them clients *and* Academy Award voters. He made sure Benigni dined with Ann and Kirk Douglas; Shirley MacLaine met him; Jack Lemmon hosted him for lunch; Cowan and his wife took him to meet Elizabeth Taylor and Rod Steiger. Not long after receiving the approval of Hollywood's standard-bearers, Benigni's film won three Oscars: Best Actor, Best Foreign Language Film, and Best Original Dramatic Score.

This is a typically genteel approach to the Oscar game, and one that would probably only work for a foreign language film, as they are quite a bit lower down the pecking order in terms of generating hoo-ha. It was obviously very effective, however. Cowan's contacts have matured with age, and he has been around so long that he has to do relatively little to achieve success. This is not the case for the slavering, lustful approaches made for bigger films sourced from Hollywood, which are inevitably hotly contested by other filmmakers. This new model of Oscar buzz is best considered in the light of what happened to *Crash*, which was distributed by Lionsgate in 2005. The film had its 2006 Oscar campaign spending revealed to the public because the company was small enough for the expense to be a considerable risk for the investors in the parent company and so had to be declared. The parent company was forced to announce that its profits would be down, because they would be spending an additional $2 million publicizing the film in the run-up to the voting. Having spent $2 million already, the company ended up spending approximately $4 million on promoting for the Oscars a film that cost a mere $6.5 million to make.

Hollywood tends to keep schtum about how much is spent on its Oscar campaigns, unless an upset or board meeting forces them into the public domain, partly because they wish to maintain the illusion that the awards are all about art, but also because the publicity campaigns have become so absolutely vast that *Crash*'s $4 million seems almost piffling by comparison. The extra $2 million spent on *Crash* was passed off as a prudent investment, as it could generate an extra $10 million in sales of DVDs and, with an Oscar nomination, a high price for television airing. Lionsgate spent most of the money on winning over Los Angeles itself, hoping that any New York votes that didn't go to *Crash* would be split evenly between the other contenders, and they played the worthy nature of the film – a dissertation on racial tension in LA – to the hilt. Their gamble paid off and it was the 'surprise' winner of Best Film at that year's ceremony, making back the money spent in spades.

Another campaign worthy of note is the one for the *English Patient*, which won nine awards at the 1996 Oscar ceremony. It was another Miramax production and took home nine of the twelve awards it was nominated for, including Best Film and Best Director. Looking at the CVs of publicists online, it's hard to find a publicist who didn't have something to do with the campaign; Miramax got everyone they could lay their hands on to contribute something towards the effort to win the film awards, and news of the picture bled into every aspect of the media. Its ubiquity, coupled with the fact that it was the type of historical, epic film that generally plays well with Academy voters, who tend to be older, guaranteed at least a few wins. That it did as well as it did is testament to the energy of the countless flacks and the wiles of the Weinstein brothers.

Certainly Miramax ran an extraordinary campaign for *Shakespeare in Love*, wooing all in their path with élan and a $15 million purse. But did they overdo it? The example of films like *Born on the Fourth of July*, which became so over-exposed that voters lost interest in it, suggests that overdoing it would have killed the campaign stone dead, but *Shakespeare in Love* won the Oscar. It seems most likely that *Shakespeare in Love* won because Miramax and its panel of expert publicists played a good, long, ingenious game with a film that was charming enough to woo the voters in its own right. It also helped that it lent itself to being seen on television far better than *Saving Private Ryan*, a film that needs the big screen to realize its full impact, which takes us back to the importance of video cassettes to Academy voters. *Saving Private Ryan* took out more trade ads than *Shakespeare in Love*, which may be an important part of the Oscar game, but not everything.

What is absolutely certain is that this Oscar spat between the studios proves beyond a shadow of a doubt the importance of the publicist in Hollywood, particularly during Oscar season, which is itself a creation of publicists. Without them, the industry as we know it would shudder to a halt and the Oscars would be little more than a small industry backslapping festival. Publicists control the promotion of the movies, the promotion of the stars and what goes on the covers of the papers. They control who the stars speak to, what they say, and how, in many cases, the reporters report. The Oscars are an excellent indicator of the hardening of attitudes in the PR world, the upward trajectory of focus and spending since the arrival of Rogers & Cowan and the promotion of *Mildred Pierce*. The Oscars have become the prime source of income for the top earners in each year's canon of films, pushing even billion-dollar blockbusters up an earning notch or two, and the only way to achieve such widespread ubiquity is through the arcane art of the publicist. To achieve it, the publicists have, of necessity, hardened up. There is no room in an Oscar campaign for a freewheeling Reichenbach stunt that would possibly damage studio finances if it backfired, nor is there room for the idiosyncratic humour of Jim Moran, or even the macho charms of Jay Bernstein. The Oscars campaign is the perfect mutant fusion of marketing, advertising and the subtle arts of PR, melded together for maximum impact, and it is, by necessity, run by boardrooms and big businesses, be they old guard like Cowan's firm or the harder-edged PMK under Pat Kingsley. It leaves no room for the wayward or the individual as the Oscars are orchestrated by companies that have almost as much power over the press as the Fixers used to. At the edges, however, there are still flacks desperate to have a piece of the pie and work at the heart of PR.

The Oscars are glorious, glittering and shiny in every respect, and they epitomize the current state of the star system to a tee. Unwary publicists can break themselves on the deceptively soft golden shine that emanates from the statuette, clawing at a chance to have some of it reflect on their client and them. Equally, though, they are more likely to have their hearts torn out by stars in whom they have invested everything, but who then leave them. Fame is a tricky mistress, and the creation of fame is a formula that needs careful work. Only the little brass statuette is guaranteed to survive.

• Twenty-Nine •

AGENT OF CHANGE

The first stop on my journey took me to one of the great Hollywood luminaries of post-war Hollywood, the über-agent Freddie Fields, one of the main proponents of change in the crossover point between the studio system and the modern period. Fields, who died in late 2007, was one of the founders of the talent agency Creative Management Association (CMA). He was born in Ferndale, NY on 12 September 1923. Fields grew up surrounded by showbusiness – his father ran a resort in the Catskill mountains, where New Yorkers fled in the summer to avoid the heat, and he would book luminaries of vaudeville and the early talkies, such as Al Jolson and Eddie Cantor. His brother Shep even made a name for himself as a bandleader.

Fields began his working life with the New York-based booking agent Abby Greschler, with whom he gained his first experiences of dealing with stars in the shape of the Jerry Lewis/Dean Martin double act. He joined MCA, a music booking agency which had expanded into television in the late 1940s, and rose to the position of vice president. In 1960, he set up CMA with David Begelman, deliberately mangling the initials of his previous employer to make the name of the new one. His clients included Hollywood luminaries such as Judy Garland, Faye Dunaway, Henry Fonda, Paul Newman, Peter Sellers, Robert Redford, Ryan O'Neill, Steve McQueen, Woody Allen, Liza Minnelli and Barbra Streisand, and he acted as a booking agent for the Beatles and Rolling Stones before moving into producing movies such as *Looking for Mr Goodbar*, *Fever Pitch*, *Millennium*, *The Year of Living Dangerously*, *Lipstick* and *Poltergeist II*.

Although it may seem strange to make an agent the first port of call in a history of the publicity industry, it actually makes perfect sense – without the rise of the talent agencies such as MCA, the William Morris Agency and CMA in the post-studio world, the modern era of publicity would never have come into being. William Morris, the first of the big twentieth century talent agencies, was born at roughly the same time as cinema in 1896 and was followed by others. They developed alongside the publicity industry, but were quicker off the mark to welcome television and the new wealth of talent that came with it. Talent agencies had their fingers in a number of pies – MCA became a record label in the 1960s for instance – but movies and the huge stars they created drove the business. It is thanks to people like Freddie Fields and Norman Brokaw from William Morris that packages began to be put together offering studio bosses the star, director and script in a single deal, meaning that the agent got 10 per cent of the entire budget of the film, a cost that was offset by the fact that the agent had saved the studio a lot of time and money finding 'the package'. Fields was also responsible for encouraging stars to ask for a share of grosses from the movies they were involved in. Both were moves that radically altered the financial landscape of Hollywood. Fields was at the peak of his influence in the 1960s and early 1970s, and without him, the publicity industry wouldn't have been able to transform from the gentlemanly affair it was in the forties and fifties to become the all-powerful juggernaut, funded by suddenly-far-wealthier stars and their need for protection.

Fields, like Cowan, has rarely spoken on the record, so it was with a sense of trepidation that I approached his house with Steve Jaffe on a bright but cold LA afternoon. This was a man who straddled the old world and the new, a man who was one of the people responsible for laying the foundations of modern Hollywood. The house looked fairly understated, very stylish but quite small, as we approached an electric gate and rang the bell. A Mexican maid greeted us and opened the door. Before Fields arrived, his small toy Pekinese, wearing a multicoloured jerkin, and two Dalmatians came and investigated us, shortly followed by a bright and sprightly eighty-three-year-old who greeted us warmly. Fields had grey hair, was incredibly thin and his piercing blue eyes were covered by trendy shades. A white T-shirt and Levis held up by white braces completed the fading-rock-star effect. I thought, If I get to eighty-three I want to look like that.

The house was extraordinary; all over the walls were trinkets of his illustrious career. Signed photos of the Beatles, Jerry Lewis, the Rolling Stones, Dean Martin and many more. The décor was appropriately eclectic – Moroccan meets Spanish – with a beautiful, partially shaded garden. There was, in proper Hollywood tradition, a full-length swimming pool outside and a number of spacious, comfortable rooms throughout the house. Fields was possessed of amazing grace and charm and his polite manner was straight out of another era. This is not what one expects from a Hollywood executive nowadays; he behaved as if he'd stepped out of a black and white film. He had a bad cough and for the first ten minutes we discussed health and doctors – he had undergone three operations for colon and lung cancer – but nonetheless he was generous with his time.

I wanted to talk about publicity, and though he said very little, what he said was significant – like many agents, he was unwilling to admit that he owed anything to publicists. A good agent will claim that no one but they can do anything for their client's career and will operate, like Ari Gold, the agent in HBO's satirical comedy *Entourage*, as if they are the only puppet masters of the star in question. However, Fields certainly had relationships with Warren Cowan and Henry Rogers when he was at his zenith, building his talent agency, and he didn't seem have a low opinion of them. He also knew about Harry Brand, Howard Strickling and Russell Birdwell.

A key moment in the development of the publicity industry, I suggested to him, was the loss of power when the Hollywood studio system broke down; at that time the power of the in-house publicist broke down. The power of the studios to grant and dismiss contracts meant the actors were powerless; they were basically hired hands and the studio publicists could do what they wanted with them. If they wanted to lie about them or finish their careers, they did. When the studio system failed, the power returned to the actors and they could control what was done in their name. It was then that the independents like Lee Solters and Rogers & Cowan took off, as publicists started to acquire serious clout in their own right and the stars realized they would need someone to manage their press or the gossip journalists would have a field day at their expense. Fields corroborated this chronology of events.

I told him I was particularly interested in the old publicists – Harry Reichenbach and his ilk – and that I wanted to get a sense of what his generation thought of them. I lured him with the suggestion that perhaps I was imagining that there was an influence, but Fields surprised me by bringing up a name I'd not heard of at that point: Maynard Nottage.

'I don't think anyone can remember what people thought about them,' he said. 'Very few are alive now. I think I'm probably one of the few who has ever bothered to look into those old guys. Reichenbach was interesting, but he died young and moved in different circles towards the end of his life. You know he worked promoting that early Disney film with Mickey Mouse? A great guy for the crazy stunts in his early days, but looking back at it, I think he'd have been heading up a studio if he'd lived.

'I met Maynard Nottage a couple of times, in the late fifties. You heard of him? He was the smaller shark, snapping at Reichenbach's heels from the early days of the movies. He was a dilapidated old man when I met him, far past his best yet still desperate to be involved in a business that had outstripped him. He came and hustled me for work and contacts, thinking that he could work his way back in through an agent's office, but his ideas were antiquated and he smelled of bad whiskey. There was no way I'd have considered hiring him. He was a shell of a man. I'd heard of him, of course, but had assumed that he'd died around the same time as Reichenbach. I asked Henry Rogers about him, but the look on his face when I did suggested that it was best I didn't say any more. Nottage? The guy didn't understand the business as it stood in the fifties at all. Didn't understand television, corporate business. Didn't even get why he had been cast aside. He'd done some great stuff in the early days, but he'd got sucked into a world of pills and prohibited booze that he supplied to his clients and he was sucked dry by the business, burned out by forty. He devoted himself too much to it – and this in a business where you've got to do that – and didn't get himself any sort of life. Even in his late sixties, which he was when I met him, he clung to the idea that he had been cheated out of a lifestyle. Kind of sad really.'

'Did you see a change when you were an agent, in the way publicity was thought of?' I asked, making a mental note of Nottage.

'Yes I did, but I saw a change in agenting as well. You look at producers and go back to producers twenty years ago and forty years ago. What I found was that now you can't become an agent if you aren't a college graduate. That's a change. You can't even get into the mailroom without a college graduation. There were a lot in the old days who didn't graduate. That's what went wrong with the agency business. You can't find good agents who've been to college – it doesn't always go. Press agents came from a place where they could do things for people. Twenty-five to thirty years ago, you employed people who could do things for you. Bobby Zarem, Henry Rogers. They were good, they could do things. You don't have to go to college. They saw what was happening in the profession. Others have gone that way since. I think they always will.'

Implicit in Fields' remarks about Nottage was a suggestion that there are publicists out there who allowed their clients to break their hearts, who gave all they had to give and then were cast aside, who were so wrapped up in the lifestyle that they couldn't escape the loneliness of losing everything. Looking back over the history of PR, it's clearly a common theme, and it still goes on, as I discovered later. I asked if he'd ever had his heart broken by his clients.

'Not that I can remember,' he told me. 'They did, but not for the reasons you think. Peter Sellers was a heartbreaker. They were all difficult people. That attracted me more.'

Fields had a reputation for taking on difficult clients, such as Streisand, Sellers and Garland, somewhat masochistically some claimed; clients who would certainly have need of the particular skills of a publicist. I asked him outright if he had ever used publicists to cover up scandals, but he was coy, answering only, 'I never protected myself. I did love Warren [Cowan] and Henry [Rogers].'

Fields did admit to using Bobby Zarem, a New York publicist with a strong renegade streak. 'Rogers & Cowan were cool, but Zarem is a maverick,' he said. 'I married Polly Bergen, and Zarem was the first person I got for her. My whole life was East Coast [early on]. Why didn't Zarem come to LA? He was in New York, that's why. Polly got an offer to do a film with Gregory Peck and Robert Mitchum [*Cape Fear*], so we went to LA and we never went back to New York.'

Fields left CMA in the late 1970s because he 'got a little bored of it. Things are found out more quickly now.' In other words, for him the speed of change left agents in the cold. The world had changed and it didn't suit him. It became a world in which accountants are the most important people and all the parties one goes to are full of accountants. He wasn't having fun any more, so he moved into producing movies, which was by far the most exciting work at the time.

Jay Bernstein, a publicist who started out at Rogers & Cowan and worked briefly at the William Morris Agency, remembered Fields well and told me a couple of stories about him and his sense of fun. 'He wanted to sign Kirk Douglas to CMA,' said Bernstein. 'Kirk was with William Morris, so he called Kirk and was pitching him on the phone. And Kirk says, "Look, I'm going to New York. Why don't you ride with me, and we'll talk about it and you can come right back." So Freddie said, "OK, fine, I'll do that." So he found the flight that Kirk was going on and he called him back saying, "I'm on the flight, I'm going to be sitting next to you. And by the way, we're going to have lots of things to talk about because they're showing the Disney movie, the horse in the grey flannel suit with Dean James or something." They both laughed. Because Burt Lancaster was best friends with Kirk Douglas and vice versa Freddie says, "You know what? I was just thinking did you see Burt's latest picture *The Scalphunters?*" And Kirk says, "No, I haven't seen it yet." So Fields says, "Let me get back to you." Fields calls him back an hour later and says, "Were gonna see *The Scalphunters*!" and Kirk says, "I'll tell you what, you don't have to come to New York – you got a new client."

'Also, James Coburn was married to Beverly Coburn at the time and lived on Tower Road, and she had a good relationship with his agent Jimmy Morrison or whoever it was. Freddie wanted to get James Coburn, but Beverly sort of ran things. She said, "Look, the guy's a fucking gangster, we don't wanna be with him," and Coburn [responded with], "But see the head of CM Analysts turned him down without even talking to him," and she's, yeah, but he is a gangster. So the story got back to Freddie. So Freddie goes over to have a meeting with Coburn at which he has no chance. So what does he do to make sure he has a chance? He takes off his jacket and he has a shoulder holster. And Coburn and Beverly cracked up. He ended up signing Coburn!'

Bernstein's story suggests that Fields might have been a gangster. That is a matter for speculation, but he certainly had dealings with gangsters – it was hard not to in an industry that attracted so much money. Certainly at our meeting he wouldn't be drawn on what influence the mob had had in Hollywood.

Fields is a perfect gauge of the changing state of Hollywood and its dealings with publicists. He tacitly acknowledged their rise to recognition, power and ubiquity without letting slip – except in fond reminiscence of people like Rogers and Cowan or brief mention of hiring Zarem for his actress wife – that they had any influence on him or the other big cogs in the celebrity wheel. His generation saw them as increasingly essential in the makeup of Hollywood, where stars had control over every aspect of their lives except what the press said about them. Fields was part of the process in the 1940s, as the studios began to disintegrate, that allowed stars that freedom – he helped give the newly released stars the sense of freedom that created the modern age of stardom. Yet he also implied that things had, in many ways, not changed, that there were circumstances where publicists would still break themselves on the walls of stardom trying to break down the barriers to get a client. By mentioning Nottage, he gave me a reference point, a hook on which to hang the threads of my journey into the heart of PR, to untangle the threads of the fame formula and how publicity related to it. Like all good adventures, the details fell into place slowly as I began to meet more and more people who had made their life in the factory of fame that is Hollywood.

Just before we left, when Fields was clearly drained by our conversation and his illness, he left me with a teaser question that led me to a perfect coda for the era of the suppress agents: 'Did you know of an actress called Gwili Andre?' he asked. He didn't say any more, just left it at that: a gnomic reference to someone I'd never heard of. I looked into her later in my stay and, trawling the libraries of LA for information, found some cuttings, dating from the late 1920s and early 1930s. I looked and looked, but that was all I could find until I came across some lurid cuttings dated 1959 and relating to her death. There were many years left blank, until her death, which had been utterly suppressed; right until the end, Strickling, Brand and others from the old studio era wanted nothing to damage the gloss of the golden age of cinema.

Gwili Andre had been a glamorous Danish artist's model, born in 1907. She had come to Hollywood in 1932, just as the studio system was getting into its fixer-dominated swing. She was one of a flurry of European actresses who had crossed the Atlantic after Garbo in 1925 and she'd achieved considerable success as a model, earning $50 an hour to be painted and photographed, as well appearing on the cover of *Vogue*, *Harper's Bazaar*, *Vanity Fair* and a number of other magazines. By 1931 she was earning $25,000 a year – a fortune at the height of the depression – for simply modelling gowns, but she wanted more and was persuaded to pursue a career in Hollywood, where her striking features were considered a huge incentive for signing her. David O. Selznick duly put her under contract at RKO and she was cast in *Roar of the Dragon* opposite Richard Dix. She failed to blossom on celluloid, however. Her looks, according to the critics, did not translate from stills to the moving image as she apparently lacked animation on screen, so her contract was not renewed. She starred in three films, but none was successful so she was reduced to lesser, unsatisfying roles. She quit the movies in 1942. Failure crippled her – she had been 'America's most beautiful model' but had told the papers in 1932 that 'people in Hollywood are not happy' and that she 'didn't find film parties very amusing'. After that, she slipped out of view, divorcing her chess champion husband and eventually marrying real estate developer William Cross. They divorced in 1949, and after that her occasional visits to Hollywood ceased entirely.

By 1959 she had disappeared into obscurity and lived in a small flat on Ocean Front in Venice, Los Angeles, surrounded by the clippings and iconography of her career. Her clippings were her life – she didn't have her son any more as her ex-husband had been awarded custody because of her ongoing struggle with alcoholism. All that she had left to focus on was her early, ultimately unsuccessful, attempt at winning eternal fame. Her neighbours remembered her as a woman living in near poverty. She told them that she 'lived on the profits of investments she made in Copenhagen "when I was younger and wiser"', the *Mirror News* reported on 6 February 1959. A neighbour told the same paper that Andre, whose married name was Gwili Cross, 'would frequently have her neighbours in for coffee, and would show them huge scrapbooks of pictures taken of her in her youth'. She only ever talked about the past. She evidently lived on those clippings and cover shots, and the memories attached to them, far more than on the interest from investments made in her youth. Andre died in a fire that consumed her and her clippings, a pyre worthy of a woman who ached to be a star, the day after her fifty-second birthday.

Andre's death is romantic and tragic in a way that Britney Spears', should it happen at any point soon, never could be, because she perished in a perfect Brunhilda moment, consumed eternally in flames born of a lost beauty. As Joe Queenan wrote in the *Guardian* in January 2008, after the untimely death of Heath Ledger: 'Movie stars, unlike rock stars, have an appeal that transcends narrow demographic parameters.' Gwili Andre may never have been the movie star she hoped to be, but the fact that she clung on to the press cuttings that suggested she might have been is proof enough. Hers was the sort of death that Hollywood despairs of: a bitter, unhappy woman, chewed up and spat out by the industry, but who nonetheless clung to the ideal life she had hoped for until it destroyed her. The studios didn't – and still don't – want to acknowledge the dark side of their rejection; they want it to be forgotten quickly as it destroys the movie industry's mystique.

The Fixers had kept their starry illuminations bright and shiny, but by 1959 their influence was over, and Andre's death was a beacon marking the fact. Ironically, her death was the only thing that caused her to resurface in the public consciousness, and her brief rebirth of fame marks the end of the era of the Fixers perfectly.

Andre is different from Britney Spears in so far as she had a body of modelling work that represented perfection, albeit deep in her past. Spears has let the media so close that they can see she is wearing no clothes, both literally and figuratively. Gwili Andre's death, tragic in its blackly ironic mini-Wagnerian perfection, and Britney Spears and Lindsay Lohan's appalling warts-and-all descent into media notoriety, illustrate perfectly the difference fifty years can make. The endless displays of flesh and naked desperation we see today are not what the Hollywood machine wants – the one constant in Hollywood is the need to present a fairytale, which is personified by the Oscar-night red-carpet parade.

This is why no flack worth their salt will take on celebrities like Spears and why her descent spirals ever faster, actively encouraged by elements of the press. This sort of chaos is not what the PR industry wants or needs – PRs are still, despite the increasingly corporate nature of the industry, in the business of selling the Hollywood fairytale and it's easy to see why, after a period of freedom personified by press agents like Jay Bernstein, the Fixers came back to the fore in the shape of Pat Kingsley, Stan Rosenfield, Michael Levine and others.

The appalling circumstances of both Andre and Spears prove, however, that the mask of fame can eat away at the face beneath and that unchecked fame can be as corrosive as brief, inglorious fame. It shows the desperate need that those who are, or have been, famous have for their chance in the spotlight. Fame is a dangerous drug and the withdrawal symptoms can be as dangerous as constant use. But what Gwili Andre did not know, and what Spears and her ilk seem instinctively aware of, despite only accessing the knowledge in the least productive manner possible, is that fame can be perpetuated, that there is a formula to keep oneself in the public eye indefinitely. It is only now, thanks to the modern era of publicists and their careful, cagey refinements of the groundwork begun in the heady days of the early twentieth century by Reichenbach *et al.*, that we can begin to understand how easy it is to implement. This may be too late to help Andre, or Spears, but, as I will show later, there is hope.

Thirty

THE LAST OF THE GENTLEMAN PUBLICISTS

The honing of the Oscar publicity campaign was Cowan's great achievement, but his innovations didn't end there. Not only did he nurture the vast majority of Hollywood's PR talent, from Jay Bernstein to Pat Kingsley, he also took famous actors and turned them into charitable juggernauts. There's a famous story about Danny Kaye meeting a representative of UNICEF on a plane that was experiencing difficulties. Kaye is alleged to have turned to the man from UNICEF as they worried about the plane and asked about the organization. On hearing what they did, he said, 'If we survive this, I'll represent UNICEF around the world.' It was a perfect match: the United Nations Children's Fund and one of the best-loved entertainers of the time, famous for his affinity with children. Of course, Kaye was a Rogers & Cowan client, as was Audrey Hepburn when she began to represent UNICEF, and the careful hand of Cowan is evident behind this story, which sounds like it comes from a film. It may of course be true, but what is absolutely certain is that the story was woven into a gem of creative publicity for Kaye, making something that would have been carefully considered for any negative implications into a beautiful, seemingly spontaneous act that lives up to Kaye's gregarious and impulsive screen personality.

Kaye was a big part of Cowan's life after he took over his PR from Henry Rogers in the mid-1960s after a falling out over a charity event. Cowan won Kaye back as a client after discovering a shared love of baseball, and there was such a bond between them that the star even accompanied Cowan on his honeymoon in 1973. Cowan's ex-wife Josette remembers, with only a hint of mild annoyance, that Kaye even cooked their wedding breakfast and that Cowan, aware that such things were likely to make a wife irate, bought her a trio of luxurious gifts to make up for Kaye's presence, including a fur coat, a Bentley and a car phone. What she remembers most vividly, however, was Kaye's charm: 'Danny looked transparent,' she said. 'He was such a beautiful creature. He would order a big stove and he'd have a big table with a Lazy Suzy and he'd be cooking. He had long fingers; he loved to conduct and he would play music. He would speak French to me. He was unbelievable. Warren loved him. You know what's amazing with Warren is that sometimes Danny would get upset with Rogers & Cowan and they'd have it out like a married couple. Nobody said "get out of my life"; it wasn't that way at all. He [Cowan] was able to do this because of his humbleness. He was very humble. He didn't have to tell you all about himself. He didn't have such an ego at all.'

Not content to sit still, Cowan's creative, innovatory streak was put to further charitable use when he started the first celebrity charity fundraisers, notably with the first pro-celebrity sports event. This was a golf tournament, staged in 1949 on behalf of the director Frank Borzage, who had fallen on hard times in the 1940s and wasn't getting much work. Bing Crosby and Mickey Rooney were among the golfers who took part in the first year and Marilyn Monroe kept score in the second. Borzage, whose output had dipped considerably in the early forties, was back in slightly more regular work thereafter.

Cowan's interest in humanitarian organizations has been a mainstay of his career, with the John Wayne Cancer Institute, the Make-A-Wish Foundation and The Society of Singers amongst others getting the benefit of his ability to network and create events. It may seem cosy by today's standards, but these charitable endeavours were as radical at the time as Laurel and Hardy throwing pies at each other twenty years before. In an *On the Record* podcast in conversation with Eric Schwartzman, Cowan said, 'Major stars are pulled at from so many directions at the same time [now]. I receive requests and they're all valid and they all make sense and they all are for good causes but I receive requests, either directed to me or, let's say, to Paul Newman. I must receive fifteen to twenty a day – people who are having a charity event and they want him to come, people who want to honour the stars and so on and there's no physical way the stars could accept all the requests that they receive.'

It wasn't all charity work, though. In 1956 Cowan, working with Frank Sinatra, was called upon to create a stir on behalf of Sinatra's first western, *Johnny Concho*. Sinatra was a hot talent, but he'd never done a western and was perhaps not the most likely man to do one. Cowan's febrile brain decided that the best way to inculcate the Italian American hard man into the ways of the west was to recruit a genuine western star as technical adviser. The consensus was that Gary Cooper, who was on the up again post-*High Noon*, would be the ideal man for the job. Sinatra barely knew Cooper, and Cowan himself had never met him, but Rogers had known him from the early 1950s, when he had worked with Carl Foreman during the McCarthy witch hunts, and this gave Cowan an in.

Cowan simply phoned Cooper, introduced himself and made the pitch, and within the week, with numerous members of the press tagging along behind him, Cooper walked on set and shook Sinatra's hand. It made international news for several weeks afterwards.

Cowan pursued new methods of publicity relentlessly, even after being made president of the company in 1964. In 1969 he launched the comedy *If It's Tuesday, This Must Be Belgium* in the private screening rooms of stars. By this time, Rogers & Cowan was a fully-fledged entertainment PR company, making a business out of showbiz and working for everyone, from the stars to the studios, TV shows to soap manufacturers, giving them an extraordinary network of people they could trade favours with. So, instead of jamming everyone into the same room to watch it, the film was shown simultaneously in the homes of various stars, and the hosts, among them John Wayne and Dinah Shore, invited all their friends along. Cowan supplied a projectionist, a caterer and a print of the film to each house, then embedded a very happy journalist amidst the throng. Given such intimate access to more than thirty stars and their friends, column inches from said journalists were guaranteed. This sort of stealth campaign, which got journalists close to the stars and the stars close to the movies without resorting to the usual tactics, played most strongly on the strength of their contact books and their recognition within the industry – it was also the template for the campaign that Miramax ran for *The English Patient* years later.

In the 1970s, Cowan took one of Russell Birdwell's early ideas and updated it for the modern jet era. Where Birdwell had painted the name of a film on a highway to get attention, hoping it would be photographed from a plane, Cowan went one step further. Spotting the potential of billboards aimed at air travellers, he took out a billboard advertising *Murder By Death*, starring Peter Falk, on a building right under one of the flight paths approaching Los Angeles International Airport because he'd heard that two million people a month travelled on that flight path. It goes a long way to proving that there's no monopoly on ideas in PR: thoughts get continually reincarnated in ways that suit the times, in much the same way as music and art are self-referential, even when the artist has no idea, or hasn't heard, of what is being referenced.

There has to be talent for Cowan's magic to work, however. 'Give me a well-endowed girl who's willing to go anywhere, and she'll get her picture in a couple of papers. You can create a little flurry. But I can't sell mediocrity,' he told the *Los Angeles Magazine*. 'Zsa Zsa Gabor is probably one of the most publicized women in history, and to the best of my knowledge, she can't get a job. No one took her seriously. So it's a matter not only of getting the name out there, but how do you make it so people are really impressed?'

'Warren was more of a businessman and had no ego,' said his ex-wife Josette. 'He was very humble which is unusual for a man like that. With Jay Bernstein, he has an ego. He's cute, you know. Lee [Solters] also worked for Frank Sinatra. They were the players in town. When I was younger I loved seeing men like Warren, the old timers, the producers of that era, the PRs, the agents – they were a different breed. They were passionate, they were caring, they loved the life. So did the actors, the directors – anyone who worked then in that era, who came from the forties and fifties. Today in the PR business, producers and directors are missing the charisma.

'Business is run by lawyers and money people now. Warren didn't worry about money. He made a lot but he didn't bother. $3,500 per month in the 1970s – that's what they paid publicists. Big actors would pay more. They were very generous to their PR people. The PRs got perks then.'

'Warren wouldn't accept any bonuses. He would allow everyone else who worked with Shirley and Danny Kaye, with him, to get bonuses, although he never took them. Paul [Newman] gave bonuses. [The clients] were very grateful. Some got mad . . . they got jealous. They'd want to know why they didn't get a cover, for example. But, you know, you can't control the newspapers; they were powerful. The Warren Cowans of this world *were* able to dictate to the papers and magazines because they had power.

'[Rogers & Cowan] made everybody Senior Vice President. Warren told me that one of the reasons he made most of the people Vice President was because the highest people wanted to deal with someone with a title. They would deal directly with him because he was the president.'

Cowan dealt in collateral rather than power and influence, believing that if you kept the collateral topped up, you'd always have influence, be it with the press, the stars, their agents, the studios or whoever mattered. In the long relay race that is PR history, Cowan and Rogers picked up the baton passed on by Howard Strickling and passed it on to people like Pat Kingsley and, indirectly, Stan Rosenfield. In this way, people like James Moran and Maynard Nottage got left behind; they were running an entirely different race. However, the niceties of that system, developed and encouraged by Cowan and Rogers, were lost in the sea of speeding communications and a changing world. They had sown the seeds of the future of publicity in soil tilled by their predecessors and they only had a certain amount of control over what grew and what the weather would do to their numerous protégés, who included Michael Levine, Pat Kingsley and James Mahoney.

It is with these protégés that Rogers and Cowan have left a lasting legacy. Their company was more than just a big business, it was also a breeding ground for the new type of publicity agent, an institution renowned for churning out people eager to make their own mark on the publicity industry. The more people they had on their books the more agents they brought through their ranks, regimented and trained in the Rogers & Cowan way of thinking. Of the names that have loomed largest and most indelibly over the last fifty years, nearly all of them had their start at Rogers & Cowan. The others were flacks who sprang up from rival firms but were keen to emulate the slick ubiquity of the company.

Rogers & Cowan was the BBC of the publicity industry, not because of any Reithian impulse, but because it was a crucible for new talent. It happened once they were settled and in a routine, after the growing pains of the 1940s and the political upheaval of the early 1950s. By the time Warren Cowan had engineered Danny Kaye into becoming a UNICEF representative, created the celebrity-driven charity golf match and, with Henry Rogers, turned the Oscar build-up into one of the most important publicity bonanzas of the Hollywood year, they were ready to pass on what they knew and keep the business thriving.

The flacks they trained came out fully versed in Rogers & Cowan's belief in the brand model of celebrity, which could be applied to charity, product placement, anything. They were tooled up and ready, thanks to the Rogers branding mantra, to take celebrities into a world where a treaty could be made between product and celebrity, allowing the celebrity to earn a great deal, just by allying their name to a loaf of bread or a bottle of cola. In an era when anything and everything is allied to a product, be it football or pop concerts, rock stars or actors, it's hard to imagine a world without celebrity endorsement, but in the bright cathode-ray glow of the television set, Rogers & Cowan and its trainees set about sculpting a brave new world of publicity. Everyone, from Orson Welles to Alfred Hitchcock, agreed to sponsorship deals, and by the 1980s it was such an essential tool for selling products that even dead stars such as Marilyn Monroe were lifted from films made long before the branding revolution and posted into adverts for beer.

Publicity in the 1960s came to be as much about brand management as it was about getting attention for the stars and creating stories. Rogers & Cowan had eclipsed everyone else, particularly the old guard of the publicity world. Russell Birdwell was, despite running a few major campaigns, withdrawing into play writing; Jim Moran cut an eccentric dash as a raconteur and talk-show guest; Harry Reichenbach was all but forgotten and Maynard Nottage was a burned-out husk living a car-crash life on the hard edge of Hollywood PR. He had disappeared into the slow death of Los Angeles' endless suburban sprawl, which pushed him further and further away from Hollywood's epicentre.

Rogers and Cowan remained hugely influential, of course, with Cowan opening his own business in 1994 and Rogers resigning from the company he founded in 1991 after Rogers & Cowan was sold to Shandwick, but still the world of PR moved on. Rogers & Cowan protégés Jay Bernstein, Steve Huvane, Pat Kingsley, Michael Levine and James Mahoney were melting rapidly into the foreground from the early 1960s on. The rules, as I'll show later, were radically redefined by Pat Kingsley, who had started out as a secretary at Rogers & Cowan in 1959, moving up rapidly to become a powerful PR agent in her own right.

Thirty-One
LEE SOLTERS

Lee Solters, who started out in PR in the late 1940s, is a prime example of the crossover period in Hollywood PR. I met Lee Solters in his poster-filled office in the midst of a business centre in Los Angeles. He moved like a shuffling ferret, constantly and eagerly, and his eyes were still filled with a fire for work. He treasured his carefully measured anecdotes and illustrated them with cuttings which he regularly drew out of a box. It looked like an old music box from which a ballerina rises when you open it. His company, currently trading as Solters & Digney, had recently marked its fiftieth anniversary, but he was still going strong. He's the sort of man who'll retire only when the reaper tells him to, and he's said he'll only retire on the day he stops learning.

Lee Solters is in his late eighties – the same generation as Warren Cowan – and was part of the days of change. He opened for business in New York in 1954, having worked as a freelance during college after the Second World War. In his long career, he has represented everyone from the notoriously difficult Frank Sinatra (for two and a half decades) to Barbra Streisand (for thirty-three years). He even maintained a working relationship with Michael Jackson for over a decade. He also worked with singer and actress Carol Channing and the producer David Merrick. A New Yorker by birth, he maintained an almost complete monopoly on Broadway publicity until the 1970s, handling shows like *Annie* and *Hello, Dolly!* and stars like Ethel

Merman and Lena Horne. Like Rogers and Cowan, he began his career by planting items in the columns published in New York and Los Angeles newspapers, and he rode the changes as effectively as them – his first major client in showbusiness was Robert Q. Lewis, an early TV star who hosted three shows concurrently in the early 1950s.

I began by asking Solters how PR became such a widespread, even ubiquitous industry. 'The country developed,' he said. 'The scope became wider so there was more need for spokesperson representation and the same happened in the entertainment industry. Someone had to make an announcement about something and that was it. I'm not oversimplifying it, but that's how it happened. [I started by going] around knocking on doors. I was mainly interested in entertainment so I focused on the entertainment publicity area. It was all luck, and I happened to be at the right place at the right time. I worked with an organization and I learned and I applied what I already knew by different methods. The most important thing at NYU was, when I enrolled, I got a part-time job with a Broadway publicity office, Irving Lehrer. Then I covered major basketball games for *The New York Times*. This is before professional basketball. I had the opportunity to edit, report, write – all the jobs on the newspaper. And a part-time job in a Broadway publicity company. High school was just a way of making connections with people. Working was much better than going to college. There were too many books by professors on ethics and law. Friends of mine today call me saying, "My son or daughter wants to major in journalism," and I'm very honest and I say, "Tell them to get a job. Get in the trenches. You'll be paid; you'll learn more; going to school you have to pay $50,000 a year."

'I was going to major in journalism. It was an appropriate tie-in. I was based in New York and I got important clients to the point where I had the virtual monopoly on all Broadway shows. Competition from many big, big players. I was lucky.'

Solters clearly loved the work; his love of it radiated from him as we spoke. This is how publicists have always survived in an industry capriciously capable of chewing up and spitting out the brightest of talents.

'Whatever I had inside of me worked for me. Long hours, hard work. Not just Broadway shows, I had motion pictures, celebrities. The entertainment industry moved to the West Coast and I had to make business trips out here. The clients liked to have you here, and I had an office in LA but I was still based in New York. I came here in 1976 but I made a lot of trips to New York, Las Vegas and San Francisco. You still have the energy to do it. It's a vocation. I love what I'm doing. I enjoy meeting the press, I enjoy coming up with ideas for motion stunts. [When I came to LA, Rogers & Cowan] were the big guns out here. They were friendly competitors, but there was enough business for both of us.'

In fact, Solters had taken on one of Rogers & Cowan's old clients, Frank Sinatra, in the sixties. Showing what seems to have been a typically calm and considered approach to work when Sinatra was receiving a lot of bad press for fighting and troublemaking, Solters suggested that Sinatra allow him to invite a columnist from the local papers on his tour to visit him before the show and meet the great man face to face. Sinatra had been inured in publicity from an early age. His record company publicists had worked hard on him, and George Evans – one of the original stuntsters who died in 1950 – had hired girls to scream and faint at his concerts. Evans had drilled these girls beforehand so that they would know exactly when to swoon, when to scream and when to do both. It's the sort of stunt that harks back to the women paid to adore Rudolph Valentino and is an antecedent of the stage-managed knicker-throwing hysterics that pursued Tom Jones in the early days, thanks to the efforts of his manager Gordon Mills. It's the sort of thing that was still smiled upon in the late fifties; the press saw through it, but let it pass as it was a harmless enough stunt. They'd pounce on it now, though.

It was unsurprising that Sinatra was hard to work with as he had a vast sense of his own worth. It was on Solters' idea, and the welter of free publicity that came with it, that Sinatra's lasting image was built – one that overrides the mob connections and his reputation for being difficult – and that is as a man of the people, because columnists from papers all over America got to meet him, chat briefly with him and then be fêted at home because they'd met Sinatra in intimate surroundings.

Sinatra had fallen out with Henry Rogers when Rogers told him the truth about why he had such a bad image in the press. 'The only thing wrong with your image is you!' wrote Rogers. 'You have been doing outrageous things, you have been making outrageous statements, you have been offending the press outrageously.' Cowan was also asked for his opinion, and he couched the answer in far softer language, without actually lying to Sinatra. The crooner wrote to them a couple of weeks later, dispensing with their services. 'It took many years for me to learn that I can be honest [with a client] but not blunt,' wrote Rogers ruefully. Solters definitely learned from the mistakes of others, taking the softer, more cautious approach that Cowan used to try and rescue the situation and run with it.

Having had a Broadway background, Solters started out working much more as an entertainment PR. 'I did some corporate but I do more now than I did then. The difference between publicity and public relations is $100k a year,' he said of the move away from the entertainment side of the business. Publicity is about noise and the excitement of the moment, whereas public relations is more about planning and carefully structuring a series of events that build to a bigger picture – the sort of thing that Strickling and Rogers & Cowan specialized in. There is still a perception of PR that relies on the image put forward in *Sweet Smell of Success*, the drop-a-story-in-and-see-something-happen approach, but the successful public relations merchants, such as Lee Solters, are as much media strategists as press agents, weaving interlocking campaigns that bring a modernity of thought to the old publicity process.

It is telling that *Sweet Smell of Success* came out in the late 1950s, casting its beady, dystopian eye on an era of publicity that was passing thanks to Solters, Cowan and their ilk. It served as a warning that was heeded by the new breed of flacks. Solters, Cowan and the others made the art of asking 'What is the story and how does it grow?' into a preternaturally forward-looking business, in the same manner as one might play a game of 3D chess. They had a sixth sense for where a story will go, what it will become. The PR model promulgated by Rogers & Cowan undoubtedly influenced Solters, as it did the flacks who came out of their company. But Solters was part of the process before the changes wrought by TV came to fruition in Hollywood and the entertainment industry. Solters is old enough to remember the industry in the early days and was clear about the effects a shrinking world and speedier media would have on the industry.

'There used to be twenty, thirty or forty gossip columns. The newspapers have shrunk, they're consolidated. Now we rely on gossip columns in New York. Page six of the *New York Post*. That's the main column. [Now, agents and producers] depend upon people who tell them what publicity is. The high people in publicity now don't know how it used to be. They think their employees are right but they don't know. There is no substitute for experience. Russell Birdwell was very creative. Harry Brand *was* 20th Century Fox, he was very tough.'

Solters clearly had a sense of history post Strickling and MGM and was a high-level worker in the Fame Factory, but was he a spiritual grandson of Barnum? Did he too create stunts? It turned out that he was and he had, and his favourite stunt involved elephants and the circus.

'We worked with the Norman Bailey circus and there was a national railroad strike from midnight on a certain day. So the cargo, the staff, the animals, everything in the circus was going to be stuck eleven miles outside New York City in New Jersey. When they declared at midnight the train stopped. So they had trucks to bring in the animals to New York and I told them hold off on the elephants. "I'll get back to you," I said.

'I called the Mayor of NYC, who was a friend of mine, and asked about the Lincoln Tunnel that leads into Madison Square Garden – I said, "Please give me permission for the elephants to go through all the tiny villages and then enter that tunnel and come up into Madison Square Garden." The Mayor told me who to call and I got permission. I got releases to the press that the elephants were coming and they would start marching through the villages and then into the tunnel. Crowds started to assemble on both sides of the street. I had tipped off all the press and I put them on a truck, TV crews, everyone. They booked stands so TV crews could have the story and be there. When the elephants came a half a mile before the tunnel, I saw the person at the toll gate. I knew they couldn't accept a $100 bill as you have to have the exact money at the toll. I told the elephant handler that they *had* to pay with a $100 bill and I was right – the elephants had to wait at the toll, they weren't let through as the toll wouldn't take the $100 bill. I got the press and TV to shoot pictures of the elephants waiting at the toll and then coming out of the tunnel. We got international publicity on that. TV is by far the most effective medium for this [sort of stunt]. It's instant and it has millions of viewers. Unlike years ago, before TV. It's not what it used to be.'

Solters may have pushed himself, but he was hard on his employees too. Jackie Greene, a leading legitimate theatre publicist in New York, started out working for Solters and remembered that there was no time off allowed for anything, to the point that if one of Solters' employees needed the dentist, he would suggest they go at the weekend. This led to stirrings of discontent – many of the staff objected to having to fork out to have their teeth treated for an additional charge at the weekend. Rather than back down, however, Solters called in an old dentist friend, who he persuaded to be available for his staff's teeth, should they need attention, at the weekend for no extra charge.

Solters may have been married to the job as much as to his family, but he was part of an early generation that allowed home and work life (when possible) to remain separate. His sense of disappointment and bitterness seemed minimal, and he came across as a determined man, ticking away like a metronome, aware that even while he slept something would be happening somewhere in the world that might affect his clients or what he was doing. He, like others of his generation, and later publicists like Pat Kingsley, had an obsession with being in control. When I asked him if any clients had broken his heart, as has happened to so many flacks before him, he simply answered, 'I've had disappointment. I had one client who was in New York and came out to LA on a tour. His show was opening in Palm

Springs in so much torrential rain. It was really terrible storms. He knew that he wasn't going to renew his agreement with us. If he'd been nice, he'd have said don't come out here, the weather is too awful. We went, as he was our client. When it was over he called us in and told us. Later I received calls from producers to see if I knew anyone who could play the piano, but I never recommended him.'

In an interview with *Television Week*, Solters recalled the early days of MGM and the way the studios suppressed stories, suggesting that the PR world of today had moved on. 'Now you've got to tell them the truth,' he said, 'and you've got to come up with an angle.' This carefully skates over the possibility of the truth at another angle looking remarkably like a lie, but that's PR: concealing what you can without giving the sense of telling anything less than the truth.

Solters had difficult clients, like Sinatra, but he was long enough in the tooth by the early 1990s to resign as Barbra Streisand's PR. However, it is only Michael Jackson he has spoken about directly, and then only briefly in an interview with *Television Week* in 2003. In it Solters said that the only reason he let the Jackson account go was because Jackson wanted him 'to lie too often. When he first married Lisa Marie [Presley] he told me to deny the marriage. For six weeks I kept denying it . . . The press knew. Then finally the *Enquirer* or the *Globe* found a judge in the Dominican Republic. He handed over the marriage certificate. When the press called me and asked me, "Why did you lie?" I said, "That's showbiz."'

The flacks that came after Solters succeeded by wedding themselves to their clients twenty-four hours a day. They were completely in their pockets and had a lot to conceal on the client's behalf, but they were also at the mercy of the stars. Solters, and Cowan, who still represents Paul Newman, had stars they were faithful to and who were faithful to them. They still had the residual spirit of the studio system lingering in their blood, whereas modern stars are far more independent creatures, feeding off a wider, more desperate shoal of publicists – thanks to the agents who had risen through the ranks at the same time as Rogers and Cowan and who understood the power of branding. They saw that the stars were their own brands and guided them to see to their own needs. If they found a publicist who could serve their brand better, the agent would persuade them to move to that person or company without a second thought. This was always the case to some extent, as Rogers found out with Rita Hayworth, but from 1960 on, it became the rule rather than the exception. Publicists like Solters and Cowan maintained a sense of loyalty to clients – they didn't want the hordes of hysterical Z-listers that plague the offices of PR firms today, because they unnerved their A-list clients, precipitating their departure to other PR firms.

On the whole, stories that leak from a disgruntled flack's mouth tend to be ones that are already common knowledge. Solters, for example, will only speak about his resignation as Streisand's PR because it's common knowledge that she can be a demanding woman to work for. Part of the reason publicists don't tend to talk is an innate fear of being found out. They're living on the edge, be it in their relationship with their clients, the media or with the accoutrements that make up their life. They're identified by their lifestyle and there's a deep-seated paranoia that if they stop there'll be nothing else to do. For the publicist, there is often little life after the career stops, as Harry Brand's continued presence on the Fox lot well past his retirement date proves. The job is a huge part of the publicist's life, and when it's gone they'll miss the company, the conversations and the control. It's a sexy lifestyle, even for the more business-minded flack – the celebrity is associated with the coverage, but the publicist is always associated with the client.

Solters didn't mention him, but there seems to be no reason why he wouldn't have encountered Maynard Nottage, who is a prime example of the brand of entropy peculiar to publicists, where their life is entirely centred around *their* lifestyle and proof that when that is taken from them, chaos reigns. Lee Solters was a little different; he was a New York hustler transplanted to LA who inveigled his way into the business. His longevity is quite possibly due to that hustler outlook, and an innate knowledge that stars are a brand with a shelf life, knowledge that allowed him to survive as times got tougher from the 1970s onwards.

• Thirty-Two •

JAY BERNSTEIN AND THE RISE OF THE NEW GENERATION

The new generation of publicists, because they were born at around the time Rogers started his company, had little or no perception of PR beyond the all-consuming prominence of the modern age. Music and cinema were on the verge of becoming much more separate entities, and within a few years, a pop star wouldn't need an adjacent film career to become astonishingly famous, as Sinatra, Bing Crosby, Danny Kaye or even, to some extent, Elvis and the Beatles had. As the speed of disseminating information increased exponentially, so the PR industry, as it was rapidly becoming, fractured and lost track of its roots. It became a world of fertile crossovers, inspired by Rogers & Cowan's manoeuvring into TV and corporate publicity in the 1950s and, in these heady days, history was something of an irrelevance.

One of the biggest exponents of this new, fractured world, which only PR could negotiate and keep connected, was Jay Bernstein. Born in 1937 in Oklahoma, he came to Los Angeles as soon as he was able, escaping his father's trade. Like so many great publicists before him, his father ran a shop; it seems unlikely that this is coincidence – the art of selling was in the blood of nearly all the early publicists, be it the circuses of Reichenbach and Nottage's youth or the shops of Strickling, Birdwell or Bernstein. All they wanted was something more glamorous to sell, and Hollywood was the natural place for them to gravitate towards.

Bernstein always wanted to be in showbiz, though not as an actor. He was one of the first stars of the PR industry to grow up entirely subsumed by the vision of Hollywood, and he wanted in by whatever means necessary.

'Since I was fifteen I've lived through the movies,' he said when we spoke just prior to his death in 2006. 'I was a fat kid and I wasn't good at sports. I would always go to movies and tell my parents that I was at sports practice.

'My mother was born in Tyler, Texas and my father, Oklahoma. His father was born in Paris, Texas. Nothing to do with showbusiness; I just always wanted to be in the business. I didn't want to be an actor because all the actors in those days were really handsome men like Errol Flynn, Clark Gable, and they would put the woman second, and then they'd put me third like Tony Randall or William Benedict or someone. So I said, if I can only be third in my chosen profession, then I better choose another one, because for five minutes I wanted to be an actor. I realized it didn't work that way. Now, if I had known they were going to have Dustin Hoffman and Al Pacino and Robert De Niro, I would have looked at it differently. I just wanted to be in showbusiness.

'After I got out of college with a BA [in history] from Claremont, I was in the Army for six months. So I did my six months in Indianapolis, Indiana.'

On leaving the Army, Bernstein was free to follow his showbusiness dream and headed off for Los Angeles. 'So I came out here. My family gave me $1,000. I went through Vegas, had $400 left when I got here. Got off the freeway, building looked nice. Took the first building that I saw. It was on National Boulevard in the hood. There was a murder the third night I was there. I was in the Mexican district. I paid $90 a month and I couldn't afford it. So I shared it with a friend from Oklahoma who came out. He slept on the floor on an air mattress. Then I couldn't get a job, so I was going to work for the Union Bank, as a teller, and before I had to do that, I got a job at William Morris.'

Bernstein had been doing the rounds of all the studios with little luck – 'obviously you can't get past the guard,' he said – and MCA had told him there would be a year's wait before they'd call him. William Morris had told him he'd have to wait six months before there would be an opening, so Bernstein, unwilling to let it go, started to flirt with the receptionist, revealing the necessary tenacity for a PR man and an early eye for the ladies.

His flirtatious encounters with the William Morris receptionist paid off. 'She got a phone call saying one of the mail-room boys had wrecked the car. She said, "Go back up there now." They had said to call in four or five months, but I was there so they hired me,' he explains.

It was the perfect start, but for the money. It has long been a cliché that the mail-room boy will be able to work his way to the top, but at $45 a week, he needed another job to survive. 'I had a relative whose father owned a ball-bearing factory downtown, so at night I'd put on overalls and from eight at night to two in the morning I was making ball bearings.' When that proved too much, he got a job at Laury's, on Le Sevigne, parking cars.

The job at William Morris was hardly fulfilling for a young man who'd been an officer in the Army. 'At William Morris I'm taking their urine samples and stool samples, buying their cigars and whatever,' Bernstein said. However, the boredom didn't last long. 'I got fired from William Morris 'cause I wrecked a car – a Volkswagen. I had never used a clutch before. So I stepped on the clutch instead of the brake and ran into the back of some guy. I said, "My God, it's my fault." The next day I told him where I worked, and he sued William Morris for six figures. So they fired me. Luckily for me, [also working] in the mailroom was the son of a famous producer who was working the summer.'

The producer was Sheldon Leonard, who worked on *The Dick Van Dyke Show* and *Make Room for Daddy*; he and his partner Danny Thomas were 'the real McCoy', big name producers with five or six shows. Leonard's son, Steve Burshad, took pity on Bernstein and invited him to dinner. Bernstein was ready to take full advantage of this opportunity and pulled out every stop to get some sort of work or opportunity.

'I had never cried – down south you don't cry – but I made myself cry at dinner, because men don't like to see other men cry. It was June and it was right before my birthday. My birthday's June seventh and this was June fifth, and I put on my only suit – a double-breasted blue suit. It was hotter than hell. [Sheldon] never told me he was going to do anything; I just felt I'd sold it though. I got the part.'

The next day, Bernstein waited by the phone, hoping that his self-belief would come to something. 'I was there from like eight o'clock, by the phone. Noon I'm getting a little nervous, about three o'clock I think I'm fucked, and about four o'clock I get a call from Sheldon Leonard's secretary. She said tomorrow you have an appointment at eleven o'clock at Rogers & Cowan. I had no idea what Rogers & Cowan was, or [about] PR or anything like that. At that time there was a woman called Tammy Brenner [with the company], it was called Rogers, Cowan & Brenner.'

It was Brenner who Bernstein met. 'She said, "Go to the office over there, there's a typewriter. Write me a story on what Sheldon Leonard thinks of comedy." So I figured I had a pretty good shot . . . I did that, came back and they hired me. And I got much more money.'

He went from earning $40 a week at William Morris to $55 at Rogers & Cowan. It was a step up, and although Bernstein didn't know anything about the job, he was prepared to learn. 'They didn't teach [PR] in Oklahoma. They didn't have a PR course. I guess [I picked it up pretty quickly]. The man who had the most influence on me in the beginning was an actor named Nick Adams. I was like his protégé and he was . . . my mentor. I was his assistant on *The Rifleman* with Chuck Connors, who I later ended up managing on *Make Room for Daddy* with Danny Thomas.

'I did that for about a year before I got transferred to what they call the Personality Department, and I was Guy McElwaine's assistant. He was handling the Rat Pack – Frank Sinatra, Dean Martin, Sammy Davis Jr. I was assisting him on his people like Natalie Wood and Shirley MacLaine. Then they gave me some people . . . they gave me Eddie Fisher, Jayne Mansfield, Gary Crosby. They're the three that I remember.'

He started off well, with three celebrities just finishing their first flush of fame and needing a spike of publicity to reinvigorate them.

Being young, eager and hungry in 1960, Bernstein was the man for the job. Like every good PR agent before him, he immersed himself in the business in an effort to outshine his peers. Like Nottage had with Reichenbach, he manufactured rivalries to keep him active, successful and moving forward, and this rivalry even extended to his superiors.

'Henry Rogers would get to work by 6.30 a.m., and I'd be there at 6 a.m. He'd leave at 5 p.m. Warren Cowan would come in at like 9 a.m. and he'd leave about 6.30 or 7 p.m. I stayed until at least 7.30 p.m. So I was in before one and out after the other.'

It was a necessary move, allowing Bernstein to learn as he went along as well as enabling him to pick up any stray nuggets of wisdom that fell from the top. He had come in at the right time and the right place – a few stunt tears had been enough to land him at the top of the heap and despite the corporate adventures in soap and television, Rogers & Cowan was still, under Cowan, a showbiz outfit. 'We were called Frankie's Flex, The Cufflink Cutie-pies, and we all wore these . . . black suits that looked as though they were painted on. And we had the cufflinks . . . the star sapphire cufflinks. The big collars and the real tight clothes.'

There was a palpable sense of showmanship about Bernstein when I met him. He was living in the house Carole Lombard had owned when she was married to Clark Gable, living the lifestyle to the max, right up until his death, and he was keen to point out his Aston Martin, his love of young women and his exquisite home, surrounded by all the paraphernalia and gewgaws of his years in the industry, as well as boasting about his bling before it became bling. He maintained a lifestyle that involved sharp clothes and beautiful women until the very end – he even asked one reporter he met not to tell the girl who was due to arrive during the interview how old he was. There's much more caution involved now, of course, and the industry isn't run on showmanship so much.

The long, benevolent shadow of Barnum lived on in Bernstein, a trace element of the carnival way of doing things. Bernstein's early career was focused on getting himself noticed, about figuring out a way to beat his peers to the big client, and his entry into this rat race started, appropriately, with the Rat Pack. This, for someone who was very much a man's man, was the right place to start.

'When I was working on *Sergeants Three* in 1960, if I tried to get close to Frank Sinatra there were too many people ahead of me. I was a kid . . . and Dean Martin didn't really want people around him; he just had Matt Gray as his guy. And Peter Lawford had a bunch of guys around him. But the one who didn't was Sammy Davis Jr. 'Cause Sammy was married to May Britt, who was a Scandinavian actress who gave up her career to marry Sammy. Their marriage was illegal in fourteen states at the time. So I get close to Sammy, 'cause I was right there. So if anyone wanted to do anything with Sammy, within a month they had to go through me. But we didn't understand black people here then. It's like, right now, I can say I lived before black people had any rights. Where I lived, the buses had seats for the coloured. I left there at eighteen, and there was only one coloured person in my college. I watched the power of the blacks, and eventually every meeting I'd go to would be headed by a black person. And later women were helping them, and they got their power and sort of pushed the blacks back to their seats at the table. Now the women run everything. And now we're on level three, which is the gays. Take a look at the movies they've made and what's going on. This whole thing and now they have a power that the blacks and the women have. And now have an equal say. I'm really glad John Wayne wasn't alive to see *Brokeback Mountain*.'

Bernstein rose through the Rogers & Cowan ranks with astonishing speed, and by 1962 established himself as a power in the Hollywood PR industry in his own right, more by luck than judgement, though it all turned out for the best.

'I didn't want to quit,' he said, 'but I had a client who . . . it's hard to tell now, I was [young]. I was very handsome and I had this client who was attracted to me. Everyone else wanted to sleep with her. I didn't because I was living with an actress by the name of Leslie Parrish, who had done the *Manchurian Candidate*, the original. She was the Queen of Diamonds [in that], and was Daisy Mae in the movie *Li'l Abner* before I knew her. We were very happy. And this client of mine kept hitting on me. I was able to handle it, but one night this client told me there was an interview that had come up last minute and she wanted me to be there and I told Leslie that I'd be back in two hours at the latest. And four hours later I came back with my leg torn out of my pants, dark suit smelling like a perfume factory, and I was actually raped. Even though it was friendly rape. It was Jayne Mansfield.

'So I got home and, hoping to save myself, I parked five blocks away. I walk the five blocks to the house, hoping I can sneak in, take a shower. But [Leslie] is sitting there right outside our house on the curb, because the cat had been killed, run over by a car, three hours before. We went into the back yard and buried the cat. Next morning she said, "You either get off the Jayne Mansfield account or it's over for us." So I went to Warren Cowan and said "You've got to take me off the Jayne Mansfield account." I told him the situation. So he called Jayne. She said, "If you take Jay Bernstein off the account I'll fire you." So the only thing that I could do to be honourable was quit. 'Cause then she could stay. And I opened my first office in my girlfriend's spare bedroom. And Warren Cowan gave me a couple of clients: Joel Gray, Jerry Rothschild.'

Cowan's reputation was and is an honourable one and he certainly set Bernstein up in style in 1963, despite his tendencies towards the showboating, lifestyle-emulating style of Maynard Nottage.

'I made a deal with Warren, because he knew how close I was to Sammy, that I wouldn't ask Sammy to come with me for one year; I wouldn't accept him. Warren was tough but fair; he warned me that I was doing a Nottage – I'm not sure what he meant exactly, but I didn't want to louse up and I wanted to part company on the best terms possible, so I agreed I'd be careful. So, after one year Sammy came with me, and had me move into his house. I had since broken up with my girlfriend and I had a studio apartment. I had one guy running errands for me who was a friend of Sammy's manager. And we put the typewriter on the ironing board and the files in the refrigerator and pulled the plug out so they wouldn't burn up or freeze. But when Sammy gave me his house to stay in when he was doing *Golden Boy* on Broadway, then I took the money from the apartment and got the money for the only office I ever had. I never liked offices. I had a big PR firm. I became a big contender with Rogers & Cowan. I had corporations, AT&T, US Steel, General Mills, Kodak, Dr Pepper, Canada Dry. [I enjoyed it] at the time. I wouldn't want to do it again. I think everything I've done I enjoyed doing it when I did it.'

It's a big leap away from personal to corporate PR, but Bernstein was ready for it; as the 1960s really started to swing, so did his business, Jay Bernstein Public Relations, and despite every aspect of the media becoming more corporate, following the model of the studios and TV in the previous thirty years, he still found a lot of stars to work with. 'I had Burt Lancaster, and because of Sammy I had Aretha Franklin, Dionne Warwick, Diana Ross, Barry White, Isaac Hayes, The Supremes, The Temptations, all of Motown, Lou Rawls. The list goes on and on.'

But change was in the air, and Bernstein was looking to push the boundaries of PR beyond those set by Rogers & Cowan.

• Thirty-Three •

STAN ROSENFIELD: POWER AND SUPPRESSION

The generation of publicists born of the Rogers & Cowan ethos spread rapidly, and as they set up their own companies, they brought in more eager young men and women determined to make their name and fortune in Hollywood. Jay Bernstein brought Stan Rosenfield into the publicity fold after an ambling path around Hollywood looking for something that suited him and Rosenfield went on to become one of the biggest powerbrokers of the new Hollywood.

'I came from Oklahoma,' Stan told me. He had an avuncular look about him and the mannerisms of a favourite older brother – he may have had something of the *Annie Hall*-era Woody Allen questioning nebbish about him, but underneath that he was clearly as solid as a rock. This was a man who would go into battle on your behalf and win, yet if you were at a party, he'd never be at the centre of the room sucking away attention. He'd be subtly working it so that his client was always in that position. 'Jay Bernstein lived down the street from me. Alan Hirschfeld grew up up the street from me. Three Jews who occupied Oklahoma. We went to Sunday school together. Hirschfeld went to New York; he went on to run Fox for a number of years, then he was President for Columbia Pictures. Jay Bernstein used to skip football practice as a youth so he could go to see movies. I didn't know what I wanted to do. I didn't want to live in Oklahoma and when I graduated my mother died so I had to stay for the summer in

Oklahoma. I moved to California but I didn't know what I wanted to do.

'I came out here without a job or direction. I ran into Jay when I came out here and he was working at Rogers & Cowan at the time. I didn't intend to get into this business. It was 1962. I was talking about this friend of mine who talked about training programmes at the William Morris Agency. I didn't know what it was, and he [Jay] told me, "It's a theatrical agency." Nothing more came of that and I took a job working for SVC, a subsidiary of IBM. I hated it so much, the people, the work, the drive in, the dress code and the drive home. I kept saying, I've got to get out . . . I'll go to law school or something else. I didn't know what to do. One day I went in and they fired me. I didn't show the aptitude! I didn't want to quit because I was afraid of hearing what they would say. They made a decision, which was in their best interests, before I made one that was in mine. From here on out, no one would make a decision in my best interests without me doing it first. Or it not being me making the decision.

'I called WMA [William Morris Agency] and said I'm ready to come and work for you. They laughed, said it didn't work like that and sent me an application form. Little did I believe it would happen and so I didn't apply for a couple of weeks.

'I was unemployed and had been sacked. I couldn't have fucked it up more if I had tried. I looked at my chequebook and I had no money. I got a call. "Hello, Mr Rosenfield, this is Jackie from the WMA." I was going to learn the history of Hollywood from the bottom up. Jackie said, "Would you be available for interview?" I knew nothing about the entertainment business. Richard Weisman was a buddy of mine – his father was Frederick Weisman, a big talent agent and Frank Sinatra's right hand. He would give me tickets to parties. I got the job because I answered two questions better than anyone ever answered. The first was: "How can you work for as little as we will pay you?" I said, "You have to invest in yourself. It's not what I'm doing now. It's an opportunity. I have to seize an opportunity when it's there. If it costs me money by not making money, then so be it. I will do it." She said to me, "You are making it very difficult for me to say no." I replied, "No, I'm not trying to make it difficult for you to say no, I'm trying to make it easy for you to say yes!"

'They gave me the job right there. It was the best answer I ever gave to any question I have ever been asked. I started and they fired me after three months. There was a screw-up delivery and I got blamed for it. I made a mistake but it wasn't really my fault. I got fired on 13 August 1963 and now I'd got a taste for it all. Gate guards at the studios knew me. I could still drive my car on to any studio lot until they realized that I was in my own car all the time, not the WMA car.

'I called agencies and asked if they had any entry positions. I then went to Creative Management Association and I talked to Lia Perwin, who later became a district attorney. She said, "Do you know who Freddie Fields is?" and I said, "Sure I know who he is. He runs an agency." I said I knew him. She asked me why I wasn't working. In the end, they hired me. I worked there for a year. It was very similar to the company we have here, nothing but A-list clients. However, they told me I was too young-looking at that point. It was 1965. They told me, "You need to be more patient; we will put you in the TV department." They told me they couldn't introduce me as an agent to the big stars in the movie department as I was too young-looking. I made a mistake and I left. I gave two weeks' notice. Lou Pitt replaced me and I realized I had made a huge mistake. I asked them for my job back, but they loved Lou so they wouldn't give me my job back and sack him.

'One night I met a secretary at CMA and we partied all night. The phone rang the next morning and it was a buddy of mine saying, "Jay Bernstein is looking for someone." Jay hired me that afternoon.

'I hated the first two years. I didn't like PR, I didn't like working for Jay. We had known each other in Oklahoma. He wasn't easy to work for. I didn't like any of it. It wasn't the hours that bothered me. It was that you made things up, you dealt with your imagination. Everyone I'd worked for believed it was "on the screen", that it's not made up. I hated it but I kept remembering Freddie Fields' words, "You gotta stick at it." I joined in 1965 and stayed there ten years. Then something happened by chance. I was reading a magazine about the golf Masters. It was about the chances of winning the Masters, and if you had won it in between the ages of twenty-six and thirty-five then you may win again. If you hit thirty-five and had never won it, then the chances are you never will. I thought, It's time. I need to start thinking about my own business.

'I must have thought about it for three years before I did it. What kind of company do I want to run? Who do I want to represent? Who do I want working there? Do I really want to do that? Do I want to produce? A lot of people don't like PR. I opened up my own office in 1975. I did what I wanted to do.

'Jay and I got on fine. We understood each other. Jay said he was the worst person in the world, as he would plot your demise at night. If you show loyalty to him, if you give to him he will give back in kind. I said to him, "Look, you've had a lot of people leave you, I have no intention of taking any of your clients." He needed to know that. He said, "Well if you won't take any from me, I will refer people to you that maybe can't afford our fee." Which he did. I took Martin Milner as he wouldn't stay [behind] if I wasn't with Jay. The other was Bruce Dern, who was a major star in those days. We had an arrangement, Jay and I, that we would share him. I agreed to it. Dern was great to have in my company. After a couple of years he didn't want to be shared any more [and became solely a Rosenfield client]. Then at the end of a couple of years [Jay] called me and said, "I'm going completely into management. I'm closing down the PR company. I'm going totally in management now. If I don't close it down do you want to run it?" I said no. Anyway, that was pretty much how I got from there to here. I got lucky.'

Rosenfield may have got lucky, but he was watching the way the wind was blowing. His comment about Bruce Dern is telling – by the time he set up in business on his own, the benign time promulgated by Rogers & Cowan was over and you needed stars on your client list to earn respect from other stars and from anyone you were in business with. Rogers and Cowan were big fish in a very small pond that was occupied by only a few other fish, who all had a gentlemanly respect for each other. By the time Rosenfield opened his company in 1975 that small pond was occupied by a vast number of smaller fish on the edge of a feeding frenzy. Any tactic that could be used was used.

'I kept my prices down at the beginning,' said Stan, confirming this, 'but later I didn't. I charged less than Rogers & Cowan and Jay. It was a gradual thing. You get lucky along the way. Most of our clients are A list. We don't have a contract with anyone. Danny DeVito has been with us since 1977, Dern since 1971, De Niro since 1991, George Clooney 1993, Geoffrey Rush 1996, John Goodman 1988, Kelsey Grammer for seven or eight years. I can't think in terms of a list. We represented Clooney a month before *ER* debuted. We have seven [publicists] including Charles Mahur. He's our editor. He's the best editor imaginable. He worked for the *LA Times*. One of the things I believe in is selling to people who know the difference. Most PR people are terrible writers. You can't send badly written press releases out.'

Stan has been consumed by his work since he joined Bernstein in 1965 but hasn't allowed the work to eat away at him. 'I can't get rich on this, but I can make good money, and I could have retired several years ago, so I'm doing it because I like it, not because I need the money,' he said. It is his steady approach that keeps him in the business, and keeps clients such as George Clooney and Robert De Niro on his books. He is the sort of flack who will start making calls six months in advance of a client going to a major film festival just to ensure they get the best suite at the swankiest hotel because it's 'what needs to be done' and he rarely loses his cool. 'It's like being a frontman in a political campaign,' he told *Daily Variety* in 2006. 'You know what you have to accomplish. You know what the needs of the talent are.' It is his strategies that keep him in command of the situation, his ability to stay utterly in control, even when a client, such as Charlie Sheen, is going through a very messy, very public divorce and is attracting a great deal of scurrilous gossip and journalists are ringing Rosenfield's phone off the hook.

He's stayed this way by keeping on top of the business and instinctively knowing where to turn next. I asked him about the differences in the business now from when he started out. 'It's a different ball game now,' he said. 'In 1973 it was different, again in

1976. It changed again in 1986 and in 1992. If you stay away too long you may never get back in because it's a different game. I'm not a publicist any more, I'm a media strategist. I'm not selling movie tickets, I'm selling someone's brand through a product. I'm interested in certain writers, photographers, but that's it. It's about control.'

Control was certainly part of the agenda at the time – people like Paul Bloch, Alan Nierob, Steve Huvane and Pat Kingsley were also following this dictum. So much money was being ploughed into Hollywood that there had to be some measure of control over the lives of the stars. In the early 1980s, it was particularly crazy. Stars like John Belushi were splashing their drug-addicted lives over the tabloids and dying in public a bit at a time. This was a time of monster hits like *ET*, and out of that otherwise sweet and inoffensive film came Drew Barrymore, one of the youngest stars to get herself into trouble with drugs. When Hollywood in general, and the publicists in particular, started to take control of the situation, such stories all but disappeared amongst the biggest money earners in Hollywood.

Rosenfield had trained under a showman – Jay Bernstein was a man prone to grandstanding and getting sucked into the lifestyle, although he had infinitely more control than Nottage – and he had learned from his mentor's mistakes and did not allow himself to be tied up in the lifestyle. Control was all.

The subtle power that Rosenfield exudes is a trait he shares with fellow Rogers & Cowan alumni Bloch, Huvane and Nierob. All of them were always there for their clients in the way that Rogers & Cowan and the Fixers were; they were subtle and they never made a fuss, even when Paul Bloch was escorting stars such as Bob Hope to Vietnam to entertain the troops. Part of Rosenfield's ethos was to request faxes of every scrap of information that passed through their hands on behalf of their clients – not only allowing them to keep an accurate eye on the various states of affairs they were operating on but also to make it clear to the clients just how much work was being done on their behalf, as clients often get to a point in their career when they wondered what the publicist is actually doing for them. Rosenfield made sure he had a paper trail they could follow, and that paperwork was a physical manifestation of the work he put in on behalf of a client, so if they accosted him he would have something to show them. All publicists have to be possessed of preternatural time management skills and an ability to make the right call at the right time, be it to the press, the studios, the stars or their agents. This is probably why Bernstein never became as powerful a PR agent as his peers – he was too much the showman, too much the lifestyle-junkie to effectively balance everyone on his books. That Bernstein remained a big name is testament to the fact that some of his clients liked his eccentricities, though not all by any means.

A good publicist will not take the crazies, the failures, the serial exhibitionists if that exhibitionist streak is not channelled into something worthwhile. At the time Stan Rosenfield got into the PR world, it was beginning to open up as a sensible career choice for a hungry young graduate. As a consequence, it paid to be selective. The lesser publicists would always have some desperate C to Z-list celebrity or wanabee to bulk out their books, but the good ones, the ones who have survived, the behind-the-scenes powerbrokers, channelled their interests exclusively into major stars.

'Yesterday a front-desk person was complaining she had two magazines to read and clip [out articles about clients],' he said. 'We know if someone is going to be in the papers, we know it already.' Rosenfield has always had a handle on the coverage his clients receive, unlike some publicists who will simply hunt through the press for cuttings and then claim they generated the ink. He also has a firm policy on who he will represent. 'You can pick up the tabloids and the weeklies, 90 per cent of those they write about we wouldn't take on our books. De Niro fits, George Clooney fits the profile. We only want a certain kind of talent here. It's about their work. Jessica Simpson is not about the work. Paris Hilton is not about the work, it's about the celebrity. I'm not interested in that.'

If the high end of celebrity – those who acquired their status through doing something special – was one of the main things that mattered to Rosenfield, then the thing that drove his need to change was the constant, rapid spread of new technology.

'The adaptation of technology is what is important. We haven't ordered a news release station [to send out mass press releases] in years. Multiple photos are out of business. We have one on the computer. You have to keep up with the technology. In 1979 what happened was I bought an IBM memory card writer. It could memorize fifty pages, then you could do mail merge. Then the Macs came in and I got one as my first computer. Databases, spell checks etc. This was all great because I could do the work of three people.

'I was working for Jay in 1971. I said I had a great idea. I said, "Let's represent the different States of America." They all have film commissions. We could get a lot of money there. This is one of those things that at the time you have no idea what you're really doing. It's a great idea but . . . Jay wanted to know when minute notes would be given out. They weren't ready and he got upset. The meeting lasted three hours so it's going to take at least three hours to transcribe the tape! He didn't think like that. I wrote a pitch letter for acquiring the States. We sent out about 40 letters to 40 states. We got at least 30 letters back and we could pick and choose. They all wanted proposals. We thought, OK, we will write one proposal and you say, "Dear Colorado" in one and "Dear Montana" in another. We have an eighteen-page proposal, so you hire some girl to do it. Kelly Secretarial service. We bring in this girl to sit behind a typewriter. She's typing all that stuff out with a different state name in each letter. You have to proof read it. It goes on for ten days all in all. Ten years later I could do the whole thing in a morning with spell check.

'A couple of months ago I was on a panel for Entertainment for Professional Publicists. When I started we didn't have anything like that. You go out today and get a job in an agency. Five years later you'll say we had such archaic ways of communications like email and internet. That's it. That's the story, you have to keep up with technology, but some things never change. I'm gonna get you a front cover and I'm gonna tell you about it. You still make creative decisions. You still have that personal thing with the client. Jay always used to say, "Did you merchandise it?" His expectation of my performance level meant I didn't tell him everything, I don't have to tell him everything.'

Whatever the differences in approach between Bernstein and Rosenfield, the latter certainly learned how to merchandise. He sells every last scrap of a story on a client to the papers, the radio, the TV, making sure all the while that the exposure they get – and he gets for that matter – is the right sort of exposure. He is an exponent of the 360-degree moment, where you let everybody know what is happening before the moment is gone – there's only one opportunity after the first spike of interest to get that attention. The difference between Bernstein and Rosenfield is that Bernstein used that 360-degree merchandising moment to get exposure for himself, whereas Rosenfield has always pursued exposure for his business.

Stan Rosenfield gave a keynote lecture at UCLA to students from the Entertainment Public Relations course, and it neatly exposes the frailties of the modern method of PR recruitment, as well as the dangers inherent in the Nottage approach. His modus operandi for hiring assistants, he told the students, was to first check if they're careful, if they could send him a letter with the correct spelling of various names, the correct punctuation and so on. If anything was incorrect, they could 'meet at a party and have a drink together . . . but I'll never give [them] a paycheque'. Careless people lose him business, he said, something he can't afford to have happen.

'OK, so now you're hired as an assistant,' he continued. 'Someone once said, "The entertainment business can only be learned. It cannot be taught." I think that's right. So here is what I want you to understand: the agency has hired you to provide assistance for low pay in return for teaching you the business. Most agencies also want to test your mettle. People you work with may try to bust you out. If they can't bust you out they will know that once you're a publicist, your clients can't bust you out either.'

His lecture also offers a superb guide to what a publicist needs to know. 'If you're going to represent talent,' he said, 'you need to know three things – well, actually, you need to know a lot more than three things, but here are the three things you *really* need to know.' They are:

1) You need to know why your client hired you, what their expectations are and if you can meet them. Expectations change, so keep abreast of the changes.

2) How does the client conduct his business? Ask! Does the client prefer email or fax, calls every hour or every week, to be contacted by an assistant, through his or her agent or manager? Learn the client's dynamics.
3) Learn about the entire entertainment business, 'because just knowing publicity is not enough. You need to know about film and television production; distribution; television ratings, film and television marketing and the agency and management business. In short, although you are functioning in only one area of the entertainment business, your advice and judgement cut across all areas.

'Learning your job is also learning to deal with the media, and there is only one thing you can learn about dealing with the media. One thing: it's exactly like a game of pool. It's not enough to make the shot, because you have to leave yourself in a position for the next shot. Dealing with the media is not just making your point today. You need to come back tomorrow. You need to be able to say "no" to somebody today in a way that will not make you unwelcome tomorrow.'

Rosenfield has a point. It used to be said among publicists when I was starting out in PR that 'I'd never fall out with anybody'. Now it's virtually impossible to achieve that happy goal, but one has to keep trying, it's all part of the journey, or perhaps the many journeys, of PR. During my time in Los Angeles, speaking to and researching some of the great men and women of the industry, I found myself beginning to understand my own complexities. I began to get a little scared, because I found so many people in both the past and present damaged by the business and their heartfelt need, their desperate urge to be involved. Harry Reichenbach died young and, like Princess Diana or James Dean but for the fact that his story is an arcane one by public standards, remains a brilliant, untouched figure, an icon of PR genius unblemished by bitterness and the sour underbelly of the fame factory. But if you live, the business begins to eat away at you, as it did with Maynard Nottage and others.

Rosenfield's balanced view is helped by the fact that he is one of the few publicists who has taken an active interest in the past. He is not willing to make the same mistakes that have haunted other flacks and left them bitter. I sensed that he was enjoying himself enough to continue working until forced out by ill-health or a lack of enjoyment. The balance he maintained, like Strickling, was enough to sustain him in perpetuity.

Thirty-Four

BERNSTEIN THE SHOWMAN

Life and work would conspire to keep Bernstein, like many of his forebears in PR, very much alone, thanks to his tendency towards self-aggrandizing stunts. When he married the model Cabrina Finn in 1993, for example, he sold the occasion to network TV, staging the ceremony underwater. The hoopla was broadcast for *Lifestyles of the Rich and Famous*. The memory of the PR stunt lasted longer than the marriage as they were divorced two years later. He was also notorious for having blondes hanging from his arms. He seems to have lived the lifestyle at the expense of a life in a manner similar to Maynard Nottage, who, ironically, died just as Bernstein was making his name. It is another reason why the PR industry needs to learn a little from the past and counterbalance some of the joyful innocent anarchy of the early days with a more careful, considered working practice without getting tied up in corporate work and the blandishments of the modern celebrity pack, whose cloned armies flock to Hollywood and glamour spots around the world, all hoping to become the next great star with a publicist hyping them to the rafters, unaware of the glass ceiling and the fact that their ubiquity makes them so much less special. '[I've] met probably one million people and heard of five million. So it's really hard now to . . . remember all of them,' Bernstein told me. He was referring to a question about whether or not he knew who Harry Reichenbach was, but it holds true for the star system and PR's involvement in it. It's always the one or two bright stars that stand out.

It's interesting to note that Maynard Nottage's name cropped up in our conversation as an afterthought, a warning against the perils inherent in succumbing to the lifestyle of the stars. I hadn't heard of Nottage at that stage of my journey, so I let Bernstein's comment pass without question, but when I listened back to it, at home in Britain with the benefit of hindsight and an armful of Nottage's papers, it struck me as extraordinary that Nottage, who had clung to his belief that someone ought to acknowledge his place in the creation of the PR industry and the celebrity game, should have his name used today as a pejorative noun for a flashy failure destined to burn out. Bernstein was in a different class, a survivor despite his outré tendencies. Was Nottage the example that kept him as close as he was ever going to get to the straight and narrow?

Jay Bernstein's approach to the PR industry, once he had set up on his own, was one of even more intensity than he had displayed with Rogers & Cowan. He pushed his staff hard and fast to achieve the best results and keep the business ticking over.

'My people all wore beepers when the doctors first got them,' Bernstein said, 'and I would have beeper checks. All the women hated me. I would have a beeper check at two in the morning, just to see if they had their beepers on. If not we would have a meeting the next day. I always felt I was different to Rogers & Cowan, because if they had to make a choice between their client and the press, they'd pick the press. They said, "Your client's going to be gone in six months to a year, but Army Archerd's going to be here for years." I didn't care. I took the client's point of view and I fought for them. 'Cause I felt, like, hey, Bob Shapiro hurt his career with OJ [Simpson] but I admire him, even though it hurt him. But hey, that's your job. That's what you're supposed to do.'

These are the choices that come back to haunt the people running the PR industry, and the reason so many of them have ended their days as lonely, embittered men. The client is always going to have their own self-interest at heart, and the PR man is paid to be part of that solar system of self-belief and protection. Bernstein certainly seemed to have been sucked into it, and when I met him there seemed, under the bravado and handsome exterior, a man betrayed by circumstances he could have controlled. It is this risk that makes the PR industry a joy and a devil to work in – you can either be dispassionate on behalf of your clients or throw fuel on the fire in their heart. Or you can crash headlong into every star you work for and burn to a crisp on entry. There's very rarely any middle ground; even Henry Rogers had a fit of pique when Danny Kaye, who was a close friend as well as a client, told him he'd prefer Warren Cowan to represent him, and Rogers and Cowan are the most successful, least bitter men in the business.

But Bernstein wooed the press too – almost as much as he fought with them. 'I had a disagreement with Army Archerd, and he didn't speak to me for twenty-five years. It was funny, I just got an award and he had to present it to me, last month.'

'Sammy Davis's manager was a guy named Sy Marsh. Sy had a son and he says, "Jay, how can I maximize that I've just had my first child?" And I said, "Well, the best thing to do is I'll give you Harrison Carol," he was a columnist at one of the papers, "I'll put it in the *Daily Variety* and *Hollywood Reporter*. So you'll get three shots at it." He said, "Well thank you." And I did it for him; we were close friends.

'Army Archerd called him the next day and said, "Sy, I thought we were friends. What is this about you had a child? Why didn't you call me?" And he said "Well Jay Bernstein told me to . . ." and that was the end of it. And Army never spoke to me again, except to punch me out once. It was funny. He punched out my lights. What happened was that we were at Red Buttons' house and he said something to me, and we were about to hit each other. Vince Edwards was just trying to stop it. But what he did is he held my arms down so I couldn't hit him. So Army just kicked the shit out of me.'

The story behind this is that Bernstein had been double-playing Archerd, who wrote for the *Daily Variety*, and a columnist for the *Hollywood Reporter* called Mike Connolly – he had placed similar stories with both men, which was against the rules of the delicate game that publicist and journalist play with each other.

There was a level of paranoia attached to upsetting journalists; on the one hand the flack wants to show the journalist who's boss, but on the other, if they come on too strong, there's a risk that journalists won't ever use that flack as a source again, as Louella Parsons and Hedda Hopper routinely proved in their time as queens of Hollywood gossip journalism. It's a game of backstabbing, fear, loathing and frantic phone calls at all hours of the day and night, with both sides trying to prove that the other is at fault and then flattering and attempting to buy the affections of their opposition. To this end, after the double play, and especially after the editor of the *Hollywood Reporter* got involved and expressed his displeasure with Bernstein, a package turned up at Connolly's house. Connolly got a call from his housekeeper saying, 'There's a huge box sat here in the foyer and it's from Jay Bernstein's office.' His response was, 'Well open it, see what it is.' The housekeeper duly did so and told him, 'It's a television set!' Connolly went to his editor and said, 'Jay Bernstein said he's very sorry, he didn't mean to double-play this item and he sent me a television set. What should I do?' The editor, poker-faced, asked, 'Is it colour or black and white?' The housekeeper had said it was a state-of-the-art colour TV and Mike Connolly's boss instructed him to keep it and called Bernstein to thank him.

'After I fell out with Army,' said Bernstein, 'I thought, I'm going to have no one. If Mike gets mad then I'm out of the trades. I called Mike Connolly [later] and said, "I'll be your number one boy." I knew I couldn't lose him. I hired a secretary to work at William Morris to get important memos that Mike would like to see. I would then put them in Mike's mailbox. Anything I wanted I got – she got paid by both places. It was a secret; I wore gloves so there were no prints.'

He also gave a Cadillac, to another journalist. '[Because] she needed a car and she was a columnist. It would be frowned on if anyone knew about it.'

Bernstein's house was a shrine to his success – fat rolodexes weighed down a nondescript desk in an office surrounded by decades of memorabilia. Framed front pages and pictures of Jay alongside every A-list film and entertainment star of a bygone generation covered every inch of wall space, with Jay beaming out of all of them with a lugubrious smile. Jay was the 'main man' to showbiz royalty, from Sharon Stone to Pamela Anderson, Michael Jackson to Stacy Keach, William Shatner to Lee Majors, Donald Sutherland to Sammy Davis Jr and Peter Fonda to Ron Howard. Even the cocktail umbrellas were connected to something he'd worked on.

I looked at Jay, and came to the conclusion, in the light of the mementoes, the lavishness of Lombard and Gable's old house and the sharpness of his dress, that he had flair which was something Rogers and Cowan didn't have, for all the extraordinary things the company had achieved. He was an ingenious and cunning man, as his stunts with the Cadillac and the TV set prove. Bernstein was also a showman, a man with a certain flair that was lacking in his early employers. I voiced this opinion, but Jay was quick to deflect it; he may have followed a different path after leaving Rogers & Cowan to set up on his own, but he remained loyal: 'I think they did have flair,' he said, 'but just in other things.'

Bernstein has a point; Rogers' and Cowan's flair lay in their unflagging diplomacy and careful machinations behind the scenes. Bernstein's brand of flair was less selfless; he was very much in the mould of the maverick publicists, inserting himself into the headlines almost as successfully as he promoted his clients. As he was quick to point out, he knew very little of Howard Strickling or Marty Weiser because 'they were studio people – I knew who they were but I didn't know them'.

Marty Weiser was actually a freelance flack-about-town, more in the mould of Reichenbach and Moran than Strickling, and a man with a sense of showmanship to rival Bernstein's. Weiser was most famous for his inspired premiere party for Mel Brooks' cult film *Blazing Saddles*, which starred Gene Wilder and Cleavon Little. Mel Brooks took a risk when he allowed Weiser to stage his stunt in a disused drive-in movie theatre. In keeping with the film, which was a pastiche on the old westerns, Weiser insisted everyone turn up not in cars, but on horseback – it was the sort of wacky stunt that's frowned upon nowadays. The evening itself was fraught for Weiser as nobody arrived on time and the movie producers began to berate him for coming up with such a stupid idea, believing no one would turn up.

However, after a few minutes, a host of people on horseback appeared on the horizon and trotted into the drive-in. They'd been shepherded by police escort as they were causing traffic chaos, so arrived late en masse. The stunt was a massive success and gained worldwide publicity, proving again Barnum's legacy: you rarely fail if you're using animals.

Truly inspirational ideas get binned these days because of the risk factor when so much money is involved. It was a pleasant surprise, and something of a relief therefore, to see two penguins ice-skating at the Rockefeller Plaza in New York for the premiere of *Happy Feet*, the 2007 animated film about dancing penguins.

One of Bernstein's less spectacular stunts came at a time when he had an umbrella account with Motown. Everything was going fine until one day Bernstein was summoned to Motown and asked to help out with The Supremes. The brief was, 'They're back, not doing great, we need a huge splash.' Bernstein and his team brainstormed but couldn't come up with anything. Bernstein, always a great ideas man, said, 'What if we got the girls to wear a million dollars of diamonds each? We can call them the million dollar girls.' He had contacts with a company who would be willing to loan the diamonds in exchange for some publicity, so he and Stan Rosenfield told Motown they could get the diamonds and some serious attention for The Supremes, who were opening on a Tuesday. One of the staff was dispatched to get the diamonds on the Monday, replete with an attaché case, which was to be handcuffed to his wrist. The only trouble was, according to Bernstein, they wouldn't give his employee the diamonds until he handed over a certificate of insurance.

'No one thought of that. We had no idea what to do. Motown would not be happy. We didn't have the insurance. We found out the insurance for one day would cost $50k. Motown won't pay and we won't pay. So we had to get fake diamonds. We got them, but we had to make them look like they were real.'

That wasn't the end of their problems, though. The press conference was a bust as no one was interested in coming. Immediately, Rosenfield put it about that the press conference had been called off because there'd been problems with the insurance – this had a measure of truth about it, but was far from the whole story. Motown went along with it all, even when Bernstein made The Supremes take the stage in an empty hall in order to be photographed wearing the fake diamonds. 'If any of those girls knew anything about diamonds we would have died,' said Bernstein. 'None of them had a clue. We got through it.' The stunt may not have been a success, but it was evident that it was only saved from being a disaster by Bernstein's chutzpah.

There's a reason why no publicist remembers the achievements of another publicist in America in the 1970s. They have to be the most important person in their story – after their clients, that is. No matter what you've done, in America, no matter how small it seems, it is perceived as a mark of greatness. An excellent example of these differing attitudes is the story of a British publicist I know of who went to a big American agency to look for a job. He made a big, impressive speech detailing his portfolio of stunts and, at the end, one of the young guns in the agency put his hand up and said, 'Bill, um, that was extraordinary. Where did all those ideas come from?' And in a very cynical, British way, the publicist dismissed it, saying, 'Well, it's not rocket science is it?' At that moment he lost the room and any chance of a job in the agency – to them good publicity is, of course, rocket science. Americans don't like anything to be simple; it has to be grand, a work of towering genius, an arcane device or idea that only the person in question could come up with. The British still, on the whole, have a self-deprecating way of working that's at odds with the way Americans do things. Every publicity agent in the US had, and still has to, appear as godlike and powerful as possible so the client believes it every time he says he's working only with them in mind.

Bernstein certainly had flair, despite his denials; he even got Nick Adams an Oscar nomination for the 1963 movie *Twilight of Honor*, in which much of Adams' part remained on the cutting-room floor. He did it by aping the Rogers & Cowan campaign for *Mildred Pierce* and buying vast amounts of space in the trades. Adams got his nomination, but unsurprisingly failed to win the Oscar. Bernstein pushed Adams everywhere he could, but because Adams was desperate and Bernstein was new to the game, he over-promised. There is no doubting his energy and dedication, but with a client who needed to be the centre of attention as desperately as Nick Adams – who died four years later of an accidental overdose, a bitter and disappointed man because he never achieved the fame and adulation he felt he deserved – he should perhaps have been a little more careful. But Bernstein fell neatly into the old traps that beset publicists. Like Nottage, he was not above becoming too involved in the lives of his clients, or of waging war on his enemies.

'I used Red Buttons' invitation to go to the party [for *Twilight of Honor*] afterwards. One of my competitors, who was twenty-five years older than I was, he didn't like that, he was jealous. He said, "You're not Red Buttons" and he wasn't going to let me into the party. I went into the pool lounge by myself and came up with an idea. I got my secretary to go into the Post Office and do a change of address for that PR guy. His mail was fucked up for some time. I'd sent it off to somewhere miles away. I got him for that. There's always a way to win.'

If this sounds like a humorous aside, a witty way of dealing with a rival, it wasn't. 'It was revenge,' said Bernstein. 'In those days I believed in revenge. I don't fuck with you if you don't fuck with me. We run on compliments. We fill our tank with compliments from people. We have what we need to keep going. This is a very lonely, painful place. I don't have anybody. It's difficult to go through stuff without a partner. I sacrificed that for my work. My clients were all my children. It went back to Farrah.'

The Farrah in question was Farrah Fawcett, who Bernstein managed at the time of her rise to fame as one of *Charlie's Angels*, getting out of the PR game entirely and dissolving the company.

'I dissolved it because I didn't have a number-two guy. A lot of people who worked with me did well. Stan Rosenfield, he has Robert De Niro, Danny DeVito, Will Smith, etc. He's doing well now. He never signed a client when he worked for me, not in twelve years. He even offered me a third of the company for $25k. It was still going to be a bad deal. You'd only get your $25k back.'

This was a poor deal for Bernstein because he was getting out of the business, but it was just one of many deals proposed at the time, as more and more publicists left the Rogers & Cowan fold and set up on their own. A thousand minor deals took place in the 1970s and the tectonic plates of publicity shifted further away from the model that accommodated people like Moran and Bernstein. It's telling that Bernstein decided to set up as an agent at this point – but, though he changed careers, he took his skills as a publicist with him.

Bernstein acquired Farrah Fawcett as a client thanks to his work with Sonny Bono. 'Because I got Sonny's career going he paid me back – because I got him working again. He got me Lee Majors as a client for publicity. Lee said, "You will have to handle my wife for nothing." That was what happened. A couple of months later I felt that this was someone who could change everything for people.'

The stars were certainly asserting control at this point, thanks to the work of agents like Freddie Fields. They became fully aware in the late 1970s of the power they had over the ever-increasing field of publicists desperate to sign them, and they used this power ruthlessly to strike deals that made the work that much harder for the flack. As soon as a major star like Lee Majors realized Bernstein was keen to sign him, he used the moment to create a break for his girlfriend. With most flacks this would create a difficult situation, where they were working for two clients but only being paid by one, meaning they'd have to acquire more stars simply to keep the hamster wheel turning. Bernstein, being a bit more canny, decided that this was the time to go into management instead.

'Once I started in management it became all about role models. Farrah was all about health and anti-drugs, everyone loved her, no one was jealous. I have a six-year-old daughter. I have no role models for her. There are no role models now. Farrah was, in her day. Her parents were married sixty-seven years. She was a good image for people. She was great.'

Bernstein's management business wasn't entirely focused on her, although it may have seemed like it at times. Bernstein's devotion to Fawcett is still palpable, and much of the wall space in his house was set aside for her image since she'd become his client again after a long gap. He had eleven other clients, who he admits were jealous of the attention lavished on her. 'But I was so hot it didn't make that much difference,' Bernstein boasted gleefully. 'I was Dr Frankenstein and Farrah was Frankenstein's monster.' Bernstein built Fawcett up to her status as a role model in a very short space of time, thanks to *Charlie's Angels*. He wanted her to be a big, big star and nurtured her ambitions for a movie career, which led to Fawcett quitting the series after only one season.

'When Farrah Fawcett left *Charlie's Angels* . . . they sued us for $13 million and sent a letter to every studio saying, "If you work with these people – with Jay and Farrah – you could be party to a $13 million lawsuit." I didn't take any notice. I put two movies together with her. However, Suzanne Somers, when she left *Three's Company*, she didn't work eight years after [she] fired me.'

Bernstein may have professed his own hotness, but he wasn't so hot that Fawcett didn't leave him. Bernstein took it very personally, proving that he was more akin to Nottage than the more corporate Rogers & Cowan. He was also interested in being a star maker and he worked hard at it, giving up his life for it. He got it, but because stars are human, they will leave you. In Farrah Fawcett and Jay Bernstein's case it was like a mini divorce and it hurt him.

'It was very painful,' Bernstein admitted. 'It was a business decision because she had a deal with Fabergé. $4.5 million. George Berry at Fabergé didn't like me. She was learning how to act in the movies. They would turn up on set wanting her to do shots for the shampoo for Fabergé. When it got close to renewing the contract, even though I made the deal they said, "We won't deal with you if Jay is still your manager." She asked me what to do and I said, "If you're asking me you know what you want to do." Then we didn't speak for three years. It was very hurtful. They never made the deal with her in the end. That kind of stuff happens to all of us. It's a daily situation.'

Bernstein was clearly a man in need of a muse, at work and at play. Farrah Fawcett was the first and, when she left, Suzanne Somers became the next in line. Bernstein clearly needed to prove to Fawcett that he could get other clients: a Machiavellian tactic to convince her that she hadn't done the right thing. When Somers left, too, however,

Jay moved into producing. Eventually, his bid to make the stars *need* him paid off, since both Fawcett and Somers returned as clients before he died and he continued to manage them until his death. His eye remained firmly fixed on the lifestyle, however. From underwater marriages to nubiles on his arm at every function, Bernstein lived the cliché with gusto, with or without his favourite star clients.

'I was never part of any group,' he said, 'and I never dated anyone out of their twenties. It pisses women off a lot. The reason I never did it . . . the reason I stayed with twenty-year-olds – and I'm getting close to seventy – is because I'm an artist . . . and the twenty-year-olds are clay. You can't sculpt people who are out of their twenties. They are not clay any more. They don't have any interest in what I'm doing any more.'

I heard a story about Henry Rogers while on my journey that seems apposite to mention at this point. Rogers called in one of his employees and tore him off a strip for letting Jane Fonda, one of the employee's clients, come and work in the Rogers & Cowan office for a day, in the same way that Carole Lombard had in Russell Birdwell's office in the late 1930s. She had told a secretary, 'You can take the day off, I'm gonna take care of all your duties and I'm going to answer the phone,' and this had annoyed Henry Rogers. It apparently upset the office because there was a movie star in there. Rogers was seething and told his employee that he was to concentrate on signing new clients while the company helped handle the clients he already had, never mind if one of the clients decided to leave. 'The most important relationship you have is with the media: the journalists we work with and the press,' Rogers said. 'You have to be willing to lose the clients.'

That is the nature of corporations; they instigate dividing lines. Lines were being drawn all over America and the world at the time – the revolutionary Vietnam protest era was coming into being at this point, hand in glove with the counterculture. Richard Nixon was stepping up to take the presidency of the USA and a sea change in the way the press worked was just around the corner. But as far as the dividing lines between PR and star were concerned, the corporate world needed to keep the two as far away as possible from each other. Of equal importance were commercial products – bread, milk, brassieres – and their attendant TV shows – one wasn't likely to form an emotional bond with them, so why do it with the clients?

The press was standing at a dividing line too, and Bernstein was among the first of the newly cautious generation to experience the change of attitude in the press in the wake of Watergate. Bernstein's major lesson in this came from Kirk Douglas during a photo shoot by Globe Photos.

'I called Kirk and said I'm coming over with [the photographer], and he said, "No, you stay in your office. Here's what I want you to do. Don't take any calls for fifteen minutes, close your door and think about me for fifteen minutes." ' Promising to do this, Bernstein went on to break the news that *People* magazine had written a very bad story about him. 'I said, "Look, do you want me to read it to you?" He says, "No, you can just tell me when they stop writing about me." You tell that story around a room and it ends up with "all publicity is good publicity", which is bullshit, because ever since Nixon was impeached, they can say anything.'

Douglas's careful balancing of the press is a precursor of the attitudes that came into play in the 1980s in the hands of Pat Kingsley, Steve Huvane and Stan Rosenfield – Douglas was always adroit at managing his image, as his continued fame, and that of his son, prove.

'The press were our friends. I mean, it used to be that journalism was a profession, and when the media became an industry, it was a whole different deal. I mean I don't want someone to call me a paedophile, so that's not good publicity. But they didn't do things like that then. They didn't write bad things. I remember working with Sinatra and no one ever said anything bad about him. They'd end up in the East River.

'When the big guy [Nixon] went down . . . that's when all these investigative shows started. They weren't around before that. There were no current affairs; *ET*, *Inside Edition*, *Access Hollywood*. Jim Bacon or Bob Thomas and that was it. They were all friends of ours. And you could work with them, you could make a deal. Hedda Hopper and I had dinner once a week for two years, and she did all sorts of things to help me.'

Bernstein's years in PR schmoozing the press helped in his next career move, post-management, as a TV producer. Bernstein turned to TV production in the early 1980s because he was depressed by the ability of the stars he forged to push him out of their lives. It is telling, perhaps, that he married ever-younger women, all of them beautiful, and that his marriages tended to last roughly the same length as his management deals. He remained creative, however, and had a way with stunts that cast him more and more in the Birdwell/Moran role.

In the early days he had paid women to throw their hotel keys at Tom Jones, and he went on to insure the legs of Mary Hart, host of *Entertainment Tonight*, for $1 million with Lloyd's of London, but it was on *Mike Hammer*, which he produced, that he made a move of lasting impact. Bernstein was very much a man's man and it was a natural fit for him to pick up the *Mike Hammer* series, since Hammer was a manly male detective created by Mickey Spillane, who fitted perfectly with Bernstein's increasingly dapper and retro-1930s lifestyle. His career as a producer nearly stalled, however, when the star of the series, Stacy Keach, was imprisoned for drugs offences. At the time there was still a morals clause in actors' contracts – a hangover from the old studio system – stating that an actor convicted as a felon could not be employed by TV companies. Bernstein, desperate to revivify the series and make back his money, launched a campaign to reinstate Keach and the show. He took a petition for the removal of the morals clause around the country, leaning on old press contacts for help.

'I said, "You only pay one price for a debt or a mortgage. He [Keach] is in prison now paying the price. He shouldn't have to pay any more." That was my message. That tour was about thirty-seven days, seventeen cities, really tough.'

The gambit worked and the show ran for several more years, thanks to Bernstein's decision to tell the blunt and honest truth. But it was a high-risk gamble – a definite case of putting everything on black on the roulette wheel and hoping for the best.

'Nick the Greek gave me a two-thousand-to-one chance of succeeding. There was no chance [before] of getting a felon convicted for drugs back on TV. By taking the morals clause out of the contracts, lots of actors went back into TV, even though they were felons.'

It's hard to imagine what TV would look like now without that action. Bernstein's unusual display of modesty is atypical, but without him Robert Downey Jr would have been denied work long ago, as would Kiefer Sutherland for his second drink-driving offence while on parole in 2007. Quite simply, actors with a propensity to get themselves into trouble owe Bernstein a huge debt. It also showed him, and others who followed him, how the power of publicity could change a point of view.

By the time I spoke to Bernstein, he had tired of TV production and was back managing Farrah Fawcett. 'Right now I don't know what to do,' he said. 'I have to do something, but I'm just managing Farrah.'

I suggested he should rest, but he was quick to dismiss that idea, as if some residual memory of the fate that befell Nottage was nagging away inside him.

'I can't afford to do that. It's very expensive to be Jay Bernstein. It can't cost less that $500,000 a year. I've made about $70 million, but I've spent $72 million. I live in a $4 million home with a Bentley and an Aston Martin. Still dating girls in their twenties. I don't know how to be a grown-up. I don't know how you do that *without* having children.'

I took a look at the mementoes littering his house and wondered aloud what would happen to them after his death, whether the house would become a museum. Bernstein stiffened and looked at me in a manner that suggested the interview was over – I had voiced the unthinkable. Like Gwili Andre and, to an extent, Nottage, the cuttings and memorabilia were an integral part of him, a way of keeping him breathing, keeping him young, just as much as the array of models he dated. It doesn't seem that he used his power as a publicist/manager/producer to extract sexual favours so much as to keep on tap an elixir of youth – you're as young as the woman you feel, to quote the cliché. Here he was much more like Nottage, albeit with a lot more smarts and time to perfect the art. There was no hint of giving up the ghost and growing old gracefully. Bernstein was in it until the end and would brook no talk of that end coming any time soon.

'I'm looking to build two more stars. The producing has become a whole other business I'm not interested in. Now you can't make a great deal. It's three companies you're doing a deal with. They're owned by someone else and then *they* are owned by someone else. Everyone else has a boss over them. In the old days you could make $4 or $5 million a year. Now you have to be in computers.'

Speaking to him, it was clear that Bernstein was very much in the Moran mould – he had become bigger than many of his clients and he loved the lifestyle. He had at one point said that Warren Cowan and others had warned him to take care not to do this, as the clients would leave and he would be subjected to envy, scrutiny and ridicule. Given that he had become nearly as big a name as some of his clients, and bigger than others, it is impressive that he maintained such a sense of hope. He was subject to the same setbacks and highs as many of his predecessors in the PR division of the fame factory, but he kept himself working whatever happened.

Bernstein had a real sense of quality about him, despite the fact that people ruthlessly made fun of him. The common perceptions of Bernstein are fake – he had class and he paid for it – but he became too famous, almost a caricature of himself. He was a showman, not a writing publicist, and in the end he was just too big a personality to disappear in the way Nottage had, or be sidelined into comedy like Moran. Perhaps it was his Rogers & Cowan training. Whatever it was, if he had any bitterness, he dressed it up in the bandages of a very American macho joviality and hopefulness that brooked no anguish. He kept on working, surrounded by the luxurious accoutrements he had gathered over the years and the clients who had abandoned him and then, finally, come back. Ironically, within a few weeks of our interview he was dead. He succumbed to a stroke and passed on, appropriately, with Farrah Fawcett at his side.

Thirty-Five

BOBBY ZAREM: NEW YORK SUPERFLACK

Not all modern PR is based in Los Angeles and it would have been foolish not to visit the true epicentre of the Sons of Barnum-era publicity, New York, especially if there was a chance to meet Bobby Zarem. To understand the shaping and changing of the system, it was essential to go there and Zarem is one of the most significant modern New York publicists, having picked up the Broadway baton from Lee Solters in the 1970s.

Zarem was another product of the Rogers and Cowan era, though he has a more barbed opinion of them. A hustler in the Lee Solters mode, he had arrived in New York from Georgia in the late 1950s, where he quickly set himself up with a welter of clients and contacts before being wooed by Rogers & Cowan. He was the man to turn to if one needed anything in the Big Apple – his list of contacts stretched from fashion to the political arena and his world revolved around parties and fixing up things for people in the best possible way. He was around Studio 55 at the height of the Warhol era and at the epicentre of every scene. Despite this star-studded, multi-faceted and seemingly over-reaching approach, he exuded an aura of underlying ruthlessness that made it extremely clear why he had become the ubiquitous name in East Coast PR and why he had never needed to commit himself to the West Coast of America. He's in his late sixties now and still a distinguished, powerful presence. He's perhaps a little heavier than he'd like, but still shows all the signs of having been a very handsome man in his prime. His relationship with New York is one of total adoration.

'I had wanted to be in New York since I was five,' he said when we met in a fashionable flat on the Lower East Side. 'I was obsessed with movies and movie stars, Broadway stars. We came here five times a year as my father had a shoe company. He would bring me autographs of Betty Grable, etc. I was obsessed with it; all the stories. I would pore over the ads for Broadway shows. I just wanted to be there. I went there when I finished Yale in 1958. I had an interview with three entertainment companies. They offered me jobs in mail offices for $30. I had a Yale degree and I thought, I can't accept a job like that, in a mail room. A friend of mine's father told me to join a training programme and get more money. That's what I did, but I hated it so much, getting in the subway really early. Then I got drafted. It was 1960. I was working in Wall Street. There was no war but I was drafted. I would have liked to have gone to Germany or something.'

Zarem made his start in a manner startlingly similar to Nottage, promoting films for clients on travelling shows before he got involved in the PR business.

'I pursued certain people – Ann-Margret, Dustin Hoffman – for a long time. I worked with Hoffman for two years in '67 to '69. I was working with him in a sales capacity. A road-show movie. They were treated like theatrical performances. He tried to sell out performances before they opened. He had a movie called *Who is Harry Kellerman and Why is He Saying Those Terrible Things About Me?* When I worked for him nobody was interested in theatre, so he dumped it in my lap. I had to send mailouts to give [people] a chance to order tickets for the shows. Instead of offering plays . . . [we] offered road-show movies instead . . . I was buying dates from theatre producers and offering membership. Jo Levine started the road-show business and hired me to sell them. I had seventeen minutes of the film to use as a sales pitch. Institutions and churches, anyone who might be interested, I targeted. I had journalist friends and I invited them to see the seventeen minutes because it was so fantastic. Newspapers started to get involved. It wasn't conscious, it was instinctive. My whole life has been like that.

'I saw that these things did have an audience. Half the actors and actresses were misunderstood by the media in my opinion. I felt it was my duty. Dustin and Ann-Margret were my first duty clients.

'I worked for Rogers & Cowan for five years before I started on my own. I had put together a manifest for the Free Southern Theatre, which I was involved in. It toured in the South and played in churches, cotton fields, anywhere they could get a black audience. I got very involved in it. I got Ava Gardner to co-chair it. Jo let me have the second night for a fundraiser. They invited Ava and she wrote me back a long letter saying she'd do anything I asked her. I asked her to be a co-chair on the committee and she gave me two dates in April. We had a supper at a hotel. Gregory Peck flew in, Lauren Bacall, Ann-Margret and the mayor turned up. Lena Horne came out of retirement. Her daughter was on the committee. *The New York Times* came . . . I'd put it together. Rogers & Cowan read the piece in *The Times* and asked to meet with me. It was 1969. [Cowan] hired me to work in their New York office.

'They never taught me a thing. But because I had such instincts, I learned on my own. They had no New York contacts. I had them all. I developed relationships with the most important people. I got big stories and items.'

Independent of spirit in the extreme, Zarem built up his own set of clients at Rogers & Cowan, using the company's muscle to interweave himself inextricably onto the New York celebrity scene. 'I wasn't aware that I was doing that consciously,' he said. 'They would call me and say these stars were coming in and I had to get them press. I got *The New York Times* on the basis of my pitch. I developed my own relationships with journalists. I managed to get news up for them. I worked my ass off and I accomplished a lot.

'Henry Rogers was a cold, conniving piece of shit. Warren was . . . he was easy to get along with. They were both in LA most of the time. Then Henry brought in commissions for getting clients. I brought in the whole Stigwood account [Robert Stigwood, producer of *Jesus Christ Superstar*]. I got Dustin Hoffman, Mama Cass when I was there. It turned out the creators of *Jesus Christ Superstar* were being forgotten. The deal was that they would bring the whole

Stigwood account to us if I got them in the press. I did get them back in the public eye and I got the account. It was arranged for me to have the account.

'[Then] Henry sent a memo to everyone saying he had made the deal with them. I'd already done it, wanted my commission and he absolutely blew. I went to the head of commissions that afternoon. I threatened to tell everyone that Rogers was a lying, low-down person and he knew I could blow him with my contacts. I got my money the next day. Then I knew I had to leave there.

'I set up my own. I didn't know about money. Never had. I offered to help Stigwood with the movie *Tommy* for a fee. Stigwood could only get his money for *Tommy* if Ann-Margret would do it. She'd never heard of [director] Ken Russell. I had to talk Ann-Margret into doing the movie and I did. In the meantime, Allan Carr [an actor's agent] met with Stigwood. Allan negotiated my fee with Stigwood for the movie. It was nothing.'

Out of nothing, however, Zarem spun gold; he invited 500 of the biggest names on the New York gossip circuit to a launch party for *Tommy* in a subway station and created an enormous stir.

'It was a huge success. This is the key because what was considered a corporate stunt in fact came out of my visual image, my ability to put things together based on the visual I had. In the movie *Tommy*, there was a scene with metal and white and glass. It was the kind of movie you couldn't describe intelligently. I put together an event in a brand-new subway station that was white, metal and glass. It was incredible. Every magazine and newspaper in the country ran pictures from it. It was that visual that caught the eye of the public. This sold the movie.'

Zarem's reputation is as the great publicist storyteller of the modern era, one of those people who solidifies the thought process. He is not a businessman as such, more a societal fixer who seems not to have made much of a fuss about what he did for people through his contacts book. He is the sort of flack who finds some creative element that makes it come alive. Great publicists that I've looked at always find a mechanism for coalescing an idea of what the movie or the product is. If you find the image of what the whole emotional element is about, it subliminally goes to the back of people's heads. Critics don't want to be told, they want to tell. They want it to be their idea. Great publicists can get critics to do that. They allow them to think it's their idea.

'I see an event catalyst,' explained Zarem. 'People don't understand it. They think if they have a party for an album, that it will do it. Without the long-term intelligent application with the press, it won't happen. They don't understand that. Just pictures of a party don't make a movie.'

He's right, Harry Reichenbach got thousands of dollars a week in 1915 by doing amazing things and getting the press to bite. Zarem's of a similar ilk. For years his press releases and pitches came handwritten, even after the rise of the personal computer. They were full of the sort of hyperbole that makes modern publicists wince and would have driven Louella Parsons to write some sort of acidic quip, but certain stars still appreciate it. Alan Alda told *The New York Times*, 'In this age of mass communications, I think people appreciate his handwritten letters.' Alda also acknowledged that Zarem had helped him make the leap from actor to director.

In the same vein, Zarem has claimed in the past that one of his finest achievements was turning Arnold Schwarzenegger into a star. He started out promoting *Pumping Iron*, the low-budget documentary about the then unknown Austrian bodybuilder. Zarem hyped the movie relentlessly, stringing out innumerable stories to the press and creating, as a consequence, a riot of publicity for the monosyllabic strongman. Without Zarem's zealous influence, there is little doubt that Schwarzenegger would have remained a weightlifter and not become the archetypal 1980s action hero or indeed governor of California.

Zarem is a dogged man – once he gets a bite on a project, he worries it until it's completed. One of his biggest successes came with the film *Saturday Night Fever*, which studio executives were convinced would be an abject failure and refused to issue colour promotional stills for. Zarem, determined that he would make a success of the movie, apparently barged into the Paramount offices and liberated some colour photos, which he then distributed. The movie was an enormous success thanks in no small part to his guerrilla tactics.

Prominent and admired by some he may be, but Zarem is not above the paranoia that creeps into a publicist's life if he takes it too seriously. Zarem claims to be the creator of one of the most enduring slogans of the late twentieth century, 'I Love New York'. But so do many others. Zarem's response to this is barbed, to say the least.

'It was the winter of 1975 and you could roll a quarter down the street and there wasn't a person or car to stop it,' said Zarem. 'People weren't coming here. It was dead. I realized something had to be done about it. I started eight days later writing to the top Broadway producers as they had the most to gain from more people coming to New York. They did gain more than anyone else. I built the campaign around theatre. It had been the one thing to draw me to New York. We had a sixty-second spot with the stars of shows singing out on New York. A guy named Steve Carman wrote the song. 800 [toll-free] numbers you could call for a brochure. Theatre tickets, hotels, restaurants, etc. People were afraid to come to New York, crime was exaggerated and people thought they would get mugged if they came here.

'I spent '76 and '77 trying to get anybody and everybody to come. Producers turned me down, but I carried on. I had a friend in the restaurant business who gave me parties for all my events – movie screenings, etc. Every event that I did I got into *People* magazine and *The Times* and he gave me free parties. I got together with the mayor and we had a game plan, which was to have supper in Central Park and a table for every US state. We would then try to get everybody famous from those states to the table to stand up and say "I love New York", in the hope we'd get TV coverage.

'One day, on the first page of the second section, there was a piece saying the ad agencies were going to move out of New York to go to New Jersey as they got tax breaks in New Jersey. I said, "This is a major backbone of New York." People agreed with me and [as] we had dinner I outlined once again all the stuff and the mayor said, "Do you mind if I take this to the State?' as he had a friend [there].

They took my plan to the State and the deputy department got passed in legislature. They would spend $16 million on it. It was all based on my plan. I wasn't looking for credit or fame or money; I just loved New York and wanted to save the city. Everybody tried to take credit for it.

'I was trying to save New York so I didn't give a fuck [about the people wanting to take credit] at that time. It didn't even cross my mind at the time to get it copyrighted.'

Zarem started in the business 'mostly out of shyness. I wrote a lot, and to this day I still write, hopefully intelligent, factual, didactic.' He is considered something of a role model in the celebrity publicity circuit. Americans often come to Britain looking for publicity and ask for a 'Bobby Zarem job'.

'I have always had a vision in my mind about what somebody or something looked like,' said Zarem. 'I have a visual of where everybody that I was working with, and what I worked on, fitted culturally.

'I never did stunts. I approached my work in a very intelligent, strong way and laid the foundations so that when something opens, the impact is fantastic. But I was accused all the time of creating stunts, which I never did. The Three Mile Island [nuclear power plant] explosion was something I was supposed to have created. It was the weekend the movie [*The China Syndrome*] opened. It was rumoured that I had created Three Mile Island as a stunt.'

It has been suggested that Bobby was the inspiration for a film about a bad day in the life of a publicist, *People I Know*, in which a seedy publicist addicted to the lifestyle comes to a bitter, painful stop. Zarem has rigorously denied that the movie is in any way based on him, as is to be expected, given the rather harsh portrayal of the central character. Al Pacino plays it as a shambling bum, stringing everyone along in the hope that he can get everything fixed for his charity event. Certain elements of the character fit Zarem – the moving and shaking to get something done, the huge list of contacts, the easy charm, the social conscience – but it departs from reality with the depiction of the flack concerned as a shambolic, neurotic and angry wreck who slowly falls apart because he has invested everything in his PR life. That, if anything, seems more like Maynard Nottage. Zarem has an energy about him that prevents him from disintegrating.

At the height of his powers, Zarem was close to the people that mattered. If he arrived at a party he would make sure *everybody* knew he was looking out for them, even if he was careful to know which hands to shake first. He's never missed an opportunity to hand over a business card, even in the lavatory. The one thing that may finally consign him to the history books is his unwillingness to embrace new technology and accept that publicity has moved on since the heady days of the late 1970s, when *Newsweek* dubbed him 'superflack'.

• Thirty-Six •

PAT KINGSLEY AND THE MODERN ERA

Publicity, as practised by the modern era of Rogers & Cowan acolytes, has joined the world of mergers and consolidation with an alacrity befitting a Hollywood consumed by homogenized stars, money and power. The brand is the key issue of modern PR, which is why, in 1987, even Rogers and Cowan sold their firm, to the British PR company Shandwick. Shandwick bought into Rogers & Cowan for the branding opportunities, putting their brands alongside Rogers & Cowan's stars. The Shandwick/Rogers & Cowan conglomeration was eventually bought by the Interpublic Group that now presides over PMK, Huvane, Baum, Halls and Bragman, Nyman, Cafarelli, all of which are staffed with graduates of the Rogers & Cowan school of PR.

The fame factory has become a super-slick operation, but the quality of the materials going in, in such pasteurized times as these, where people can become famous for turning up and getting out of a car *sans* knickers or even for licking a stamp – opening envelopes being the place where everybody goes these days – is much lower, as there are far fewer genuine stars available. All of this means that publicity has never been more essential and stars have never been more aware of their potential and how to make the most of it, causing them to travel between publicists until they find someone who can reinvigorate their image.

In a time when Tom Cruise can ditch his publicist – Rogers &

Cowan-trained Pat Kingsley, who ran PMK until late 2007 – and almost immediately lose his lustre and his contract with Paramount, thanks to a few ill-judged leaps onto a sofa and other displays of over-enthusiasm, it becomes rapidly apparent that the publicists, at their best, can keep a loose cannon firing in a straight line. They may sometimes be perceived as rodents, scuttling around behind the skirting boards of power, but these alleged rodents long ago learned to put the bell on the cat – corporate and fat or feral and prone to go out on the tiles at night – and then persuaded it – and more importantly the world – that it was actually a lion.

Robert Downey Jr is one such 'lion'. But for an artful publicist, his off-stage antics with drugs would have consumed his career and his talent as an actor, and yet he has rarely been out of work. Anne Heche, however, remains a kitten and could do with a more fleet-of-foot team of advisers – she reportedly announced that she was from outer space on TV while plugging a book a few years ago and would have been better served keeping as quiet as possible.

Pat Kingsley would have been the woman for the job, had she not retired. Described as 'the stern-faced queen of the PR business', Kingsley was born in North Carolina in 1932 and, before getting a job as a secretary at Rogers & Cowan in 1959, she worked in Reno, Nevada for the Department of Agriculture, vaccinating cattle in their disease eradication programme. At Rogers & Cowan, she swiftly rose through the ranks, helping Marilyn Monroe's cat give birth, working with Doris Day, Natalie Wood and Frank Sinatra. She swiftly became a 'top publicist' as Warren Cowan put it, but she is more than that; at her peak she was one of the most powerful women in Hollywood and is in great part responsible for the fact that the industry is now more powerful than the media.

She has got there through a mixture of hard work, mergers and by slowing the business down as the world turns faster and faster. She left Rogers & Cowan in 1971 and set up her own firm, Pickwick Public Relations, with Lois Smith and Gerri Johnson, dealing with clients like Jane Fonda. She then merged that company with Maslansky, Koenigsberg to form PMK in 1980. That Kingsley is the top woman in a field too often portrayed as a men-only club, where the women staffers are merely there to look pretty and take clients to lunch, only cements her iconic status. Others have risen to prominence in her wake, including Pam Alexander and Bumble Ward, and perceptions of the PR industry have changed radically as a result.

Kingsley may be an innovator, but she is of the Rogers & Cowan school, believing less is more and realizing that overexposure can easily kill a career. Consequently she chose to drastically limit the number of interviews her clients would give, thus creating a feeding frenzy whenever one of them was put up for interview. She witnessed the vulgarities and excesses of the 1980s and set her plan in motion late in the decade when she took control of Tom Cruise's PR. In this way, she took control of the media, apparently even telling one editor that she didn't understand why it should be him that chose the cover story for his journal. She rewrote the rules of publicity entirely – if you can't stop celebrities making mischief, she reasoned, then at least you should try and stop the journalists from making mischief.

There have been fight-backs. In 1999 the *Today* show refused to bow to her dictum that they could not ask Calista Flockhart about her weight, so Kingsley pulled the then rake-thin actress from the show. Stanley Kubrick's last film, *Eyes Wide Shut*, came out in the same year, starring Tom Cruise and Nicole Kidman, at that point the hottest couple in Hollywood. The *Today* show wanted to interview them, but Kingsley refused and as revenge they refused to interview any of her clients on the show. They only reversed the ban when Tom Cruise was promoting *Vanilla Sky* – he was too big a draw to let slip away. Like stags locking horns and grunting, PR and the media have always been in some form of conflict. It is perhaps stretching the simile to say that Pat Kingsley became far and away the dominant stag in the herd, but she certainly won more than her fair share of battles with the press.

Less is more is a reasonable modus operandi in an age of celebrity at all costs, where TV shows promise fleeting fame. The stars of the modern era to have lasted are the ones who have put themselves in the care of stern publicists like Kingsley, who can read the mood of the times and respond accordingly, fitting the square-peg star into whatever gap presents itself in the market. The biggest names sell the most papers and people respond to pictures of them with unanimous devotion; this would soon fade in the heat of constant exposure. And even when there is exposure, the rules of maintaining perfection are stringent. The publicist in the Pat Kingsley mould is an image controller: the crossed legs of their charges must be held an inch apart when they appear on TV so the top leg will not appear fat; tiny teeth must not be exposed by laughter; certain chat show hosts should be allowed to get the laughs; publicists should inspect the teeth of their charges for stray bits of food. There is no margin for error.

Kingsley learned this art of necessary silence early, from no less a star than Doris Day. She and Day got on very well, attending sports events together and working cheek by jowl, but when the star was about to turn forty, *Life* magazine got in touch with Kingsley and announced that it would like to devote a whole issue to this momentous event. Kingsley was excited – it would have been the first cover of *Life* magazine she had managed for a client – but Day refused to play ball. She asked Kingsley why she should to do it, and Kingsley's response was, 'Because you're number one.' Day responded, 'Then what's the point?' and wouldn't even consider it as a favour to her publicist.

Kingsley is more in the tradition of the suppress agents of the 1930s and has, on occasion, been called Dr No – she exudes an air of control that frightens journalists and calms clients and which would have endeared her instantly to Howard Strickling. Of course, her clients have more freedom now than they would have done and she has a beady eye on the star rather than a studio. She accrued so much power through the mergers she orchestrated for her companies that her reach extended across the whole of Hollywood as well as the corporate world. It has been reported that her clients have even asked her for script advice, and she has been known to negotiate vast webs of product placement in clients' movies. Thirty per cent of PMK's business was corporate and consequently Cadillacs were used to chauffeur her stars to the Oscars; she also negotiated with the makers of *Minority Report* that her client, Tom Cruise, would walk through one scene in the film and see adverts for another client, Guinness, then buy clothes at yet another client, Gap. On the tensile strength of such an invisible web, the whole of Hollywood can be held up, with capitalist society clinging gleefully to its legs like the pendulum of a clock.

In an article in the *Observer* in 2005, the journalist Gaby Wood describes telling an LA-based friend that she was due to meet Pat Kingsley. Her friend gasped and said, 'Here, that's like saying you're coming to meet the Queen.' She has taken on many roles over the years – from sports fan to hothead, mother to professional – a necessity when dealing with clients whose interests vary wildly. But this willingness to change is just a small element of what made her so formidable. She actively pursued a course, from 1992 onwards, of making sure journalists signed 'consent forms'. A number of journalists had been free to abuse their positions prior to this act of prevention; indeed it was their job to do so.

Like the scorpion who asks a fox to swim it across the river on the promise that it won't sting the fox, only to do just that and drown them both, so the journalists were duty-bound to swipe at their interviewees.

Kingsley felt that enough was enough – she was determined to protect her clients' privacy at all costs, which is what endeared her to them so much. She was the first to do this in such a brusque, businesslike fashion – there were none of the behind-the-scenes deals that attended MGM's suppression model – and of course any number of flacks followed suit, or tried to emulate her methods in a bid to accrue as much power and loyalty as she had.

The media's growth had outstripped Hollywood's ability to make stars in the 1980s, as the number of chat shows and magazines proliferated, and they were fully aware of how much a huge name could do for their circulation. However, there was a dearth of stars, so Pat Kingsley was able to set the terms under which journalists could interview her clients, and those journalists who signed consent forms tended to fawn outrageously, knowing they could work their way up to a priceless interview with a major star if only they bumped up the profile of one or two lesser ones first.

Journalists from various magazines tried early on to set up a code of practice preventing them from collectively caving in to the demands of the publicist, but Kingsley was a firm believer in divide and conquer and she recognized that all it would take to pull such an alliance apart was the offer of one exclusive interview. The code, which was mooted in 1992, was never, as a consequence, implemented. Hollywood has taken this practice and run with it, making sure that as many journalists as possible are kept on a golden leash, their consent forms signed and their copy approved prior to submission.

'I'm told it's not unusual now for someone to say, "If you want so-and-so, you have to take so-and-so." That is immoral,' Warren Cowan said in the *Los Angeles Magazine* a few years ago. 'I have never played one client against the other. I feel strongly about not misusing power. I always go back to creating news. On the way in this morning I was thinking, What am I going to do with Sidney Sheldon? I'll come up with something – the 350-millionth sale of his book or something.'

Victor Davis, showbusiness writer for the *Daily Express* and later the *Mail on Sunday*, gave anther side of the publicity game in the *British Journalism Review* in 2003, shortly after he retired. 'When I first landed the job,' he wrote, 'I was summoned to the Carlyle Hotel in New York to see my proprietor, Sir Max Aitken, who inherited the kingdom from his father, Lord Beaverbrook.

'"You will be subject to many temptations," he said, handing me a Scotch. "In Hollywood they will try to bribe you. You will be offered money. You will be offered drugs. You will be offered women. You will, of course, not let the side down." Scout's honour, I said. Or words to that effect. A week later, in Hollywood as Mister Showbiz, I was greeted warmly by the major studios' international publicists. Flowers, baskets of fruit and bottles of booze welcomed me to my suite at the Beverly Hills Hotel. One publicist apologised: "In the old days we would have sent a girl. Now we only do it for the big distributors."

'In a long career, I was never offered money, drugs only a couple of times (always declined, I hasten to add), and a girl only once – by an Italian producer (also declined). The real temptation in my experience was insidious charm. Many workers in the film industry are amusing, clever people and often terrific company. What journalists should never forget is that these same charmers also have large-salaried jobs and the continuing prosperity of a wonderful industry to protect. They rightly fight their corner, but you must also fight yours. It is often dismaying when you are compelled to upset someone you genuinely like – it is much less bothersome to keep everybody happy by surrendering one's critical faculties. But that shouldn't be the name of the game.'

He cites several examples in the article, which is as humorously savage an exposé of the industry as one might hope for from a good Fleet Street journalist, including a publicist for United Artists whisking him off to LA to see *Man of La Mancha* in the hope that Davis would serialize it in the *Express* prior to its release. On arrival, Davis was subjected to a full-beam schmooze, getting rides in a stretch limo, a suite at the Beverly Hills Hotel, meals at famous restaurants and being taken to a screening with other journalists and a host of A-list celebrities. The film was a dud, a squawking turkey ripe for the slaughter, yet the A-listers all whooped and hollered and got to their feet to applaud at the end. Davis recounts the pressure upon him from the publicist, Charles Bertram, and doubt at his own judgement all the way back to London. Davis refused to push the movie, which was, as predicted, a flop. 'Two years later,' he writes, 'I was having a drink with . . . Charles Bertram and I asked: "Did you and all those celebrities really believe that you had a hit on your hands?" "No, luv," said Charlie. "Piece of shit, wasn't it?" '

Davis also remembers arriving at the Cannes film festival and trying to arrange an interview with the star of a film, only to be told, 'Sorry, you're not distributor-nominated.' Davis was victim of the sweetheart contracts made with various publications by the star of the film's publicists who 'didn't fancy taking a chance on an unreconstructed loose cannon such as myself. They were ensuring that their girl was exposed only to hacks who'd been purged of any tendency towards scepticism, irony or insufficient adoration'.

At the following year's Cannes, Davis wasn't going to let this tendency stop him getting an interview with Mel Gibson and he, being long in the game by then, went behind Warner Brothers' backs, using personal contacts to secure an interview outside the strictures of the publicity team's set of arranged interviews. The interview, when it appeared in the *Mail on Sunday*, outraged Warner Brothers and the scooped publications, who accused Warners of 'deliberately stitching them up'.

'Warners then made a serious error of judgement. They wrote to the various aggrieved editors, with a copy to my guv'nor, Stewart Steven, rightly pleading their innocence but alleging that my exclusive was in fact invented, a scissors-and-paste job.

'Stewart called me in. I explained in detail the old-fashioned take-no-prisoners journalism that had secured me my scoop. I also played him the tape of Mel telling all. Stewart reached for our lawyers. He demanded and got an apology from Warners on my behalf and they were obliged to contact again their favoured editors to withdraw their libellous letter.

'This unfortunate episode sharply brought home to me that the years when [I] could interview film stars without inhibition had come to an end. We had operated virtually unfettered. Publicity people existed to facilitate, not to lay down surrender terms for a journalist's independence. But slowly in the 1980s Hollywood began to get the upper hand . . . The surviving handful of A-list names became weapons in circulation wars, precious commodities to be wooed and flattered by the media.'

The problem is as much capitulation by the media as the supremacy of the publicity machine, which is embodied most perfectly by the rise of Tina Brown at *Vanity Fair*. On her arrival at the magazine as editor, she instigated a programme of advance promises to secure major stars for interview, from the promise of the cover to copy approval, photographs by renowned photographers, digital enhancement of the pictures, stylists, couture wardrobes and the choice of interviewer. Any magazine or journal wanting to get in on the action had to match that or better it to stand a chance of getting an interview. *Rolling Stone* once had fourteen interviewers rejected by Tom Cruise, who finally settled on one who would write what he wanted him to write.

Prior to the arrival of Tina Brown, journalists had, to some extent, shaped things to their own agenda. In so doing they had had their own way for a long time and were therefore mightily surprised when Pat Kingsley and her peers reweighted the scales. A great many journalists now look nostalgically to an age where press agents simply fed them stories, which is not a helpful or healthy outlook. After a long period of playing second fiddle, the press agents became, of necessity, so skilled at feeding these stories that they exploited the situation. It's not necessarily a productive position, but a natural one when they are protecting brands and stars who have become brands. There should always be a balance, however, for the sake of the stories that both professions rely upon. Everyone is complicit now in brand protection and takes liberties to maintain it; the journalists forget that they took liberties in the first place and now, in the wake of Pat Kingsley, the publicists take them too.

The greatest art a publicist can learn is how to say no without offending anyone. Paul Bloch was a master of that simple word, as I discovered when I worked with him. When I first set up my company, Borkowski, I had a sign strung across my office, 'Learn the answer no!' The ability to say no delicately, with tact and diplomacy, comes with age, so it's not surprising that Pat Kingsley, Stan Rosenfield and others of their ilk took command of the industry when in their fifties. It's all too easy to say yes to everything, but there's poetry in the art of saying no to people and not pissing them off, despite the fact that an exclusive has been given to their main rival. Kingsley, however, took this art to the point where she was very firm in her manner, far beyond the firm-but-avuncular style of Stan Rosenfield.

Kingsley, like many of her peers, has rarely been willing to discuss anything outside her own sphere of influence, and I was unable to interview her for this book; regrettably, given her extraordinary influence on PR and starmaking. I had met her when I was working with Michael Flatley in 1995 and 1996 and he, eager to break America, had chosen to be represented by her (an understandable decision given that I was in no position to further his career in the US). I found her unreceptive to discussion and a little aloof then but, in researching this book, it has become clear that this guardedness is a common condition amongst the Hollywood PR giants; the more they have to lose, the less they're likely to speak on the record. Their power is born of their silence and aloofness and even if they are prepared to talk, it is usually through a carefully constructed filter.

So who, now, has the power? It all comes down to the strength of the talent on the publicist's lists: whoever one is representing gives one power. A long list of A-list celebrities guarantees a large slice of the power, because modern TV, radio, cinema, magazines and newspapers and – most hungrily now – the internet, needs the famous to the point of desperation. No matter how big or small the audience is, the media in its myriad forms absolutely has to feature famous people, from Britney Spears to Tom Cruise and on down to the murky depths of fame for the sake of it, because no one better or more talented can be found. The media can get on its high horse if it wishes and say it's not prepared to cover celebrity stories, for whatever reason, but it will buckle. Who has the power also depends on who the media thinks it is talking to; the publicist or the chair the publicist sits on. If the office is where the talent comes to be represented, rather than hiring an individual publicist, then whoever sits in the chair is the power. Power is transient and depends utterly on how many enemies the publicist has made, how many favours they have tried and failed to achieve and how eagerly they take up the new media tools. It's a combination of these things that marks the publicist's future.

As we have seen, in the early days of the publicity industry, a measure of anarchy reigned and a book, film, star or photograph was given a beautiful lie to clothe them, emperor-like, by the stunt-masters extracted from Barnum's circus. For Reichenbach and Nottage, it seemed as if every crowd had a silver lining and every journalist was desperate for what they offered – with a few notable exceptions. In the 1930s, at the height of MGM's power, the publicity offices operated a policy of suppression to counter the worst excesses of what had gone before, and there was such a range of stars that any journalist who wanted to could interview any one of them; consequently journalists held a great deal of power, predominantly gossip divas such as Louella Parsons. She was absolutely clear about what sort of publicist she liked, as this quote from her autobiography, *The*

Gay Illiterate shows: 'The material for my column comes from visits on my part to the studios, news telephoned in, rips from friends, and from my pals, the press agents. I don't always like their press agent material. But I like every one of them. They are the hardest working boys in any business. Harry Brand, of 20th Century Fox, is one of our closest friends; so is Howard Strickling of M.G.M. . . . and while they may try to sell me on a story that I won't use, I know they'll never try the old Barnum and Bailey tactics of trying to get me to print stuff that insults my intelligence.'

In the 1960s and 1970s, a Hollywood flack's best hope of swaying journalists was attempting to bribe them and intimidate them with swathes of celebrities. Communications had sped up to the point where it was impossible to keep control of the stories, unless you were in the privileged position of Rogers & Cowan or Lee Solters and had come to prominence after the Second World War, when gentlemen's agreements ran the industry Nowadays, in an industry entirely driven by stories, the publicists are at the height of their powers, as socially acceptable as Henry Rogers could have hoped for and fêted within the industry. But they have created a weird isolation around their clients, a bubble of unreality that cannot be pricked and which makes all the stories sound rather over-familiar.

The general public are fed so many stories that the truth becomes hard to discern, and yet more emphasis than ever is placed on truth. Like novelists, the early publicists lied profusely, creating their own brand of truth to guide the chaos that produced the Hollywood myth. This myth has sustained itself on the bedrock of publicity. Publicity has burst out of Hollywood and brought its wayward, controlling methods of storytelling to every element of modern Western life. Politicians, corporations, booksellers, bread-makers, bookmakers, artists, writers, racehorse trainers, televangelists, religions and soldiers all rely on it. But it's a different animal now.

One of the by-products of this is a brand of celebrity journalism that's afraid to say anything the star and the publicist doesn't want said, breeding a mealy-mouthed culture where the public only learns about the frothy surface. One journalist, from *GQ*, was even barred by Pat Kingsley from interviewing her roster of clients for having the temerity to contact an old schoolfriend of Tom Cruise as research for an interview, even though the interviewee merely stated that Cruise – then known as Thomas Mapother III – was 'a nice guy'. It is truth, unlike the delightful *Virgin of Stamboul* stunt that Reichenbach cooked up or many of the stories about MGM's stars, be they sinister or benign, but it's a parsimonious truth that goes no further than revealing the star's favourite cheese and how much they loved their co-stars (and that's not in the Clark Gable sense). The risk of taking a stranglehold on the publicity system is that, at some point, either the fame or the interest in it is going to stop. Nothing proves this more than the increase in prurient stories on stars in meltdown, those past their best and those no longer represented by a big-name publicity firm.

Journalists have been sucked into the fold and consumed by the industry; they have become an extension of it, rather than a necessary foil that will occasionally stand up and say no to the worst excesses of a publicity-hungry celebrity who has started to believe his own hype, or a money-hungry multinational, or a mendacious, oleaginous politician. Like the modern armies in the Gulf, publicity agents in the Kingsley mould seek to embed journalists in their camp, aiming to assert control over everything that's said or thought about their client. They attempt to woo them in with exclusives and then, if the journalist has anything interesting or wayward to say, to bowdlerize that sentiment.

It all still boils down to the art of story-making, the successful spreading of a story by word of mouth, like a virus. It was always the same, from Barnum's plough-hitched elephant drawing a crowd to Reichenbach's epiphany in his early years, following the man with the bricks; from Strickling's suppressions on behalf of the MGM stars in collusion with Louella Parsons *et al.* to Bernstein's impassioned defence of Stacy Keach. The stories were all designed to spread, develop, envelop or obscure on behalf of the client. It has always been thus, be it through the pages of the newspapers, over the telegraph wires, on the radio, the television or the internet. A celebrity needs to be able to sneeze and have the rest of the world catch their cold, and fame and the carrier stories that serve it must use technology, and the publicist best equipped to conduct the necessary germ warfare, to spread them as far as possible.

'All I know is that I worked very hard and I recognized I was able to be optimistic, after [looking] at the real facts,' said publicist Michael Levine, who worked for Rogers & Cowan in the late 1970s before setting up on his own in 1983. 'The game isn't easy, and the game isn't fair. If you think you're gonna win at a high level at forty hours a week, you're an idiot. If you think you're going to win this game taking your birthday off or taking a month off at Christmas, you're an idiot. You may be a likeable idiot, but you're an idiot. The game isn't fair. What motivates people in the end? People! You, me, every person in this room, every person I was working with; [all] were motivated by three principal things. There are three currencies in this world that matter to people in terms of their animated behaviour: Cash. Love (and sex). Fame (and power). And since I sold fame, I was in a good place to provide all of the possible elements to motivate people.

'I started a PR firm when there were no computers, no fax, no email, no Fed-Ex, no *USA Today*, no MTV, no Fox News, no CNN. It was a different place. We had typewriters. The speed changed, as did the number of media outlets. Celebrity obsession has magnified a hundred times. I think that the opportunity for celebrity to become a brand is more significant today. I wrote a book on branding so it's a subject I know a fair amount about. If you had said to Elvis or The Beatles, "You guys are a brand," [they'd have replied] "We are what?" Calvin Klein is a real man but also my – and perhaps your – underwear. He's a man and a brand.'

He's absolutely right. The industry is only as effective as the technology it uses and if something new comes in, then the publicist must adapt.

There have always been showmen in the publicity industry, from Reichenbach to Moran, Birdwell to Bernstein, but they are less significant now because their own lives became as important as the ones they were promoting – and there's nothing most stars like less than someone who works for them hogging the limelight. Their influence has been extraordinary, but it's as messy as the circuses from which they inherited their extravagance. They are the sons, grandsons and great grandsons of Barnum and the publicity industry was founded in the chaos they engendered.

Howard Strickling, Henry Rogers, Warren Cowan, Michael Levine and Pat Kingsley took a different approach, one firmly grounded on the bedrock of the past, but which has adapted more successfully to the rigours of capitalism and the modern world. This new breed of publicist is adored by their clients because they save their extravagances *for* their clients. There are no underwater weddings, relentless womanizing or Grand Guignol for the publicists who do their level best to hide in the shadows while having fingers in every available pie. They are little known or entirely anonymous to the world at large and it is that which allows them to dissemble freely on behalf of their clients. With the showmen, even the greatest lies could be picked out, turned over and laughed at. Now it's not so easy to do. All that is certain is that to succeed requires hard work.

According to Michael Levine, who came to prominence in the heady days of the early 1980s when competition was at its fiercest, throwing himself into the ring like a hurricane, doing everything necessary to be at the peak of the game and better than the others, 'It becomes a question of, "What do you want most? And what will you give up to get it?" If you want something as much as you want that next breath of air, you are motivated. I've never seen anyone achieve success at a high level who hasn't had a burning rage and obsession.'

The whole history of PR has been one of obsession, from Reichenbach to Levine, Strickling to Kingsley – all of them have been determined to succeed and many have been burned by the candle they flew into. Out of this obsession, a fame factory was born, one that has been refined and remodelled over the years. But every factory has a formula for success.

• Thirty-Seven •

THE FORMULA

The journey I have taken to the roots of PR is not a nostalgic one; it has never been my intention to delve into the past to see how much better everything was back then – such utopias are as inaccessible as they are fallacious. The early days of PR, though exciting, were only a starting point on a fascinating journey through the shaping of the twentieth century. The industry, as well as the mindset of the Western world, has been driven forward at a remarkable pace by the new technologies that have proliferated every few years. My aim was to chart the people who have made the PR radar ping, shaping the industry for good or for bad, and in doing so reshaping society. To do that it's been necessary to find out what made the original publicists tick and what lessons, if any, they passed on to their successors. There have been omissions on this journey, but that is because, excellent as many of the unmentioned publicists are, they simply don't epitomize the business and how it has changed as well as those publicists whose heads I have forced above the parapet.

All the stories I have included, when played against each other, illustrate that the decline in the fame of the individual follows a certain trend, and that fame can be continued ad infinitum in the hands of a careful, clever flack. I spent a year poring over cuttings, pondering this notion as I studied the various methods and madnesses of the publicists featured in this book. I started to wonder if Andy Warhol – an artist by calling but a master of the stunt and the sound-bite – was right; does everyone get fifteen minutes of fame? It occurred to me that it should be possible to look at fame statistically, to analyse the evidence we have all witnessed in the media, to see if fame's decline can be quantified. The answer, I discovered, is that it can be, and that Warhol was partially right – but the first spike of fame will last fifteen months, not fifteen minutes.

After that initial rush of fame, a new thermodynamic reaction must be set off under the famous thing or person, most likely by a publicist, if they are to remain in the public eye. All the research I have conducted into this, and the analysis of a select group of willing mathematically-minded researchers, has revealed a relatively simple formula that illustrates how fame, left unattended, goes into decline, and why those who wish to remain in the public consciousness must be prepared to pay for it. They just need to pay the right people to come up with something new.

The formula is not as nice and accurate as, say, $E=mc^2$ but, after all, I am applying an exact science to an inexact phenomenon. It nonetheless seems rather appropriate that the PR industry, which has coalesced into a slick, corporate, powerful and effective machine in the century or so since its chaotic inception, should have a scientific formula which it can employ to ensure it does what it has always said it could – keep people famous. The formula is most potent now because of the realization – impressed upon a generation of publicists by Rogers & Cowan – that stars are brands and have a sell-by date. Hollywood is run by lawyers and agents nowadays – these are the people who have the funkiest parties, but they understand spreadsheets, not stories. Pat Kingsley and Stan Rosenfield rose to power thanks to their understanding that a brand needs a story and that storytelling is a key element of fame in our disparate, distracted world where real-life soap operas are played out in the papers. This formula illustrates that without intervention, in the form of further publicity, fame follows an exponential slide to obscurity. It also shows how the repeated, carefully altered telling of stories can prolong the brand's period of fame.

The formula was derived from the study of a host of celebrities, using an extensive cuttings archive. The subjects tested for the formula included Kevin Spacey, Halle Berry, Paris Hilton, Nicole Kidman, Richard Branson, Mel Gibson, Martha Lane Fox, Lindsay Lohan, Tom Cruise, Abi Titmuss, Angelina Jolie, Anthea Turner, Brad Pitt, Peter Mandelson, Hugo Chávez, Noel Edmonds, Chris Evans, Charles Ingram, Jeffrey Archer, Jade Goody, George Michael and Angus Deayton. A study was also made into brands like Red Bull, Stella Artois, Heineken, American Express and Adidas. Each brand was measured by their appearance in print in the papers from 2000 onwards. The formula for illustrating the decline in fame from its peak works out as follows: $F(T) = B + P(1/10T+1/2T^2)$ where:

F is the level of fame.

T is time, measured in three-monthly intervals. So T=1 is after 3 months, T=2 is after 6 months, etc. Fame is at its peak when T=0. (Putting T=0 into the equation gives an infinite fame peak, not mathematically accurate, perhaps, but the concept of the level of fame being off the radar is apposite.)

B is a base level of fame that we identified and quantified by analysing the average level of fame in the year before peak. For George Clooney, B would be a large number, but for a Fabulous Nobody, like a new Big Brother contestant, B is zero.

P is the increment of fame above the base level, that establishes the individual firmly at the front of public consciousness.

This formula fits the data remarkably well, giving a precise numerical value to the 15 month theory: if I put in T=5, (corresponding to 15 months after the peak), it gives F=B+P(1/50+1/50), which works out at F=B+.04p. In other words, up to 96% of the fame boost achieved at the peak of public attention has been frittered away, and the client or product is almost back to base level.

The study showed pretty conclusively that any specific boost to fame is sustained for approximately fifteen months and that each celebrity or brand was surprisingly similar in the way that their fame decayed. Out of this study, I came to realise that Warhol was wrong, although he was getting there – his assertion that, in the future, everyone would be famous for fifteen minutes has proved a mite optimistic. Fame still, on the whole, relies on someone being possessed of an extraordinary talent, even if that talent is as simple as owning an extraordinarily photogenic face, although this is not always the case, as *Big Brother* has proved. However fame can be sustained and refreshed, just as long as there is something new to give it the necessary impetus. The formula is the perfect totem for the publicist's art, illustrating that a flack can keep their client famous with just a few well-placed spikes of coverage. Without these, their client will be a has-been after fifteen months.

It seems so obvious when you look at it like this – why else do *Big Brother* contestants vanish without trace within a year and a half? They have their moment of exposure on the claustrophobic set and then, when they exit the house, the luckier ones hire a publicist willing to slum it in the hope of a quick buck. But if they do nothing but wallow in that one moment of fame, they will be forgotten, because there is always something or someone new waiting round the corner to take the public's attention away. Jade Goody, who failed to win *Big Brother* in 2002, became famous for being loud, vulgar and faintly ridiculous, the person who should have won but failed to. That image tired quickly – in about fifteen months in fact – and she cannily reinvented herself a little and remained in the papers and the gossip journals, famous for collapsing when she ran the London Marathon without bothering to train and other such innocent, ludicrous feats of failure.

The public tired of this too, so Goody, who realized she needed a boost to stay in the fame game, published an autobiography and decided to return to the celebrity strand of *Big Brother* in 2006. Here, having deviated from the fame formula by trying something the public recognized her for, she made her first mistake. Trapped in the *Big Brother* house with a selection of celebrities whose waning fame was, for the most part anyway, based on a talent, be it for acting, singing or whatever, she felt like a fish out of water and quickly ganged up with two other celebrities on the show, one famous for having breasts, the other for being part of a short-lived pop band. Trapped into repeating herself, Goody reacted with all the anger of a badger that's been cornered and lashed out at the person in the house she felt threatened by: the Bollywood star Shilpa Shetty. What followed was one of the most spectacular celebrity meltdowns this side of the Atlantic. It featured a display of racism and naked fear brought on by the suspicion that she was being looked down on and was cringe-makingly painful to watch. It led to Goody's expulsion from the house and from the front pages of the gossip journals and tabloids. At present, there seems little chance of her relaunching into true fame again – notoriety just doesn't count where the formula's concerned. She has done far better than some of the people who actually won *Big Brother*, however. Who now remembers Cameron Stout or Brian Dowling? Without the boosts that Goody got to her fame, those winners have disappeared from the public consciousness at a rate of knots.

Big Brother contestants are perhaps the closest the modern era has come to offering Warhol-style fame for everyone, if only for fifteen minutes, while the formula works best with major stars. In the period of study, the supermodel Kate Moss, for example, rose to an extraordinary level of fame when police dropped a case against her some months after she was photographed allegedly sniffing forbidden substances. From a very public, famous presence prior to the incident, averaging nine mentions a month in the *Daily Telegraph*, she became hugely famous and was mentioned continually. Her fame has run at twice its previous level ever since and she has gone on to bring out her own range of designer labels. Ulrika Jonsson was another study – having been famous in the late 1990s, her presence dipped under the radar a little by 2002. She then had an affair with the England football manager Sven-Göran Eriksson and published an autobiography alleging that an unnamed TV presenter had raped her. This spike of fame, coupled with a lot of mentions in the paper, led to her having a year of intense fame, which was only beginning to tail off by 2006.

The fame formula would also explain why pop and rock musicians are pushed by their labels to put out an album every two and a half years and tour it in between. They get a break at some point, then they return with a new product or a new spin on the product, such as a live tour. The trouble with that is that the record companies also want them to repeat their original success, note for note if needs be, and this doesn't always counteract the formula – there must always be something new, and if the records sound too similar the slide the formula so clearly illustrates continues. Only a few bands buck this trend, such as the Arctic Monkeys. Radiohead are a good example of a band who always offer something new – their album *In Rainbows* was released as a download only in late 2007, for whatever price the customer was prepared to pay. Thousands downloaded the album for anything between 49p (the fixed administration cost) and £10. Radiohead, who had left their major label for an independent, were at risk of disappearing if they hadn't been careful and clever, but as a consequence of this stunt, they refreshed their image hugely. The album, when it was released on CD in early 2008, went straight to number one.

Madonna is an excellent example of a celebrity working the fame formula to perfection. From her early days as a sharp-witted Eighties party girl, she has moved onwards and upwards in her quest to stay famous, creating controversy through videos of her kissing a black Jesus, her *Sex* book and her flirtation with lesbianism, changing style for every album, acting parts in movies, adopting children, writing books for children and becoming a member of the English landed gentry by dint of marriage and money and taking to it like a duck to water. Even her sporadic film roles, lambasted though many of them have been, are part of her success. Each new innovation has caused her fame to spike and kept her in the media spotlight, which she shows no sign of leaving, even though she guards her privacy more and more jealously.

Heather Mills is another good example. However much stick she may have received for having the temerity to divorce Paul McCartney, she has appeared in the media regularly with a new angle on her situation, be it dancing on a television show or simply asking for vast amounts of money in her divorce hearing, and she will doubtless continue to hit the front pages even now that the divorce is finalized.

The formula is applicable to brand names as well: Reebok did consistently well in the study until the second quarter of 2006, when its mention rate in the papers disappeared thanks to no soccer matches being played at Bolton Wanderers' Reebok Stadium. And if anyone doubted that Rogers & Cowan were sensible to tie celebrity and product together, the fact that Britney Spears' range of cosmetics took the largest share of the UK market in 2007 despite, or just as likely because of, her very public meltdown, proves that they were right beyond doubt. Britney is a woman doing something new every week; whether it's shaving her head or attacking cars with an umbrella, she is utterly at the forefront of the formula. The mere fact that there are stories expressing surprise that people still love her enough to buy her perfume should push her fame still further. The only thing that might stop it is an untimely death, but even that will only serve as a pausing point, because a celebrity martyr lives on for ever, if only in the headlines of the *Daily Express*.

The continued interest in the decadent soap opera that is Britney's life – or those of Amy Winehouse, Kate Moss or Lindsay Lohan – shows most effectively the need people have for stories. The lives of stars are the fireside fables of the twenty-first century, the contagious god myths that spread and spread and get better with every retelling. This is what Jim Moran, Harry Reichenbach and Maynard Nottage understood, although they were more interested in the one-off event, the initial spike that creates fame. The way they created stories and stunts to get them on the wires should be a salient lesson for the people who came after them and who recognize the potential to make money from the stars and their stories. Now that the media is instantaneous and global there needs to be a less chaotic, chancy method of exploding a story than those practised in the early days of the publicity industry. The planners and long-term thinkers, from Rogers & Cowan on, would do well to take a fresh, anarchic approach like their forebears and apply a scientific method to it. Publicists need a new propulsive spike to keep them moving forwards too.

The fame formula runs like a game show in which the rounds last fifteen months – a kind of *Who Wants to Be a Millionaire* where all the options are Phone a Friend. As long as the friend is a good publicist and you have a reasonable amount of general knowledge, you're going to win as long as you make it to the necessary plateaux where your fame is guaranteed. Of course, thanks to the internet, the audience doesn't need to be asked – it is quite free to proffer its opinion from the sidelines. It certainly helps if the celebrity in question keeps a selection of publicists on hand to further their career; Frank Sinatra, on his steady rise to international fame, was repped by an endless stream of publicists, each one spreading his fame in different directions and into different markets. Fame is contagious, and Sinatra cannily spread the germ of his fame as widely as possible, allowing it to spread almost out of control. Nearly every publicist mentioned in the latter half of this book worked with him at one time or another.

Circumstances have changed since the heyday of Sinatra, however, and the power now lies with anyone who wants to take it. All they need do is learn about fame and its applications and the tools necessary to shift fame virally. All of the publicists I spoke to noted how constantly shifting technologies have helped them and made it clear that their ability to adapt to them has kept them in business. As they get older, however, that revolutionary zeal has been replaced by a more reactionary stasis. In a world where the ability to become famous, or create a stir on behalf of someone famous, is made ever easier thanks to the vast array of new media – from the desktop publishing that revolutionized the 1980s when it appeared on Apple Mac computers to mobile phones and high-quality cameras in mobile phones, from social networking sites such as MySpace, Facebook and Bebo to YouTube, email and virtual reality worlds like Second Life – a formula for creating fame is a necessity. It is a vast, uncontrollable new world with endless ways of doing things, limited only by the ability of the programmer to program the code and the constantly increasing power of the desktop computer. This newness adds to paranoia and confusion, certainly, but when information can be at one's fingertips wherever one is and whenever one wants it, the world is going to be changing at the speed of thought.

Films like *The Blair Witch Project*, which started life on the net, teasing people with the possibility that it was real, and *Cloverfield*, a trailer for which appeared on the internet and gave nothing away, showing only a group of scared-looking twenty-somethings reacting to the Statue of Liberty's head landing at their feet as something rips up New York, and a release date, have appeared out of nowhere thanks to the internet and have had a huge impact on increasing and adding variety to methods of publicity. They were obsessively spoken about on blogs the world over and achieved enormous success. *Snakes on a Plane* appeared in much the same way, teasing net-based fans with the opportunity to add to the film by suggesting scenes they'd like to see in it. That the film was not so special, as one might expect from the title, doesn't take away from its impact on the publicity world.

Publicists like Pat Kingsley and the suppress generation that came out of Rogers & Cowan still maintain a stranglehold on information, but they are missing out on the fact that the people want a soap opera and the internet provides that for them, while the carefully orchestrated puff pieces that come from the higher-end gossip papers do not. The internet is something they can't control, although they try – the acidic Rotten Tomatoes site was bought out by Rupert Murdoch's NewsCorp, which effectively put a stop to its scurrilous invective because it scares them.

The superheroes of cinema, created by the original publicists, have, thanks to the rise of the internet, been replaced by super-victims, such as Britney Spears and Lindsay Lohan, and it's part of the human condition to be fascinated by that. Will X find permanent happiness? Will Y win their fight against drugs or booze? Will Z avoid madness and self-destruction? Publicists in the Kingsley mould want to cover this up, deny it all, but failure is necessary in the celebrity world, in much the same way that fairy stories are tainted with the horrific. The hero or heroine must fight against extraordinary odds to win – just look at the Greek gods; superhuman though they may have been, they also were prone to the most human of foibles such as pride, greed, envy, jealousy and self-destruction, and were all the more popular for it.

The future of the publicity industry is unknowable; all that we can reasonably predict is that if technology continues to develop at the same exponential rate, things will continue to change at an astonishing rate too. Simpler and more effective tools will arrive, making it easier for anyone with determination to achieve success and notoriety. As Brian Eno said, 'Don't start from meaning. It will appear. Whatever is now at the edges will in time become the centre. The future will be made with simple equipment, unqualified people, small budgets and bad taste. Adjust your ideas as much as you like; this is a reality. TV entertainment is too fast, too slow, too dull, too bright, too brash, too tame.'

Reality stars like Jordan and Jade Goody prove beyond doubt that those determined to become famous will do so, but they must take it upon themselves to understand that they've got a fifteen-month turn-around in which to keep it running. Most astonishing for all concerned is the fact that no punter now has to be silent. Everyone has the tools to shape a star's success or comment on someone's failure. They have the power, derived from that simple but incredibly versatile tool the internet, to make or break someone, from the lowliest reality TV star to Tom Cruise or Britney Spears. They even have the power, thanks to the ability to share files on peer-to-peer networks, to destroy the status quo of Hollywood and the music industry. The skill of the future for the publicist will be honing the ability to undermine and neuter vituperative blogs and persuade people that a product is worth buying or a star's life is worth buying into. Right now, the people in power are struggling to get their heads around this concept, but there will be a time, soon, when they will come to terms with the new agendas and wider goalposts. Although we all have the vast expanse of the web on which to express ourselves, the ghettos will become tighter and smaller – publicists will, of necessity, become specialists. But even if you're a specialist with a tiny little brand, a small-fry operator, you've got to get a foothold on the Worldwide Web. Fame and the promotion of fame is like the Everest quest: some people have only the energy and talent to get to the foothills, while some have the talent and drive as well as a plethora of determined publicists and agents, to reach for the top . . . one fifteen-month phase at a time.

Celebrity, as we understand it now, was invented the moment D. W. Griffith moved his camera to take a close-up of one of his stars in the early years of silent film, transforming the base metal of the actor into the gold of celebrity. From then on, they were pursued and worshipped the world over, their pearlescent faces filling screens in the same way one might imagine a god's face. That's when the star was made and, whether it's fifteen minutes or fifteen months of fame, it's that close-up that started it all. What the publicists have done is create a world that lives beyond that one enduring image, which encompasses fairy tale and morality tale, fable and truth. It's something that Reichenbach and Nottage instinctively recognized and capitalized on, something the Fixers sought to control and that Rogers & Cowan applied to an endless number of other things, from toothpaste to television.

What the future holds is unguessable – technology's tectonic plates shift too quickly and throw up too much new landmass overnight for it to be sensible to try – but the world is always going to want to know about the famous and there will always be a need for publicists to help manage that fame. King Arthur had Merlin, Valentino had Reichenbach. And even though it's a long distance between Barnum, Reichenbach, Nottage and the present day, someone, somewhere will need a publicist's help. It is worth remembering, though, that if you succeed in this business everything else goes on hold. PR is an all-consuming vocation and it can be exhausting.

It's not quite devil worship, as some would have you believe. It's not quite the Aleister Crowley-esque profession of popular legend, but the seeds of that are there. There's an arcane thrill about the practice of publicity; it's not fair or easy and can even be dangerous, but you'll have a fantastic ride along the way, *and* you get to mould people, but beware, there's no way out. It is a drug and as such must be handled with care, but the possibilities, now more than ever, are endless. The power really does lie with anybody who wants it and is willing to learn about fame, and the steps necessary to achieve it.

It's an exciting time to get involved in PR, with the goalposts changing every day and room for new ideas continually appearing. Fame, and the applications it can be put to, is expanding all the time, like the after-effects of Griffith's first close-up. New particles of unformed matter appear constantly and all an eager flack need do is fix on one of them and apply some well-timed, carefully constructed publicity to see if they can form a whole new constellation of stars from them. The only thing to remember, when embarking on such a course, is that fame requires sacrifices – its Gwili Andres and Britney Spears.

In 1996 Richard Edelman, writing in *Esquire*, summed up the modern era perfectly: 'In this era of exploding technologies,' he wrote, 'there is no truth except the truth you create for yourself.'

Bibliography

The story of Nottage is derived largely from his own papers and I thank Linda Fairweather and family for access to his archives. Much invaluable help was also given by the Margaret Herrick Library, Fairbanks Center for Motion Picture Study which was the source for many of the articles and theses below. I also used *Moving Picture Weekly*, *Photoplay* and *Modern Screen* for background. Most invaluable for information about Strickling and Mannix was a fascinating book called *The Fixers* by E. J. Fleming. His research has done much to throw light on how these two men operated behind the scenes at MGM.

Books

Allen, Robert Clyde. *Horrible Prettiness: Burlesque and American Culture.* The University of North Carolina Press, 1991.

Alter, Judy. *Vaudeville: The Birth of Show Business.* Franklin Watts, 1998.

Balio, Tino. *Grand Design: Hollywood as a Modern Business Enterprise 1930–1939* (History of the American Cinema Volume 5). Scribner, 1993.

Barnum, P.T. *Selected Letters of P.T. Barnum.* Columbia University Press, 1983.

Barnum, P.T. *Struggles and Triumphs.* MacGibbon & Kee, 1967.

Barnum, P.T. *The Life of P.T. Barnum.* University of Illinois Press, 2000.

Baxter, John. *Hollywood in the Thirties.* Zwemmer, 1968.

Bone, Howard and Waldron, Daniel G. *Sideshow: My Life With Geeks, Freaks & Vagabonds in the Carny Trade.* Sun Dog Press, 2001.

Boorstin, Daniel Joseph. *The Creators: A History of Heroes of the Imagination.* Random House, 1992.

Boorstin, Daniel Joseph. *The Image or What Happened to the American Dream.* Weidenfeld & Nicolson, 1961.

Brownlow, Kevin. *The Parade's Gone By . . . .* University of California, 1992.

Churchill De Mille, William. *Hollywood Saga.* Dutton & Co, 1939.

Clarke, Gerald. *Get Happy: The Life of Judy Garland.* Little, Brown and Co., 2000.

Clemens Warwick, Karen. *P.T. Barnum: Genius of the Three-ring Circus.* Enslow Publishers, 2001.

Cooper, Miriam, with Hendon, Bonnie. *Dark Lady of the Silents: My Life in Early Hollywood.* Bobbs-Merill Co., 1973

Csdia, Joseph and June Bundy. *American Entertainment: A Unique History of Popular Show Business.* Billboard, 1978.

Desmond, Alice Curtis. *Barnum Presents General Tom Thumb: Typescript, 1953–1954*. Macmillan, 1954.
Dietz, Howard. *Dancing in the Dark*. Quadrangle, 1974.
Doherty, Thomas. *Pre-code Hollywood: Sex, Immorality, and Insurrection in American Cinema, 1930–1934*. Columbia University Press, 1999.
Drop, Mark. *Dateline Hollywood: Sins and Scandals of Yesterday and Today*. Diane Publishing Company, 1994.
Edmonds, Andy. *Frame-up!: The Shocking Scandal That Destroyed Hollywood's Biggest Comedy Star, Roscoe "Fatty" Arbuckle*. Avon Books, 1992.
Fishbein, M. and Ajzen I. *Belief, Attitude, Intention and Behaviour: An Introduction to Theory and Research*. Longman Higher Education, 1975.
Flamini, Roland. *Thalberg: The Last Tycoon and the World of MGM*. Andre Deutsch, 1994.
Fleming, E. J. *The Fixers: Eddie Mannix, Howard Strickling and the MGM Publicity Machine*. McFarland and Co. Inc., 2004.
Fountain, Leatrice Gilbert. *Dark Star: The Untold Story of the Meteoric Rise and Fall of the Legendary Silent Screen Star John Gilbert*. St Martin's Press, 1985.
Frank, Gerold. *Judy*. W. H. Allen, 1975.
French, Philip. *The Movie Moguls: An Informal History of the Hollywood Tycoons*. Weidenfeld and Nicolson, 1969.
Gabler, Neil. *Walt Disney: The Biography*. Aurum, 2007.
Goodman, Ezra. The Fifty-year Decline and Fall of Hollywood. Simon & Schuster, 1961.
Green, Abel, and Laurie, Jr, Joe. *Show Biz: From Vaude to Video*. Henry Holt and Company, 1951.
Groh, Lynn. *P.T. Barnum, King of the Circus*. Garrard Pub. Co, 1966
Hamann, G. D. *Hollywood Scandals in the Thirties*. Filming Today, 1996
Hampton, Benjamin Bowles. *A History of the Movies*. Arno P. NY, 1976
Harris, Neil. *Humbug; The Art of P.T. Barnum*. University of Chicago Press, 1981.
Hays, Will H. *The Memoirs of Will H. Hays*. Doubleday, 1955.
Higham, C. and Greenberg J. *Hollywood in the Forties*. Tantivy Press, 1968.
Hirsch, Phil (ed). *Hollywood Uncensored; The Stars, Their Secrets and Their Scandals*. Pyramid, 1965
Hofler, Robert. *The Man Who Invented Rock Hudson: The Pretty Boys and The Dirty Deals of Henry Willson*. Da Capo Press, 2005.
Hollander, Paul. *Discontents: Postmodern and Postcommunist*. Transaction Publishers, 2002.
Holledge, James. *The Notorious Harlow, and Scandal in the Hollywood Jungle*. Horowitz Publications, 1965.
Jacobson Fuhrman, Candice. *Publicity Stunt: Great Staged Events that Made the News*. Chronicle, 1989.
Kanin, Garson. *Hollywood: Stars and Starlets, Tycoons and Flesh-peddlers, Movie-makers and Money-makers, Frauds and Geniuses, Hopefuls and Has-beens, Great Loves and Sex Symbols*. Viking Press, 1967.
Kominsky, Morris. *The Hoaxers: Plain Liars, Fancy Liars and Damned Liars*. Branden Press, 1970.
Koszarksi, Richard. *An Evening's Entertainment: The Age of the Silent Feature Picture, 1915–1928*. Scribner, 1990.

Koszarski, Richard. *Hollywood Directors, 1914–1940*. Oxford University Press, 1976.
Kunhardt, Philip B. and Peter W. *P.T. Barnum: America's Greatest Showman*. Knopf, 1995.
Laws, Richard Wayne. *A Study of Celebrity*. University of Michigan, 1972.
Lewis, Robert M. *From Travelling Show to Vaudeville: Theatrical Spectacle in America, 1830–1910*. Johns Hopkins University Press, 2007.
Maney, Richard. *Fanfare: The Confessions of a Press Agent*. Harper & Bros, 1957.
Mann, William J. *Kate: The Woman Who Was Katharine Hepburn*. Faber and Faber, 2006.
Marshall, David P. *Celebrity and Power: Fame in Contemporary Culture*. University of Minnesota Press, 1997.
McLean, Adrienne L. and Cook, David A. *Headline Hollywood: A Century of Film Scandal*. Rutgers University Press, 2001.
Parsons, Louella Oettinger. *The Gay Illiterate*. Doubleday Doran, 1944.
Reiss, Benjamin. *The Showman and The Slave: Race, Death, and Memory in Barnum's America*. Harvard University Press, 2001.
Rogers, Henry C. *Walking the Tightrope*. William Morrow and Co, 1980.
Rojek, Chris. *Celebrity*. Reaktion Books, 2001.
Ross, Steven J. *Working Class Hollywood: Silent Film and The Shaping of Class in America*. Princeton University Press, 1999.
Rotha, Paul. *The Film Till Now: A Survey of World Cinema*. Spring Books, 1967.
Russell, Don. *The Wild West*. University of Texas Press, 1970.
Schickel, Richard. *Intimate Strangers: The Culture of Celebrity*. Doubleday, 1985.
Scott Berg, A. *Goldwyn: A Biography*. Hamish Hamilton, 1989.
Siegel, Scott, and Siegel, Barbara. *The Encyclopedia of Hollywood*. Facts on File Inc., October 2004
Slout, William L. *Olympians of The Sawdust Circle: A Biographical Dictionary of the Nineteenth Century American Circus*. Borgo Press, 1998.
Smoodin, Eric Loren. *Regarding Frank Capra: Audience, Celebrity, and American Film Studies, 1930–1960*. Duke University Press, 2004.
Sobel, Bernard. *A Pictorial History of Vaudeville*. Citadel Press, 1961.
Stanley, Robert H. *The Celluloid Empire: A History of The American Movie Industry*. Hastings House, 1978.
Sutton, Felix. *Master of Ballyhoo: The Story of P.T. Barnum*. Puttnam,1968.
Walker, Mike. *Malicious Intent: A Hollywood Fable*. Bancroft Press. 1999.
Wallace, Irving. *The Fabulous Showman: The Life and Times of P.T. Barnum*. Alfred A Knopf, 1959.

Articles

'Shakespeare in Trouble', Julian Borger, *Guardian*, 11 March 1999
'Heartbreak Town', Russell Birdwell, *New York Journal*, 8 and 15 June 1935
'Birdwell', *Variety*, 31 August 1938
'Saving the Nation', *MP Herald*. 17 September 1938
'Birdwell Handles Korda Publicity', *Hollywood Reporter*, 12 April 1940
Boxoffice, 4 July 1942
'Ex-King Carol Tries to Press-Agent Self into USA', *PM*, 13 November 1943
'Hollywood Strips for War Victims', Florabel Muir, *Citizen News*, 24 March 1945

'Actresses Play Strip Poker to Assist Clothing Appeal', *Los Angeles Times*, 29 March 1945
'The Great Bamboozler', Maurice Zolotow, *Saturday Evening Post*, 10 December 1949
'Moran the Magnificent', Wade Jones, *Park East: The Magazine of New York*, February 1953
'Variations on a Zany Cat's Meow', Ed Wallace, *New York World-Telegram*, 5 February 1954
'Jim Moran Hosts a Miserable Party', Erskine Johnson, *Mirror News*, 3 June1960
'The Little World of Jim Moran', Richard Gehman, *Playboy*, September 1961
'Spearheads', Ivan Spear, *Boxoffice*, 11 September 1961
'Moran Masking His Activities', Lee Belser, *LA Mirror*, 27 October 1961
'Hollywood's Most Fabulous Bird', Charles Samuels, *Fawcett Publications Magazine*, 1962
Bill Kennedy's Mr LA column, *LA Herald Examiner*, 17 June 1964
'Interview with Russell Birdwell on David O. Selznick', *Hollywood Reporter*, summer 1965
'Birdwell: Word War's Old Soldier', Jack Smith, *Los Angeles Times*, 3April 1966
'Birdwell Denies His Play About a Publicist is Autobiographical', *Variety*, 29 March 1968
'Publicist Russell Birdwell – Instant Fame for a Fee', Don Alpert, *Los Angeles Times Calendar*, 28 April1968
'Hollywood Magic Lantern', Russell Birdwell, *Variety* 1972
'Jim Moran: From Bedcover to Hardcover', James Bacon, *LA Herald Examiner*, 10 September 1973
'Used for Brand Evaluation,' Fishbein, M. and I. Ajzen, *Journal of Consumer Research*, 1975
'The Power of Public Relations', Katharine Mieszkowski, *FastCompany* Issue 14, April 1998
'Publicity Stunt Master Jim Moran Dies at Age 91', *Hollywood Reporter*, 19 October 1999
'Jim Moran; Publicist of Outrageous Stunts', *Los Angeles Times*, 20 October 1999
'James S. Moran Dies at 91; Master of the Publicity Stunt', Douglas Martin, *New York Times*, 24 October 1999
'Meet the Enforcer', Ed Helmore, *Observer*, 3 June 2001
'Sharper Image Man', Amy Wallace, *Los Angeles Magazine*, November 2001
'They Love You', Tad Friend, *Observer Magazine*, 8 December 2002
'When PR Was Young: Warren Cowan and Lee Solters', Alex Ben Block, *Television Week*, 16 June 2003
'Solters and Digney Announces Expansion', PR Newswire, 4 March 2004
'The Agency Business: Sustaining Client Relationships after Primary Contacts Depart', Craig McGuire, *PR Week*, 13 December 2004
'The Entertainment Publicists Professional Society (EPPS) Presents Legends of Entertainment Publicity Panel; *Variety* Columnist Army Archerd to Moderate', PR Newswire, 25 October 2005

Internet Resources

'The Culture of Celebrity', Joseph Epstein, www.theweeklystandard.com
'New York's School for Scandal Sheets', Mark Caldwell, *New York Times* www.nytimes.com
'Sharper Image Man', Amy Wallace, *Los Angeles Magazine* www.lamag.com
'Lindsay Lohan: Is Any Publicity Good Publicity?' Mark Carter, www.associatedcontent.com
'Richard Dyer's Theory of Movie Stars', Barry Mauer, www.associatedcontent.com
'Did MGM Executive Eddie Mannix Kill George Reeves, TV's Superman?', Jon Hopwood, www.associatedcontent.com
'Frederic Remington's Wild West', Brian W. Dippie, www.americanheritage.com
'Evolution of the Movie Star – How Hollywood Stars First Came to Be', Associated Press, www.associatedcontent.com
'Study: Celebrities More Narcissistic', Associated Press, www.livescience.com
Interview with Warren Cowan, Eric Schwartzman, www.OnTheRecordPodcast.com

Other Sources

American Vaudeville-Theatre in a Package: The Origins of Mass Entertainment by Frederick Edward Snyder, PHD Thesis, Yale University, 1970.
Benjamin Franklin Keith, Vaudeville Magnate: The First Fifty Years 1846–1896, Vera Moorehouse, MA Thesis, Eastern Michigan University, 1975.
Circus Sideshow Advertising Theories and Practices During the Late 19th and Early 20th Centuries by Dara Nan Dulitz, MA Thesis, University of New Orleans, 1981.
A History of Buffalo Bill's Wild West Show, 1883–1913, William E Deahl, Jr, Ph.D. dissertation, Southern Illinois University, 1974
'The stars look down', Victor Davis, *British Journalism Review*, vol 14, no 2.
'Believability in Advertising: The Too Good to be True Phenomenon' Coney, K. A. and R. F. Beltramini, in *Marketing Communication – Theory and Research*, edited by M.J. Houston & R.J. Lutz, American Marketing Association, 1985

Index

Printed in Great Britain
by Amazon

76674041R00248